Jerry Baker's

BACKYARD
BIRD FEEDING
BONANZA

www.jerrybaker.com

Other Jerry Baker Good Flower Gardening & Birding Series™ books:

Jerry Baker's Year-Round Bloomers
Jerry Baker's Flower Garden Problem Solver
Jerry Baker's Perfect Perennials!
Jerry Baker's Flower Power

Jerry Baker's Good Gardening Series™ books:

Jerry Baker's Dear God...Please Help It Grow!
Secrets from the Jerry Baker Test Gardens
Jerry Baker's All-American Lawns
Jerry Baker's Bug Off!
Jerry Baker's Terrific Garden Tonics!
Jerry Baker's Giant Book of Garden Solutions
Jerry Baker's Backyard Problem Solver
Jerry Baker's Green Grass Magic
Jerry Baker's Terrific Tomatoes, Sensational Spuds, and Mouth-Watering Melons
Jerry Baker's Great Green Book of Garden Secrets
Jerry Baker's Old-Time Gardening Wisdom

Jerry Baker's Good Health Series™ books:

Nature's Best Miracle Medicines
Jerry Baker's Supermarket Super Remedies
Jerry Baker's The New Healing Foods
Jerry Baker's Cut Your Health Care Bills in Half!
Jerry Baker's Amazing Antidotes
Jerry Baker's Anti-Pain Plan
Jerry Baker's Homemade Health
Jerry Baker's Oddball Ointments, Powerful Potions, and Fabulous Folk Remedies
Jerry Baker's Giant Book of Kitchen Counter Cures

Jerry Baker's Good Home Series™ books:

Jerry Baker's Homespun Magic
Grandma Putt's Old-Time Vinegar, Garlic, Baking Soda, and 101 More Problem Solvers
Jerry Baker's Supermarket Super Products!
Jerry Baker's It Pays to be Cheap!
Jerry Baker's Eureka! 1,001 Old-Time Secrets and New Fangled Solutions

To order any of the above, or for more information on
Jerry Baker's amazing home, health, and garden tips,
tricks, and tonics, please write to:

Jerry Baker, P.O. Box 805
New Hudson, MI 48165

Or, visit Jerry Baker on the World Wide Web at:

www.jerrybaker.com

Jerry Baker's

BACKYARD
BIRD FEEDING
BONANZA

1,487 Tips, Tricks, and Treats
for Attracting Your
Fine-Feathered Friends

by Jerry Baker,
America's Master Gardener®

Published by American Master Products, Inc.

Published by American Master Products, Inc. / Jerry Baker

Executive Editor: Kim Adam Gasior
Managing Editor: Cheryl Winters-Tetreau
Writer: Sally Roth
Copy Editor: Barbara McIntosh Webb
Interior Design and Layout: Sandy Freeman
Interior Photography: Monte Taylor
Cover Design: Kitty Pierce Mace
Illustrator: Len Epstein
Indexer: Nan Badgett

Publisher's Cataloging-in-Publication
(Provided by Quality Books, Inc.)

Baker, Jerry.
    Backyard bird feeding bonanza : 1,487 tips, tricks, and treats for attracting your fine-feathered friends / Jerry Baker.
        p. cm — (Jerry Baker's good gardening series)
        Includes index.
        ISBN 978-0–922433–57–5

    1. Birds—Feeding and feeds. 2. Bird feeders.
3. Bird attracting.   I. Title.

QL676.5.B194 2004   639.9'78
                    QBI04–200168

Printed in the United States of America
4 6 8 10 9 7 5   hardcover

Contents

Introduction...vii

CHAPTER 1
Cheepers' Keepers · 1
Good for You...2
Good for Your Garden...5
First-Time Feeders...7
Four-Season Feeding...12

CHAPTER 2
Menu Mainstays · 21

Superior Sunflowers...22
Miracle Millet...35
Budget Stretchers...42
Feeder Free-for-All...45

CHAPTER 3
Seed-Eater Specialties · 51
Finches to the Feast...52
Never-Fail Niger...54
More Tiny Treasures...56
Starting Out with
Specialty Seeds...62

Marvelous Mixes...68
Finch-Friendly Feeders...71

CHAPTER 4
Plain & Fancy Fats · 84
Super-Simple Suet...85
Simplest Suet Tweets...102
Ever-Popular Peanut Butter...106
High-Calorie Helpers...112
Cooking for a Crowd...116

CHAPTER 5
Nuttin' but Nuts · 124

The Big Bang...125
Thrifty Feeding...130
Bargain Buys...135

CHAPTER 6
Sweets for the Tweets · 148

Surefire Sugar Water...149
Nectar Know-How...152
Jamming with Jelly...160
Fruits for the Feathered...164
Calling All Fruit Eaters!...170

CHAPTER 7

Do-Si-Dough · 177

Golden Grains...178
The Staff of Life...181
From Breadbox
to Bird Feeder...183
Pantry Possibilities...189
Home Cooking...195
Serve-It-Up Secrets...196

CHAPTER 8

Extra Enticements · 205

Irresistible Insects...206
Rustle Up Some Grubs...211
Insect-Enriched Treats...218
Mineral Musts...220

CHAPTER 9

The Old Watering Hole · 225

Sip and Splash...226
Water Habits...231
Water for All Seasons...234

CHAPTER 10

Vamoose, You Varmints! · 238

Wearing Out Their Welcome...239
Birdseed Bandits...245
Predator Protection...249

CHAPTER 11

Oh, Give Me a Home · 253

Top Ten Tenants...254
The Dastardly Duo...270
Best Birdhouses on the Block...274

CHAPTER 12

Feathering the Nest · 279

Sweetening the Deal...280
Back to Basics...288
Holders for the Heist...294

CHAPTER 13

Mighty Fine Station Design · 302

Functional Feeding Stations...303
Installation Insights...310
Prettify the Practical...316
Second-Story Solutions...320

Sources...324
Favorite Backyard Birds...329
Index...361

Introduction

It was Grandma Putt who first showed me how good it feels to give birds a helping hand. When I was just a whipper-snapper, Grandma would hand me a slice of stale bread and help me break it into bits for the birds that always flocked to our yard. Later, when birdseed hit the store shelves, we set up a feeder together. It was my "job" to keep it stocked, but it was Grandma who taught me what birds like best to eat, whether it was certain seeds or last night's leftovers.

🐦 I've racked the ol' brain for every scrap of Grandma's wisdom I can remember to pass along to you in the pages of this book. And I've added to her teachings with lots of tips I've learned myself over the years. You'll find a treasure trove of ideas to put into use right away, so that you, too, can call yourself the birds' best friend!

🐦 In Chapter 1, you'll learn how a bunch of simple sparrows (or cardinals, bluebirds, or any other backyard pals) can lower your blood pressure, make your tomatoes healthier, and improve your life in lots of other ways. If you're a beginner, you'll discover the best ways to get started in this lifelong hobby. And if you're a seasoned seed-stocker, you'll learn some new tricks for making birds sing your praises year-round.

🐦 In Chapter 2, we'll get down to the nitty-gritty and talk about the main dishes on the menu. You'll find out which two types of seeds will satisfy nearly all of your feeder visitors, and why they're so popular. I'll show you how to shop smart, too, so that your birdseed bucks will really s-t-r-e-t-c-h.

🐦 In Chapters 3, 4, and 5, you'll find a long menu of special foods, such as out-of-the-ordinary seeds, high-calorie suet and other fats, and irresistible nuts, all guaranteed to catch the eye of some beautiful birds. I'll let you in on which foods birds like best, and I'll give you plenty of ideas for serving those foods, so that you can attract the birds you like most.

No yard would be complete without those fabulous humming-birds, so Chapter 6 focuses on their faves and other temptations for birds that prefer their food extra-sweet.

Grandma Putt would be proud of Chapter 7, which focuses on using up leftovers from the breadbox and pantry. Here's where you'll learn how to give an ordinary, unappealing slice of stale bread a real Midas touch.

You bluebird fans—and I'm one of 'em!—will appreciate Chapter 8, where I pass along my latest brain-storms for bringing these beautiful birds right to your feeder. Insects are the key, but that doesn't mean you'll need to haul out the butterfly net! I'll show you how to get in on the big new wave in bird feeding by adding easy-to-serve, protein-rich insects to your feeder menu.

Chapter 9 will tell you every-thing you need to know to have the best doggone watering hole in the neighborhood. I'll let you in on my secret weapon, the low-level birdbath, so you can enjoy the fun of splashing, sipping birds. You'll also find out about another nifty device that will attract plenty of attention from shower-lovers.

It's Jerry-to-the-Rescue time, as I pass along possible solutions to feeder pests in Chapter 10. Most of us won't be dealing with anything worse than cats or starlings; but if it's a bear in your backyard, I'll show you how to discourage that feeder varmint, too!

You'll keep the backyard bird bonanza going year-round with the ideas in Chapters 11 and 12. Here, I'll show you how to choose birdhouses tailored to your favorite tenants and why location, location, location can help get you the birds you want. You'll also learn some tricks for keeping out birds you don't want. We'll go on a scavenger hunt, too, to collect a batch of nesting materials that the birds will be fighting over come spring.

Of course, we want our bird-friendly yards to look good, too, so Chapter 13 will give you plenty of ideas for keeping your feeder area looking classy, not trashy. Looks aren't everything, though, so you'll also find plenty of ideas for selecting feeders that are easy to use.

By the time you put all my tips into practice, every bird in the neigh-borhood will give your backyard bonanza two thumbs (er, wings) up! But you don't need to wait until you read every page to get started. As soon as you begin using a few of my tricks, your yard will be on its way to becoming a solid-gold center of bird attention. So turn the page, and get ready to welcome a wave of warblers!

CHAPTER 1

Cheepers' Keepers

When you become a bird keeper, you quickly find out that you get a lot of benefits in exchange for supplying those inexpensive, easy-access eats. Feeding birds gives us entertainment, pest protection—and, believe it or not, lower blood pressure!

That's why I'm starting this book by talking about the benefits to both you and your feathered friends. In this chapter, you'll discover how bird feeding can lead to better health, more fun with the family, and maybe even a new bird-related hobby. You'll find out why feeding birds is good for your garden, too. Later in this chapter, you'll find tips for getting started, whether you're a first-timer or just need a refresher course, and you'll learn how to keep your birds coming back for more all year long.

Good for You

Let's be selfish here. Bird feeding is just plain fun. Birds may have an easier life because of our feeders, but the big bonanza is the way a bird feeder instantly makes life more interesting for us! I can't resist watching those little winged wonders outside my window, and I have a feeling you're just as hooked as I am. The extra little zing that birds bring to our lives actually works wonders on our health. Read on to find out how keeping a feeder can calm you down, cheer you up—and keep your mind sharp as a tack!

MOUNTAIN CHICKADEE

Super Stress-Buster

Look, right there—see that chickadee? Oops, there he goes. Well, he'll be right back—see? There he is again! And now, look, a whole flock of goldfinches just flew in!

That's the way bird-watching works, whether you're sharing the view with your family or talking to yourself. And that's exactly why experts say it's so good for us. We forget all about our busy lives and our weekday worries, and get lost in the action that's happening right outside the window. Try it yourself: Ten minutes with the towhees, and you might even have the peace of mind that's needed to balance the checkbook!

Just Say "Om"

No need to get with a guru, according to scientists who've measured heart rate and blood pressure of meditating or bird-watching volunteers. Watching birds at the feeder, for old hands and newbies alike, works just as well at calming down the heart rate and blood pressure as practicing the art

of meditation does. Both meditation and feeder-watching work their magic, so they say, by shifting our conscious focus off of ourselves, thus calming the chaos in our busy brains. 🐦

Calling Old Dogs!

Now, where did I put those car keys? I'm gettin' a little forgetful these days, so it's a comfort to know that sorting out sparrows can help keep me sharp. When I first started this hobby, I could tell a cardinal from a jay, and remember which one was the robin, but all those little birds just looked alike.

The more I watched them, though, the more I started to notice the little details that set them apart. I was *learning*—and that's the key to fending off the fog of an older brain. It may take me a little longer than most to match my birds to their pictures in a field guide, but this ol' dog can still learn a new trick or two! 🐦

Winter Blah-Beater

Unless you're lucky enough to live where flowers bloom all year long, winter means plenty of gloomy days. Some of us are look-

JERRY
TO THE RESCUE

Q. **I bought a field guide so I could figure out who's who at my feeder, but it's hopeless. There are too many birds in the book!**

A. Put down that book for a minute, and pick up a pencil instead. Make a list of all the birds you already know. You'll be surprised how many you can rattle off right away—robin, cardinal, jay, sparrow, blackbird—and those are just for starters. Nearly all field guides are organized by bird families, so that foundation is all you need to dig in. Small bird? Turn to the sparrows section. Shaped like a robin? See you in thrushes. Black bird? Aw, that's too easy!

Keep a field guide close at hand. Whenever you have a few minutes to spare, page through the pictures (skip the ducks, gulls, shorebirds, hawks, and owls at the beginning—hey, that's half the book right there!) and read the names beside them. Even though you're just looking, not studying, your mind will store that info to pull out later. It still surprises me when I spot a bird I've never seen before, and my trusty thinking cap chimes in "evening grosbeak," or whatever the bird is. So far, I'm batting better with birds than I ever did with birthdays!

CARDINAL

ing at snow, while others get a mostly gray landscape, but days are short everywhere, and the winter blahs can all too easily get a grip on you. Feeding birds helps fend off the moody blues. It's hard to stay down when you look out the window and see a busy bunch of cardinals or jive-talkin' jays. That long stretch after the holidays, when it starts to seem as if spring will never get here, is a great time to set up a feeder or expand your offerings. I get so distracted by watching to see who'll be the first to spy my new concoction that, before I know it, the days are getting longer again and the air says "spring thaw."

Never-Ending Education

Learning their names is just the beginning of gettin' educated about birds. It's fun to figure out who eats what, too, and that'll keep you busy for at least a few years! Meanwhile, you'll also be absorbing knowledge about their actions, such as who are the feisty ones and who are the friendly sort. Learning about birds is likely to lead you to reading about them, too, so you can learn other people's stories and compare them to your own. And no more scrabbling around for small talk at that get-together: Just ask who feeds birds, and you're off and running!

Get Connected

The Internet is brimming with bird sites where you can find fellow feeder-keepers. Look for a site that has a message board attached, where members can post notes to chat with

each other, ask and answer questions, and share tips and "Guess who's at my feeder!" news. Friendships are easy to make online, and you can hook up with folks you'd never have met otherwise. Just don't forget to look up from your computer now and then, though, to check on your bird feeders!

Good for Your Garden

Bird feeders are great for our gardens. Every bird that stops by for seeds is likely to spend some time scouting around the yard, as well, to find natural grub. Want proof? Just watch where that chickadee goes after he grabs a sunflower seed at your feeder. He may look like he's doing acrobatics on the branches, but he's really looking for bugs. Insects are a big part of the wild diet of birds, and that hankering is happy news for us. Here's the scoop on how our feeder friends help out around the yard.

Hide 'n' Seek

After dining at your grand buffet bird feeder, birds fly off to find a meal from Mother Nature. They're experts at ferreting out insects from their hiding places. Nuthatches scour the bark on your trees, woodpeckers snatch up ants, grackles flip over leaves to get at beetles: Your feeder friends cover every possible niche where bugs might be hiding. When the pest-control posse cleans up the place, it's *adios* to the aphids on your plum tree, *sayonara* to the Japanese beetles on your roses, and *see you later, alligator,* to plenty of other pests.

"Pest" Birds Earn Their Keep

Starlings and house sparrows have a habit of showing up in hordes at the feeder, which is why some folks consider them pests. But all feeder birds, even these two, work hard at eating insects when they're not gobbling your goodies. If you love your roses and despise the Japanese beetles that chomp their petals, you may want to think about adding feeder foods to *attract* starlings and house sparrows! Introduced to America from other countries, these imported birds do a great job of eating imported insects. House sparrows seek out adult Japanese beetles to munch, while starlings use their long beaks to grab the immature beetle grubs from underground.

Grandma Putt's BIRD BITS

Even-Steven

Ever notice how some years your yard is overrun with beetles, and the next year you can hardly find any? Grandma Putt always said that insect populations definitely have their ups and downs. And she knew that these natural cycles can leave a gap where birds are concerned, and they may have to range farther from home to fill their tummies. So she made sure her feeders were always full—feeder foods help even out the boom/bust cycle in bugs by making sure birds have a source of nutrition they can depend on.

Bugs in the Balance

Bad bugs are way more numerous than good ones, but that's the way nature intended it. In her eyes, the only thing that matters is keeping a balance between predators and prey. The insects we call good bugs, or beneficials, are those that prey on the bad bugs, which really aren't all that bad if you're not trying to keep your roses from being overrun by aphids. With all the pesticide fixes available for pest problems, good bugs are unfortunately getting sprayed into oblivion right alongside bad bugs. Birds help restore the natural balance between beneficial insects—the praying mantises, ladybugs, and others that dine on pesky sorts—and the ones we think of as pests. A single chickadee can down a dozen aphids in one brief stop, and that's just for starters. With birds holding down the pest population from overrunning the world, the beneficial insects have a better shot at keeping our gardens from falling prey to the bad guys.

HOUSE SPARROW

First-Time Feeders

Putting out your first feeder is a big deal. It takes less than half an hour to set one up and stock it, but the anticipation is almost as good as it is on Christmas Eve waiting for Santa. In neighborhoods where birds are already living or visiting, you may have curious customers as soon as you go back inside, or it might take a few hours before they spot the handout. If you live in an area where birds are scarce, such as a brand-new subdivision that's lacking trees, it can take several days for birds to find the feed. But don't get discouraged while you wait—some feathered friends will eventually show up, and that's a real red-letter day! Here's how to get started, and how to keep going, right through all four seasons.

Nurture 'Em, Cowboy!

Feeding birds may be a little harder to brag about than hanging tough on a bucking bronco, but the reality is that it feels doggone GOOD to nurture smaller creatures. If this is your first feeder, you'll be surprised at how proud you'll feel when the birds find their way to it for the very first time. After that, it just gets better and better, because the birds will build in numbers, and more kinds will come by. Before you know it, you'll be adding feeders and spending your weekends in the birdseed aisle, instead of the hardware store.

Low Budget? No Biggie

You can set up the Rolls-Royce of feeding stations for less than $500, and that's including one of those astronomically priced feeders you see in the fanciest shops. For a couple of well-made basic feeders, you can get away with under $50. Of course, if you're the least bit handy, or if you try the make-it-yourself alternatives in this book, your feeders don't have to cost you a penny!

DO IT YOURSELF

Faux Focus

After you snap your twentieth pic of birds at the feeder, you might hanker for a wilder setting, one that looks a little more natural. An easy solution is to "plant" a large, dead branch by the feeder. Most of us have a likely candidate hanging around somewhere; maybe a tree that needs major pruning, or a branch blown down in a storm. Since you're not planting this for posterity (only for a season's worth of snapshots), you don't need to worry about whether the wood will rot. Here's how to set up your faux wild setting:

DIRECTIONS

Step 1. Dig a hole about 12 inches deep, very close to the feeder, so that birds will be able to use your branch as a convenient landing or launching pad.

Step 2. Have a helper hold the bottom end of the branch upright in the hole while you stand back to gauge the effect. Then, when you have the branch positioned to your liking, fill in the hole with the soil you removed.

Step 3. Stomp the soil down very firmly. Pile a few rocks around the base of the branch for extra stability if it looks a little shaky.

Step 4. Get ready for some great shots. Snap new arrivals or birds waiting for their turn on the branch. (You can also hang a tube feeder or suet feeder on the back side of the branch, or smear some peanut butter on it, for extra incentive.)

Seeds, Camera, Action!

Taking pictures of your feathered friends can be the start of a whole new hobby. It's a great excuse to dust off that camera. Feeder birds offer lots of color and lots of action, right up close. You'll get satisfying results with simple snapshots or digital pics, and it's so easy that kids like to try their hand at it, too. Here's how to do it:

◆ Install the feeder right outside a window, as close as you can get it. Make sure the window opens easily, so there's no glass blocking the action.

◆ When you're ready to snap a picture, stand to one side of the window, so your big hulking form doesn't scare away your subjects.

◆ If your camera isn't auto-focus, set the focus before the shot by zeroing in on the feeder or the spot where birds usually land. You may need to do a bit of adjustment when birds arrive, but at least you'll have a head start.

VARIED THRUSH

◆ Consider a shutter-release cable for your camera, if it's adaptable. This "extension cord" screws into the thumb button, so you can set the camera in front of the action and stand several feet away to click. Most 35mm nondigital cameras can use this inexpensive aid.

◆ Install a prop to make your pictures more "wild" looking. See "Faux Focus" on the opposite page for details.

Breakfast Is Served

Filling those feeders can cost hundreds a year—or practically nothing at all. Try this trick: Put out only as much seed as you can afford, at the same time every day (morning and late afternoon are best, because that's when birds eat most). Once the scoop is gone, birds will glean every overlooked crumb, then disperse. It won't take them long to figure out what time of day you fill the feeders. Just like those horses banging their buckets in the barn, your birds will be ready and waiting when it's feeding time.

Everyone's a Winner

We get a lot out of feeding birds, but birds benefit from the partnership, too. They get a reliable feast without having to work for it. In harsh weather, they never go to bed hungry. And until the neighborhood cat comes a-prowling, birds are more protected from the risk of predators at the feeder than they are when foraging in the wild. No wonder customers come along almost as soon as we set up a feeder! 🐦

BIRD BITS

Seed Stampede

Boy, it used to make Grandma Putt hotter than a frying pan when she called "Dinner!" and no one came running. When folks aren't waiting at the table with their mouths watering for your fine home cookin', it's natural to feel unappreciated. I wonder if that's why she took her feeders down in summer, when eager eaters are few and far between? Whatever her reasons, Grandma Putt waited until well into fall to set up her feeders. By then, birds are done with family duties, and days are getting shorter and nights chillier. In fall, birds come flocking when you bring out their breakfast. So if you're setting up a feeder for the first time, mid- to late fall is a gratifying time to begin. Wait until the leaves turn colors and the nights are crisp, and I guarantee your precious seed won't get snubbed.

Sure Cure for Shut-Ins

If I had a million dollars, I'd put a feeder at every old folks' home, hospital, or wherever else folks are confined indoors. For my money, a tufted titmouse beats a television any day. Birds are alive, a part of the real world, and not the soap opera scene. I'd wager that's why they're more fun to watch than any amount of "must-see" TV. If you want to do a real good deed for a friend or family member, set up a feeder by the window closest to their favorite easy chair—and keep it filled. Extra-large tube feeders and hopper feeders with generous storage capacity are the best choices for those who won't be tending it themselves; they'll need refilling only about once a week or so. 🐦

Social Climbers

No yard to put a bird feeder in? No problem! With a little coaxing, you can tempt birds to your second-floor balcony or deck. Birds aren't afraid of heights (hey, these guys have wings, after all!), but they *are* wary about visiting a highly unnatural place with no nearby trees or shrubs. Hungry stomachs usually win out over natural reluctance, but it will take longer for you to gain a steady trade than it would at ground level.

Birds are social creatures, so once the first brave souls arrive, others will follow. Native sparrows, which usually stick close to the ground, are unlikely to ever be regulars, but you may eventually draw jays, cardinals, chickadees, finches, and most other familiar feeder birds. And be sure to include a nectar feeder in your aerie; hummingbirds have no qualms at all about sipping at new heights. ✍

JERRY
TO THE RESCUE

Q. **Won't feeding birds make them dependent on us for food?**

A. Out of habit, yes. But as a sole source, no. Our feeders are simply a supplement to natural foods. Even the most exotic seed mix takes a backseat to fresh, juicy insects, weed seeds, and ripe berries. If you're ever in doubt, just watch a bird after it leaves your feeder. You'll see it hasn't forgotten the wheres, whats, or hows of foraging for its own food. Only in hard times are our feeders vital to birds, so make sure yours stay stocked during wild winters or whenever an ice storm strikes. You may be the only source of food during those times.

Kids These Days

I don't care how jaded they seem to be by the video games and computers of today's world, kids still like to do things with their parents or grandparents—as long as it's fun and they're not scolded every minute for not doing it right! Filling a bird feeder and watching birds is something you can't mess up, so it's perfect for prying young'uns away from the electronics. Get Johnny or Jasmine to help you fill the feeders in the morning or after school, then spy on the diners together. Keep in mind that young ranch hands have a short attention span. It's better to call them to the window to "Come see this!" every hour or so than to make them sit still for half an hour at a shot. ✍

Creative Champ

Snow and ice storms will test your mettle—mostly in the area of being prepared! I get caught short sometimes when bad weather hits, but I no longer consider shoveling my way to the seed store. Instead, I look in my larder for a chance to get creative. A few stale crackers, a handful of dog food, some cooking oil, and *voilà*—haute cuisine for chickadees! You'll find plenty of tips in this book to help you cook up or dress up everyday foods to make them more palatable to birds. And while you'll probably get cold tootsies keeping the feeder cleared and filled, you'll definitely feel all warm inside thinking about the bird bellies that won't go hungry because of you. 🐦

FOUR-SEASON FEEDING

The changing clientele at your feeder makes every season a surprise. Some reliable regulars, such as cardinals, jays, and house finches, will be around all year long, but many of the most interesting birds are drop-ins for shorter duration. Make sure you get your share of birds year-round by shifting your feeder menu to suit the seasons. Here's what you need to consider.

GRAY JAY

Fall-into-Winter Festival

The peak feeder season begins in late September as days shorten, leaves change color, and fall migration swings into high gear. Feeders fill up with young adult birds from the neighborhood, as well as with travelers passing through. When winter settles in, birds turn to feeders to conserve energy they'd otherwise expend seeking out wild foods. So expect to empty a lot more sacks of seed during this season, when standing-room-only is likely to be the rule at your feeders! 🐦

Cold-Weather Aids

As winter approaches, switch your feeder menu to a hearty, high-calorie diet. Here's a checklist to help you decide how to fill your feeders:

◆ Stock up on basic seeds, plus seed specialties. You'll host plenty of large and small seed-eaters in winter, so be ready!

◆ Put out a generous supply of suet and other fats, which are literal lifesavers when temperatures dip below freezing.

◆ Try mealworms and other insect foods to attract some unusual birds, such as that neighborhood mockingbird that's decided to stick it out instead of moving south.

◆ Now's the time to try some of your home cooking on the birds! Hungry birds need extra calories in winter, and they'll appreciate the concoctions you make just for them. You'll find plenty of recipes for nutty, fruity, seedy, and suetty goodies throughout this book. 🐦

Lawn Chair Lean-To

All-weather lawn furniture that you leave out in the yard makes nifty instant roofs when you need more sheltered feeding space in a hurry. When a blizzard rolls in, I shuffle on out to the garden bench and scrape out some of the snow below, letting the seat stay blanketed with white. Then I scatter some seed on the ground, below the bench "roof," so that all those sparrows, juncos, doves, and other hungry birds have a protected spot to peck in.

Pre-Blizzard Conditions

No need to watch the weather channel when you have a bird feeder! One glance is all you need and you'll know when snow is on the way, or an ice storm is brewing. More birds than ever will begin to flock to the feeder the day before the bad weather arrives, and the numbers will keep building right up until the flakes begin to fall. When you see a passel of sparrows, juncos, and other regulars cracking seeds as if their lives depended on it, you can bet your bottom dollar that they're right! Within hours, their wild food will be buried or hard to get at, so they stock up big-time before the storm. 🐦

PURPLE MARTIN

Survival School

I'd like to believe that my feeders are vital to birds, but the unvarnished truth is that birds usually don't need me for survival. Most of the time, they can get along just fine without a handout. My feeder guests are loyal only because they like my food! Sometimes, though, a handy handout does make the difference between life and death. Here's when:

Ice storms. A coating of ice makes it impossible for birds to get at seeds or insects on plants or on the ground. Ice-coated branches may look beautiful to us, but the stuff spells disaster to birds.

Deep snow. White stuff that piles up deeper than a few inches makes it darn difficult for birds to find enough food on their own. Sparrows, juncos, towhees, doves, and other ground-level birds have the worst of it, because the seeds they depend on are buried too deep to dig out.

Extreme cold. Frigid nights can cause birds to literally drop dead, unless they have their inner furnace well stoked before retiring for the night. Heat them up with an extra helping of high-fat foods before dusk.

Spring cold snaps. Bluebirds, purple martins, robins, and other birds that rely mainly on insects can get caught by surprise when the spring weather shifts back into winter gear, even for a day or two. Mealworms and other insect foods at the feeder, supplemented by suet and other high-fat goodies, can be their salvation. 🐦

Spring Superlatives

Every day in spring holds the possibility of an "Oh wow!" bird at the feeder—an indigo bunting, rose-breasted grosbeak, scarlet tanager, or other bird that doesn't normally frequent feeders year-round. Many of these super songbirds are here today, gone tomorrow, as they stop off for a fast fill-up along their migration route. Others may hang around for a week or longer, until they disperse to court and nest. In most parts of the country, the spring season begins in late February to March as the earliest migrants, including purple finches and fox sparrows, arrive. Bigger, bolder birds come a little later, usually from April through mid-May.

Pesticide Payback

You may be an organic gardener, but pesticides could be popular with your next-door neighbor—and everyone else on the block. Insect-killing sprays, dusts, and other potions eliminate a lot of the natural food of backyard birds. Stocking your feeder helps to offset those pesticide losses, especially if you include suet, mealworms, and other soft foods. If insects are scarce, birds may turn to your feeder to supply the protein-rich morsels they'd otherwise have harvested naturally.

Summer Slowdown

Fair-weather friends? Not hardly! When the weather is foul, birds flock to the feeder, but in fair weather, they're nowhere to be found. Feeder traffic slows to a crawl in summer because birds' natural foods are everywhere in abundance. Birds can fend for themselves just fine once bugs are out and about. Besides, we aren't so cooped up ourselves when the days are long and warm, and we're likely to spend more time outside, rather than indoors, watching the feeder. No need to pack it in, though. A handful of

---

Sprightly Swap

New birds means a new menu. Spring is a good time to add another open tray feeder, so you'll have plenty of serving space. Keep your basic and specialty seed feeders brimming, but add some of these interesting extras to pique the curiosity of the passersby:

✳ Offer mealworms and other insect foods— they're a huge hit in spring, especially when a cold spell sneaks in. They're the best bet for enticing purple martins to make a pit stop, and they'll also get gobbled up by bluebirds, catbirds, yellow-rumped warblers, Carolina wrens, and brown thrashers just in from migration.

✳ Set out the suet and suet-based treats. They're popular with the same songbirds that appreciate insect foods.

✳ Fill the nectar feeder so it's ready and waiting when hummingbirds arrive.

✳ Add some orange halves for the orioles, and your feeders will be brimming with spring beauties!

loyal regulars—birds that live in the neighborhood—will still stop in daily. Grandma Putt, being the frugal sort, cut off the seed supply as soon as feeder birds began dwindling around lilac time. I keep mine going, though, because I still enjoy sharing breakfast time with the birds.

Help for Pooped Parents

Raising babies is just as much a full-time job for birds as it is for us. Come to think of it, it may be even worse! Sunup to sundown, it's a never-ending round of foraging and feeding, because those baby beaks are always hungry. Parent birds that are nesting in your neighborhood may not nourish their babies with feeder foods, but they will take advantage of the easy eats for their own needs.

Summer Menu Switcheroo

Seed-eaters eat seeds year-round, but in summer, they also seek out softer foods that are more like their natural summer staples of insects and fruits. You'll notice that the consumption of basic and specialty seeds drops off dramatically in summer. Reduce the seeds, but add these foods to entice colorful summer birds to your feeder:

◆ Mealworms and insect foods, which will be snatched up fast by parent birds feeding nestlings, and by the adult birds themselves.

◆ Fruit and fruit-based treats (like jelly) will win the loyalty of orioles, thrashers, bluebirds, catbirds, Carolina wrens, and

Grandma Putt's BIRD BITS

Goldfinch Garb

Those little birds squabbling over the tube feeder in October sure ACT like goldfinches. They even SOUND like goldfinches. But they sure don't LOOK like 'em!

In fall and winter, the male goldfinch is definitely a bird of a different color. Like other songbirds, goldfinches shed their feathers after nesting season and grow a new set for the coming year. But instead of donning a fresh yellow-and-black suit, males reach into the closet and grab an understated olive green outfit, similar to the female's year-round dress.

When winter shifts to spring, you'll see these boys looking progressively blotchy as their winter feathers are replaced by a new suit of yellow and black for breeding season. WOW!

mockingbirds. These same soft-food eaters will also enjoy bird breads and doughs made from the recipes in this book.

◆ Suet and peanut butter treats; overworked parent birds adore these high-energy snacks.

◆ Nectar will be much appreciated by hummingbirds and orioles. (For recipes, see "Nectar of the Gods" on page 153.) 🐦

WHO EATS WHAT

An all-purpose menu of black oil sunflower seeds and millet will fill the bellies of nearly all feeder birds year-round. But adding some variety will not only attract unusual birds, it also will combat competition from other neighborhood feeders and boost the number of birds at your feeders. Here's how to fine-tune the feed, in order of each bird's preference.

BIRD	FALL/WINTER FEEDER FOODS	SPRING FEEDER FOODS	SUMMER FEEDER FOODS
Blackbirds, grackles	Usually absent from feeders; where present, feed cracked corn, millet of any kind, black oil sunflower seeds, bread-based treats, chicken scratch	Same as in winter	Usually absent from feeders (natural food is abundant)
Bluebirds	Usually absent from feeders; where present, feed mealworms and other insect foods, peanut butter treats, suet and suet-based treats, bread-based treats, fruit	Mealworms and other insect foods, peanut butter treats, suet and suet-based treats, bread-based treats	Uncommon at feeders (natural food is abundant), but may come for mealworms and other insect foods
Brown creeper	Mealworms and other insect foods, suet	Same as in winter	Usually absent from feeders (natural food is abundant)

(continued)

WHO EATS WHAT, *continued*

BIRD	FALL/WINTER FEEDER FOODS	SPRING FEEDER FOODS	SUMMER FEEDER FOODS
Buntings	Absent from feeders (migratory)	White proso millet, other millets, black oil sunflower seeds, niger and other small specialty seeds	Usually absent from feeders (natural food is abundant)
Bushtit	Suet	Same as in winter	Same as in winter
Cardinal	Sunflower seeds, any kind; safflower	Same as in winter	Same as in winter
Carolina wren	Usually absent from feeders; where present, feed mealworms and other insect foods, suet and suet-based treats, bread-based treats, fruit	Mealworms and other insect foods, suet	Usually absent from feeders (natural food is abundant)
Catbird, thrashers, mockingbird	Usually absent from feeders; where present, feed suet and suet-based treats, mealworms and other insect foods, bread-based treats, fruit	Mealworms and other insect foods, fruit, suet and suet-based treats, bread-based treats	Usually absent from feeders (natural food is abundant); may come for mealworms and other insect foods
Chickadees	Nuts, peanuts, peanut butter, suet and suet-based treats, any kind of sunflower seeds, bread-based treats, mealworms and other insect foods	Same as in winter; may be absent from feeders after migration, except within breeding range	Same as in winter
Doves, pigeons	Cracked corn, millet of any kind, milo, chicken scratch	Same as in winter	Same as in winter
Finches	Niger, black oil sunflower seeds, flax and other small specialty seeds, sunflower chips, striped sunflower seeds, millet of any kind	Same as in winter	Same as in winter

BIRD	FALL/WINTER FEEDER FOODS	SPRING FEEDER FOODS	SUMMER FEEDER FOODS
Grosbeaks	Sunflower seeds of any kind	Same as in winter	Usually absent from feeders (natural food is abundant; migratory)
Hummingbirds	Usually absent from feeders; where present, feed nectar	Nectar	Same as in spring
Jays	Nuts, peanuts, any kind of sunflower seeds, corn, peanut butter-based treats	Same as in winter	Same as in winter
Juncos	Millet of any kind, other small specialty seeds	Usually absent after midspring except within breeding range; where present, feed millet of any kind, flax and other small specialty seeds	Absent except within breeding range; where present, feed millet of any kind, flax and other small specialty seeds
Kinglets	Mealworms and other insect foods, suet	Usually absent from feeders after midspring (natural food is abundant)	Usually absent from feeders (natural food is abundant)
Nuthatches	Peanut butter, suet, nuts, peanuts, any kind of sunflower seed, mealworms and other insect foods	Same as in winter	Same as in winter
Orioles	Absent from feeders except in southern Florida (migratory)	Mealworms and other insect foods, oranges, nectar, grape jelly	May be absent from feeders (natural food is abundant), or may continue visiting for same foods as in spring
Pine siskin	Black oil sunflower seeds, niger, millet, rapeseed and other small specialty seeds	Usually absent after midspring, except within breeding range; where present, same as in winter	Usually absent from feeders (natural food is abundant)

(continued)

Who Eats What, continued

BIRD	FALL/WINTER FEEDER FOODS	SPRING FEEDER FOODS	SUMMER FEEDER FOODS
Purple martin	Absent from feeders (migratory)	Mealworms and other insect foods, crushed eggshells	Usually absent from feeders (natural food is abundant)
Robin	Mealworms and other insect foods, suet and suet-based treats, fruit, bread-based treats	Frequents feeders when natural foods are scarce; mealworms and other insect foods, suet and suet-based treats, fruit, bread-based treats	Usually absent from feeders (natural food is abundant)
Sparrows	Millet, flax, other small specialty seeds	Same as in winter	Same as in winter
Tanagers	Absent from feeders (migratory)	Mealworms and other insect foods, white proso millet, sunflower chips	Usually absent from feeders (natural food is abundant)
Towhees	Millet, flax, other small specialty seeds, mealworms and other insect foods	Same as in winter	Usually absent from feeders (natural food is abundant)
Vireos	Absent from feeders (migratory)	Mealworms and other insect foods	Usually absent from feeders (natural food is abundant)
Wild turkey, pheasant, quail	Cracked corn, millet, milo, chicken scratch	May be absent from feeders; where present, same as in winter	Usually absent from feeders (natural food is abundant)
Woodpeckers	Suet, mealworms and other insect foods, nuts, peanuts, peanut butter, any kind of sunflower seeds, corn	Same as in winter	Same as in winter
Yellow-rumped warbler	Mealworms and other insect foods, suet	Same as in winter	Usually absent from feeders (natural food is abundant)

CHAPTER 2

Menu Mainstays

Back when I was just a whippersnapper, I ate a peanut butter-and-jelly sandwich for lunch every day, and it suited me just fine. When it comes to feeding birds, sunflower seeds and millet are the backbone of the feeder menu, just like that jar of Jif® was to me. They're easy to buy and easy to feed, and just about every bird that comes to your feeder will gobble them up. They're proof that your menu doesn't have to be fancy to bring lots of purty birdies to your backyard!

In this chapter, you'll learn how to attract a five-star clientele of cardinals, jays, chickadees, and dozens of other pals on a budget. When you're ready to add some special fixin's to these menu mainstays, the other chapters will tell you all about the extras that make feeding the birds so much fun.

Superior Sunflowers

The first time I tackled a whole lobster, I was ready to quit before I got to the good part. Claw crackers, nut picks, messy fingers—whew, that was a lot of work. No wonder the tail is everybody's favorite part: It's easy to access and is a great big reward! I like to think of sunflower seeds as the "lobster tail" of the feeder world. One good crack and the shell splits to reveal a supersized seed kernel, packed with plenty of protein and fat. Super size, super nutrition, and super easy to get at—a winner in every way!

ACORN
WOODPECKER

Strike Oil with Black Gold

The next time you're filling the feeder, take a sunflower seed and smash it with your thumbnail on a piece of paper. That streak of grease may horrify you calorie-conscious souls, but to birds, food with extra fat is extra good. If you want to get technical about it, a sunflower seed is about 25% protein, and can be almost 50% fat. I don't know if that counts as a winner on the Atkins diet, but those good, greasy sunflower seeds are a real champ, according to birds that chomp on them.

Back in Black

Back in the dark ages of bird feeding, oh, long about 30 or 40 years ago, striped sunflower seed was all I ever saw for sale. Then black oil sunflower seed came on the scene, and now striped seed has almost become an endangered species in birdseed land. Black oil seed is everywhere, at El Cheapo prices, if you know how to shop (don't worry, I'll tell you how to get real deals later in this chapter). But if you want striped seed, you'll have to search for it—and shell out more of those precious bucks.

More birds prefer black oil seed, but farmers still grow the striped kind for human treats. Wonder who eats more seeds in a week: the baseball team spitting shells in the dugout, or the feathered gang at the feeder? 🐦

Back Porch Picnic

A sturdy, pressed-paper plate, such as a Chinet® plate, makes an ideal quickie bird feeder. The plate will last for weeks if it's in a spot that's protected from rain. Just use thumbtacks to attach the plate to your wooden porch railing, right next to your usual sitting spot. Scatter a handful of black oil sunflower seeds in it, then wait for the feasting to begin. 🐦

One Size Fits All

You can stop reading right here if you want to simplify your bird-feeding life: Just put out black oil sunflower seed, and sit back and enjoy the action. When birds find a feeder that's heaped full with black oil sunflower seed, they've reached the mother lode. You'll strike it rich with

BIRD BITS

She Eats Like a Bird?

That old saying was a compliment in Grandma Putt's day, or maybe a comment on picky eating habits. Turns out that eating like a bird means just the opposite of what we think it does: Birds eat almost constantly, and they eat a lot!

For birds, maintaining their usual body temperature of about 105° to 110°F—by stoking it with food—is a dawn-to-dusk job. Their metabolism is geared much higher than our own because birds are so small to begin with, so they lose body heat faster.

Watch a bird and you'll see that it gets more exercise in 5 minutes than some of us couch potatoes get in a week. It swings from branch to branch, flies without a second thought, hops hither and yon, and is just generally a little perpetual-motion machine. It takes a lot of juice to keep that kind of mini-engine going!

cardinals, woodpeckers, and at least 20 other species of feathered feasters when you start feeding black oil seeds. WOW! That's almost every bird in the neighborhood—quite a payoff for putting out just one kind of seed.

Why the rush to get to this black gold? If that chickadee scarfing down sunflower seeds would stop a minute and explain, he'd whistle a tune like this:

High meat-to-shell ratio. That's the fancy phrase for it, but all

Spring Fling

Spring and fall migrations are tough times for birds. Their wings beat along a route that covers thousands of miles in just a few weeks, so finding high-energy food is even more important than usual. In fall, weed seeds and wild berries are abundant every wingbeat of the way. But by the time spring rolls around, wild foods have been pretty much picked clean. That's when your feeders take center stage, attracting even birds that usually fend for themselves.

So make sure your feeders are stocked with big, meaty, high-calorie, black oil sunflower seeds from March through April, and you may be rewarded with a sighting of a hungry scarlet tanager, rufous-sided towhee, or rose-breasted grosbeak, as well as dozens of other tuckered, tummy-rumbling migrants.

birds care about is that there's a plump, supersized kernel waiting under that thin shell.

Higher oil content. Fat is the fuel for birds' daily fast-action lives, and all those calories keep their motors running. Black seed is higher in oil than striped, so it's more beneficial to birds.

Smaller size. Black seed is smaller than striped, so more kinds of birds can get it into their beaks. With black oil seeds, sunflowers aren't just for jays and cardinals anymore. Now song sparrows and even tiny chipping sparrows can grab a share, too.

Thinner shells. Black seed has thinner shells than striped, so more kinds of birds can crack it. In the old days, those little gray juncos (which I grew up calling "snowbirds") used to have to pick through the leavings to find bits of overlooked kernels. Now they can eat right beside their big-beaked pals. 🐦

Ready for Rush Hour

Feeders are busiest first thing in the morning, when bird bellies are running on empty after a good night's sleep. To fill the tank fast, they flock to the feeder to get the grub. So fill your feeders as early in the morning as you can to make sure that the birds' breakfast is ready at rush hour, which lasts from dawn to midmorning. And if you're a sleepyhead, restock your feeder the night before so that you don't leave any hungry customers hanging. 🐦

Roll Call Roundup

Everyone eats black oil sunflower seed. Well, almost everyone. I've noticed that the only birds that don't are those that naturally chow down on soft foods: insect eaters like purple martins, worm eaters like robins, and fruit eaters like catbirds and orioles. Still, I make sure that black oil sunflower seed is always in the feedbag, because so many kinds of birds do love it—more than 50 different species in all! And you never know whether a bird will have a change of heart and decide to try a taste—I've watched a scarlet tanager enjoying the stuff, after "experts" tried to tell me they wouldn't touch it! But even without those rare birds, the list of regulars is a long one. Keep your eyes open and you're sure to see some of these birds cracking those seeds:

DICKCISSEL

- ✔ Cardinal
- ✔ Blackbirds
- ✔ Buntings
- ✔ Chickadees
- ✔ Dickcissel (yep, there really is a bird with this name!)
- ✔ Finches
- ✔ Flickers
- ✔ Goldfinches
- ✔ Grackles

- ✔ Jays
- ✔ Juncos
- ✔ Native sparrows
- ✔ Nuthatches
- ✔ Pine siskin
- ✔ Titmice
- ✔ Towhees
- ✔ Varied thrush
- ✔ Woodpeckers

And, of course, let's not forget our ever-present pardners, the house sparrows and starlings, who maybe aren't quite as welcome at the ranch as these other birds are. 🌱

Anti-Starling Stripes

Stick to striped sunflower seeds if you want to discourage starlings or house sparrows from visiting your feeder. They can't crack the bigger, harder-shelled striped seeds as easily as they can the black oil type, so with any luck, they'll fly off to gobble someone else's birdseed. Meanwhile, cardinals, jays, and woodpeckers will still be able to enjoy the feast at your feeder. 🌱

Bottom Feeders

Plastic soda bottles may be worth a few cents when you return the bottle (in certain states), but you'll get a million bucks' worth of fun from turning two or three of them into quickie feeders. Just saw off the bottom of an empty bottle with a kitchen knife, and presto—it's a feeder! I like to line 'em up on my deck rail to coax those chickadees and titmice right up close. Big, heavy birds aren't likely to use these bottle-bottom feeders, so you can attach them in a snap with thumbtacks. Just fill 'em up with black oil sunflower seeds, the favored snack of the perky little birds you'll get as customers. ✑

JERRY
TO THE RESCUE

Q. **Which is better, black oil or striped sunflower seeds?**

A. No need to haul that 50-pound bag back to the store—birds will eagerly devour either kind! As for "better," consider the following before you buy:

• Black is better for your budget—it's less expensive per pound.

• Black is better at serving more customers. Smaller seeds and thinner shells means more seeds to the scoop, so you won't have to refill your feeder as often.

• Black is better in cold weather. More oil = higher calories = warmer birds!

• Black is better for more kinds of birds. Smaller seed-eaters, like buntings and finches, can easily crack the shells.

Pie Pan Pin-Up

My recycling bins are so inspiring, I thought up another use for an everyday object that usually lands in the trash. You may already be recycling aluminum pie pans as bird scarecrows in the garden, but did you ever think about making them into bird feeders? When you fasten them down so that they can't twirl in the wind, birds soon get comfortable perching on the edge and picking at seeds inside of them. The transformation is finished in a flash: Just use a staple gun to attach the pan to the sill of your deck or porch railing, and fill it with any seed mix. ✑

Slippery Slope

That first feeder can lead to a long slide into obsession, but I don't let that stop me! I've even taken that "slippery slope" to heart, and put it to work in the form of my main birdseed mover: a discarded sledding saucer. The sturdy plastic disc works great at moving heavy bags of seed over the snow to my more distant feeders. As winter snow piles up, even crossing the yard can feel like hiking to the "Back 40," so I keep the sled handy right by the seed storage cans. I load it up with seed-mix jugs and bags, plus suet and home-made goodies I want to distribute, then grab the rope and slide along on my rounds. By the way, the sled also slides just fine on paths covered in wood chips or bark mulch and on grass, though you will leave a flattened track behind. For extra-slick sliding, spray the bottom of the sledding saucer with a silicone spray made for cross-country skiis or a vegetable oil before you load it up. 🐦

Big Beak, Big Seeds

Take a look at the birds munching on those sunflower seeds, and you'll see that many of them are big birds with big beaks. Think of an evening grosbeak or its kissin' cousin, the cardinal, or take a gander at the size of a red-bellied woodpecker or a jay. These are the Hoss Cartwrights of the homeplace, way bigger than the

Grandma Putt's BIRD BITS

Sunny Susie Picked a Peck of Sunflower Seeds

I never was much good with tongue twisters, so I'll stick to just the facts, ma'am. A single sunflower head holds somewhere around 2,000 seeds, according to the folks that spend their spare time counting these things. Me, I'll take their word for it. And farmers know for a fact that an average yield of sunflowers is 1,400 pounds per acre—and can be as much as 3,000 pounds per acre. I'll let you folks figure out how many seeds that is. All I know is that those big yellow daisies sure keep my birds mighty happy. Plus, they're patriotic: Check the fine print on the bag, and you'll see that the sunflowers we buy for birdseed are grown in the great "breadbasket" states and provinces of North America. They're native to the Southwest, where Navajo, Sioux, and other Native Americans were spitting shells long before Europeans arrived on the scene.

EVENING GROSBEAK

bantamweight sparrows, juncos, and chickadee Little Joes that bustle among them. Not only are they bigger in body size, but these seed-eating heavyweights have bigger, stronger beaks, too, which means more crunch power.

Birds are no dummies when it comes to singing for their supper. Big birds would rather eat big seeds than spend more time pecking at tiny ones. Put out plenty of plump sunflower seeds and you'll keep this hungry horde happy. 🐦

Weather or Not

It's easy to overfill open feeders, such as the classic tray type that's so popular with birds and feeder hosts. Why, scooping and pouring out seeds is just plain FUN! But before you get carried away, check the weather forecast. Leftover seed that gets soaked by rain or buried under snow is no help to the birds. So, if wet weather's in the forecast, lean toward the skimpy side, about 1 cup per feeder. Once you have a handle on how much your birds are eating, you can supersize the servings to match their appetite, whatever the weather may be. 🐦

Swiss Army-Knife Anatomy

Whether you call it a bill or a beak— and don't let anybody tell you that one word is better than the other, they're both correct—that pointy little thing is handier than a spork when it comes to serving up the grub. With no clever fingers or multipurpose pocketknives, birds make do with sheer, um, bill power.

A bird's beak can pick up food in one dainty motion, or peck away to get lots of little bites fast. It can nibble off the shell as daintily as a debutante, or it can whack open a walnut like a pile driver. And it's great for multitasking, too: Birds can pause from eating to run that beak over their feathers like a comb, or dip into your birdbath to take a sip. Come to think of it, if our noses were as handy as a bird's beak, I wouldn't have to fiddle with my confounded pocketknife contraption nearly so often! 🐦

COME 'N' GET IT!

Black-and-White Banquets

Black oil sunflower seeds, striped sunflower seeds, and white proso millet are the "Big Three" at the main birdseed table. I like to fiddle with the amounts of each kind of seed—and maybe add some hulled sunflower chips for extra incentive, or try out other types of millet—to attract particular birds to my feeder. Reminds me of my favorite Mexican restaurant: Many of the dishes have the same basic ingredients, but it's how you combine them that keeps the customers coming back!

NOTE: All of my recipes are made to fit into a plastic gallon milk jug for easy handling and pouring, and for waterproof, bug-proof storage. A gallon jug holds about 12 cups of seeds; you may need to shake it now and then while filling, so that the seeds settle.

Tanager Treat

Bright-colored songbirds that eat mostly insects and berries, tanagers usually stay in the treetops—but sometimes, especially in early spring, they come down to earth for a meal at the feeder. Tempt them with this mix, which includes the extra enticement of no-work, hulled sunflower chips.

6 cups of sunflower chips
4 cups of black oil sunflower seeds
1 cup of white proso millet

Mix the sunflower chips and sunflower seeds together in a large bowl with your hands, then stir in the millet. Pour into a clean, dry, plastic milk jug and cap tightly for storage.

Finch Favorite

Finches are famous for warbling a few notes while they're at the feeder. Listen—I think they're singing your praises! The combination of hulled sunflower chips plus seeds with shells will keep finches happily pecking away at this mix. It's a fine feast for goldfinches, house finches, purple finches, and other small songsters.

6 cups of black oil sunflower seeds
3 cups of white proso millet
2 cups of hulled sunflower chips

Mix all of these ingredients together. Pour into a clean, dry, plastic milk jug and cap tightly for storage.

Serve-'Em-All Seed Mix

Store-bought seed mixes are usually pretty skimpy on the sunflower seeds, and they may be filled out with cheaper seeds that aren't bird favorites. My Serve-'Em-All Seed Mix will be eaten down to the last bite. It suits almost every bird that visits birdfeeders across the country, and it's easy to make changes to this basic mix, depending on which birds are at your feeder. When sparrows or juncos are thick, I boost the millet; when cardinals come in for the winter or evening grosbeaks arrive en masse, I pump up the sunflowers.

9 cups of black oil sunflower seeds*
3 cups of white proso millet

1. Pour the sunflower seeds into a plastic pail or other container big enough to comfortably hold the quantity you're making.

2. Pour in the millet, and mix with your hands until the millet is distributed throughout.

3. Funnel the mix into a clean, dry, plastic milk jug. (After a time in storage, the millet tends to sink to the bottom of the container, so just shake up each jug before filling the feeders.)

4. Cap the jug tightly. You can store it outside in a metal trash can with a lid, or on a shelf in the pantry or a kitchen cupboard, until you're ready to use it.

*About 11 to 12 cups of seed will fill a single milk jug; allow a little headroom for shaking. If you want to mix up a bigger batch, just use more cups of each ingredient.

Quail Ho!

If you live in quail country, you've probably already spotted these birds bustling around your feeding area, their jaunty top-knot feathers bobbing as they scurry to and fro. Give them a feast all their own in a low feeder or directly on the ground, where they can gather in groups to eat.

6 cups of cracked corn
**3 cups of milo (a close
   cousin of millet)**
**2 cups of white
   proso millet**

Mix all of these ingredients. Pour into a clean, dry, plastic milk jug and cap tightly for storage.

Shell Game

When birds crack open sunflower seeds, they drop the shells—usually in the feeder. And sunflower seed shells look an awful lot like sunflower seeds from a distance! To make sure I'm not shortchanging my birds, I do an in-person inventory every day. Shells easily brush away when I lightly swipe my hand across the feeder tray, and then I can really see how much of the good stuff is left. ✐

Buy in Bulk, Save a Buck

Sure, you can find sunflower seed packed in tidy stacks of plastic bags on the shelves,

Save at Stock-Up Sales

Seed sellers often have sales on black oil sunflower seed because it's the most popular bird food. Watch for specials on 25-pound bags in early fall, when feeder season kicks into high gear as folks spend more time indoors and birds spend more time at feeders. Many sellers continue to run sales on big bags of black oil sunflower seed throughout the peak fall and winter feeding seasons. They figure that once you come through their door to get your bargain-priced sunflower seed, you'll probably drop some greenbacks on a new feeder or special treat foods, too.

but if you're as tight-fisted as I am, you'll want to check for giant-sized bags before you load up your cart. You might save only pennies a pound when you buy the giant, economy-sized box of laundry detergent; but with sunflower seed, when you buy in bulk, you can save 50 cents a pound or even more! ✐

Jumpin' Jehoshaphat—It's Jays!

They're big, they're beautiful, they're blue (mostly)—and boy, are they a bunch of bullies! When jays fly in to the feeder, you can bet just about every bird in their path will head for the hills. Jays aren't a danger to other birds at the feeder, but their size and shrieks sure are scary. To prevent those daily panic attacks, I keep a feeder just for jays, stocked with the sunflower seeds and nuts they love best. It helps keep them away from the millet and mixed seeds where the smaller, shyer birds can eat in peace. ✐

BLUE JAY

Stingy Seed Shopping

Saving money is always smart, so I figure that by now, I must be a real genius. Even my pennies holler "No more pinching!" when they see me coming. Here are some of the tricks I've picked up to help my wallet stay fat and my bird-seed budget stay slim:

Shop at seed specialists. Bird-supply stores and pet-supply stores usually sell sunflower seed in bulk at much more reasonable prices than smaller sellers of seed, such as grocery stores, because they move a lot more of it. At my local bird-supply store, a 25-pound bag of black oil sunflower seed sets me back about $10 to $12. At the supermarket, I'd pay $4.99 for a 3-pound plastic bag. That's $1.66 a pound at the supermarket vs. 48 cents a pound at the bird store—guess where I do most of my shopping?

Find a feed mill. Feed mills and farm stores, often run by farmers' co-ops, may have ultra-low prices on sunflower seed, especially if you live near a breadbasket area in the U.S. or Canada, where sunflower seed is commercially grown. Check the Yellow Pages of your phone book to find one near you.

STELLER'S JAY

Save time and $$ with your telephone. Different stores charge way different prices—sometimes as much as a $10 difference on a big bag of sunflower seed—so let your fingers do the walking: Phone around to check prices before you head out to load up the wagon. 🐦

Share a Sack, Save Your Back

Don't fret if you're not the strongest wrangler on the ranch. There are plenty of ways to help even us not-so-young'uns get a bargain bag of seeds without having to heft a heavy sack. Here are my tricks to make hauling a big bag easy on me and my back:

◆ Lots of folks feed birds. Look around your neighborhood and find a friendly face, then ask if you can share a sack. Let them do the hauling, and you chip in your half of the cost.

◆ Take along a stash of plastic grocery bags and a seed scoop when you go to stock up. Ask your seed seller to open the big bag, then transfer the seed to your small bags (just don't make a mess!). I generally make about five small bags out of one big 25-pound sack, because I know I can easily handle lugging a 5-pound bag of potatoes—or sunflower seed. Oh, and be sure to double-bag the loot. You don't want to have to clean up a spill if your plastic bag decides to let loose.

◆ If you're a little shy about doing the transfer in the store, ask the merchant to load the big bag into your vehicle for you. Then you can divvy it up in the privacy of your own driveway. ✍

Naked: Worth the $$?

Hey! Put those socks back on, please—I'm talking about naked *seeds!* For a premium price (about $1.50 a pound), you can buy sunflower seeds with their shells already removed. These hulled seeds, or sunflower chips as they're often called, seem like they should be even more attractive to

JERRY TO THE RESCUE

Q. **Where'd all of these sunflowers come from—they're popping up all over my yard!**

A. Makes you wonder, doesn't it, how the seeds strayed so far from the feeder? Some of those plants sprout from seeds that birds drop when they carry them off to eat elsewhere, but most of them are actually planted by jays. Bluejays, scrub jays, pinyon jays, Steller's jays, gray jays, and all other birds with "jay" in their name don't usually stay and crack seeds at the feeder. Instead, they stuff them into their beaks and fly off. It's not that jays are gluttons—it's just that they normally hide the leftovers so they can come back and eat them later. A favorite hiding place is right in the ground. The jay pokes the seed or seeds in with its beak, then flies back to your feeder for another mouthful.

Meanwhile, when the time is right, any overlooked sunflower seeds begin to sprout, and before you know it, there's a bunch of cheery yellow faces smiling around the garden. Once they grow up and go to seed, you'll see a whole circus of birds attracted to them. The birds will deftly pluck out seeds for weeks, until that giant seedhead is empty. It's a real treat to watch.

birds than the ones that require work. But in my years of tending feeders, I've found that birds don't seem to prefer them to shell-on seeds, unless they can't crack the usual kind. When a flock of goldfinches shows up, for instance, they'll happily crack their own as well as pick up the labor-savers. But bluebirds, which struggle to crack big seeds, eagerly eat the chips.

No-Mess Naked

You may want to add hulled seeds to the repertoire for a reason that has nothing to do with eating preferences: Naked seed means no mess! Most of the debris under and in the feeders is sunflower seed shells. Switch to hulled seeds and you'll attract the same birds with much tidier results. So, if you feed birds on a balcony, patio, or deck, hulled seeds will save you time sweeping up.

Capacious Cookie Sheet

Got an old cookie sheet you can donate to the cause? If there's not one in your cupboard, you can pick them up for pocket change at garage sales. Nail the cookie sheet to an outside windowsill, and you have a modernized version of the old-fashioned feeding shelf. Fill it with whatever seed you like; all kinds of birds will use this roomy feeder.

MIRACLE MILLET

When I was new to this obsession—er, hobby—of bird feeding, I used to buy bags of any brand birdseed mix to fill my feeders. After a while, I noticed that many of the seeds, like the wheat and oats that often were in the mixes, were ignored by birds. Then I realized that about the only seeds birds ate out of these mixtures were the sunflowers, which were few and far between, and the tiny, round, pale gold (or sometimes reddish brown) seeds called millet. The lightbulb clicked, and I stopped feeding wasteful seed mixes and switched to buying pure millet (and sunflowers, of course). It's the most popular food at the feeder for all my favorite native sparrows, such as the white-throated sparrows that visit all winter and the song sparrows that nest in my yard. My beloved juncos, those chipper little birds with the gray backs and snowy bellies, love it, too, as does just about every small bird that comes my way.

Millet Mania

Millet comes in several sizes, and even more than one color. The most familiar is white proso millet, but even that may be extra-big (although still a small seed) or downsized, depending on the source. Then there's red millet, and German millet, and Japanese...the list goes on, but you don't have to fret. Birds eat all kinds and colors of millet, so just pick the one that's least expensive. White proso is the only one usually sold by the pound as well as used in mixes. The others are grown in smaller amounts than the standard crop of white proso, so they're usually added to finch and general-purpose seed mixes. If it says millet on the label, or millet in these pages, figure that any millet is a good millet.

WHITE-THROATED SPARROW

A Little Goes a Long Way

When Grandma Putt filled our plates for Sunday dinner, she adjusted the serving sizes for each of us. I'd look at the others' heaping plates and beg for more, but she'd shush me and say, "Eat that first, and then we'll see." Usually, her first guess was right, and I couldn't eat another bite.

"Eat that first, and then we'll see" is a good guideline when you begin offering pure millet at your feeder. According to those in the know, a pound of millet has about 80,000 seeds. That's a lot of bird bites! And that's why your 10-pound sack of millet will easily outlast 25 pounds of sunflower seed. Birds can polish off a pint of sunflower seed in 10 minutes, but it will take them days to peck through the same amount of millet. This little grain is one of the best bargains in Birdseed Land—it serves so many customers with such a small amount.

Small Seeds for Small Beaks

As soon as you start making millet a staple at your feeder, you're bound to notice an increase in the number of small birds eating at your place. Big birds with big beaks will usually eat more big sunflower seeds than they do millet, though some larger customers, including towhees, prefer these small seeds. But it's the little guys that love it best. Small birds with small, weak beaks—mostly sparrows, juncos, and buntings—will seek out the millet, even if you offer oil-rich sunflower seeds along with it. The little seeds are the perfect size to fit their beaks and, more importantly, their cracking strength.

Specially for Sparrows

Most of us think of house sparrows when we hear the word "sparrow," but think again! Native sparrows of more than 20 different species fill every kind of niche you could possibly imagine. They live in or among cities, open fields, swamps, forests, sagebrush, chaparral, and sand dunes—but all of them love millet! Sparrows are notoriously tricky to sort out, because nearly all are variations on the "little brown bird" theme. Once you get them up close at the feeder, though, you'll be able to get a good long look, so you can tell who's who. Start by identifying the most common millet munchers—the song sparrow, white-throated sparrow, and white-crowned sparrow—and then see how many other spiffy sparrows you can sort out.

Millet or Milo?

"Milo" sounds sorta like millet, but don't get the two confused. Both are the seeds of annual grasses, but that's where the similarity ends. Milo is bigger than millet, and dull instead of shiny. It's a faded reddish brown color. Beauty's only skin deep, but milo gets the thumbs down for another reason: Most birds don't eat it. I've learned that it pays to read the fine print: If milo is listed as an ingredient in birdseed mixes, I buy another brand.

But some birds do devour milo—blackbirds, quail, bobwhites, and doves are the usual takers at the feeder, just as they are in the farm fields where this crop grows. If you want to tempt these birds, add milo to your menu. But self-respecting sparrows, juncos, and buntings usually turn their beaks up at this seed and say, "Hey, where's my millet?"

BOBWHITE

COME 'N' GET IT!

Low-Cost Luxuries

Lots of birds are attracted to seed mixes made on the cheap. Lucky for us and lucky for them, some of their favorite foods are sold at bargain prices. Here are some I keep on hand for the big eaters that don't demand haute cuisine.

Pigeon-Toed Treat

Pigeons (or rock doves, as serious birders call them) and gentle mourning doves are often among the regulars at feeders in most towns. House sparrows are everyday visitors in backyards here, too. Make them all happy with this inexpensive mix.

5 cups of cracked corn
4 cups of black oil sunflower seeds
2 cups of millet

Measure the ingredients into a plastic pail or large mixing bowl, and stir with your hands until it's blended. Fill your feeder and store the leftovers in a clean, dry, plastic milk jug, capped tightly.

Craving Cardinals

Bright red cardinals grace many a Christmas card, thanks to the unbeatable color they lend to a snowy winter scene. Keep your yard accented with redbirds by offering this mix of big seeds for their big beaks.

5 cups of cracked corn
4 cups of striped sunflower seeds
2 cups of black oil sunflower seeds

Mix all the ingredients well. Scoop out a serving, then store the extras in a clean, dry, plastic milk jug, capped tightly.

Sparrows Supreme

Pour this mix into a low feeder to bring sparrows of all sorts flocking to your yard. These small brown birds of various sorts often show up in droves, especially in fall and winter. This mix is just the ticket when you're feeding a crowd—it's low-cost but has high appeal, and it serves a multitude!

5 cups of cracked corn
4 cups of millet
2 cups of black oil
    sunflower seeds

Mix all the ingredients well and serve. Store leftovers in a clean, dry, plastic milk jug, capped tightly.

Cheepest Trio

Try this mix to cut costs and still keep all your feeder birds coming back for more—even if your neigh- bors are serving the birds a higher- priced menu! The corn gives this mix an extra dose of oil, so it's a good one to serve in cold weather. Expect to see woodpeckers and nuthatches eating

right along with the jays, cardinals, sparrows, and other regulars.

6 cups of cracked corn
4 cups of black oil sunflower seeds
1 cup of chicken scratch (available at
    feed stores)

Measure the corn, seeds, and scratch into a plastic pail or large, deep bowl. Mix with your hands until well-blended. Funnel into clean, dry, plastic milk jugs and cap tightly for storage.

Turkey Trot

They may not be as plump as the Butterball® on the Thanksgiving table, but lanky wild turkeys eat a lot—and once they discover your feeder, they're likely to show up with the whole family in tow. Satisfy their hunger pangs with a generous helping of cheap cracked corn and chicken scratch. You don't even need to mix this recipe—just scoop and scatter! They'll clean it right off the ground or peck it out of a low feeder. Pheasants, doves, and quail like this mix, too.

6 cups of cracked corn
5 cups of chicken
   scratch (available at feed stores)

Stir it up and scoop it out. This'll keep your biggest birds satisfied all season.

Major Millet Eaters

If you're a bird and your beak is weak, millet is the way to go. Birds with big crunch power, and even small sorts like chickadees and titmice (which are perfectly capable of whacking open nuts and acorns), will seek out the sunflowers. Those who naturally eat small weed seeds and insects will be big customers at the millet line. So expect to see some of these hombres among the millet mob:

✔ Blackbirds	✔ Doves	✔ Mockingbird
✔ Bobolink	✔ Finches	✔ Redpolls
✔ Buntings	✔ Grackles	✔ Sparrows
✔ Carolina wren	✔ Horned lark	✔ Thrashers
✔ Cowbirds	✔ Juncos	✔ Towhees
✔ Dickcissel	✔ Meadowlarks	

Scratch 'n' Sift

"Waste not, want not" seems to be the motto of the small sparrows and juncos that are reliable feeder regulars. These small birds sift through seed with a hop forward and a slide back, scratching up the shells and flicking their beaks to get to

DARK-EYED JUNCO

the good stuff. Naturally, that less-than-finesse maneuver causes some seeds to spill over the edges of feeders. Not to worry. These same small birds like to do their scratch-'n'-sift right on the ground. They'll search diligently below your feeders until every edible grain of millet is gone. 🐦

The Breakfast of Champions

Way before Cheerios® and Wheaties® hit the shelves, millet was in big demand as a popular grain for cereal. It's been grown for thousands of years around the world, but wasn't in favor in countries that depend on processed food—like boxed cereals—until recent years. Now it's making a comeback, thanks to its incredible nutritional content. Those unprepossessing seeds contain more essential amino acids than wheat, oats, barley, rye, or rice, and are one of the most easily digested of all the grains. So after you fill your feeders with the golden goodness of millet, check the fine print on your breakfast cereal box. You may be dining on the same dish! 🐦

Snowstorm Life Saver

There's nothing worse than getting caught with an empty birdseed bag when a blizzard blows in. Your feathered friends are looking to you for help, and you can't even get out of the driveway to restock the cupboard. So when the season shifts to winter, I put an unusual traction-aid device in the trunk of my car: two spare bags of birdseed! Twenty-five pounds of sunflower seed go over one of the back wheels, 25 pounds of millet over the other. Not only does my car do better on slick roads, but I can rest easy knowing that I have plenty of extra seed if it's needed. Not a winter driver? Store your just-in-case supply in a covered metal trash can, and keep it for emergency use only; use up any that's left in the spring.

First-Rate for Fussbudgets

The shells of millet are so light that the chaff cracked off by birds quickly blows away in the slightest breeze. But if you want to make sure your feeder area is neat and tidy, you might want to give hulled millet seed a try. The seed is cleaned so that all that remains is the goodness of the grain. Birds can peck it up and simply swallow it down the hatch. You'll pay more, but only you can decide whether a chaff-free patio or deck is worth the price. 🐦

Color Considerations

Both red and white millet are proso millet (*Panicum milaceum*), with practically no difference except for their color. White proso millet, which is not white but pale golden tan, is the most common millet you'll find. Red millet is a pretty, shiny chestnut color. Birds eat both with relish. (Or should I say, with enthusiasm?) But if I have a choice, I go for white rather than red, because birds seem to spot any dropped seeds better, and very little goes to waste. White proso millet is also the most common variety, so birds are already accustomed to eating it, and they can be as fussy as toddlers when you put an unfamiliar food in front of them! 🐦

Fancy Fingers

You might spot another kind of millet in the pet-bird department: finger millet, which is harvested with the seeds still on their long, fingerlike seedheads. Cage birds enjoy working out the little seeds, and feeder birds—which are perfectly content with less-expensive loose millet as their mainstay—will nibble at it, too. Finger millet makes a fun gift for your bird-feeding friends, who

JERRY
TO THE RESCUE

Q. **Help! My birdseed has bugs! I can see tiny worms or caterpillars crawling around in it, and little moths are flying around it, too.**

A. Those "worms" are the larvae of the tiny meal moths you see flying around. They're attracted to seed for the same reasons that birds are: It's highly nutritious. These bugs will eat the innards of your precious birdseed, leaving the empty husks. Luckily, there's an easy solution that requires no harmful pesticides—and very little effort! Just set out a few of my sticky, pheromone-scented "Flour & Pantry Moth Traps" (available at www.jerrybaker.com) near your seed supply to nab the flying pests. In the future, shop smart so you don't bring problems home. Watch for moths flying around the birdseed aisle, and examine the bag for insects, their cobwebs, or powdery excrement. All of these clues point in the same direction: Shop elsewhere for bug-free birdseed.

can tack the sprays to the edges of their feeder like a fringed skirt. To get even fancier, staple the plump "fingers" side by side to cover the wooden roof of a feeder, for sparrows and other millet-eaters to peck at. 🐦

Huff and Puff

The millet shells that birds nibble off to get at the meaty part of the seed are so lightweight that the wind usually takes care of blowing away the chaff. But if your feeder is parked in a sheltered spot, or if you're hosting a lot of birds, that tray that looks so temptingly filled with seeds may actually be heaped with shells. Pretend you're the Big Bad Wolf to solve the problem: Just close your eyes, take a big breath, and blow the shells away. 🐦

BUDGET STRETCHERS

Sunflower and millet are inexpensive choices, considering that some fancy birdseed mixes can cost as much per pound as a steak dinner. But I like to see how low I can go by adding foods that birds will readily eat, but that cost even less than those two staples. Unfortunately, not much fills the bill. But I've found a couple of choices that attract birds and keep feeding costs dirt "cheep."

Crazy for Corn

I've met plenty of folks who didn't like eating raw tomatoes, but I've never run across anyone who didn't like corn. Corn on the cob, corn chowder, corn pudding, cornbread, hush puppies—oops, sorry, that's my wish list, not the birds'. Corn, as all dieters know, is plenty high in calories and corn oil. That's great news to birds.

Cardinals and woodpeckers are about as big at corn appreciation as yours truly. Doves and pigeons enjoy it, too, as do some native sparrows, buntings, and juncos. Mockingbirds and thrashers will also eat corn, as long as it's cracked into small pieces. And if you're lucky enough to have wild turkeys or pheasants in the neighborhood, a pile of cracked corn will bring them calling. 🐦

NORTHERN
MOCKINGBIRD

Woodpecker Winner

Dry corn on the cob is a year-round favorite with woodpeckers, who will work at a cob for hours, wiggling out the golden stuff one kernel at a time. You can find the cobs at bird-supply stores, where you're likely to pay about 30 to 50 cents an ear. For an even lower price, ask for "ear corn" at a feed mill. Push the cobs onto the pointed ends of long nails driven through a board, or use a commercial corncob feeder, so that squirrels can't carry off the cobs wholesale. You'll get weeks of entertainment from acrobatic woodpeckers for a very small investment. 🐦

⊗ DO IT YOURSELF ⊗

Fast, Free Funnel

Pinching pennies is my favorite pastime, so I fashioned this simple funnel out of a plastic bottle from the recycling bin. A few quick strokes with a kitchen knife, and she's ready to pour!

MATERIALS

2-liter plastic soda bottle, rinsed and dry, cap removed
Sharp kitchen knife

DIRECTIONS

Step 1. Slice off the loose, narrow plastic band from the cap at the neck of the bottle.

Step 2. Stick the knife into the bottle about 3 inches from the bottom, and saw smoothly around the bottle to remove the bottom. (Save the bottom; it makes a good feeder for bird treats—see page 26.)

Step 3. Turn the top of the bottle upside down, and you're ready to go. This funnel fits neatly into the opening of a gallon plastic milk jug, so you can measure and mix your favorite recipes right in the jug.

Looks Like Chicken Scratch

BIRD BITS

Back in Grandma Putt's day, many families had their own small flock of chickens. Grandma never minded feeding the hens, she said, because they came running as soon as she called, and gobbled up the food so fast she knew she was appreciated. Country folk call it "chicken scratch," a blend of corn, wheat, and sometimes other grains, ground to a moderately fine texture. When I was scratching my head for cheap alternatives to fancy birdseed, I remembered Grandma Putt's chicken scratch stories. I bought a few pounds of scratch at a nearby feed mill for practically pennies. Soon, I was tossing out scratch just like Grandma did, except I was serving sparrows, juncos, blackbirds, and even the occasional robin, instead of chickens.

Cracking the Cost

Cracked corn is about as cheap as it gets. You can buy it in bulk for about half the price of sunflower seed, or as little as $6 for 50 pounds. Shop at feed stores for rock-bottom prices. All birds that eat corn will crunch on the cracked variety. Some outlets offer cracked corn in coarse or finer texture; buy the coarser variety, because the cornmeal-like kind will be worthless to birds if it gets wet.

Decoy Dish

Starlings and house sparrows are also corn aficionados. That's great news for us feeder hosts, because we can use a tempting dish of gleaming gold kernels to lure these birds away from other feeders, making more room for the preferred birds at the sunflower seed tray. The only catch: You may have to play out Hansel and Gretel to lure the starlings and house sparrows to their new feeding place. It's simple to do: Just lay a trail of cracked corn from the usual feeder to their new spot. Keep their corn feeder full so they're more likely to stay there and not come see what's for dinner at the better restaurant.

Low Seating for Easy Eating

Most of the birds that will come for your corn generally eat near to the ground in nature. Help them feel at home by pouring the golden goody into a low feeder or onto a flat rock.

Supersized wild turkeys and pheasants will be just as appreciative of the natural feeding level as the doves, sparrows, and juncos that peck at the corn beside them. 🐦

Cornmeal Cons

Cracked corn, whole-kernel corn, dried corn on the cob: yes, yes, yes. But corn*meal* is a no-no in the bird feeder. Not because birds won't eat it (a few birds will), but because it absorbs moisture so easily and soon becomes a sodden, useless lump. Save your cornmeal for mixing into homemade treats, like those for which you'll find recipes in Chapters 4 and 7. 🐦

RING-NECKED
PHEASANT

FEEDER FREE-FOR-ALL

Eye appeal is often the main reason we choose a particular feeder—should we go for the red barn or the green gazebo? Ohh, and look at that one with the copper roof! My friends, birds don't care about looks. From the bird's-eye view, it's all about function and location. Can they eat in a comfortable position without getting crowded out? And is the feeder in a place where they feel safe? Providing a banquet table that feels like home is the fastest way to round up a herd of birds at your spread. Filling that feeder, or those feeders, with their favored foods will keep them making return visits. 🐦

Feeder Checklist

Bird feeders should be easy for you to use, as well as for birds to dine at. Before you shell out your hard-earned $$ for a fancy feeder, examine it to see if it's as practical as it is pretty. Here's a checklist to point you in the right direction:

☐ Is there room for at least a dozen birds to perch at one time, without running out of elbow room?

JERRY
TO THE RESCUE

Q. **Many years ago, when I was a young girl, I remember my mother tending a "feeding shelf" nailed to the window-sill. Isn't that still a good way to go?**

A. You're absolutely right, except for the fact that folks today are a little fussier about their houses than they were in the good old days. Nothing more than a rough, wide piece of board nailed (and sometimes bracketed) to an outside win-dowsill of the family home, the feeding shelf holds a lot of seed, it has plenty of room to perch, and best of all, it brings the birds right up to eye level.

A drawback to bringing back the feed-ing shelf is the advent of vinyl and alu-minum windows. Nailing into a stout old wooden sill is one thing, but marring those modern windows is another. I solved this sticking point by supporting my shelf with a pair of fancy brackets, available at any home-supply store. I also gussied mine up by tacking strips of store-bought molding (lath strips would work, too) around the edges, to give birds a place to perch.

A big advantage to the feeding shelf is that you don't even have to step outside when it's refill time: Just open the win-dow and scoop seed onto the shelf.

☐ Does the design allow birds to access the seed in a normal posture, or will they have to be contortionists to grab a bite?

☐ Does the feeder hold enough seed so that you don't have to refill it more than once a day? A quart of seed capacity is usually a good starting point.

☐ Is the feeder well made, with a sturdy hanger or hooks?

☐ Can you refill the feeder with-out taking it off its mount? Ease of use counts for a lot on a cold or hurried morning.

☐ Is the feeder easy to fill with one hand? Remember, you'll probably be holding a scoop full of seeds in the other.

☐ Does the feeder allow you a good view of your guests, or will the view be obscured by the roof or other parts? 🐦

Bigger Is Better

You should make your main feeder a tray-type design, of the biggest size that you can manage. A wide-open or roofed tray has plenty of room for a big batch of birdies to eat at the same time. It also allows raucous feeder guests like jays to share the space with quieter types, which can easily move down to make room for the pushier birds.

And you won't have to refill a tray feeder as often as a dinkier design, either—a big plus when it's –10°F, or raining cats and dogs! 🐦

Weather or Not

Keep your birds comfy in rainy or snowy weather by making sure at least one of your feeders has a roof over the eating area. Seed that gets wet can turn moldy, and birds won't eat bad seed. 🐦

Fill It and Forget It

Feeders with built-in storage, or hopper feeders, are highly popular with feeder hosts. You fill the hopper just once every week or so, and fresh seed flows out the bottom as birds clean up what's in the tray. But eyeball the size of that tray

⊗ DO IT YOURSELF ⊗

String-'Em-Up Coffee Can

Save the metal cans from ground coffee and their plastic, snap-on lids for a feeder that's fast to make and that looks good, too. Just wrap the can with natural-colored twine, winding the twine round and round from the top to the bottom of the can, until the whole thing is tightly covered. Cut an entrance hole by removing about half of the lid's surface in a half-moon shape, but be careful not to cut through the rim of the lid, so it still stays securely in place. Tie a piece of twine around the middle of the can for hanging; it will hang sideways. Fill the can about half full of sunflower seeds or any seed mix, snap the lid on securely, and soon your birds will be enjoying the buzz from their coffee can feeder.

LEAVE HALF OF PLASTIC LID INTACT

BRIDLED TITMOUSE

before you open your wallet. Some feeders of this style have a hopper that's so large, or a tray that's so small, that only a few birds at a time can cling to the edges. If an open door is your preferred policy, pick a hopper feeder with a generously sized tray attached.

Small Feeders for Special Guests

Add a small-birds-only design to your feeder array, and chickadees, titmice, and Carolina wrens will always be able to get to the goodies, even if every bully on the block is fighting for space at the other feeders. Clear plastic globe hanging feeders, with an opening sized for small bodies, are a worthwhile investment. Or try a crafty alternative: the time-honored hanging coffee can (see "String-'Em-Up Coffee Can," on page 47).

Hoosegow Hangout

Some folks prefer not to share their generosity with starlings, who can quickly wear out their welcome by inviting all their friends and relatives over to your house. If that's the case, then "barred" feeders are made for you! These designs have an outer shield of thin metal bars spaced closely enough to keep out starlings and noisy jays that can frighten off other birds, but they don't keep out smaller birds. Sure, it looks a lot like the Dodge City hoosegow, but small birds would rather be safe behind bars than be bullied.

YOUR BEST TABLE, PLEASE!

Where you put your feeders is just as important as what you fill them with. A feeder in a bird-desirable location will fill up fast with customers, while even the most delectable treats will have a hard time luring birds to a poorly placed feeder. Of course, you'll want to put your feeder where you have a great view of it. After you pick your favorite window to view it from, consider what will make the birds feel comfortable. A feeder that's placed closest to the level at which they naturally find food will make them feel most at home.

Three feeders—one near ground level, one about waist-high, and the third on a higher post or windowsill—will guarantee you the most birds, and the most kinds of birds. But in winter or other times when food is scarce, birds overcome their hesitation to leave their usual haunts and will seek out feeders no matter where they're placed.

SEED-EATING BIRD	NATURAL SEED-EATING LOCATION	FEEDER PLACEMENT
Blackbirds	Ground level	No more than about 5 feet above the ground; best near ground level; mounted
Bluebird	Ground level, low shrubbery, brush	5 feet or less above ground level; mounted
Cardinal	Highly variable, from treetops to ground level	Any height; mounted or hanging; will visit 2nd-story feeders
Carolina wren	Ground level, low shrubbery, brush	Any height; mounted or hanging
Chickadees	Treetops, tree branches at least 3 feet above the ground	Hanging feeders that sway are quickly adopted, as are mounted feeders; will visit 2nd-story feeders
Flickers	Tree trunks and branches	Any height; mounted; will visit 2nd-story feeders
Goldfinch	Highly variable, from treetops to ground level	Any height; mounted or hanging; will visit 2nd-story feeders

(continued)

YOUR BEST TABLE, PLEASE!, *continued*

SEED-EATING BIRD	NATURAL SEED-EATING LOCATION	FEEDER PLACEMENT
Grackles	Ground level, low shrubbery	5 feet or less above ground level; mounted
Grosbeaks	Highly variable, from treetops to ground level	Any height; mounted; will visit 2nd-story feeders
House finch	Highly variable, from treetops to ground level	Any height; mounted or hanging; will visit 2nd-story feeders
Jays	Treetops, shrubbery, brush	Any height; mounted; will visit 2nd-story feeders
Juncos (snowbirds)	Ground level, low shrubbery, brush	5 feet or less above ground level; mounted; despite preferring low feeders, will also visit 2nd-story feeders
Mockingbird	Highly variable; forages from rooftop to lawn	Any height; mounted; will visit 2nd-story feeders
Nuthatches	Tree trunks, main branches	At least 3 feet above the ground; mounted or hanging; will visit 2nd-story feeders
Pheasant	Ground level	Less than 1 foot above ground level
Quail	Ground level	Less than 2 feet above ground level
Sparrows, native	Ground level, low shrubbery, brush	5 feet or less above ground level; mounted
Thrashers	Low to moderately low shrubbery and brush, vines	5 feet or less above ground level; mounted
Titmice	Treetops, tree branches	At least 3 feet above the ground; mounted or hanging; will visit 2nd-story feeders
Wild turkey	Ground level	Less than 1 foot above ground level
Woodpeckers	Tree trunks, branches	Any height; mounted; will visit 2nd-story feeders

CHAPTER 3

Seed-Eater Specialties

A generous spread of sunflower seeds and millet is the "meat and potatoes" menu for birds. It'll keep 'em happy—as long as there's not a better bird feeder next door! Your neighbors may wonder where their goldfinches have gone when you fill your feeders with special seeds, but all's fair in love and feeder wars, and I'll take any advantage I can get!

In this chapter, you'll discover a treasure trove of small seeds, and find out which special birds will come flocking to them. You'll learn how to read seed-mix labels, so that your precious bucks go for the best ingredients, and how to make your own money-saving mixes.

Finches to the Feast

Small, easy-to-crack seeds are the natural food of finches. Sparrow-sized and smaller, these birds have beaks built just for this job. In the wild, they eat lots of weed seeds. At feeders, they'll come in droves for similar, small-sized seeds.

Goldfinches and house finches are the most familiar finches, and they have plenty of pretty little cousins. Putting out niger (thistle), flaxseed, or other finch favorites is a great bargain, because a couple of scoops of special seeds bring me dozens of goldfinches, plus their active, colorful kin, including redpolls, pine siskins, and purple finches. Here's the lowdown on the hoedown.

AMERICAN
GOLDFINCH

Nibble, Nibble, Like a Mouse

Watch a finch in action, and you'll see right away that its eating style is different from the grab-and-go habit of stronger-beaked small birds such as chickadees and titmice. Instead of snatching a seed and taking it away to whack open, finches eat more like mice or rabbits: There's barely a break in the action as they nibble the shell off one seed, then pick up another, staying put in one place for many minutes, or even an hour at a time. To suit this nibbling style, I keep my special seeds in separate feeders from my main-dish menus. That little trick prevents these higher-priced treats from getting lost in the seed tray shuffle.

Betcha Can't Feed Just One!

Once the first finch finds your feeder, his pals won't be far behind. These birds hang out in groups that can swell to incredible numbers during spring and fall migration. In summer and winter, you're likely to host a half-dozen goldfinches, a smattering of purple finches and pine siskins, and a whole horde of house finches, one of the most populous birds in America. Come migration time in early spring (and again in fall), your goldfinches may swell to a gang of hundreds, as more and more passersby stop in to see what all the activity is about.

Desirably Dainty

Goldfinches are as welcome as sunshine when they show up at my place. Their energetic ways and cheerful voices are a surefire pick-me-up. No matter how many cardinals and juncos are already at my feeders, when a flock of finches arrives, my yard seems to come alive. Plus, goldfinches and their finchy kin are the neatest birds I know. Even though they hang out in gangs, they're no muss and no fuss. They squeeze in together at the feeder without shrieking or squawking, and they don't spray seed shells all over the place. One more big plus, especially for those of us who have feeders on our decks or patios: Their droppings are barely noticeable!

JERRY
TO THE RESCUE

Q. The little black seeds that my goldfinches like so much are sold as thistle seed, niger seed, and lately, Nyjer™ seed. What's the difference?

A. Only the name. All those labels refer to the seeds of *Guizotia abyssinica*, a mouthful for any marketing department. Good ol' *Guizotia* is a tall, bushy, yellow-flowered daisy, most definitely not a thistle. I'd wager that "thistle seed" was somebody's bright idea of how to grab the birdseed market, because true thistle seeds were widely known to be a favorite of goldfinches. But that turned out to be a bad idea—few feeder-keepers wanted to risk a plague of thistles. Seed sellers then switched to "niger," an English variation of the name used for the plant in its homelands. Nowadays, "niger" is beginning to give way to "Nyjer," a name trademarked by the Wild Bird Feeding Industry of North America. The new phonetic spelling eliminates any chance of an offensive mispronunciation of niger.

Never-Fail Niger

Niger, formerly called thistle (and recently updated to Nyjer™ in some circles), is the winner by a mile among special seeds. The itty-bitty, long, skinny black seeds look something like iron filings, and they're just as magnetic! Pour some in your feeder and you're guaranteed to attract goldfinches until every speck is eaten. Here's where to find it and how to feed it.

LAWRENCE'S GOLDFINCH

Buy It by the Bag

Since niger is the most popular specialty seed for finches, it's often added to mixes. You'll get a better bargain by shopping for bags of pure niger seed, which costs from 50¢ to $1.50 per pound, than by investing in premium-priced mixes in which the main ingredients are likely to be lower-cost sunflower seeds and millet.

Muscles Aren't a Must

No need to fret about lugging a huge, heavy sack of seed when you go shopping for niger. Most feeder-keepers buy it in sealed plastic bags of 1 to 5 pounds; it's usually no cheaper to buy larger quantities in bulk. Better yet, a pound of niger usually lasts at least a couple of weeks at the feeder.

The Big Oil Boom

High oil content is the reason for niger's success. Those little black seeds may look dusty and dry, but they're about 30 percent oil! That's a real boon to birds, who need a high-fat diet to keep them humming. And it's the reason why this humble little seed is such a huge hit with small-seed eaters. Native sparrows, juncos, towhees, and other birds that prefer to eat at tray feeders will also appreciate a helping of niger when those winter winds howl. The extra calories help the birds stay warm on wintry nights. 🐦

Fill 'Er Up— Once a Month!

I fill up my basic-menu feeder at least every morning for the staple singers, but my specialty feeders need refills much less often. In winter, when my finch feeders are busiest, I refill them every several days. In summer, when traffic slows down, I can get by for weeks without adding another scoop. Niger and other small seeds are the way to go if you want to reduce feeder-filling duties. They're just the ticket for those of us who have trouble getting around, or who'd rather not brave the rain, snow, or cold every morning. 🐦

Snowbird Solution

You lucky snowbirds fleeing to sunnier climes won't need to worry about your finches going hungry when you take a winter vacation. Just put out an extralarge helping of niger in a big, self-contained tube feeder before you make your getaway. Your feathered friends will then have plenty to snack on while you're moving on down the road. 🐦

Grandma Putt's

BIRD BITS

Buy Now, Serve Later

Hard to believe, but the niger we now think of as a staple has been filling up feeders only since the 1960s. Up until then, this power-packed seed stayed on the other side of the world, feeding millions of humans in Ethiopia, India, Kenya, and other regions where it grows like a weed, needing no fancy fertilizers and not much water to make a major crop. Eventually, someone noticed that birds flocked to niger fields, too, and the rest is history.

Because most niger seed is imported and not grown at home, niger prices fluctuate more than those of sunflower seeds and millet. When the yearly yield is lower than usual, or the food demand is higher, we pay more for this seed. I make "cents" of shifting prices with a little trick Grandma Putt would be proud of: When prices are low, I buy extra and store it in zip-top plastic freezer bags. When seed prices climb, my bargain seed is still snatched up by goldfinches, even after spending more than a year in cold storage.

More Tiny Treasures

Now that your finch feeders are well stocked with niger, think about branching out to other small specialty seeds. Flax, canola, amaranth, and other unusual grains—and even good ol' grass seed—are finch favorites, too. You'll have to hunt a little harder to find other seeds to experiment with; none of them has cracked the birdseed market in a big way, although many are used in ready-made seed mixes.

In this section, you'll meet some small seeds that have proven popular with finches and other small birds. Part of the fun of fine-tuning your feeder menu is discovering oddities, so keep your eyes open for other small seeds to experiment with, too! You'll find suggestions for further explorations in this section, and finally, tips on where to buy specialty seeds at the best prices.

LESSER GOLDFINCH

Canary Seed for Wild Canaries

I won't mention some of the nicknames I've been given, but like you Slims and Reds out there, I sure can identify with the gorgeous goldfinch. Beloved by all, this little bird's list of monikers runs into the dozens. Two older nicknames are "thistle bird" (in German, that's *Distelfink,* or "thistle finch"), a reference to its favorite eats, and "wild canary," a nod to its looks. Goldfinches share their sunny color with canaries, and they share some food habits, too. Look for canary seed listed on birdseed bag labels, and you've found another way to their little hearts. 🐦

Canoodling with Canola

Canola is another seed that, like niger, has undergone a name change for cosmetic reasons. Actually a mustard, the parent of this small round seed is widely known as rapeseed. A genetically improved variety is called canola, and the name has spread to replace rapeseed in many cases. In the grocery store aisles, you'll find "canola oil," but on birdseed bags, "rapeseed" may still be listed. Any seed labeled as canola, rapeseed, or mustard will be a hit with all finches. High oil content is the reason that goldfinches, pine siskins, redpolls, and other finches seek out mustard seeds of any kind.

First-Rate Flax

Chances are, you don't need any convincing of the benefits of flaxseed. Its human health properties have been much touted—better digestion, weight loss, and lower blood pressure are just a few of its claimed benefits. While finches don't have those health concerns, they do go for these shiny, flat, oval seeds because the seeds are chock-full of oil, just like other finch favorites.

A Minuscule Millet

Millets, as we talked about in Chapter 2, are among the most popular menu items at the feeder, sought by dozens of backyard bird species. The newest member of the millets to arrive at wild-bird stores is German millet, an itty-bitty variety that's a warm, honey brown color. Like the more common white and red proso millets, German millet is a great source of oil. Its small size makes it appealing to small birds, and it's a good ingredient to add to finch mixes. And, not only does German millet pack a myriad of seeds to the pound, but its seeds are so small that they can be easily extracted from the tiny slits in a niger tube feeder.

Dandelion Time

Bright yellow dandelions in bloom are your cue to stock up on niger and other small seeds—the finches are coming! Spring migration of finches, siskins, and buntings starts around the time those familiar weeds show their buttery faces. Fill the tube feeders and you're bound to get a lot of takers in this season. If your offerings are generous, expect to see the numbers climb day by day as more finches stop in to see what all the fuss is about. Migrating goldfinches, indigo buntings, and other spring songbirds will stick around for a few weeks until their wanderlust gets stronger than the lure of free eats.

DO IT YOURSELF

Taste Test

With the variety of bird-seeds available, you may be wondering which seeds your finches would most want to find in their feeders. Do this little experiment using a homemade divided feeder and you may be surprised at the results!

MATERIALS

Simple open tray feeder, without a seed hopper, clean and empty

3 strips of cardboard, about 2 inches high, as long as your feeder is wide

1 cup each of black oil sunflower seed, millet, niger seed, and sunflower chips (or other seeds of your choice)

Ruler

Marker pen or pencil

DIRECTIONS

Step 1. Measure the length of the feeder. Divide by 4. Make three marks on the rim of the feeder to indicate the four equal feeder divisions.

Step 2. Make "walls" within the feeder with the strips of cardboard: Insert a strip of cardboard across the tray of the feeder, within the rim, at each of the three equidistant marks. The strips of cardboard should stand in place, supported at their ends by the rim.

Step 3. Place the feeder in its usual spot. Fill each of the four compartments with 1 cup of each different kind of specialty seed: black oil sunflower in the first compartment, for example; niger in the second; and so on.

Step 4. Monitor the feeder daily to check how much of each seed has been eaten. Note your results. Repeat the taste test for at least a week, noting the results daily and refilling the compartments as needed.

Step 5. After a week, empty the feeder and refill the compartments, but in a different order than you used the first time. Monitor and record your observations as before. Compare your findings at the beginning of the test and on the last day: Did they change? Chances are the answer is yes, as birds became more familiar with the more-unusual choices. No matter how your results fluctuated, by the end of the test, you should have a clear answer to this question: Which seeds do your finches prefer?

Sampling Safflower

Safflower seed is definitely not a case of love at first sight with birds. But it may become a favorite at your feeder if you give birds time to get used to it. This white, pointed, mid-sized seed has a thick hull that's so hard to crack, usually only cardinals, parrots, and squirrels will attempt it. Start with a scanty quarter-cup or so scattered on top of your basic feeder mix in a tray feeder to pique cardinals' curiosity. Once birds break the barrier of the unfamiliar, you can give them bigger servings of this oil-rich seed.

Montezuma's Miracle

For a royal treat of ancient origins, seek out amaranth. This grain comes from a plume-flowered, red-leaved relative of the garden cockscomb (*Amaranathus cruentus* and other species). Incas ate it ages ago, and it's still cultivated for human food in South and Central America. The tiny seeds are smaller than poppy seeds, and savored by siskins, goldfinches, buntings, and other birds because of their unusually high protein content. They're making their way into human foods in this country, too.

JERRY TO THE RESCUE

Q. My feeders are super busy all winter long. But by summer, most of my birds have disappeared. Why aren't there as many birds at my feeder in the summertime?

A. Feeder traffic is perching-room-only in winter, and only slightly less busy in fall and early spring. But in late spring, the flow of birds shuts off like a spigot. What gives? Just the facts of life! Late spring through summer is the time for birds to nest. They're more involved with courting, mating, and raising a family than hanging out all day at Ye Olde Feeder. They forage close to home because of the danger of leaving nestlings alone. And once the weather warms up, bugs abound. Sorry, but no feeder goodies can match the appeal of a nice fat caterpillar or a bellyful of beetles!

Seed-eaters may be scarce in summer, but nectar feeders are humming. Now's the time to get to know your local hummingbirds and orioles. Why not invest those birdseed bucks in inexpensive binoculars so that you can have a close-up view of your fine-feathered friends?

Ali Baba's Bright Idea

I never had much luck using Ali Baba's magic words to reveal any riches, until I tried out "Open sesame!" at the feeder. I got gold(finches) galore! Sesame is another small seed that's so rich in oil, it's almost an instant favorite with birds. Add untoasted sesame seed to mixes, or feed it separately to draw in a wealth of gleaming goldfinches and sapphire-hued buntings.

Grandma Putt's BIRD BITS

Nay to Oats?

Horses say "Neigh!" for oats, but most songbirds snub them unless they're baked into breads or mixed with peanut butter or other superior foods. Back before the Model T automobile, though, one bird species developed a huge habit for eating oats. House or English sparrows thrived on the still-edible oats they were able to extract from the manure that littered the streets. The sparrows were so accustomed to depending on the food that their population noticeably declined when horseless, no-mess carriages took control of the highways and byways.

If you happen to like house sparrows and their long history with us, serve oats (or groats, which are hulled oats) at your feeder. The chirpy sparrows are still fond of the seeds. Doves, pigeons, blackbirds, and quail, all birds that typically forage in farm fields where oats may be grown, will also snack on the grain at feeders. Finches, unfortunately, usually say nay to oats if something better is around.

Pep It Up with Poppy Seed

Sandwich rolls just wouldn't be the same without a sprinkling of round, black poppy seeds decorating them and adding crunch. And finches enjoy these nutritious seeds just as much as I do! Look for the little seeds, which may be gray to black and occasionally brown, in bulk spice bins at supermarkets. They're a desirable addition to finch feeders, especially when you munch your lunch on a poppy seed roll on the other side of the window!

Going against the Grain

Grains seem like they should be a natural with birds, especially since corn—just an overgrown grass, or grain—and grass seed are high on the list of favorite edibles. In the wild, birds do seek out grain fields and nibble on some of the crop; but at the feeder, wheat, oats, barley, rice, and other grainy goodies are apt to go untouched. What's the deal? It's simply a matter of preference, due to the lower oil content of many grains. Given a choice, as they have at the feeder, birds are just like kids (and like yours truly)—they'll eat the "dessert" first! When times are tough, though, as in winter snowstorms, grains are a good filler to have on hand. And in baked goods and other homemade bird recipes, such as those in Chapters 4 and 7, you'll see that oats, wheat, and other generally ignored grains are readily eaten—as long as they're mixed with more tempting foods. 🐦

LARK
BUNTING

Cooking Lessons

If you're wondering what other small seeds are gleaming with oil inside, look for hints in the cooking oil section of the supermarket: If a seed contains enough oil to press for commercial

use, then birds are bound to appreciate the seed it was pressed from. Canola oil, safflower oil, corn oil—ring any bells, feeder-fillers? Check the oil selection at ethnic grocery stores, too, and you may discover a new seed to tempt your finches or other feeder birds. 🐦

Borrowing from Bagels

My breakfast bagel is always a treat, no matter what flavor I pick. Usually, I go for the ones with a scattering of crunchy, tasty seeds for extra zip. One morning, I was cleaning my plate when I did a double take and looked a little closer at the seeds. Sesame, flax, poppy seeds—hey, these were big bird favorites, too! Now, before I take my first bite, I examine just what's on that bagel. Chances are, if it's good enough for me, my feeder birds will be fond of it, too. That's how caraway seeds came to my attention—and ended up as an occasional treat in my finch feeder. 🐦

Starting Out with Specialty Seeds

Finding special, small seeds, and introducing them to your birds, isn't quite as simple as pouring out a scoopful of sunflower seeds. In the following pages, you'll find out where to track down these tasty morsels, and how to get a good buy. You'll also learn about introducing your new menu items to your faithful feeder birds, so that both you and they are happy with the results.

REDPOLL

Pay Less for More

Comparison shopping can save you big bucks in the specialty seed department. Prices vary widely from store to store, especially for the less common varieties. Seek out stores that sell the seeds in bags or in bulk, rather than buying them in little spice-rack bottles (unless you just want to give your birds a little taste at a hefty price). Even though you won't be serving as many of these seeds as you do the staples, it still makes "cents" to shop around. Oh, and don't forget to check the spice rack in your kitchen—if you haven't used those sesame seeds in five years, why not donate them to the cause?

Affordable Abundance

Small birds have big appetites, but there's no need to fear for your wallet. The tiny seeds they like best have thousands of seeds to the pound, so a little bit goes a long way. Niger, flax, and other specialty seeds cost more than basic birdseed, usually about $1 to $1.50 per pound when you shop smart. But because these itty bitty goodies are so tiny, you get a lot of bird bites out of one small scoop. They're treat

seeds, sure, but once you get past the initial sticker shock, you'll find that a single scoop can really be s-t-r-e-t-c-h-e-d.

Scouting Out Seeds

You won't have any trouble finding niger, one of the "Big Three" of birdfeeding (after sunflower seeds and millet), but it takes a sharp posse to find the hiding places of the other specialty seeds. Eventually, wild-bird suppliers will no doubt wise up and add these niche seeds to the wider market, but in the meantime, here's where to send the search party:

Pet-supply stores. Scour the cage-bird supplies aisles to find canary seed, usually in a small box of plain canary seed or mixed with other goodies. Or, read the ingredients on bags of finch seed mix in the wild-bird department; it's often added as an extra enticement.

Farm-supply and feed stores. Canola (rapeseed) may be found at farm-supply stores and feed mills. Check the Yellow Pages to find one near you.

Hardware and home-supply stores. Grass seed is a seasonal item sold for lawn use. Check home-supply and hardware or discount stores. To prevent possible ill effects in birds, buy organic or the most chemical-free seed you can find; avoid those pretreated with fertilizers or other additives.

Health-food stores. Flaxseed is a bargain at health-food stores, where it's a popular product. Amaranth is a health-food store staple, too, but look for the whole seeds, not the already-ground flour. And don't buy "popped" seeds, which are great people snacks, but not to birds' liking.

Bulk-foods aisle. Check out the bins in the bulk-foods aisle of some grocery stores, and you're likely to rustle up some great bargains and maybe even some new treats to try. Flaxseed, for example, sells for as little as 50¢ a pound in bulk bins; packaged with a pretty label, it may run $2 and up per pound.

Spices and seasonings section. Here's where to hunt for oddball seeds that you want to experiment with.

Sesame seed, for example, is another small seed that's ultra-high in oil. If your birds take to it (and mine sure do!), you can then explore buying bigger quantities at smaller per-pound prices.

Ethnic grocery stores. Explore the shelves of Asian, Indian, and other ethnic markets, and you're likely to find bulk seeds at low prices. These stores are often a reasonably priced source for mustard and poppy seeds.

Bakeries. Ask your local baker if they'll share the name of their source for bakery toppings—poppy seeds and sesame seeds, to name just two. Your baker may even be willing to part with a pound of seed at a fair price.

Redpoll Roundup

I was pleased as punch to host an explosion of redpolls at my feeders a few years back. One winter morning, about a dozen birds showed up; by the end of the week, I was hosting more than 100, and had to make an emergency run to the birdseed store to keep up with them.

The next winter I waited, but the redpolls never arrived. It wasn't me, it was them: Like other birds of the far, frozen North (the evening grosbeak, red-breasted nuthatch, pine siskin, snowy owl, and purple finch), redpolls are nothing if not unpredictable. One theory is that when their natural diet of conifer seeds is scarce, they head south; otherwise, they stay put. Be ready when the redpolls roll in by keeping a good supply of finch-favored seeds on hand—and in the feeders, too. They'll join goldfinches at the niger tube, but they'll also go for mixes of small, oil-rich specialty seeds in any type of feeder.

Picky Pecking

Even experts have a hard time agreeing on what foods birds like best. Everyone knows sunflower seed, millet, corn, and niger are roundly welcomed, and nuts and suet are amply appreciated extras, but after that, the pecking order gets a little fuzzy. In the wild, birds eat thousands of kinds of seeds. But as feeder offerings get more creative, ranking the top treats gets trickier. Bird preferences for specialty seeds often vary from one region to the next, even among the same kind of birds. When you're trying something new, avoid disappointment by starting small: Offer just a handful of the new seed, until your birds decide whether or not they like it. If they do, then you can fill the tube to the top!

Space-Age Seed Shopping

Now that we're in the twenty-first century and using our computers instead of the ol' Pony Express®, you might try looking for seed sources online. You'll find many sources of bulk seeds online, but it's time-consuming to search for sellers, and the shipping costs can be prohibitive. If you want to give it a whirl, search for the name of the seed you're interested in, plus the word *pound*. (Or search for birdseed retailers online.)

The drawback of buying online is that you usually have to buy in big quantities, and it takes a long time for finches to finish off, say, 20 pounds of canola seed. If you have the space to store the seed or friends to share it with, buying online can offer big savings, even with the shipping costs. One more space-age suggestion: Use your search results to find nearby distributors of the seeds you're seeking.

Patience, Please

Cardinals like safflower seeds, or so I hear. But when I generously poured out the hard white seeds, cardinals barely gave them a glance. Across town, though, friends tell me that safflower seeds disappear down cardinal gullets lickety-split. Chances are, my birds just haven't yet figured out that the unfamiliar seeds are edible. They're sticking to the tried-and-true, instead of branching out. Sooner or later, though, they're likely to sample these unfamiliar seeds. The lesson here is that once you step beyond the staples, trying out new seeds is a matter of playing wait-and-see. So be patient! It can take weeks before a new offering is adopted.

CARDINAL

COME 'N' GET IT!

Totally Tubular

Nothin'-but-niger suits the tastes of most finches just fine. These recipes are variations on that single-note theme, which will keep the feeding fun for you and add variety for the birds. Use these recipes to fill tube feeders. Just be sure to check the seed openings of the feeder to make sure they're the right size for your recipe.

Budget Breakfast

Sneak in some millet to extend your supply of the more expensive niger seed. This basic combo attracts all finches, siskins, and buntings; look for juncos and sparrows nibbling up spilled seeds. Use a feeder with small openings to reduce spillage.

7 cups of niger
5 cups of millet (white proso millet,
**   if openings are large enough;**
**   German millet if they're tiny slits)**

Pour the seeds into a large bowl or clean bucket. Use your hands to mix the seeds, then funnel the mix into a plastic gallon milk jug for filling feeders. Cap tightly for storage.

Grainy Goodness

Humans have used these ingredients to make their daily bread for millennia. See how long it takes your finches to discover the goodness of these grains. Use a feeder with small openings to reduce spillage.

5 cups of amaranth
5 cups of millet (white proso millet,
**   if openings are large enough;**
**   German millet if they're tiny slits)**
2 cups of niger

Measure the seeds into a large bowl and stir well with your hands. Transfer to a plastic gallon milk jug for filling feeders. Cap tightly for storage.

Full Flavor for Finches

A variety of small seeds will satisfy the tastes of all finches, plus pine siskins. Serve this mix in a tube feeder with small openings.

3 cups of German millet
3 cups of niger
2 cups of flaxseed
1¹/₂ cups of canary seed
1 cup of poppy seed
¹/₂ cup of rapeseed (canola)
¹/₂ cup of amaranth
¹/₂ cup of sesame seed

Wear rubber or garden gloves to make this mix to avoid the irritating silica grains of the canary seed. Measure the German millet, niger, flax, and canary seed in a large bowl, and stir well to combine. Add the poppy seed, rapeseed, amaranth, and sesame seed, and mix lightly. Funnel into a plastic gallon milk jug for filling feeders. Cap tightly for storage.

Souped-Up Sunflowers

Fill a tube feeder with large holes (often called a sunflower seed feeder) with this delectable concoction, and you'll have cardinals, grosbeaks, and other sunflower-seed aficionados jockeying for space with the finches.

6 cups of black oil sunflower seed
3 cups of white proso millet
1 cup of safflower seed
2 cups of niger

Measure all of the seeds, except for the niger, into a large mixing bowl. Stir with your hands until well combined. Pour in the niger seed, and stir lightly. Transfer to a plastic gallon milk jug for filling feeders. Cap tightly for storage.

MARVELOUS MIXES

Shelf space is limited in seed stores, and if they sold each specialty seed individually, they'd soon run out of room. The same is true at your backyard feeding station: too many seeds, not enough feeders. The solution? Serve 'em up in mixes! Ready-made mixes usually cost more than making your own, but they can be a real time-saver. Or maybe you'd rather do it yourself. Either way, this section will tell you everything you need to know about shopping smart for store-bought mixes, *and* stirring up your own concoctions.

LEAST FLYCATCHER

Lasso the Lingo

To make sure you're getting a good mix for your money, you'll definitely want to read the label and examine the seed mix before buying anything. Ingredients are listed in descending order: There's more of the first ingredient on the list than the second, and so on. The label might include a handy list of ingredients by percentage, but if it doesn't, do a quality check yourself to make sure you're not buying a pricey bag of mostly millet. If the seed is visible, eyeball the bag to see what's what. If the bag is opaque, ask a clerk to open a bag so you can see for yourself.

Magnify the Possibilities

I've gotten in the habit of slipping a small magnifying lens into my pocket when I go birdseed shopping for specialty seeds. Why? Because that small print on bags and boxes can be hard to read! Squinting or asking for aid takes too much time when I'm concentrating on finding seeds and comparing prices. You can buy a perfectly adequate magnifying glass with a handy handle at any drug or discount store, for just a couple of dollars. At my age, it's worth it! 🐦

Creatures of Habit

Birds will try almost anything once, if it's in a feeder they're familiar with. Wait until you have a daily flow of finches at a certain feeder before you start monkeying with the menu. Once I have finches accustomed to visiting a certain tube feeder, I add a new flavor to the feeder now and then: a scoop of round black poppy seed, for instance, instead of niger. That's how I found out just how popular poppy seed is with my feathered friends. 🐦

Keep Your Cool

High-fat seeds can go rancid when stored in warm, damp surroundings, especially in humid summer heat. You won't need to worry about the seeds in your feeders, because the birds will keep them moving, but you'll want to store your extras in a cool place instead of in the hot sun. I buy specialty seeds whenever I find them at a good price, and I keep them in a metal trash can on the shadiest side of the house until I'm ready to make my mixes. If I buy or mix more seed than I can use in a few months, I

Grandma Putt's

BIRD BITS

The No-Feeder Feeder

The most common bird feeding method used to be to scatter the seeds or bread crusts right on the ground. Grandma Putt always said the best way is the simplest way, and ground feeding sure is simple, but consider these points before following suit:

❀ Seed poured on the ground not only attracts birds fast—it's also an instant favorite of mice and other rodents. To keep them at bay, try a very low tray feeder or scatter only as much seed as birds can clean up in one day.

❀ Birds like to feed at different levels, depending on what they eat in the wild. Treetop-dwellers will naturally prefer to feed at a higher location than, say, doves, which are right at home eating on the ground, so you may not attract the birds you want with ground feeding.

❀ Seed absorbs moisture from dew or wet soil when it's directly on the ground. It'll start to sprout or mold much faster than in a raised feeder.

On the plus side, snow and ice storms are the time to throw seed to the ground! After a bad storm, birds are relying on your feeder. So pack down the snow or shovel out a stretch around your feeder and spread out the seed so there's enough elbow room for all.

divvy up the surplus into zip-top plastic freezer bags and store them in the freezer. Luckily, because these seeds are so small, they don't take up much room, so I still have space for that carton of non-fattening ice cream!

WHICH SEED IS WHICH?

It's not always easy to tell one seed from another. Use this handy guide to help you decipher what seeds are in the mixes you're buying. That way, you can be sure you're getting what you pay for—and getting the seeds your feathered visitors will appreciate the most!

SEED	DESCRIPTION
Canary seed	Elongated, pointed at one end; similar to grass seed, but often shinier; golden tan **NOTE:** Wear gloves to handle; tiny silica granules can irritate skin
Flax	Flat, oval, shiny; medium or golden brown
German millet	Often in finch mixes; tiny, round with pointed tip at one end; warm honey-brown
Grass	Long, pointed seeds; dull tan or grayish tan
Millet	Often in finch mixes; small, round with pointed tip at one end; shiny; pale tan, golden tan, or reddish brown
Mustard (canola, rapeseed)	Small and completely round; black, gray, tan, or whitish
Niger (thistle, Nyjer™)	Small, thin, and long; dull to moderately shiny; dark gray to black
Poppy seed	Small, round; black, gray, or brown
Safflower	Midsized, a little smaller than black oil sunflower seeds; plump with a pointed end; white to cream-colored

Finch-Friendly Feeders

Finches are a little on the shy side, particularly when compared to pushy types like jays and blackbirds. To make sure they get plenty of chow, give them their own chuckwagon, where they won't have to fight for every bite. Tube feeders will do the trick. These nifty gadgets hold plenty of the small seeds that finches love best, and their design means that mainly finches will use them. Add a tray feeder filled with finch favorites, and word will spread like wildfire about your great grub. In the following pages, you'll discover why tube feeders are so valuable, and how to make your own freebie feeder. You'll also learn about other feeders that increase the perching capacity, so you can accommodate all those special birds that your special seeds will attract!

The Tube Solution

Most bird feeders are pretty much alike—a tray that holds seeds, with or without a hopper to hold the extra. But tube feeders are radically different. They came into vogue right along with niger seed, because feeder hosts needed a way to dole out the relatively costly seed without waste. Well-made tube feeders seem expensive, at about $25 and up. Don't let the price tag scare you off: A high-quality product is worth every penny! Cheap tubes are made of lightweight plastic that can crack, or which squirrels can gnaw through like butter. Better ones have better plastic tubes, and they also have metal perches, metal guards around the feeding holes and perches, and metal caps at the top and bottom. The metal protects the seed and deters squirrels, but just as important, it adds weight so that the feeder is less inclined to sway in the breeze, scattering seeds in all directions. ✒

GOLDFINCHES

DO IT YOURSELF

10-Minute Tube Feeder

Add this nifty quickie to your finch feeder lineup: The birds will instantly recognize its cylindrical shape and give it a try.

MATERIALS

Plastic 1-liter soda bottle and cap, label removed, rinsed and dry
Measuring tape or ruler
Marking pen
Sharp pocketknife
Spool of florist's wire (available at craft shops and discount stores)
1/4" wooden dowel, 9" long
Gravel

DIRECTIONS

Step 1. With the cap on the bottle, measure 2 inches from the base of the bottle, and mark the spot. Repeat on the opposite side of the bottle.

Step 2. Measure 2 inches above that mark, and make another mark. Repeat on the opposite side.

Step 3. Using the knife, cut a vertical slit about 1/3 inch long at each of the upper marks.

Step 4. Make a second slit, parallel to and right next to the initial cut. Curve the second slit inward at both ends, to join the first. Remove the tiny scrap of plastic. Repeat on the opposite side.

Step 5. Make a vertical slit 1/4 inch long at the lower mark on each side of the bottle. Add a second, horizontal, slit across the first one to form a cross through which you will insert the dowel. Repeat on the other side.

Step 6. Leaving the first 12 inches or so of wire hanging free, wrap the florist's wire tightly around the neck of the bottle for several turns. Snip it off, leaving another 12-inch-long end hanging free.

Step 7. Twist the two free ends into a handle above the cap of the bottle, dou-

bling the wire several times for extra strength. Allow enough free space between the handle and the cap so that you can remove and replace the cap when needed.

Step 8. Insert the dowel through both 1/4-inch slits, and center it so that its

(continued)

NIGER

GRAVEL

⊗ **10-Minute Tube Feeder, continued**

ends protrude equally from each side of the bottle.

Step 9. Remove the cap, and fill the bottom of the bottle with gravel to a depth of about 2 inches. This area is inaccessible to feeding birds, so there's no need to fill it with seeds.

Step 10. Fill the rest of the bottle with niger seed, then replace the cap, being careful not to invert the bottle.

Step 11. Hang the bottle from a hook.

Refill the feeder as needed. Just remove the cap and use a funnel or long-spouted watering can to pour in the seed.

Limited Access

Hey, move over! No, YOU move over! That's what those finches at the tube feeder are saying to each other with their flashing wings and threatening beaks. It's single-seating only, and there are just a few perches on these seed-saving feeders, which means hungry finches have to wait their turn or squabble for space. I always have a tube or three filled and waiting; but when finch traffic is high, I take care of the overflow crowd by offering their favorite niger and other seeds in roomy tray-type feeders, where the eating etiquette is come one, come all. 🐦

Eyeball the Openings

When tube feeders first came on the market, they all had tiny slits for birds to feed at, sized for niger seeds to be withdrawn one at a time. As feeder hosts learned to love these stay-dry, seed-stingy feeders, designers created tubes with openings large enough for sunflower seeds and other seeds to fit through. But pour niger in a tube feeder with big openings, and the teeny-weeny seeds will spill out in a rush. Pour sunflower seeds in a tube sized for niger, and birds will quickly get discouraged trying to yank the monster seeds out of the Tom Thumb openings. Since the feeders look alike at first glance, you'll need to read the label or examine the openings to see exactly what kind of seed they're designed for. 🐦

Cheapies for Chirpers

I depend on good-quality tube feeders, but I can't resist picking up cheapies when I run across them. Even if they last only a season or until the squirrels discover them and gnaw through the thin plastic, I add a lot of perching room for just a few bucks. Tube feeders dole out niger seeds to only six or eight customers at a time, so my seed supply lasts longer, and the birds keep coming back for more. Those that can't find an empty perch pick up dropped seeds below the tube or scour the other feeders for millet and sunflower seeds.

Eke Out the Treats

When your bird clients are a manageable handful, you'll find that a little seed goes a long way. But when the traffic starts to get thick, gregarious finches can empty your feeders faster than you can afford to refill them with those precious little seeds. I like to stretch my birdseed bucks, so I add millet to the mix in feeders with small eating holes. In tubes with larger openings or in come-one, come-all feeders, where birds can peck at will, I stir in plenty of black oil sunflower seeds. As long as there's at least a tantalizing taste of their favorite niger and other small seeds, the finches stay loyal to my feeders.

PINE SISKIN

Hang 'Em High

Any bird with "finch" in its name has no fear of heights and will instantly adopt a feeding station on a second-story deck or balcony. Pine siskins, too, are high fliers. If you're just beginning bird feeding at the heights, hang a tube feeder in a highly visible spot: on the outside of a raised deck rail, or suspended from a shepherd's hook clamped to the rail. That'll get their attention, and once they find you, you'll be friends forever—or as long as the feeder is filled!

COME 'N' GET IT!

Open Season

Serve these mixes in tray-type feeders, where finches can peck at will. Dole them out as needed to feed the overflow crowd from tube feeders. Or serve generously when finches are flocking in fall and spring. Store the extras in plastic gallon milk jugs, tightly capped, in a cool, dry place.

Every Finch's Fave

Expect to see goldfinches, pine siskins, purple finches, house finches, and drop-dead-beautiful buntings dining on this all-purpose finch mix. Doves, towhees, and tanagers may also stop by for a sample.

4 cups of niger
2 cups of white proso millet
2 cups of black oil sunflower seed
2 cups of flaxseed
2 cups of grass seed

Measure the seeds into a dry, clean bucket or large bowl. Mix well using your hands. Store in a plastic gallon milk jug, tightly capped.

Cheep Crowd-Pleaser

A dozen goldfinches are delightful, but 100 of those hungry beaks can make you wonder what you've gotten yourself into. This recipe serves a horde without breaking the bank. Other finches, siskins, and buntings will partake, too.

5 cups of white proso millet
4 cups of black oil sunflower seed
2 cups of niger
1 cup of grass seed

Measure the seeds into a dry, clean bucket or large bowl. Mix well using your hands. Store in a plastic gallon milk jug, tightly capped.

Sparrow Style

Though not as flashy or as charming as their finchy cousins, native sparrows are just as interesting at the feeder. Serve this spread in a low tray feeder and see how many of these low-key characters you can attract. Towhees and red-winged blackbirds enjoy this mix, too.

5 cups of millet
3 cups of cracked corn
2 cups of black oil sunflower seed
2 cups of flaxseed

Measure the seeds and corn into a dry, clean bucket or large bowl. Mix well using your hands. Store in a plastic gallon milk jug, tightly capped.

Pumped-Up All-Purpose Mix

Here's a mix that will satisfy every bird that arrives at the feeder, including those finicky finches. Goldfinches, pine siskins, and buntings are fond of this mix, because of its bonus of niger seeds.

5 cups of black oil sunflower seeds
4 cups of millet
2 cups of cracked corn
1 cup of niger

Measure the sunflower seeds, millet, and corn into a dry, clean bucket or large bowl. Mix well using your hands. Stir in the niger. Store in a plastic gallon milk jug, tightly capped.

Blowing in the Wind

Ever notice how the level of seed in your tube feeder takes a sudden dive sometimes? The likely culprit could be whistling over your shoulder right now. Wind can blow lightweight tube feeders willy-nilly, causing the seeds to spill out of the feeding holes faster than you can say "whoa!"

Stop seed spillage in stiff breezes by adding weight to your tube feeder. Before you fill the feeder with that precious seed, drop in some small but heavy stones to just below the first feeding hole. The extra weight will help add stability when the wind blows. ❧

Give Hawks the Heave-Ho

Sometimes a tragic consequence of being a feeder-keeper is bearing witness to hawk attacks—and I'm talking about hawks attacking birds, not feeders! Sadly, finches often attract a hawk's attention, because they're so active and there are so many of 'em. Once a hawk has discovered the great "hawk feeder" you've got going, your choices are few. The simplest solution is to stop feeding the birds: Take down the feeders, clean up every bit of spilled seed, and within days, the birds will realize the welcome mat's been pulled out from under 'em. You won't have to witness any more disturbing hawk attacks, or feel guilty for being the indirect cause of other birds' demise. After a week of slim pickin's, the hawk is likely to head elsewhere, although it may return if you put the feeders back in place. ❧

Hasta la vista, House Finches!

When house finches first appeared at feeders in the East and Midwest years ago, we greeted them with open arms. Then these immigrants (from California, by way of New York, where they were released into the wild) exploded, and soon every feeding station was swamped. Adapting way too well, house finches now make their homes across the country.

To keep them from gobbling up all of your special finch seeds and from hogging every seat at the diner, try a topsy-turvy move: Attach a wire around the bottom of any tube feeder, and hang it upside down so that the perches are above the seed holes. Acrobatic goldfinches and siskins won't be deterred, but house finches will think twice and look for seed elsewhere. You can also buy specially designed anti-house-finch feeders, but it may not be worth the investment: Word from some quarters suggests that house finches are getting the hang of this trick, too. ❧

COME 'N' GET IT!

Homemade for Habitat

The wild places, if any, that are near your home determine what birds you see in your backyard. City folk, for instance, feed more pigeons than their country cousins do. No matter where you live, these treats are tailor-made to attract birds typical to the habitat around your home.

Suburban Savories

The backyards of subdivisions are popular with finches, siskins, and buntings from fall through spring. Try this recipe when you notice new customers finding a place among the usual cardinals and jays.

4 cups of millet, any kind
2 cups of niger
2 cups of flaxseed
2 cups of black oil sunflower seed
1 cup of canary seed
1 cup of rapeseed (canola)

Measure all ingredients into a large bowl and mix thoroughly, using your hands. Pour some into a tube feeder with large openings. Serve the rest in a tray-type feeder. Some of the small seeds will drop from the tube feeder; watch for towhees, doves, juncos, and native sparrows doing clean-up duty below.

Farms & Fields

Sparrows—both native species and the ubiquitous house sparrow—blackbirds, quail, and even pheasants will flock to this recipe. The nicety of niger added to the mix will ensure that goldfinches and indigo buntings are happy with it, too.

3 cups of cracked corn
2 cups of black oil sunflower seed
2 cups of niger
4 cups of millet, any kind

Measure all ingredients, except for the millet, into a large mixing bowl, and stir with your hands until well combined. Pour in the millet and stir lightly to distribute it throughout the mix. Serve in a tray-type feeder.

In-Town Treats

Doves, pigeons, and house sparrows—three of the most common city birds—will find plenty to feed on in this dish. So will any goldfinches or house finches in the neighborhood, plus the other usual suspects. In spring and fall, this tempting recipe will also catch the attention of rose-breasted grosbeaks and other out-of-the-ordinary migrants that may be passing through.

3 cups of millet, any kind
3 cups of black oil sunflower seed
3 cups of cracked corn
1 cup of niger
1 cup of flaxseed

Measure the millet, sunflower, and corn into a large bowl and mix well using your hands. Pour in the niger and flaxseed and mix lightly. Funnel some of the mix into a tube feeder with large openings so that finches can dine without competition. Serve the rest in a tray-type feeder, where other in-town birds can find a place to perch.

Forest Fauna

This one-recipe-fits-all mix appeals to all your usual feathered fauna, from big woodpeckers, grosbeaks, and jays to diminutive chickadees, nuthatches, pine siskins, redpolls, and Cassin's and purple finches.

2 cups of whole-kernel corn, off the cob
1 cup of cracked corn
1 cup of white or red millet
1 cup of niger
1 cup of flaxseed
5 cups of sunflower seed, any kind

Measure all ingredients, except for the sunflower seeds, into a large bowl and mix well using your hands. Stir in the sunflower seeds. Serve in an open, unroofed tray-type feeder with plenty of room for perching.

Swinging Socks

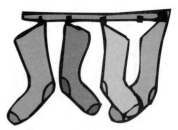

Instant gratification at a great price—that's the allure of niger socks. Made from soft nylon mesh with a drawstring top, these instant "tube" feeders are a cinch to hang to increase perching capacity at your place. Finches cling to the netting wherever they can get a grip, and pull out the tiny niger seeds through the mesh. More than a dozen birds can easily find elbow room, instead of the usual six to eight perching places on tube feeders. Look for prefilled socks in garden catalogs, or save a few pennies by buying empty ones and stuffing your own. ✍

Fall Is for Flocking

Goldfinches are gregarious birds. When nesting season is finished in late summer, they stick together in a small family flock. As fall migration kicks in, one family joins another, and so on, until the flocks number in the dozens to hundreds of birds. You'll hear their lilting calls as they roam, looking for food. When they spot the banquet at your bird feeder, they're bound to pay you a visit that may last for weeks. Eventually, most of the migrants will move on, but winter resident finches may stick around through the cold months. Try the specialty seed recipes scattered throughout this chapter (especially those that stretch the precious niger with tasty alternatives), to keep them satisfied through the seasons.

Corral the Competition

Birds that are perfectly capable of cracking bigger seeds, and perfectly satisfied with the less-expensive alternatives, will also scarf down your special seeds if you give them the chance. They'll quickly rule the feeder if you mix the goodies with the basics, because the less aggressive finches yield the field to the bigger bullies. Tube feeders are the simplest way to give finches a place to call their own, where they can eat at leisure. Other birds have difficulty maneuvering their bodies into position on these hanging holders, and will soon retreat to more physically accommodating feeder styles, even if the spread there is less tempting. ✍

It's a Stick-Up!

Nothing's more fun than watching birds up close—REAL close! I keep a batch of small suction-cup feeders on one of my windows, so I can go nose to beak with the birds. They're the perfect size to hold one or two goldfinches, pine siskins, or other perky little birds that don't mind getting close to people. The clear plastic lets me get a good look at whoever drops by.

Stick-on feeders have to be lightweights or the suction cups will lose their grip, so their seed reservoirs are small. That's why I bunch 'em up on one window—more action in one location, and my refill chores are consolidated.

Finch-Seed Filchers

Look on the ground below your tube feeder and you'll spot a bunch of birds that don't use finch feeders, but do love finch food. Small juncos and sparrows are the major small-seed eaters,

DO IT YOURSELF

Seed-Catching Saucer

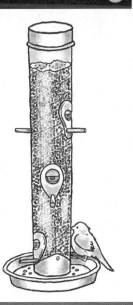

No matter how careful you are, your tube feeder is destined to be a seed spiller. Birds will sometimes pull out extra seeds as they feed, which then fall to the ground. Catch those spills, and you'll save seeds and add more feeding space at the same time. Here's how to do it:

Buy a clear 6-inch plastic plant saucer at a discount or home-supply store or garden center. These thin, lightweight saucers are remarkably inexpensive, usually less than $1. Glue the saucer to the bottom of the tube feeder. An all-purpose fast-holding glue such as Aleene's Tacky Glue™ should do the trick. That's all there is to it. Now, dropped seeds will fall into the saucer, where finches can perch on the rim to retrieve them.

SPOTTED TOWHEE

but they may be joined by bigger birds that prefer to eat small seeds at ground level. Blackbirds, doves, and quail are the usual larger ground-feeding guests, but keep your eyes open for more uncommon visitors, too. These special birds usually visit singly to feast on finch leftovers, not in groups like doves or juncos. Keep checking below the finch feeder and you may spot one of these:

✔ California towhee

✔ Eastern (rufous-sided) towhee

✔ Green-tailed towhee

✔ Spotted towhee

✔ Summer tanager

✔ Varied thrush

Not only are these birds a treat to see, they're valuable vacuum cleaners for dropped seeds that might otherwise be wasted. 🐦

FAVORED BY FINCHES

The colorful little birds we know as finches will happily come to your feeder when you pour out the specialty seeds. But just like kids, these guys'll squabble over who gets the favorites! Here are the finchy favorites that I've noticed are tops with my birds (yours may have slightly different appetites), and some clues on how to identify the special seeds by sight when they're in a mix.

FINCH	FAVORED SEEDS (IN ORDER OF PREFERENCE)	FEEDER STYLE AND PLACEMENT
Cassin's finch	Black oil sunflower seed, niger, flaxseed, canary seed, grass seed	Tube or tray, at least 3 feet above the ground; will also visit 2nd-story feeders
Goldfinch	Niger, canary seed, grass seed, flaxseed, rapeseed (canola), poppy seed, amaranth, sesame seed, caraway seed	Tube or tray, at least 3 feet above the ground; will also visit 2nd-story feeders; also feeds on the ground

FINCH	FAVORED SEEDS (IN ORDER OF PREFERENCE)	FEEDER STYLE AND PLACEMENT
House finch	Niger, black oil sunflower seed, millet of any kind, grass seed, flaxseed, canary seed, poppy seed, rapeseed (canola), amaranth, sesame seed, caraway seed	Any kind, anywhere
Indigo bunting	White proso millet, German millet, canary seed, grass seed, amaranth, poppy seed	Tube or tray, at least 3 feet above the ground; also feeds on the ground
Lazuli bunting	White proso millet, German millet, canary seed, black oil sunflower seed, grass seed	Tube or tray, at least 3 feet above the ground; also feeds on the ground
Painted bunting	Niger, white proso millet, German millet, canary seed, grass seed, black oil sunflower seed, amaranth, poppy seed	Tube or tray, at least 3 feet above the ground; also feeds on the ground
Pine siskin	Rapeseed (canola), mustard, niger, German millet, white proso millet, black oil sunflower seed, canary seed, grass seed, poppy seed, amaranth	Tube or tray, at least 3 feet above the ground; will also visit 2nd-story feeders
Purple finch	Black oil sunflower seed, white proso millet, niger, grass seed, canary seed	Tube or tray, at least 3 feet above the ground; will also visit 2nd-story feeders
Redpoll	Niger, black oil sunflower seed	Tube or tray, at least 3 feet above the ground; will also visit 2nd-story feeders

CHAPTER 4

Plain & Fancy Fats

Fats are fundamental at your feeder, no matter what the "food police" are warning us about our own intake! Serve your birds suet and other fats, and you'll see lots more woodpeckers, nuthatches, titmice, and chickadees. Fats will also bring you birds that might otherwise pass you by, like those that rely on soft foods instead of seeds. Bluebirds, orioles, tanagers, thrushes, thrashers, warblers, and even a bustling band of bushtits may all be tempted to the table. Why, it's a regular roundup!

In this chapter, you'll learn why suet is such a standard at the feeder: It's easy to buy, easy to serve, and costs only a few pennies a day. Plain and simple, it's just about unbeatable for you and the birds! You'll also discover why peanut butter packs such a big punch at the bird buffet, and how you can use it in tempting treats.

SUPER-SIMPLE SUET

Fast, cheap, and easy; that's suet in a nutshell. It takes just a minute to slip a suet block into the feeder, and I'm set for another month or two of woodpecker watching. Not to mention enjoying the company of chickadees, titmice, and nuthatches all year long, and thrilling to the sight of tanagers, orioles, bluebirds, robins, wrens, thrushes, and thrashers from spring through fall. And here's another big plus—a block of suet only sets me back about a buck!

In this section, we'll consider the differences between store-bought suet blocks and meat trimmings from the market. You'll also find out how to choose and hang a suet feeder, so that you get a super show from your suet-eaters.

Suet Savvy

According to the strictest standards, "suet" is the layer of solid, white fat around a cow's or sheep's kidneys. In the old days, it was called "tallow" and was prized for making candles. Others say suet is not raw fat, but rendered fat, the product that results when fat scraps are melted and impurities are strained out. Birds go by a more lenient definition, and so do I. Any animal fat will do, no matter what part of the beast it comes from. My feeder friends eat the raw, rough trimmings I get from the butcher just as eagerly as they do the tidy, packaged variety of melted-and-molded suet. In my book, "suet" simply means solid fat from animals.

All-Season Staple

Suet-loving birds will visit your feeder year-round, but the traffic will increase and decrease with the seasons. Here's why:

◆ From late fall through winter, finding food is the main motivation for birds. Natural foods are getting scarce, so birds range widely to fill their bellies. Your customer base will come from a

BLUEBIRD

much larger area than your own neighborhood, because birds are no longer sticking to nesting territories.

◆ When the weather turns extra cold, your suet feeders will host an overflow crowd. High-fat foods supply a lot of calories, so expect a boom when the big chill sets in.

◆ Spring suet is still popular, at least until resident birds take up nesting territories. Some winter regulars will say goodbye as they leave on spring migration. So as the days lengthen, you'll see fewer birds pecking at your suet.

◆ Midspring brings the possibility of unusual birds at your suet feeders. Vivid tanagers and orioles, musical wrens, charming catbirds, and other birds that spent the winter in warmer climes are winging their way back to nesting grounds. You'll want to add special suet recipes now, to tempt them into stopping over.

◆ As soon as insects become abundant, most suet-eating birds are likely to leave your feeders. Traffic will slow to a crawl, but you can expect to see an occasional woodpecker or other daily regular stopping by.

◆ From late spring through midsummer, during nesting season, watch for parent birds grabbing a bite or possibly bringing the youngsters by after they leave the nest.

◆ As fall sets in, suet feeders become more active. Birds will drop by during migration, or settle in for the duration. 🐦

Prepacked Convenience

Ready-made suet blocks are hard to beat. They're inexpensive—as little as $1 apiece—and simpler to serve than a TV dinner. Just peel off the plastic, remove the tray, and slip the cake of fat into your feeder. Start to finish: less than 5 minutes!

You can find commercial suet blocks, about 5 inches square by 1 to 2 inches thick, in the birdseed aisle of any discount store, garden center, supermarket, or even the hardware or drug store. The block of fat is held within a plastic tray, and a greaseproof plastic wrapper keeps it nice and neat. 🐦

Extra Added Attractions

Some of us go for the plain M&Ms®, others pounce on the ones with peanuts. Same with birds: Plain and simple suet is just fine, thank you, but extra goodies—mmm! You'll find commercial suet blocks made with all kinds of extras and marketed as suet for bluebirds, suet for orioles, and so on through the feeder roll call. Just as with seed mixes, it pays to read the label on souped-up suet blocks. Sometimes, unappealing seeds of the cheapest kind are used, or the additions are so scanty that you're better off buying a block of plain suet and fancying up the fat on your own. You'll find lots of easy recipes to do just that in the next section, "Simplest Suet Tweets" (see page 102). 🐦

Chopped Suetty

SEASONAL SUGGESTIONS

Every bird in the neighborhood can use some extra calories in winter, but not all birds can hang onto a suet feeder. When bitter cold sets in, when ice or snow falls, and, sometimes, just because I'm nice, I help out my feathered friends by being extra-generous with suet—and serving it their way! If you want to surprise your sparrows, juncos, bluebirds, and other nontypical suet-eaters, pull out your chopping block and get to work. A block of plain suet is easy to dice into small bits with a sharp knife: Just cut parallel lines about $1/4$ inch apart across the block, slicing all the way through the suet, then turn the knife perpendicular, and do it again. Presto—bird-sized suet bits! Scatter them in a tray feeder or directly on the ground, and watch the fun begin.

Greasy Kid Stuff

Some feeder-keepers avoid feeding anything but plain suet, or suet that's been coated, not mixed, with extras. The reason? They believe that birds might stick their beaks in so far to get that nugget of nut or other goody that their head feathers will get greasy. That slicked-back 'do isn't a good choice for birds, because fluffy feathers

JERRY
TO THE RESCUE

Q. I keep my suet feeder filled in summer, because some birds still come to it. They don't eat much, though, and my suet melts in hot weather and makes messy drips on the patio. Any suggestions?

A. I keep my suet going in summer, too, but I do one thing different: I move the feeder! When the sun starts to heat things up, I poke a tall, black, iron hook (a bargain at less than $10 at any garden center!) into the ground well away from any wood or walking surfaces. It takes just seconds to hang a wire suet cage on the hook, and the birds follow the move pretty quick. And choosing a location that's in the shade most of the day cuts down on melting, too. You can also cut down on the amount of fat in your feeder; just store the extra in your freezer until you need it for the winter rush. Try these simple changes, and you'll have it made in the shade with suet, even on hot, sultry days!

provide vital insulation. Maybe the birds are just smarter at my feeder, but I've never seen one dig deep enough to get the greasy kid stuff effect. If you're concerned, though, stick to serving suet that has the extra attractions only on the outside, not throughout the fat. 🐦

Cheaper by the Dozen

To save a bit of pocket change, ask your suet-block seller if you can buy a whole box of the stuff. Don't worry, you won't need to rent a truck—usually the blocks are packed 12 to a box. Because suet is such a bargain to begin with, you'll save just a few pennies per block. Buying by the dozen will probably net you only a dollar or two of savings, but, hey, every little bit helps, right? 🐦

Trimming the Fat

Suet blocks are so neat and tidy, and so widely available, that the old ways of supplying fat are rapidly falling by the wayside. It's good to know, though, that you can still get suet-in-the-rough by asking for it at the meat counter of your favorite market. The scraps of tasty white fat trimmed off of steaks and roasts are just as appealing to birds as the prepackaged blocks, and they're just as easy to fit into a feeder. Some stores sell the stuff alongside hamburger and other people meats, because they've recognized that there's a market for it. But if you can't find it in the grocery case, just ask! ✒

SONG
SPARROW

Smart $avings

Shhh—don't tell the suet-block makers, but they could probably double their price and still keep their customers. Why? The stuff is just so darn convenient! You'll save money, though, by buying fat scraps from the butcher instead, especially if he gives away fat scraps, or sells them for pennies on the pound.

But there's a point where the savings of buying raw suet may not be worth the fuss. Should the sticker price for fat scraps ever hit $1.50 a pound, I'll pass them by and buy the 12-ounce blocks of pure suet for $1.29—still a little more per ounce, but well worth it to me in convenience! ✒

Truth in Advertising?

I've used quite a collection of "fancified" suet blocks from commercial manufacturers over the years, but no matter what price I pay, they all seem to use cheap ingredients to fill out the mix. Read the labels, and you'll see that cracked corn and milo—two of the cheapest seeds out there—are usually used in the "special" blocks for orioles, bluebirds, or other birds. Sometimes, "peanut flavoring" or other flavors are also listed, instead of the real thing. Now, my birds will eat just about anything that's smeared with suet, so the labels aren't exactly incorrect, and the packaged blocks are seductively convenient. I still buy them if I'm fresh out of fat. But for my suet feeder mainstays, I make my own! ✒

COME 'N' GET IT!

Basic Banquets

These easy treats satisfy all suet-eating birds, from wrens to wood-peckers and everyone in between. And, because they don't include expensive extras, they'll save you money! These recipes make enough to stuff a standard wire suet cage; if you want to make more, just multiply all ingredients. And if you have any leftovers, freeze them in zip-top plastic freezer bags.

Come One, Come All

My favorite all-purpose mix, this high-fat, high-protein recipe will appeal to exotic tanagers and orioles, bluebirds, thrashers, robins, Carolina wrens, catbirds, and mockingbirds, plus the usual gang of woodpeckers, nuthatches, titmice, and chickadees.

1 cup of suet or fat scraps, chopped
1 1/2 cups of cornmeal, regular grind (not coarse or fine)

Put the suet or fat scraps in a deep bowl. Pour the cornmeal into the bowl, and mix it thoroughly with the fat. Use your hands to firmly pack the mix into your suet feeder, or mold into balls or blocks. Freeze them individually in zip-top plastic freezer bags for later use.

Suet 'n' Sunflowers

Here's a better-than-basic mix, with sunflower chips that are ready to eat right along with the suet (those in commercial mixes often have shells that require cracking first—wasting the suet on the shells). It'll please nuthatches, titmice, and chickadees.

1 1/2 cups of suet or fat scraps, chopped
1/2 cup of sunflower chips (hulled sunflower seeds)

Put the suet or fat scraps in a deep bowl, and add the sunflower chips. Use the back of a large, strong spoon, and with a "creaming" motion, smash the sunflower chips into the suet, or mix the suet and sunflower chips with your hands. Use your hands to pack the mix into your feeder, or mold into balls or blocks and freeze them in zip-top plastic freezer bags.

Feedbag Full o' Oats

Oatmeal isn't a top food for birds, but, apparently, suet improves its flavor tremendously. Adding oatmeal to suet makes the fat go farther, so more birds get a bite. Use this mix to feed a crowd in winter, or to pinch a few pennies anytime. It costs me only about 25¢ to make, using fat scraps from the market. At that price, I don't mind serving it to starlings—**even they** need to keep warm in winter!

1 cup of suet or fat scraps, chopped
$^1/_2$ cup of oats, regular or quick-cooking

Put the suet or fat scraps in a deep bowl, and pour in the dry oatmeal. Work the mixture with your hands until the suet and oats are thoroughly combined, or use the back of a large, strong spoon to smash the oatmeal into the suet. Stuff the mix into your feeder, or mold into blocks or balls, and freeze them in zip-top plastic freezer bags.

Sparrow Suet

Save this recipe for winter feeding, when temperatures drop and small birds need an extra boost of body-warming fat to keep cozy at night. The hulled proso millet means that sparrows and juncos can eat every bit, without cracking any shells.

2 parts packaged suet
1 part cornmeal
3 parts hulled white proso millet

Melt the suet in the microwave by putting it in a microwave-safe bowl and heating it on high for 60 **sec**onds. Continue heating in 15-second increments, if necessary. Add the cornmeal to the melted suet, stirring to combine. Add the millet, and mix thoroughly. The mixture will be crumbly, not as cohesive as cookie dough. Spread the mixture onto a nonstick cookie sheet. Set the cookie sheet in the freezer until the suet mixture is frozen. Working quickly so that the suet doesn't thaw, break the mixture into bits of about $^1/_2$ inch diameter or smaller. Scoop the bits into plastic zip-top freezer bags, and return them to the freezer. When cold weather comes, scatter the suet bits in a tray feeder or directly on the ground (or snow!) to serve sparrows and juncos.

Corny Suet

Woodpeckers adore this inexpensive mix. The corny bonus will make downy, hairy, red-bellied, and red-headed woodpeckers extra happy, and it'll appeal to flickers, too.

1 cup of suet or fat scraps, chopped
3/4 cup of cracked corn

Put the suet or fat scraps in a deep bowl. Pour the cracked corn into the bowl, and use your hands to combine thoroughly. Pack into a wire suet cage, or mold into blocks or balls and freeze them in zip-top plastic freezer bags.

Kitchen Sheriff

I was irked by the thought of paying more than $1.50 a pound for El Cheapo cracked corn (which I can buy in bulk for less than 25¢ a pound), just because it was mixed with some suet. So I did some detective work in the kitchen, melting and measuring suet blocks, to see whether I was jumping to conclusions.

In all cases, no matter what I'd paid for the block, each of those 11- or 12-ounce blocks contained only about one-third suet. That's only a quarter-pound of suet—about a dime's worth, by my grocery store's prices! The rest was cheap filler. The one that won the worst-case award, though, was the premium-priced "Peanut Treat" block, which included more corn, more milo, and more wheat than the few-and-far between peanut pieces in the mix. ✎

Cages & Contraptions

Suet is one of the best buys in the bird feeding business, and so are suet feeders. For less than $5 (as little as $2, depending on where you shop!), you can buy a sturdy, long-lasting wire cage that's sized to accommodate ready-made suet blocks. Flip open the hinged top, slide in the block or homemade treats, and you're good to go. Make sure the one you choose has a plastic or other coating on the wire, so that your hands don't stick to the metal in winter.

Start your suet setup with a basic model, which will be heavily used by chickadees, titmice, nuthatches, and woodpeckers. Suet-eating songbirds that aren't as acrobatic as these guys will appreciate a more horizontal feeder that doesn't swing; you can dedicate a tray feeder to these birds, or add a perch to a hanging model. 🐦

Nothing but Net

Need a bunch of suet feeders fast? Cut an empty net sack, the kind that onions come in, into squares of about 6 inches or so. Cut a suet block into chunks, or pile a few fat scraps in the center, gather the corners together like a hobo sack, and secure with a twist-tie. Tie a string for hanging around the neck of each bundle, and attach to any handy branch or hook. 🐦

Latch onto a Log

Check your bird-supply store for a "suet log," a versatile contraption that serves several birds at one time and looks nice and natural. They're usually about 1 foot long and 3 inches in diameter, and they're made by drilling holes about $1\frac{1}{2}$ inches across and an inch or so deep into a solid section of a tree branch. You smoosh suet or other high-fat foods into the holes, and the birds cling to the log to eat. A suet log can hang either vertically or horizontally, and because it's all-natural, it blends right into the garden.

If you're handy with an electric drill, you can make a suet log yourself lickety-split. Add an eye-hook and wire loop for hanging, and you're done! 🐦

Grandma Putt's

BIRD BITS

Befriend a Butcher

Up until a few years ago, meat came into the market in big slabs, needing finishing work to slice off the fat and carve up the meat into pot roasts and T-bone steaks. Just for the asking, you could go home with a huge helping of fat scraps—a winter's worth of woodpecker food for free! Grandma Putt taught me that money-saving trick, but nowadays, it's a little harder to put into practice.

Modern supermarkets usually get their meat pretrimmed of fat, so the scrap supply is much slimmer. And there's usually a price to pay, too. But if you have a neighborhood butcher shop, or a market that takes pride in its custom-cut meat selection, you're in luck! Lots of these places still trim their own meat, leaving an ample supply of leftover fat that's ideal for your birds. If you're a good customer of a small shop, you might still get fat scraps for free. But such a prime bird treat is worth paying the small price they're usually asking for it.

DO IT YOURSELF

Posture Prop

Ever take a close look at a woodpecker's tail? Those stiff, pointy feathers are powerful aids for helping the hammerhead hold its grip when the bird is whacking away at trees, or suet. Woodpeckers are so fond of suet that they'll soon figure out how to get a grip on a hanging, swaying feeder. But given their druthers, they'd prefer a solid place to prop their tails. You can find special woodpecker-style suet feeders, with an extended board below for extra support, or you can make your own posture prop in just a few minutes. Here's how.

MATERIALS

Wire suet cage
Pencil
4 metal eyehooks, $1/2$" to 1" or larger opening, with a screw-in shank; about 2" long overall

DIRECTIONS

Step 1. Choose a porch, deck, or feeder post location for the feeder. Hold the wire cage against the post, and use a pencil to draw a horizontal line on the post along the top and bottom of the cage. Set the cage aside.

Step 2. Screw in two of the eyehooks just below the bottom line, spacing them about 2 inches apart.

Step 3. Screw in the other two eyehooks just above the top line, spacing them about 2 inches apart.

Step 4. Fill the feeder.

Step 5. Position the eyes of the hooks so that they are parallel to the lines on the post. Slide the feeder against the post, until it's centered on the hooks. Turn the eyes of the hooks perpendicular, so that they hold the feeder snugly in place against the post.

That's all there is to it! Now your woodpecker friends will have a handy post to prop their tails on while they peck at the suet. When it's time to refill, just turn the eyes to the horizontal position and slide out the feeder.

Inclement Increase

I'm a big fan of salads in summer, but when cold weather sets in, give me those heartier foods, please! Those extra calories get burned off just trying to keep warm. Outside, where there's no thermostat to nudge upward, birds need our help to make it through the wintry blasts. So when winter sets in, I add lots of suet feeders around the yard, even in places I can't watch from a window. I want to make sure that there's plenty of fat for everyone, so all my bird friends stay well fed and warm. 🐦

DOWNY WOODPECKER

In Praise of Plastic

Wooden suet feeders are lovely to look at, but that pretty wood will soon become stained with grease. I don't mind the darkened stain as long as it's only on the feeder. But when it comes to my porch or deck, I'm a neatnik! I've found a few creative ways to keep things tidy, including using the shallow foam trays from packaged meat or produce. Here's how to capitalize on these freebies:

◆ Nail a foam tray to the deck rail, to hold high-fat treats.

◆ Use thumbtacks to attach a tray to the post behind your suet feeder to block those greasy contact stains.

◆ Thumbtack a tray to the porch or deck floor below the suet feeder. It won't catch all of the greasy crumbs, but it'll help.

◆ Keep your trusty tacks handy, and use a few to anchor a foam tray inside your tray feeder. Serve the greasy goodies on the tray, to keep the seed in the rest of the feeder clean. 🐦

Get a Grip

Handling suet is messy business. No matter how careful you are, your fingers are still likely to get greasy. That's why I now put my hands into plastic bags before I fill the feeder. Small plastic food-storage bags will do the trick, but I prefer to use the longer plastic bags that protect my newspaper on rainy mornings. They slip on easily and cover my sleeves, so my sweater cuffs stay suet-free, too. 🐦

COME 'N' GET IT!

Peanut Butter Panache

Peanut butter has a long line of hungry admirers—and I don't mean the human kind! Bluebirds, tanagers, and other beauties are especially drawn to it, but all of your regular suet eaters will also take to the stuff.

Bottom Line

Cornmeal extends the higher-priced fats in this simple mix. Many birds gladly eat corn, and they like it even better when it's coated with tasty fats. Watch for woodpeckers, chickadees, titmice, and nuthatches when you serve this in hanging feeders; at feeders with a place to perch, be alert for a glimpse of a catbird, Carolina wren, tanager, thrasher, or beautiful bluebird.

**2 cups of cornmeal, regular grind
   (not coarse or fine)**
³/₄ cup of peanut butter
¹/₂ cup of suet or fat scraps, chopped

Measure the cornmeal into a deep bowl. Mix the peanut butter into the cornmeal. Add suet to the mixture, and mix well to combine. With your hands, mold the mixture into a block about the size of your suet feeder. Put into the feeder and serve, or freeze the block in a zip-top plastic freezer bag for later use.

Awesome Twosome

A little bit of peanut butter goes a long way toward tempting special birds to the feeder. Try this treat to coax bluebirds, tanagers, orioles, thrashers, catbirds, and Carolina wrens. Be sure to poke in a perch, or serve in a horizontal feeder where these less agile fat-lovers can get a grip.

³/₄ cup of suet or fat scraps, chopped
¹/₄ cup of peanut butter

Put the fat into a small, deep bowl. Add the peanut butter and mix well, using your hands. Form into a block to fit your suet feeder, or freeze the block in a zip-top plastic freezer bag for later use.

Yo-De-Lay-Hee-Hoo!

Give your feeder an alpine accent by adding "muesli," a cereal of Swiss origin, to your mix. This blend of untoasted rolled oats and other cereals, plus dried fruits and sometimes nuts, combines easily with suet and peanut butter to make a nutritious, palatable bird breakfast. Listen! Is that a yellow-rumped warbler that I hear yodeling?

¹/₂ cup of lard
¹/₂ cup of suet or fat scraps, chopped
¹/₄ cup of peanut butter
1 cup of muesli, any brand

Measure the lard, the suet or fat scraps, and the peanut butter into a deep bowl. Use your hands to mix thoroughly. Pour in the muesli, and combine it with the fats. Use your hands to work the cereal into the fat, until it is thoroughly distributed. Form into a block to fit your suet feeder, or freeze the block in a zip-top plastic freezer bag for later use.

Sorry, Starlings!

Suet eaters are solitary diners, with two notable exceptions. In the West, bands of small gray birds called bushtits roam the neighborhoods, sweeping through the shrubbery, seemingly always in motion. It's no big deal if they descend en masse onto your suet—these birds are barely chickadee-sized, and they're in perpetual motion, so a visit is a fleeting pleasure.

But not so with starlings. These common blackish birds are as gregarious as bushtits, but they're way bigger and way hungrier, not to mention much noisier. Should starlings find your suet, you'll hear loud squabbling as the birds fight for space, and the fat will be gobbled up fast. I solve the starling situation by giving them their own feeder of greasy good stuff, and by adding extra suet feeders around the yard (they can't hog 'em all!). I also hang a suet feeder that holds the fat inside a cage of metal bars, which blocks starlings, so that small birds can dine at their leisure. 🐦

Topsy-Turvy

Did you ever have a bright idea that turned out to be not so smart? Sometimes, I wonder whether the inventor of the upside-down suet feeder might be in the same company! It seems like a stroke of genius: a hanging suet feeder that allows access only from the bottom, with a closely covered roof and sides to block bigger birds from the suet cage within. The theory is that chickadees and other acrobatic types can cling below and nibble away, but starlings are excluded.

The stumbling point is that the birds that are able to use these topsy-turvy feeders might never notice the suet! I gave one a try, and even the chickadee regulars, who were accustomed to coming for a high-fat handout, showed no interest in investigating. Maybe there just wasn't enough room to get a grip down below, what with the suet pressed up against the wire grid. If you're plagued by starlings, you might want to give an upside-down suet feeder a try. You may have better luck than I did, but my advice is *caveat emptor!*

JERRY TO THE RESCUE

Q. Something is eating all of the suet out of my feeder at night. What could it be, and how can I prevent it?

A. Well, you could set up a stakeout to find out exactly which critter is getting your goodies, but my guess for Most Wanted Suet Thief is that masked bandit, the raccoon. Coons are plentiful in both city and country, and boy, do they love a tasty supper of suet. An opossum might also be the culprit, or you may have to look no further than your neighbor's kitty cat.

What to do? Put that feeder where they can't get at it. That's easier said than done, especially since all three varmints are good climbers and darn clever when it comes to getting food. If your feeder is mounted on a post, the sure cure is to invest in a squirrel baffle, a flared collar that attaches around the post and can't be climbed over (at least, not without a struggle!). For a hanging wire-cage feeder, try extending the chain with a thin length of wire; even the most agile coon will think twice about walking *that* tightrope.

Double Your Pleasure

Double your fun by stringing two or three wire suet feeders together. It'll give the birds more places to perch, and you'll get a kick out of watching the antics as the diners trade places. Just hook the chains of the second and third suet cages to the bottom of the feeder above them. Shorten the chains of the second and third feeders, if you like, by threading them through the cage once or twice before connecting your cage cascade. ✒

WESTERN
TANAGER

Insta-Perch

Lotsa birds love suet, but getting at it can be tricky for the less athletic members of the tribe. To make sure that my bluebirds, tanagers, orioles, robins, catbirds, mockingbirds, and Carolina wrens can frequent the fat without difficulty, I add perches to my hanging suet feeders. It's as easy as picking up a stick!

Simply choose a fallen stick at least 6 inches long. A twiggy one is fine; birds are adept at perching on even the skinniest sticks. Push the thicker end of the stick into the suet, so that it's securely anchored. It's a simple solution with instant results! ✒

Anti-Sway Solution

Revolving restaurants, such as the one in Seattle's Space Needle, may be fun for occasional dining, but I'll take my everyday table solidly anchored, thank you! Many birds feel the

same: They may visit a freely swinging suet feeder because the food has such high appeal, but they'd rather peck at a block of fat that isn't blowing in the wind. So I use an unobtrusive thin, short, black bungee cord (about $2 at discount or hardware stores) to hold my wire cage feeder to a post. The cord hooks onto the sides of the feeder and hugs the back of the post, leaving suet access (and refills!) unimpeded. ✒

COME 'N' GET IT!

Winter Warmup

Suet and peanut butter are extra appealling to birds in cold weather, thanks to the heat their high calories generate. Try these treats to keep your flock feelin' cozy during the gray days and long nights of winter.

Titmouse Time

In England, "tit" means a small bird. This one's as soft and gray as a mouse, and a sprightly favorite at the feeder.

1 cup of peanut butter
1 cup of cornmeal
1 cup of sunflower chips
¹/₄ cup of cracked corn

Combine all ingredients in a bowl, and mix thoroughly. Pack the mix into a wire suet cage, and sit back to watch the show.

Suet Snowman

This one's lots of fun, so call the kids to help! We're making a snowman from suet to feed woodpeckers, chickadees, and any other bird that dares to take a nip of Mr. Snowman's belly.

1¹/₂ cups of suet or fat scraps, chopped
2 raisins
1 almond sliver
4 hazelnut (filbert) halves
Half of an English walnut shell,
    nut meat removed
2 twigs, 6" long, branched at tip

Bet you can guess how this one goes. Form the suet into three balls: the biggest one for the base, a middle-sized one for the belly, and a smaller one for the head. Set the base in an empty tray feeder, pushing it down to make firm contact and to flatten the bottom. Set the suet-ball belly on the base, and push into place. Top it off with the head, pushing gently to make sure it adheres. Gently push in the raisins for eyes, make a nose from the almond sliver, and push a parade of hazelnut halves down the front, for buttons. Crown the snowman's head with the walnut shell, for a slightly undersized hat. Finally, push one twig into each side of the belly ball to create arms—and perches!

Flicker Flapdoodle

You've probably heard a flicker, even if you've never seen one. Just holler its name at the top of your voice, three or four times in a row, fast, and you've got it! Not only does this big brown woodpecker say its name, it also flickers when it flies, thanks to a white patch of feathers above the tail. Try this suet-rich mix to bring this bird to your feeder.

1 cup of suet or fat scraps, chopped
$^1/_2$ cup of cornmeal
$^1/_2$ cup of cracked corn
$^1/_4$ cup of nut meats, any kind, chopped
$^1/_4$ cup of raisins

Put the suet in a deep bowl, pour in the other ingredients, and mix thoroughly. Form into a cake to fit your suet feeder. Serve in a wire suet cage or other suet feeder, secured against a post or tree, so that it doesn't swing under the weight of landing flickers.

Strictly for Starlings

Donate your fatty kitchen scraps to a good home—down the gullet of starlings! This low-cost mix will readily feed a crowd of gaping beaks.

4 parts cracked corn
2 parts cornmeal
1 part ham fat trimmings, chopped
1 part peanut butter

Put all of the ingredients in a bowl, and mix thoroughly with your hands. The mix will be crumbly. Scatter it directly on the ground, if you already have starlings visiting. Or set out a sample in a tray feeder, until the birds make the exciting discovery and call in all their relatives!

Blackbird Buffet

Like starlings, blackbirds can move in on a feeder in high numbers. Keep your flock of redwings, cowbirds, or grackles content with this cheapie high-fat mix.

4 parts chicken scratch
2 parts cracked corn
1 part suet or lard, melted
1 part corn oil

Pour the chicken scratch and cracked corn in a bowl, and stir to combine. Pour in the melted lard and corn oil. Stir until all dry ingredients are moistened. To serve, crumble about 1 cup at a time, directly on the ground or in a low tray feeder. Freeze leftovers in zip-top plastic freezer bags.

Robin Roundabout

Gentle robins love to pig out on bacon fat, especially in winter, when worms are hard to come by! Prepare this treat only occasionally, so as not to overload them with salt from the bacon. Robins are most likely to visit your feeder for the first time in winter.

4 parts bread crusts
1 part bacon fat, melted

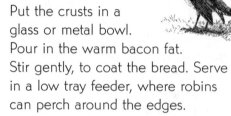

Put the crusts in a glass or metal bowl. Pour in the warm bacon fat. Stir gently, to coat the bread. Serve in a low tray feeder, where robins can perch around the edges.

SIMPLEST SUET TWEETS

Plain suet is solid gold where birds are concerned, but with a little mixing and fixing, you can shine it up from low-glow 10-karat to a gleaming 24-karat gold standard. Add extras such as nuts and fruits to a block of plain suet, and your suet feeder will be the most popular place in town with all the usual woodpeckers, chickadees, and nuthatches. And, your special recipes may even catch the eye of beautiful bluebirds, vivid orange orioles, and other out-of-the-ordinary tweeters. My easiest treats require no cooking at all—just a sharp knife, a mixing bowl, and 10 minutes of your time. What are you waiting for? Let's get going!

Peanut Party

Call the kids for a stompin' good time. They'll love helping you prepare this simple suet-and-nut mix—and the mix will make your feeder a fave with chickadees, nuthatches, and titmice. Have Junior unwrap a block of plain suet, let little Susie measure out a cup of unsalted peanuts, and then sharpen your chef's knife. Here's all you do:

1. Chop that suet block into bits. For fast action, anchor the tip of the knife with your finger on the far side of the block, and work the handle up and down like a papercutter. Turn the cutting board 45 degrees, and repeat.

2. Meanwhile, pour the nuts into a heavy-duty zip-top plastic bag, seal the bag shut, and let the kids smash the nuts by stomping on them (they'll love this!).

3. Scrape the suet tidbits into a mixing bowl, and pour in the crushed nuts.

4. Have everyone don a pair of disposable plastic gloves, and dig in! Mush the suet with the peanuts until they're mixed pretty good.

5. Make two thick patties out of the peanutty suet, about 5 inches across and $^1/_2$ inch thick, shaping them with your hands just as you would a burger. Put one or both patties into a suet feeder, clean up the counter, strip off your gloves, and watch the peanut party begin. ✐

Corn-Studded Suet

I like to make this treat around Halloween, because it brings back fond memories of "tick-tacking" houses with a handful of corn tossed against the window—and it also makes me dream of that oh-so-sweet candy corn! All you'll need is a few handfuls of whole corn kernels (birds love Indian corn, too, so snitch a bit from your door décor if you need to) and a store-bought block of plain suet.

Unwrap the suet, but don't remove it from the tray. Poke the kernels one by one into one side of the suet, leaving their thick ends sticking out about $^1/_4$ inch so that birds can easily grasp them. Make patterns or rows if you like, or just go for an all-over effect. When you're finished, remove the tray and carefully slide the suet into a wire holder. It won't be long before any red-bellied or red-headed woodpeckers in the neighborhood come by to collect the corn—unless the jays beat them to it! ✐

Gimme One Good Raisin

Or how about a whole cupful? Coarsely chop the raisins, then set an unwrapped block of suet on top of them. Put a dinner plate on top of the suet and press down hard, so the raisins are pushed into the fat. Repeat on the other side of the block. Now you have a treat that will give the jaunty Carolina wren, manic mockingbird, and quiet catbird a good "raisin" to come visiting.

Suet and fruit are a natural combo, because both foods appeal to many of the same birds. You'll find more fruit 'n' fat recipes in Chapter 6. 🐦

DO IT YOURSELF

Suetty Sandwich

I don't begrudge any birds their daily bite of fat, but I do mind when chickadees, nuthatches, and other dainty eaters can't get a bite in edgewise. To give them a fighting chance, I rigged up a hanging sandwich-style feeder that discourages larger, less agile birds. A block of wood serves as a spacer between the sandwich boards, and prevents waste by having suet only where birds can reach it. Popsicle® sticks on the outside help those little feet keep their grip. You can buy similar sandwich-style feeders, but I get more pleasure out of making my own. Here's how I did it.

MATERIALS

1 piece of 1" scrap lumber, about 3" × 3", for a spacer block

2 pieces of $1/4$" or $1/2$" oriented-strand board, a.k.a. OSB (the stuff that looks like a mosaic of splinters), each about 5" × 5"

Waterproof glue

1 galvanized screw, 2"

6 to 8 Popsicle sticks, available in packs at craft or discount stores

1 small C-clamp, with opening of about 2"

Wire for hanging

Suet or fat scraps

DIRECTIONS

Step 1. Glue the 3 × 3-inch spacer block of wood to the center of one 5 × 5-inch piece.

⊗ Suetty Sandwich, continued

Step 2. Apply a 2-inch-square patch of glue to the center of the other 5 × 5-inch piece. Set it carefully on top of the spacer block, aligning the edges with the other 5 × 5-inch piece on the bottom. Push down firmly in the center with your hand, to make contact between the spacer block and the glue.

Step 3. Use a screwdriver to insert the screw in the center of the "sandwich." It will go in easily with a cordless electric screwdriver. With a little muscle power, you can insert it with a manual one.

Step 4. Arrange half of the Popsicle sticks on one outside surface of the sandwich, laying them flat and parallel to one another, with a bit of space between them. Glue each one into place. Turn over the sandwich, and attach Popsicle sticks to the opposite side.

Step 5. Set aside overnight, to allow the glue to dry.

Step 6. Stuff suet or fat scraps into the sandwich around all of the edges.

Step 7. Attach the C-clamp to one of the sides. Screw it into place so that the sandwich is as thick at the edges as it is in the middle. Allow some of the fat to hang or squeeze out around the edges, just like the gooey-good stuffing of a real sandwich, to catch the eye of suet-eaters.

Step 8. Wrap the wire around the C-clamp, to form a loop for hanging.

Step 9. Refill as needed, by poking fat scraps or pieces of suet block into the empty edges. Your fingers are best for this operation.

Ever-Popular Peanut Butter

Here's one of the higher-priced foods for birds, but it's definitely worth paying for. Peanut butter costs a lot more than suet ($3 to $5 a pound, versus $1 or so), and it disappears down the beaks of birds much faster, too. But, boy, will this high-fat food win you the loyalty of the birds on the block! Plus, it's one of the very best foods for luring bluebirds to your larder.

In this section, we'll talk about some of the special birds that can't resist a spread of good ol' PB (hold the J, please!), along with serving suggestions tailored to their habits. You'll also find my tips for making this food more affordable and, of course, I'll share lots of recipes that will garner you the gratitude of those feathered flocks of PB lovers. Let's start by meeting some of those birds, and finding out how they like their lunch.

Count Your Wealth–In Bluebirds!

Bluebirds are the biggest prize in the eyes of many of us feeder-keepers. Their breathtaking color, the bluest of blues, is a big reason for their popularity, but their personality is just as delightful. They're gentle birds, not feeder hogs or fighters, and best of all, they're remarkably unafraid of people. Soft foods are essential for bluebirds, and PB is one they adore. A simple mix of coarse cornmeal and peanut butter, crumbled into an open tray feeder, will get their attention fast—if you live in their neighborhood.

Catbird Seat

I still get fooled when I hear that mewing from my bushes— don't tell me the neighbor's cat is stalking my feeders again! Nope, it's only the catbird, living up to its name. One of the newest birds to learn how convenient a feeder can be, the slim, gray catbird is becoming less of a rarity at the soft-food trough. Fruity PB-and-suet mixes are a good bet to grab this guy's attention. Catbirds and their cousins, the mockingbird and brown thrasher, can't use cage feeders, because they have feet built for perching, not clinging. So be sure to offer your treats in a tray for these unusual feeder visitors.

COME 'N' GET IT!

Basically Bluebirds

Try any or all of these quick recipes to satisfy the bluebirds at your feeder, any time of year. Don't know if bluebirds are in your area? If they are, they're bound to find it. If they're slow to appear, woodpeckers, chickadees, catbirds, and other soft-food eaters may beat them to it!

Got the Blues

Bluebirds approve of practically any combination of suet and peanut butter. This is my old reliable recipe, using nutritious cornmeal to stretch the servings.

6 parts cornmeal, coarse grind
4 parts suet or fat scraps, chopped
1 part peanut butter

Mix all of the ingredients thoroughly. Form into blocks or balls, and offer in a low or mid-height tray feeder, or in a suet feeder with a perch.

Ultramarine Dream

Super-swift to mix, this recipe is a good one to keep on hand for a snowstorm, when bluebirds may descend in droves to your lifesaving feeder.

2 cups cornmeal
$^1/_2$ cup suet or fat scraps, chopped
$^1/_2$ cup peanut oil

Put all of the ingredients in a deep bowl, and thoroughly combine them. Crumble into a low or mid-height tray feeder, or stuff into a suitable suet holder.

Sapphire Supply

The addition of fruit makes this mix particularly pleasing in winter, when wild fruit is hard to find.

1 part peanut butter
1 part cornmeal, regular grind
1 part cornmeal, coarse grind
1 part chopped raisins

Put all of the ingredients into a bowl, and mix thoroughly. Form into patties, or crumble into a low or mid-height tray feeder.

BOREAL CHICKADEE

Chock-Full of Chickadees

I love chickadees, you love chickadees, everybody loves chickadees! Seems like we can never get enough of these friendly, perky pals. A dab of peanut butter, or a PB-enriched treat, is just the ticket for getting you an ongoing sideshow of these acrobats. To make sure they get their share and don't have to elbow away larger birds, sneak some pats of peanut butter into bark crevices here and there, or put them in feeders that (literally) bar the big guys.

Sneaky Steal

Peanut butter may be pricey, but it'll pay off big-time if you live in a neighborhood of feeder-keepers. Tempting PB-based treats are a sneaky way to bring the birds over the fence to your place. The stuff is simply irresistible, and the birds will linger until every crumb is gone. Then they'll be back tomorrow, to see what you've set out! Of course, the high-fat spread is also packed with good nutrition, so you don't have to feel too guilty about hogging the show.

Chunky or Creamy?

Birds will gladly eat both, so you don't need to worry about which kind of peanut butter you're using. Birds that naturally eat nuts,

such as chickadees, woodpeckers, nuthatches, and titmice, will love the chunky version, but will eagerly dine on creamy, too. Those that stick to soft foods, including bluebirds, tanagers, catbirds, and Carolina wrens, may eat around the nuts or swallow those chunky bits right down with the rest of it. Sometimes, I fine-tune my recipes: Since I serve the nut-eaters in hanging feeders and the other songbirds in tray feeders, it's easy enough to give them what they like best. But when time is short, or the weather is rough, any kind of peanut butter is better than none at all!

Solid Gold Spread

One look at all those bags of yellow corn-meal on my pantry shelf, and you might think I was aiming to win the next Cornbread Cookoff! But those sacks aren't for competitive cooking—they're the backbone of my easiest, one-size-fits-all recipe. I scoop out a few generous globs of generic peanut butter into a bowl, then pour in the cornmeal, a half-cup at a time, mixing after each addition.

The exact measurements vary, depending on how oily the peanut

JERRY
TO THE RESCUE

Q. I put out lots of bluebird foods in my feeders, but I'm still waiting to see my first one. What am I doing wrong?

A. Probably nothing! Keep in mind that late winter to early spring is the peak feeder season for bluebirds, although birds may also be regulars from fall onward or even year-round. When natural food is abundant, bluebirds generally are much less interested in your feeder.

If you're serving their favorite soft foods in a highly visible open tray feeder, and you've gone through the prime winter/spring season and still haven't gotten a glimpse, then the problem is probably one of location. Peanut butter and suet treats, mealworms, and fruity goodies can get you bragging rights to blue-birds—as long as you live near natural bluebird habitat. Open land is the key, with nearby woodsy areas or hedgerows. That means out in the country, folks, because these boys rarely come to town. If you live near a golf course or cemetery (two top bluebird hangouts!), or in uncrowded suburbs, you might also be within bluebird range. Stand at your feeder and take a look around. Can you see open land within about a half-mile? If the answer is yes, keep your hopes up!

butter is; so I mix by feel, rather than by science. When the "dough" gets too stiff to mix with a spoon, it's ready for serving. I grease my hands with vegetable oil, so the stuff doesn't stick, and mold some of my mix into patties for my wire suet cages. Then I scoop out the leftovers into a tray feeder or other open feeders for a real feast. Here's a sampling of the customers that'll come for this treat:

✔ Bluebirds
✔ Carolina wren
✔ Catbird
✔ Chickadees
✔ Juncos
✔ Mockingbird
✔ Nuthatches
✔ Robin
✔ Sparrows
✔ Starlings
✔ Thrashers
✔ Thrushes
✔ Titmice
✔ Towhees
✔ Woodpeckers

Sticky Subject

You know that if you slather that bread a little too thick with peanut butter when you're making yourself a sandwich, you'll be reaching for a glass of milk to wash the sticky stuff down. Experts disagree over whether peanut butter can be a sticking point for birds, too, but some feeder hosts pass up peanut butter altogether to avoid any risk. But there's no need to go that far! Mixing in other ingredients, such as suet or cornmeal, makes peanut butter perfectly safe. And, in all my years of feeding birds, I've never once seen any beaks biting off more than they can safely swallow. I still spread plain peanut butter on a post at my feeding station, but I make sure to smooth it on in a thin layer so birds are forced to take small bites. As Grandma Putt used to tell me when I reached for that second piece of pie, "Everything in moderation, Jerry." It's a good rule at the feeder, too!

Penny-Wise Peanut Butter

Store-brand or generic peanut butters cost a lot less than the national, well-advertised varieties. Stick with the cheapies when you're mixing it up for birds, and you can save as much as half the cost! At my supermarket, a 16-ounce jar of Brand X costs about $2; the high-priced spreads right next to it on the shelf run almost $4. Guess which one is for the birds?

DO IT YOURSELF

Perching Pole

Here's an easy way to serve peanut butter spreads, suet, and other high-fat, spreadable foods in a way that makes them accessible to all birds. Make sure to put the post where you'll have a good view of the birds enjoying the fruit of your (very little) labor.

MATERIALS

Wooden post, about 4" × 4" (an existing feeder support post is fine)

Several twiggy branches, about 4"–6" long and less than 1/2" diameter at larger end, leaves removed

6 small nails

DIRECTIONS

Step 1. Dig a hole about 1 foot deep and set in the post, if you're not using an existing one. Refill the soil, and stamp down firmly.

Step 2. Lay one of the twigs against the post, about 1 foot down from the top, with the branching end extending past the post, and visible from your window viewpoint. This will be a perch.

Step 3. Secure the perch by hammering a small nail into the thicker end as you hold it against the post. (A heavy-duty staple gun may also do the trick, if your sticks are skinny.)

NAIL

Step 4. Repeat with the rest of the twigs, placing them at staggered intervals on the post.

Step 5. Spread a small, thin layer of peanut butter, suet, or other fats within reach of each perch. Be stingy with your servings, because extra goodies are likely to be licked off at night by prowling coons or cats.

Bigger Isn't Always Better

Look on the lowest shelf at your supermarket, and you may spy giant-sized jars of peanut butter. Before you stock up, check those shelf tags and see what the price per ounce is, compared to smaller sizes. I was surprised to find out that sometimes the biggest jar just isn't worth it—its price per ounce is exactly the same as the smaller, easier-to-handle sizes!

But when the giant jar is the cheapest option, I take it home. Then I transfer its contents to smaller jars I've saved, so I don't have to wrestle with a heavy 5-pounder every time I want to make up a mix. Since my recycled jars aren't sealed as tight as new ones would be, I store them in the fridge, so the PB doesn't go stale before I get to the bottom of my supply. ✍

HIGH-CALORIE HELPERS

When I'm caught short on suet, or scraping the bottom of the peanut butter jar, it's reassuring to know that other fats will fill the bill. In this section, you'll discover other possibilities from the pantry, and laudable leftovers that supply plenty of those precious calories to our bird friends. Chickadees, nuthatches, titmice, and woodpeckers will be your best customers for these foods. So will starlings, unless you serve the treats in a feeder that discourages them. Try the recipes I've included, and have fun inventing some of your own!

Loaded with Lard

I hate to admit it, but sometimes the "antiques" I see in shops look very much like items I used to use! Take the lowly lard bucket, for instance. Nowadays, this metal pail is more

PURE
LARD

likely to hold a country-style flower arrangement than the solid white fat I was familiar with. A few cooks still swear by lard, because of the magic it works in pie crusts, and some restaurants rely on melted lard for frying. But in most home kitchens, good old lard has been replaced by solid vegetable shortening.

You can still buy lard in neatly packaged, 1-pound blocks at many markets (look for it near the bacon). You can substitute lard for suet in any of my recipes, or serve it all by itself at your feeders. In winter, it'll bring fat-lovers winging in from far and wide! 🐦

Spring Fling

High-fat foods are a must in winter, but they're pretty popular in spring, too. Insects are still in short supply in most places, and spring migrants are streaming back fast and thick. Many of those birds, such as tanagers, bluebirds, and orioles, are soft-food eaters, so they'll be grateful for a generous helping of greasy goodies. Until the spring season is in full swing and lilacs are once again in dooryard bloom, keep birds happy with those high-fat treats!

SEASONAL SUGGESTIONS

Bringing Home the Bacon

Like lard, bacon comes from pigs. Feeder birds don't care what animal is contributing to their high-fat intake, but they do like their fats served soft. Crispy bacon strips won't attract interest, but the fat left over from frying is right up their alley. Because bacon fat is so high in salt, I usually save mine to use sparingly in mixes, rather than feeding it as is. After breakfast, just pour the fat into a metal can, cover it, and set it in the fridge to harden until you're ready to use it. 🐦

Sunday Dinner Scraps

Save some calories in your own diet, and pre-trim the fat from that nice big ham before you bake it. Ham fat is softer than suet, but you can still serve it in a wire cage feeder. Simply add the scraps to your current suet cage, or fill a second cage if you prefer. You can also mince or dice ham fat to boost the fat potential of bird recipes, although it won't

STARLING

work as a binder to hold other ingredients together. One of my favorite ham-fat recipes, which you'll find in this chapter (see page 101), is strictly for starlings—they love the stuff! 🐦

Soup Bone Bribe

How about contributing a meaty soup bone to the cause? Just don't bother cooking it first: Big-beaked starlings love to peck out every good bit of meat, fat, or marrow in the raw. In winter, when it warms my heart to see every bird well fed, I set a big soup bone on the ground, far away from the feeders. Starlings will mob it until it's stripped, and— sneaky me!—the other birds can eat at the feeder in peace. 🐦

Desirable Drippings

I like the idea of birds helping me trim my waistline, so instead of making gravy with the pan drippings from that roast, I pour off the fat to use in bird recipes! Every tablespoon of the drippings holds about 100 calories—calories that I don't need, but which birds sure do, especially on a cold wintry day. Just drizzle the fat over cracked corn, right in the feeder, for a woodpecker pick-me-up in winter. Or use it in place of melted suet in any of my recipes. 🐦

Hamburger Helpings

Lots of folks are surprised to learn that many birds eat meat, but the protein-packed insects they devour are just a few steps away from hamburger. Be extra-stingy when you serve meat at your feeder, because it goes bad quickly and can attract every varmint within sniffing distance. And always serve it raw, not cooked: The only takers for a Quarter-Pounder® are the birds that frequent McDonald's® parking lots!

I save my hamburger helpings for desperate straits: after a blizzard or during an ice storm, when birds are unable to find food. Then, scattered by the handful or mixed into concoctions, my humble hamburger can be a lifesaver for bluebirds, robins, Carolina wrens, catbirds, woodpeckers, and other meat-eaters. I was taken aback by how quickly the birds fell upon plain hamburger, but then I decided those little squiggles look a lot like caterpillars!

Pepperoni Potential

Pepperoni and sausage are hits at my home feeder because, like hamburger, they're high in fat. The 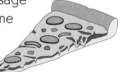 shapes of these meats are unfamiliar to most birds, though, so they can be reluctant to try a taste. I remedy that reticence by tearing or chopping the meats into small bits for serving. A tray of cracked corn, sprinkled with leftover breakfast sausage and the remains of last night's pizza topping, makes a solid breakfast for jays, woodpeckers, and other large meat-eaters.

Calorie-Rich Cooking Oils

Cooking oils are made from lots of bird favorites—corn, safflower, sesame, peanut, and walnut, to name just a few—but birds won't sip liquid oils. What can you do with these high-cal helpers? It's easy! Use them to moisten dry ingredients that birds eat, such as cornmeal, bread crusts, or other grain-based foods. Sparrows, juncos, chickadees, and other birds will be quick to notice the addition of extra fat, especially in winter, when they need every calorie they can corral.

Grandma Putt's

BIRD BITS

No Fats down the Hatch!

Or I should say, no fats down the drain. In the old meat-and-potatoes days, meals were big, greasy productions, often topped with a rich pour of gravy. Nowadays, we skim the fat on those rare occasions when we do make gravy. But what to do with all that grease? Grandma Putt kept her extra drippings in a metal can, and for good reason. I learned my lesson the hard (and expensive) way when I poured fat down the drain. That was some mess, cleaning out the curvy trap where it'd collected. Now, when I need to skim the fat from meat stock before making gravy, I follow her lead and pour the fat into a metal can to save for my bird recipes, instead of fattening a plumber's trust fund. The greasy-good stuff is ideal for replacing melted suet in my recipes, or for moistening dry kibble dog food to make a special brunch for starlings, jays, crows, and other big eaters.

Cooking for a Crowd

Getting a handle on the techniques and tools makes mixing up recipes a lot easier, whether you're cooking for a crowd of friends or for a flock of feathered friends! In this section, I'll share what I've learned about making fat-based treats, and tell you how to store them for later use.

Give Me a Hand!

I used to melt my suet before proceeding with treat-making, but one day, when I was in a hurry, I discovered that it doesn't take much effort to mix the little extras into unmelted fat. Suet, fat scraps, and lard may look solid, but they yield easily to my hands or the back of a spoon. Skipping a step is just the kind of time-saving trick I like best!

Stirring the mix is about as laborious as mixing stiff cookie dough. Here's the basic by-hand method that works best for me:

1. Unwrap a commercial suet block, remove the tray, and drop the block into a small mixing bowl.

2. Measure and pour in the extra goodies you want to add to the fat.

3. Use the back of a sturdy spoon (I use a metal tablespoon from the silverware drawer) to smash the extras into the suet. This is the motion that cooks call "creaming," employed when mixing sugar into butter, for instance.

4. To make sure the extra ingredients are thoroughly distributed, so that every bird bite has a little something in it, finish mixing by using your hands in a grab-and-squeeze motion. I don a pair of disposable plastic gloves, or slip my paws into plastic bags to keep them grease-free.

COME 'N' GET IT!

Rolling Along

Here's your chance to practice your Play-Doh® skills: All of these recipes are a good consistency for rolling into balls, or patting into blocks. Each mix yields about three tennis-ball-sized bird treats. For an instant hanging feeder, wrap each ball in a piece of plastic netting, such as that used for pea fences, gathered at the top, and secured with a twist-tie. Suspend from a hook for easy access, and poke a stick into the ball to accommodate perchers, such as bluebirds, tanagers, orioles, and catbirds.

Oriole Ovals

When these sweet singers arrive in midspring, it's time to roll out the treats! This one'll keep 'em chirping, and may attract tanagers, too.

2 cups of cornmeal, regular grind
1/2 cup of orange juice
1 cup of suet or fat scraps,
    chopped

Put the cornmeal in a bowl, and pour the orange juice over it, stirring to moisten the cornmeal as you do so. Mix in the suet, and mold into balls— or ovals, for a change of pace! Serve in an oriole-accessible feeder, or poke a perch into the ball.

Tanager Tantalizer

Tanagers usually turn up in early to midspring, about the time the trees are just beginning to show a haze of green. Greet them with these high-energy goodies.

1/2 cup of suet or fat scraps,
    chopped
1/2 cup of cornmeal, regular grind
1/4 cup of peanut oil

Thoroughly mix together all of the ingredients. Pack into balls, or make a block for your perchable suet feeder.

Downy's Dream

Diminutive downy wood-peckers are among the most reliable feeder guests across the entire country. Treat them well by offering high-fat balls made of their favored foods.

1 cup of suet or fat scraps, chopped
1 cup of chopped peanuts
1 tbsp. of peanut butter

Mix all of the ingredients thoroughly, using your hands. Form into a block to fit a wire suet cage, or make peanutty balls for an appropriate feeder.

Nuthatch Hustle

Dapper little nuthatches are always busy. I hustle 'em over to my feeder by offering this delectable concoction.

1 cup of sunflower chips
$3/4$ cup of suet or fat scraps, chopped
$1/2$ cup of cornmeal, coarse grind
$1/4$ cup of peanut butter

Thoroughly combine all the ingredients, using your hands. Serve in a wire suet cage, or liven up the look by forming the mix into balls for hanging.

Appliance Aids

You may be able to enlist your electric mixer or food processor to whip up your suet mixes, same as you would cookie dough. These handy appliances will save your arms from working so hard, but don't forget—you'll have a bigger clean-up job on your hands later, what with all those beaters, bowls, and blades. And, greasy suet has a habit of gumming up the works, so you may need to stop to clean off the moving parts occasionally. Always remember to unplug before doing so, and be careful around those blades!

Here's how to make the mixing go more smoothly:

◆ Only use these appliances for mixes that include at least 1 cup (or 1 part) of cornmeal, oatmeal, or other "meal"-type ingredients. Without these dry foods, the suet will form into one greasy lump around the blades or beaters.

◆ Alternate dry ingredients with fat, to keep the blades or beaters spinning freely.

◆ Use unfrozen suet in a mixer, but keep the fat frozen for a food processor so that it doesn't gum up the works.

◆ When suet and dry ingredients are well mixed, empty the food processor, and finish the mix by hand, or with a portable mixer.

◆ Add the finishing touches last: the tasty tidbits of chopped nuts, fruits, or other yummy stuff. 🐦

In the Grease Pit

Working with fats is a hands-on process, so don't expect you or your kitchen to stay too tidy! Here are a few tricks that I've learned for keeping clean-up to a minimum:

JERRY
TO THE RESCUE

Q. **Melting suet on the stovetop takes a lot of time, because I have to stand there watching it and stirring. Can I use my microwave as a shortcut?**

A. You bet! Using your microwave to melt the fat is safer than rendering suet on the stove, where splattering grease can pose a fire hazard—not to mention a messy clean-up. Commercial suet blocks work best for this; just be sure you buy blocks that contain only suet, and no added ingredients, such as cracked corn or seeds (there's often very little suet in such blocks). Here's how to do it:

1. Remove a block of plain suet from its wrapper and tray. Set aside the tray; you'll use it later.

2. Set the block in a microwave-safe bowl, breaking it into chunks if needed to make it fit. Melt the suet on medium power (not high). The total time needed for melting will vary, depending on the power of your model; start with 60 seconds, then check, and continue by 15-second spurts if most of the suet is still solid.

3. When the suet is mostly liquefied, set the bowl in the refrigerator until it begins to thicken (about 30 minutes or more, depending on your temperature setting).

4. Remove the bowl from the fridge, and stir in the chopped nuts, peanut butter, or other treats. Cool to lukewarm, and pour into the tray you set aside. Once it hardens, it's ready to serve.

SCOTT'S
ORIOLE

◆ If you're using a store-bought suet block, break it into several chunks with your hands in a deep bowl. If you're using fat scraps, chop them coarsely on a cutting board before proceeding.

◆ A deep, 2-quart bowl (about the size of many brands of plastic storage containers) is ideal for mixing, because it corrals the ingredients into a concentrated area.

◆ Cover counters with sections of newspaper; then, when it's time to clean up, pour the stray bits right into a tray feeder!

◆ You may want to wear disposable plastic gloves when cooking up your specialties: Suet and peanut butter are greasy and sticky. 🕊

It's a Party!

Friends of mine have a fat-fixin' party every fall. One chops the fat, another globs out the peanut butter, a third measures the treats, and the others mix, mold, and package the stuff. In a couple of hours' time messing around in the kitchen, they make enough to stock their feeders for months to come. It's a kid-friendly party, too, because messy, hands-on fun is what these recipes are all about! 🕊

Bag It

Winter is peak season for suet feeders, so I make sure I have plenty of extra blocks on hand. To save time on those frosty mornings, I also stock up on inexpensive wire suet cages before the big rush begins. After I've mixed up some goodies for the birds, I stuff the cages with the mix, and slide cage and all into a plastic freezer bag. It's ready to go anytime! A quart-sized bag is a perfect fit for most wire cage feeders.

SEASONAL SUGGESTIONS

E-Z Freeze

Keep your store-bought suet blocks and your homemade mixes in the freezer, and they'll stay good for at least a year. Plus, your hands won't get nearly so greasy when you handle frozen fat mixes. I like to mix up a big batch of suet treats at one time, so I have plenty of extras on hand to add a little extra to my feeder menu.

I've come to depend on zip-top plastic freezer bags, because they're so easy to use. I pull out quart-sized bags to store my homemade blocks, and I use larger bags when I've made a more generous supply. Don't worry if treats made of mostly fat stick together when packaged; to separate for serving, just insert a butter knife, warmed under hot tap water, between them. 🐦

Separate Rooms, Please

Fatty treats made with cornmeal, oatmeal, or other dry ingredients freeze as hard as rocks, unlike those made without "meal"-type additions. And boy oh boy, can they be frustrating to separate for serving! To forestall conniption fits, I use a separate bag for each treat, so that pulling one out for serving is a pleasure, not a pain. 🐦

HIGH-FAT FAVES

I'm a potato-chip man myself, but that high-fat food doesn't even make the list of bird favorites (except with starlings, and everyone knows they'll eat anything!). If you're wondering which high-fat foods will have birds flocking to your feeder, take a look at this menu.

BIRD	HIGH-FAT FOOD (IN ORDER OF PREFERENCE)	SERVING SUGGESTIONS
Bluebirds	Peanut butter, suet, other fats	Serve suet plain or chopped; combine suet, peanut butter, or other fats in treats with chicken scratch, cornmeal, finely chopped nuts, fruit, or sunflower chips; use an accessible feeder that the birds can perch on, such as a tray feeder
Bushtit	Suet	Serve plain; use a hanging cage feeder
Catbird	Suet, peanut butter	Serve suet plain or chopped; serve suet, peanut butter, or other fats in treats with fruit or insect foods; use an accessible feeder that the bird can perch on, such as a tray feeder

(continued)

HIGH-FAT FAVES, *continued*

BIRD	HIGH-FAT FOOD (IN ORDER OF PREFERENCE)	SERVING SUGGESTIONS
Chickadees	Peanut butter, suet, other fats	Serve plain or in treats with bread, cracked corn, cornmeal, chicken scratch, chopped nuts, or sunflower chips; use any type of hanging or mounted feeders
Jays	Peanut butter, other fats, suet	Not usually big fans of plain fats; serve in treats with bread, chicken scratch, corn, cornmeal, fruits, sunflower chips, shelled nuts, or other foods; mounted feeders are most accessible
Juncos	Suet, peanut butter, other fats	Serve suet finely chopped; use suet, peanut butter, or other fats in treats with bread, chicken scratch, cornmeal, cracked corn, hulled millet, or sunflower chips; serve in tray feeder or at ground level
Mockingbird	Suet, peanut butter, other fats	Serve suet plain or chopped; serve suet, peanut butter, or other fats in treats with bread, chicken scratch, chopped nuts, cornmeal, cracked corn, fruit, insect foods, or seeds; for such a large bird it's remarkably agile, so any feeder will do
Nuthatches	Peanut butter, suet, other fats	Serve plain or in treats with cracked corn, cornmeal, chicken scratch, sunflower chips, insect foods, or chopped nuts; use any type of hanging or mounted feeders
Orioles	Suet, other fats	Serve suet plain or chopped; serve suet or other fats in treats with fruit or insect foods; use an accessible feeder that the bird can perch on, such as a tray feeder
Robin	Suet, other fats	Serve suet plain or chopped; serve suet or other fats in treats with bread, chicken scratch, chopped nuts, cornmeal, cracked corn, fruit, insect foods, or seeds; use an accessible feeder that the bird can perch on, such as a tray feeder, or feed at ground level
Sparrows	Suet, peanut butter, other fats	Serve suet finely chopped; use suet, peanut butter, or other fats in treats with bread, chicken scratch, cornmeal, cracked corn, hulled millet, or sunflower chips; serve in tray feeder or at ground level

BIRD	HIGH-FAT FOOD (IN ORDER OF PREFERENCE)	SERVING SUGGESTIONS
Tanagers	Suet	Serve plain, chopped, or in treats with fruit or insect foods; use an accessible feeder that the birds can perch on, such as a tray feeder
Thrashers	Suet, peanut butter, other fats	Serve suet plain or chopped; serve suet, peanut butter, or other fats in treats with bread, chicken scratch, chopped nuts, cornmeal, cracked corn, fruit, insect foods, or seeds; use an accessible feeder that the bird can perch on, such as a tray feeder
Thrushes	Suet, other fats	Serve suet plain or chopped; serve suet or other fats in treats with bread, chicken scratch, chopped nuts, cornmeal, cracked corn, fruit, insect foods, or seeds; use accessible feeder that the bird can perch on, such as a tray feeder
Titmice	Peanut butter, suet, other fats	Serve plain or in treats with bread, chicken scratch, chopped nuts, cracked corn, cornmeal, or sunflower chips; use any type of hanging or mounted feeders
Woodpeckers	Suet, peanut butter	Serve suet plain; combine suet or peanut butter in treats with chicken scratch, chopped nuts, cornmeal, cracked corn, fruit, insect foods, or sunflower chips; mounted feeders are most accessible
Wrens	Suet	Serve plain or chopped; use any kind of feeder (wrens are very agile)
Yellow-rumped warbler	Suet	Serve plain or chopped; use hanging or tray feeders

CHAPTER 5

Nuttin' but Nuts

Nuts are the fastest way to get your feeder noticed, and the burst of activity that you'll see after putting out nuts is like nothing else. You think sharks are bad? Wait'll you see a nutty feeding frenzy! It's the best entertainment you'll ever get for a buck.

Sometimes, I think I may be a little nutty to serve nuts at my feeder. Do you know what these things COST?! And nuts get vacuumed up super-quick—unless you employ some of the slow-down techniques I'll tell you about in this chapter. You'll discover, too, which nuts are best suited for your feeder, and how to serve 'em up right. And, naturally, I've figured out ways to save money on the deal, which I'll share with you. But for starters, let's take a look at the fantastic birds that are true nut fanatics—and learn some of my tricks for slowing them down!

THE BIG BANG

"Big" is right! The first birds that'll come flocking for your nuts are the heavyweights of the feeder scene: jumbo jays, woodpeckers, and, if you live in the West, the Clark's nutcracker. There'll be little guys scooting around, too, particularly chickadees, titmice, and the appropriately named nuthatches, all of whom are nutty about nuts.

In this section, you'll discover why this food is so highly rated, and meet some of the characters that compete for nuts at your feeder. You'll also learn how to use their feeding habits to counter their consumption, so your nuts last a whole lot longer!

What's All the Fuss?

Nuts are high in fat (75 percent or better!), packed with protein, and loaded with vitamins, minerals, and other substances that do good things for health—our own included. Lately, we've learned that a few almonds a day will do wonders for our blood pressure and help fight osteoporosis; that pecans can lower our cholesterol; that peanuts make us less prone to heart attacks; and that cashews can boost our iron-poor blood and even cure scurvy.

But I suspect that there's another reason besides nutrition for the popularity of nuts. I'm still waiting for science to catch up with my theory that birds also like nuts because they taste good! 🖋

CLARK'S
NUTCRACKER

A Lively Bunch—Year-Round!

I like all of my fine feathered friends, but my favorites (shhh—don't tell the others!) are the birds that liven up my feeder-watching. Big, bold jays, high-octane chickadees, natty little nuthatches, friendly titmice, and flashy woodpeckers: They're still a thrill after all these years, thanks to their lively personalities and over-the-top antics. And, for most of us, these birds are a year-

Familiar Favorites?

Grandma Putt's BIRD BITS

Grandma Putt had her own theory about why birds love nuts, and I've heard the same idea from other folks, too. Doling out a few fragrant walnuts into the feeder caused her to flash back to shelling black walnuts as a kid, stained fingers and all, and she decided that birds must have their own memories of nuts, too. Black walnuts, pecans, beech-nuts, hickory nuts, and acorns are all American born and bred, so they've been a natural food of American birds for eons. No wonder birds fall upon them so eagerly at the feeder—they're just recognizing a familiar favorite food.

Not so fast, my little chickadee—what about peanuts (from Africa), almonds (from the Mediterranean), Brazil nuts (you guessed it), and so on through the nut bowl? Seems that our feathered friends go wild over these imports, too. It's an interesting point to ponder while you dole out those exotic nuts to an impatient crowd!

round treat. The birds in this loyal, lively bunch are the main consumers of nuts at the feeder. Furnishing a few nuts will keep them visiting throughout the year, even when natural foods are abundant. They're not picky, so expect to see them feasting on any nuts you care to share! 🐦

Rapscallion Rodeo

The biggest of the nut fiends, the jays and Clark's nutcracker, are impossible to overlook, and they're part of the reason that feeding nuts is so much fun! These are big, rowdy birds, accompanying their takeoffs and landings with ear-splitting screeches and loud scoldings. Often, they keep up a constant hollering back and forth to each other as they feed or fly. Seems to me they just like hearing the sound of their own voices!

Want to see some fast action? In the morning, when birds are busiest, set out a handful of peanuts in the shell. Within minutes, you're likely to see jays winging in from all directions. 🐦

Tree-Planting Tribe

Jays have an unusual habit when it comes to whole nuts. They hide them away—usually in the ground—to eat later. Jays (and squirrels, which do the same) are serving a larger purpose when they bury their nuts:

They're planting nut trees, which sprout from any buried nuts that are overlooked. That way, there'll be plenty of nuts for the following generations of jays to enjoy. Great system! But, in the meantime, the nuts are disappearing from your feeder, fast. To moderate the jays' consumption, use the same trick as for smaller birds: Chop the nuts into smaller pieces. The jays won't be able to replant the forest as easily, but they will stick around longer at your feeder! 🐦

COME 'N' GET IT!

Budget-Friendly Basics

Keep your costs low by adding only a few nuts to your seed mixes. Chop them first to extend the appeal of the mix: Birds will instantly grab whole peanuts for themselves, but chopped nuts guarantee that more customers will get a sample. I chop my nuts moderately fine to make them stretch a little bit further, using my blender to grind them to a good consistency. If I leave my finger on the button too long, they become nut meal, and then nut butter. Both are usable in treats (try them mixed with suet), but for these recipes, you'll want to *chop* your nuts, not turn them into *mush*.

Gorgeous Gluttons

Jays seem to materialize out of thin air whenever I put out whole peanuts in the shell. I think they can spot those things from a half-mile away! And when one bird flies in, his friends won't be far behind, and your peanuts will swiftly disappear. So add them to other jay-favorite foods, to encourage lingering.

4 parts black oil sunflower seeds
1 part peanuts, chopped
1 part peanuts, in the shell

Pour the sunflower seeds and chopped peanuts into a bowl, and stir to combine. Add  the whole peanuts, stirring once or twice. (Jays will grab them first no matter what, so don't spend much time trying for an equitable distribution!) Serve in an open tray feeder.

Tube-Feeder Treat

Keeping nuts AWAY from certain birds is a big aid in making them last a little longer! Here's a mix you can pour in a tube feeder to treat chickadees, titmice, and cardinals.

1 part black oil sunflower seeds
1 part walnuts, coarsely chopped
1 part pecans, coarsely chopped
1 part peanuts, coarsely chopped

Combine all ingredients thoroughly. Serve in a tube feeder made for sunflower seeds, so that the feeder ports will be big enough to allow birds to tug out the nut pieces.

Goober Boost

Adding peanuts to your seed mixes will win the hearts of your feeder regulars—at least until they pick out all the nuts!

4 parts black oil sunflower seeds
2 parts white proso millet
1 part peanuts, chopped or ground

Measure all ingredients into a bowl, and stir well to combine. Serve in a tray or tube feeder.

Woodpecker Powwow

See that demure downy woodpecker industriously working at your nut-studded suet? Believe it or not, this common feeder visitor has more than 20 woodpecker cousins! Adding nuts to your menu, especially acorns, peanuts, and walnuts, is a good way to make sure you get your share of woodpecker visitors. Serve the nuts whole, or chop and add them to suet mixtures for extra incentive. Depending on where you live, you might catch a glimpse of the fabulous red-headed woodpecker, the striking acorn woodpecker (guess what its favorite nuts are?), and maybe even an eerie white-headed woodpecker.

Hernando's Hideaway

It's not only jays that play hide-and-seek with nuts—so do woodpeckers, titmice, and nuthatches. But instead of burying the booty, these guys stash it in cracks and crevices, to seek out later. Now, I enjoy watching a nuthatch or downy woodpecker decide where to hide its treasure, but often the bird flies too far away from the feeder for me to watch the game. That's why I include both hidable whole nuts, to satisfy their natural instinct, and chopped bits that can't be snatched and carried off.

Please, Do Loiter

Whole shelled nuts or large nut pieces are such a prize that birds don't linger when they come across them. They grab and go so that they can eat the nut without competition. Watch the chickadees at your feeder, and you'll see that they select a nut, then carry it off to eat, holding it in their feet against a perch, and pecking off bits. To put the brakes on these small birds, serve them chopped nuts. Instead of carrying off these morsels, chickadees will down them right at the feeder.

JERRY
TO THE RESCUE

Q. What's the best kind of nut to feed to birds?

A. Birds can be fussy about other menu items, but in this case, any nut is a good nut! You may notice that individual birds prefer a particular nut, and pick that one first. But other nuts don't go begging. These no-waste nuggets are the hottest items at the feeder, no matter what their name is. To attract the widest variety of birds, two nuts stand out from the crowd: peanuts, as you might expect, and acorns, which many of us may not think of as a popular bird food. Both appeal to almost 50 species of birds.

Acorns aren't grown commercially because they're difficult to store, (they're strongly inclined to sprout once they fall from the oak!), so they're a temporary feeder offering, at best. That leaves peanuts as the No. 1 nut, even though the peanut is officially a legume, not a tree nut. So make the peanut your first choice, not because of its wide appeal—other types of nuts aren't far behind in the popularity parade—but because of its price and availability. But add variety by offering any other nuts you want; birds will eagerly devour them all!

THRIFTY FEEDING

If you have a bulging bank account, go ahead and feed birds all the nuts you want; they'll keep your feeders brimming with birds, especially in fall and winter, when nut-eaters are at their peak. But if you're like most of us, with more limited means, you'll want to figure out a system of serving nuts that doesn't break the bank. In this section, I'll pass along my tried-and-true suggestions for serving, er, conserving!

GRAY CATBIRD

And the Winner Is...

Want to keep your nut feeding as reasonably priced as possible, and simple, too? The answer, in a nutshell, is peanuts! Peanuts are beloved by every nut-eating bird, as well as by some—including catbirds and mockingbirds—that rarely eat any other nut. The shelled nuts only cost about $2 per pound, and a pound contains hundreds of nuts, more than enough to satisfy a lot of feeder guests.

Shell Game

Whole, shelled almonds and hazelnuts are almost always carried away from the feeder, either to peck or to hide. But birds just as eagerly carry away these nuts when they're still in the shell. Taking advantage of that habit is one way I save money—without reducing my viewing pleasure. I follow a crude rule of thumb to figure out which is the better buy: If the no-shells type costs more than twice the shells-on variety of the same nut, I buy the ones with shells.

Consider It Candy

Seeds and suet are staples, but nuts are truly treats. They're nice extras, but birds will get along just fine without them, and they'll still visit your feeder even if the nuts are nearly nil. You can get big pleasure from a small amount of nuts, so don't hesitate to keep a tight rein on your supply, pardner!

Nut Feeders

Pile a handful of nuts on a tray feeder or your deck rail, and they'll be gone in a flash. That's fine, if you like to watch an enthusiastic crowd, and I do! But I also use a special nut feeder, so the birds have to work a little harder to get their goodies, which gives me more time to watch them.

Nut feeders are vertical tubes made of wire mesh, and topped or trimmed with wood, plastic, or metal; they're priced at about $15 and up. Birds cling to the mesh or sit on perches, and extract the nuts through the openings in the mesh. They work well for nuts as large as whole shelled peanuts; you'll need to chop larger nuts to fit. And look for squirrel-proof models, with an outer cage of vertical bars to keep out these varmints, if you're plagued by them.

JERRY
TO THE RESCUE

Q. **Are salted nuts bad for birds? They're often on sale, but I don't buy them.**

A. Now here's a subject a lot of us can identify with! Doctors are often advising us to pass on the salt shaker, because of salt's propensity for increasing blood pressure, among other not-so-good things. Unless you're feeding seagulls at that feeder, keep salted nuts off your regular bird menu. Seagulls, which make their living from salty sea foods, have special anatomical adaptations that allow them to expel excess salt. But our feeder birds aren't so blessed, and too much salt can wreak havoc on their health.

Although some birds actually seek out pure salt to supplement their diet (you'll learn about this habit in Chapter 8), it's best to let the birds make that decision for themselves! So avoid feeding salted nuts as a regular course at your feeder. An occasional serving of the salted variety won't hurt your feeder friends, but do them a favor and keep salted nuts salted away for your own use!

Out of Sight

Jays can't gobble up nuts they don't see, or at least that's my theory for why they stay away from my coffee can feeder (find out how to make it on page 47). You can also sneak a few nuts into a small suction-cup window feeder, a regular restaurant for nut-loving chickadees, titmice, and nuthatches, which is usually overlooked by jays. 🐦

DO IT YOURSELF

Net-Wrapped Feeder

Plastic garden netting, sold for supporting peas and other climbers or as an anti-bird device for fruit trees, is a quick solution to the greedy habits of jays. Use the netting to cover a typical wire suet cage, and you'll have a nut dispenser that makes these big birds work for it! Here's how.

MATERIALS

1 wire suet cage
Plastic garden netting,
  ⁵/₈" mesh, about
  6" × 18"
Twist-ties

DIRECTIONS

Step 1. Cut the netting into two pieces—one that covers the back and sides, and one that covers the front so you can still open and close it.

Step 2. Place the cage on the netting piece that will cover the back and sides, with the front door of the cage facing up. Bring the netting up the sides and back of the cage, cut as necessary, and attach it to the cage with the twist-ties. The back of the cage, the bottom, and the sides should now be covered with netting.

Step 3. Open the cage. Attach the second piece of netting on the outside of the open "door," using twist-ties to hold it in place. Cut off and discard any excess netting.

Step 4. Fill the feeder with whole peanuts in the shell. Close, hang, and watch the jays figure it out!

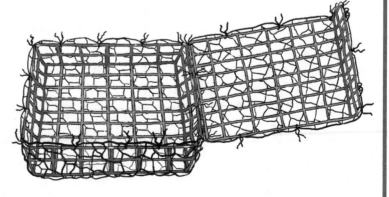

Suet-Cage Slowdown

It's hard to hold back from feeding jays whole unshelled peanuts, which they love above all else at my feeder. I still offer them their favorite, but I slow down the jays by putting the nuts in a wire suet cage with smaller openings than the typical cage. Look for openings of ¹/₂ × 1 inch (you'll find a mail-order supplier for this feeder in the Sources section of this book, on page 324, or ask at a bird-supply store). The smaller grid keeps whole unshelled peanuts in place, and forces the jays to extract them one at a time, with a little effort. 🐦

OREGON
JAY

Save Money with Mixes

Use those precious nuts for adding punch to mixes of seeds or fats. You'll find a cornucopia of creative recipes in this chapter, and in Chapters 4 and 6, that incorporate delicious nuts with other popular bird foods. As little as a quarter-cup of chopped nuts can make the difference between a so-so suet feeder and one that has a line of customers waiting in the wings. Sprinkling a quarter-cup of chopped nuts over your seed trays will bring a boom in birds, too. Peanuts, walnuts, hazelnuts, and almonds are good choices for adding to seed or fat mixtures, because they require little prep work and are, usually, relatively low-priced. 🐦

Chop Down Those Prices

Want to make your nuts go further? Haul out that chopping block! Chopped nuts will save you money because the bigger birds, such as jays, won't be able to carry them off wholesale. And smaller birds, such as chickadees and juncos, will benefit, too, because they won't have to waste time whacking big nuts into littler bits. Choose whichever one of these methods suits your skills and your appliance collection:

◆ Chop nuts by hand with a sturdy, sharp chef's knife or cleaver.

◆ Put a cup of nuts in a heavy-duty plastic zip-top bag, squeeze out the air, zip securely, and crush with a rolling pin.

◆ Use a food chopper, either hand-powered or electric.

◆ Process nuts in a blender, 1 cup at a time; set to "chop" or "grind," depending on how fine you want the final results.

◆ Pull out the food processor, and chop nuts according to the instructions for your machine.

BIRD BITS

Get Choppin'!

It's time to resurrect one of the kitchen aids that was indispensable before the days of convenience foods: the food chopper. Food choppers keep the nuts contained, so you don't have to retrieve them from every nook and cranny of the counter. This simple device consists of a jar or bowl with a lid, through which a handle is attached to blades inside the bowl. At Christmas time when I was a boy, the sound of Grandma Putt's food chopper sang in our kitchen. Those sharp blades made quick work of chopping walnuts and pecans for our favorite cookies and mincemeat. You can still find hand-powered food choppers at country stores and at some modern discount stores.

I've upgraded my old hand-powered chopper to an electric model. If you're interested, check the small-appliances section of a discount store for an electric chopper. These handy, labor-saving machines cost less than $10, and they can process nuts faster than you can do it by hand.

Bold-Faced Bribes

I offer a handful of nuts every morning at my feeder, because I like the company with my coffee. I also use nuts for bribes on special occasions, when I have plans such as these:

Starting a new feeder. In winter, some birds will home in on nuts faster than on seeds. If you're setting up your first feeder, or adding another at a new location, tempt the takers with nuts added to your seed staples.

Bonding with the kids. Nothing like instant results to get a youngster hooked on feeding birds! Let your young'uns spill out the nuts, while you refill the seed feeders. Then watch together at the window.

Impressing the guests. Treat your houseguests or visitors to a real show at the feeder by getting out there and offering nuts while your guests watch the feeder.

Setting up a second-story feeder. Get jays, chickadees, and woodpeckers to your high-rise in a hurry with a handful of delectable nuts.

Hand-taming. Nuts have such incredible appeal that they can entice birds into overcoming their natural wariness of people. You'll find out just how to do it later in this chapter, using nuts as the bribe (see "Hat Trick" on page 140).

Crack 'Em Up

Walnut, hickory, oak, and other nut trees along highways and byways are favorite bird areas when the crop is ripe, because the passing cars do the job of cracking the nuts. The crushed nuts are popular with just about every bird around, including sparrows, juncos, and wild turkeys, as well as the more usual woodpeckers, jays, and chickadees.

Nuts in shells are often available at low prices, so I take a tip from the crushing cars and smash some nuts myself. A few whacks with a hammer, and I can enjoy a circus of birds picking through the shells until every bit of nut meat is gone.

Bargain Buys

Controlling the amount of nuts you feed to birds is a major way to pare costs, but you can also save mucho bucks by buying smart to begin with. Per pound, nuts are generally at least three times as expensive as niger, and as much as five times the price of black oil sunflower seeds. Read on to learn my tried-and-true ideas for whittling down your nut budget!

Go with the Flow

Except for peanuts, which usually hold steady at about $2 per pound, nut prices seem to zoom up and down with no rhyme or reason. One week, the hazelnuts in my grocery store's bulk bins might be less than $5 per pound; the next week, they've shot up to over $7. The nuts in the bin are the same ones I looked at last week; it's only the price tag that's new.

Nuts vary widely in price depending on the season and the size of the harvest. When the supply of a certain nut is slim, you can expect to pay a premium price. When it's a bumper crop, prices fall. Since birds eagerly eat whatever kind I bring home, I make "cents" out of this situation by buying whatever nuts are cheapest.

COME 'N' GET IT!

Premium Treats for Prime Times

Save these higher-priced treats for prime feeder-watching times, such as when you eat your own breakfast, when your kids are watching, or when you just need a little pick-me-up. They're simple to mix up, and guaranteed to please your chickadees, jays, and other nut-lovers.

Good 'n' Pretty

Sometimes, I make my mixes to appeal to my eye, as well as to my birds' taste! This one combines eye-catching slivered almonds with fat hazelnuts, colorful Spanish peanuts, and other goodies. It's so pretty, I like to offer it in a clay plant saucer right on my patio table, where I can admire it—at least for a few minutes, until the birds scarf it up!

1 part hazelnuts (filberts), whole
1 part Spanish peanuts, raw or
    roasted, with reddish skin still on
1 part sunflower chips
1 part slivered almonds

Combine all of the ingredients, and lift and stir gently to mix. Want to focus on your larger feeder guests? Serve in an open tray feeder. Want to single out smaller birds? Serve in a small hanging feeder. Want a free-for-all? Carefully pour out some of the mix onto a flat-topped deck or porch rail, and see who grabs it first!

Big Treat for Little Guys

Chickadees, nuthatches, and titmice are among the most stalwart of the feeder crowd. These small birds visit daily through fall and winter, and in the warm months, too, if you live in their nesting region. All three are major nut- and sunflower-seed-eaters.

2 parts sunflower chips
1 part peanuts, raw or roasted
1 part almonds, chopped

Mix all of the ingredients thoroughly. Serve in small amounts in a stick-on window feeder. The small birds won't have to compete with jays, and you'll get a close-up view, so you can learn to tell these similar, mostly gray guys apart. Titmice have pointy crests on their heads, nuthatches have long beaks and short legs, and any other high-energy little gray bird that comes for this mix is likely to be a chickadee!

Extra Incentive

Make a budget treat by adding just a small amount of nuts to the mix. Here's one I like (and so do my downy woodpeckers, nuthatches, chickadees, and titmice).

8 parts black oil sunflower seeds
2 parts sunflower chips
2 parts chopped walnuts

1 part sliced or slivered almonds,
    coarsely chopped
1 part slivered almonds

Combine all of the ingredients, stirring until well mixed. Offer this special treat in a wire-mesh nut feeder, or in a small hanging feeder, such as a plastic dome or the coffee can feeder shown on page 47.

Woodpecker Windup

Increase the number of hammer-heads at your place by using a free hand with nuts and their favorite seeds. Here's a reasonably priced treat I dole out to woodpeckers year-round, with an extra helping when those big, brown woodpeckers known as flickers are migrating in fall and spring.

4 parts dry corn kernels
3 parts peanuts, chopped
3 parts peanuts, whole
2 parts black oil
    sunflower seeds

Mix all of the ingredients thoroughly. Serve in a wire-mesh nut feeder, or pour into a tray feeder.

Blue Jay Bounty Hunting

This nutty treat will win the hearts of bluejays, Steller's jays, scrub jays, gray jays, and pinyon jays. Whichever jays you have in your neighborhood, you're bound to see them within minutes of offering this mix. The sliced almonds will slow down these grabby gluttons; they're harder for a jay to pick up with its big beak. Plus, the almonds look funny, so jays may not figure out right away that they taste just as good.

4 parts black oil sunflower seeds
2 parts sliced almonds
2 parts peanuts, raw or roasted
1 part peanuts, in the shell, unsalted
1 part hazelnuts, whole,
**   in the shell or shelled**
1 part walnuts, in large pieces

Combine all of the ingredients, and stir until blended. Unless you've won the lottery lately, you'll want to dole this out by offering one or two handfuls at a time. Serve in an open tray-type feeder to accommodate the big-bodied jays.

Acorn Bash

Now, here's a fine way to work out your frustrations: Just grab a hammer and whack some nuts! I like to prepare my ingredients for this one outside, where I don't have to worry about denting the linoleum or cracking the counter with my blows. Oh, and after you finish your hard knocks, sit back and enjoy the view of birds feeding as they would in the wild!

2 parts acorns
1 part pecans, in the shell
1 part English walnuts, in the shell

1. Set all the nuts on a section of newspaper on a flat surface so they'll be easy to collect when you're done whacking. Hammer each nut with a not-too-heavy blow so that you don't smash the nuts to smithereens. What you're after are bigger pieces—split or partly broken shells; nut meat peeking out, but not bashed to oblivion.

2. Pour the broken nuts and their shells into a bucket. Carry the bucket to a spot that you can view comfortably from indoors, then pour into a low tray feeder, or directly on the ground (if you don't mind cleaning up shells later). It's surprising to see how many birds like nuts-in-the-rough: Watch for woodpeckers, chickadees, titmice, nuthatches, juncos, sparrows, cardinals, doves, jays, and maybe even wild turkeys!

Recipe for Redheads

Nearly all woodpeckers have some splash of red on or around their head, but a couple of the birds are unmistakable redheads: the well-named red-headed woodpecker and the misnamed red-bellied woodpecker, which has only a hard-to-see pinkish stain on its belly, but does have a bold red neck and nape. They'll both revel in this recipe, and so will other woodpeckers at your feeder. The nuts in this mix may also be snitched by jays, chickadees, titmice, nuthatches, juncos—and even wild turkeys, which adore acorns!

2 parts chestnuts, raw, in the shell
1 part acorns, in the shell
1 part English walnuts, in the shell
2 parts dry corn kernels
2 parts black oil sunflower seeds

1. Set a dish towel on a sturdy cutting board on a nonbreakable counter or floor. If you have tile or stone throughout the kitchen, or want to be sure you don't cause damage—there's hammering involved!—make this recipe outside.

2. Lay the chestnuts in a single layer on the dish towel. Fold the towel over, and tuck the edges underneath. Whack this "package" of nuts several times with a hammer, to split their leathery shells. Open the dish towel and pour the nuts, with shells and all

debris, into a mixing bowl. Don't worry if not all of the nuts are split; woodpeckers are adept at doing it themselves!

3. Repeat the process with the acorns. Add them to the bowl.

4. Repeat with the walnuts, or use a nutcracker to break each nut. Add them to the mix.

5. Add the corn and black oil sunflower seeds to the bowl. Use a long-handled wooden spoon (nut shells can be sharp) to mix all ingredients.

6. Serve this treat in an open tray feeder, or pour it directly on the ground at the base of your woodpeckers' favorite suet feeder.

Hat Trick

Nuts are so hard for the birds to resist that they'll eventually overcome any reluctance about using YOU as a feeder. Try this trick in winter, especially after a snow-storm, when birds are most motivated:

1. Remove all other feeders, so that you'll be the only food source in sight. Then, dress for success: Wear warm clothes and footgear, and crown your head with a cowboy hat (wear a knit cap underneath if you like).

2. Pour about a quarter-cup of shelled, coarsely chopped walnuts into a tray feeder, and sit or stand beside it. When you're settled comfortably, drop a generous handful of nuts on your hat brim or crown, wherever they'll stay put. Now comes the hard part: Don't move! Stay as still as you possibly can, no matter how much your nose is itching. Keep your eyes focused downward, and avoid meeting the eyes of any birds that come into your viewing area. Stay as long as you can, but if you get no takers after 30 minutes or so, retreat, leaving the nuts in the tray, and try again the next morning.

3. On the next go-round, the birds will probably not be as alarmed at your presence, and they'll be quicker to descend on the nuts. With any luck, you'll soon have a chickadee hat ornament! Once the birds are eating from your hat, make it a habit to wear the hat—with nuts on its brim—every time you fill the feeders.

Homegrown Help

Keep your eyes peeled for small nut-growing operations in your neck of the woods. Lots of folks keep a few nut trees in the yard, and sell the crop at roadside stands or farmers' markets. You'll usually save money over retail prices, and, if you're willing to take the nuts in the shell, you may be able to buy them for a bargain price. Early to late fall is the peak season for harvesting nuts, and prime time to buy. But you may still find nuts well into winter at farm outlets, for as long as the fall crop lasts.

Don't Pay for Packaging

Pretty has a price, when it comes to nuts. Compare the cost of fancy bags or cans with those of nuts in the unadorned bulk bins, and you're likely to find a real way to save some dough. At my supermarket, the packaged nuts may run as much as 50 percent more than the price of those I have to scoop out myself. Hey, for that kind of money, I can do my own bagging, thank you!

Holiday Cheer

You'll be grinning, all right, when you see the prices for nuts around the time of the two big baking holidays: Thanksgiving and Christmas. Grocery stores and discount stores sell nuts at a bargain during these seasons. Shelled English walnuts are usually an especially good buy—sometimes available for less than half their usual price! Watch for sales on almonds, hazelnuts, and pecans, too.

CAROLINA
CHICKADEE

Profiting from Charities

Selling nuts to benefit a good cause is popular in some areas, especially in pecan-pie country! When the crop comes in, charity groups weigh out and package the nuts, then sell them at reasonable prices for holiday baking, to raise money for their causes. Watch for notices of such sales in late fall, in the calendar section of your local newspaper or in local "shopper" publications or bulletin boards. I've picked up shelled pecans for $3 a pound at such a charity sale, when the same nuts were going for $6 a pound in the supermarket!

Cheapest Price? FREE!

Nothing's cheaper than free! Nuts are no doubt growing wild somewhere near you, no matter where you live. You'll find a chart of the general geographic ranges of native nut trees on page 147, or you can just look around to see what's growing in your neighborhood. Don't forget that oaks are nut trees, too!

If the trees aren't on your property, be sure to get permission from the landowner. Then, enjoy a crisp fall day by having a nut-gathering expedition. And here's a tip for you folks with creaky joints: Kids love to help fill the buckets!

COME 'N' GET IT!

Nutty Balls & Blocks

Add nuts to suet, peanut butter, and other fats to make a nutritious dough that's fun to mold into balls or blocks to fill your feeders. These molded treats are best served in cool weather, from fall through early spring, when you won't have to worry about them melting or turning rancid before they get gobbled up.

Peanutty Porcupines

Slivered almonds in this mix make the finished balls look like porcupines—well, maybe a little! Chickadees and titmice are likely to pick out the almond slivers and peanuts and carry them off, like kids grabbing their favorites from the candy bowl.

4 parts peanut butter
4 parts oatmeal
1 part peanuts, raw or roasted
1 part slivered almonds

Measure all ingredients into a deep bowl. By hand, or with an electric mixer, combine to form a stiff dough. Mold into lumpy, spiky "porcupine" balls for serving.

A&W Float

That's "A," as in almonds, and "W," as in walnuts, so don't start salivating for root beer and ice cream! This tasty treat is for the birds—nuthatches, chickadees, titmice, and any other nut-eaters that pull up for curb service.

1 store-bought pure suet block
¹/₄ cup of almonds, chopped
¹/₄ cup of walnuts, chopped

Unwrap the suet, and remove the tray; set aside the tray. Put the suet in a microwave-safe bowl, and cook on high for about 40 to 90 seconds (time varies depending on the strength of your microwave oven). Meanwhile, scoop the chopped nuts into the empty suet tray. When the suet is melted, set the bowl in the fridge to cool off quickly. It will begin to turn from clear to cloudy as it cools. When the fat is still lukewarm and easy to pour, carefully pour it on top of the chopped nuts, filling the tray to the very brim. Let your floating A&W nut block harden at room temperature or in the freezer, then serve in a wire suet cage.

Acrobats Only

Chickadees, titmice, and bushtits are adept at clinging to the smallest swaying twig, so I decided to take advantage of that skill to bar bigger birds from this extra-nutty treat. Save this one for winter, when the demand for fats is at its peak.

4 parts suet
3 parts chopped
 peanuts
2 parts cornmeal,
 regular grind
 (not coarse or fine)
1 part chopped walnuts
1 part peanut butter

Measure all ingredients into a bowl, and use your hands to mix it all up. Shape some of the mix into a small ball, about the size of a golf ball. Set the ball on a nonstick cookie sheet. Repeat, until all of the mix is used up. Poke a length of thin wire, about 18 inches long, through the center of each ball, so that the free ends extend from each side. Twist the ends together securely to make a loop for hanging.

Set the cookie sheet in the freezer overnight. Remove the nutty nuggets one at a time, and loosely coil up the wire, then store them in the freezer in zip-top plastic freezer bags. To serve, re-thread the wire through the treats and hang the whole shebang from an iron hook or other holder that allows it to dangle in midair—just for acrobats!

Super Stuffing

Chestnuts were once a staple for American birds, until blight wiped out nearly all of these once-common trees. Birds still take fondly to chestnuts, which you can find at many farmers' markets in fall.

1 cup of chestnuts, raw
1 cup of suet or fat scraps, chopped
¹/₂ cup of cornmeal, coarse grind

Cut the raw chestnuts in half, and use the tip of a teaspoon or a small melon baller to scoop out the nut meat. Set aside. Mix the suet and cornmeal by using your hands, or with the back of a spoon. Mix in the chestnuts by hand, using a light touch to prevent breakage of the nut-meat chunks. Serve in a wire suet cage.

Pileated Possibility?

For many bird-watchers, the giant-sized pileated woodpecker, a shining black bird with a bold red crest, is the Holy Grail at the feeder. If you live near woods, where this bird makes its home, try this mix; it has plenty of the pileated's favorite pecans to coax it into view. If no pileateds show up, you can depend on other woodpeckers, as well as chickadees, nuthatches, and titmice, to enjoy the results of your efforts.

1 cup of suet or fat scraps, chopped
$1/2$ cup of pecans, finely chopped
or crushed (or pecan meal,
if available)
$1/2$ cup of pecans, halves or
large pieces

Using the back of a spoon, "cream" the crushed pecans or pecan meal into the fat. Or mix well, using your hands. Pour in the large pecan pieces. Lift and stir, working carefully to avoid breaking the nuts into small pieces, until the pecans are evenly distributed throughout the fat mixture. Spread about $1/2$ cup of the mixture directly on a tree or post, about 3 feet from the ground. Put the remaining mixture into a wire suet cage, and attach the cage about 1 foot above your suet smear. Fasten it securely so that it won't move under this extra-large woodpecker's weight.

Salty Savings

Ever notice that unsalted nuts cost more than the salted kind? It sure doesn't seem to make sense, does it? I've noted the same thing with some brands, and at some stores. Maybe it's because there are fewer customers for unsalted nuts, so the supply is lower. At any rate, I've figured out some bargain-hunting tricks to salt away savings on unsalted nuts. To glean a good buy on unsalted nuts, shop at natural-food stores, or as we used to say, "health-food stores." Most of these stores sell unsalted nuts in bulk, by the pound, for reasonable prices. You can also find unsalted nuts in bulk at some grocery stores. As their popularity grows with us health-conscious honchos, even those cans of super-salty snack nuts may be joined by an unsalted version—for the same price!

Make Your Wallet Smile

When I'm feeding a lot of nut-lovin' birds, it's comforting to my wallet to know that I can make my own special suet mixes for a whole lot less than the store-bought kind. And, it takes just a few minutes to mix up enough to fill a suet feeder. I keep a supply of chopped peanuts and other chopped nuts, raisins, sunflower chips, and chopped dried fruits in zip-top plastic storage bags, so they're ready when I'm in a cookin' mood. Then all I need to do is cut up some fat scraps into a bowl and mix it up. For the $2 price of one special suet block, I can make *five* nutty-good blocks of my own! ✍

CRAZY FOR NUTS

Just as with other feeder foods, your birds' tastes may be different from those at another feeding station. In this chart I've listed the nuts that are most popular in my backyard. Use these nut suggestions as a starting point, keeping in mind that most of us limit our feeder menu to lower-priced peanuts and walnuts. For all we know, macadamia nuts might be even more appealing!

BIRD	NUTS EATEN	HOW TO PREPARE	HOW TO SERVE
Blackbirds	Acorns, almonds, beechnuts; possibly other nuts	Acorns: in shell; all others, chopped	With seeds or cracked corn; tray feeder
Bluebirds	Peanuts, pine nuts (pinyons)	Chopped	With fats; suet feeder or tray feeder
Carolina wren	Peanuts	Chopped	With fats; suet feeder or tray feeder
Catbird	Peanuts	Chopped	With fats; suet feeder or tray feeder

(continued)

CRAZY FOR NUTS, *continued*

BIRD	NUTS EATEN	HOW TO PREPARE	HOW TO SERVE
Chickadees	All	Shelled; whole or chopped	Alone, with seeds, or with fats; any kind of feeder
Doves and pigeons	Acorns, peanuts	Chopped	With seeds, cracked corn, or chicken scratch; low or mid-height tray feeder
Grosbeaks	Acorns, beechnuts, hickory nuts, pecans; may eat other nuts	Chopped	Alone or with seeds; tray feeder
Grouse, pheasant, turkey	Acorns, beechnuts, hickory nuts, pecans; may eat other nuts	Whole or chopped, with or without shells	With seeds, cracked corn, or chicken scratch; low tray feeder or directly on ground
House finch	Almonds, peanuts	Finely chopped	With seeds; tray feeder
Jays	All; particularly fond of peanuts in the shell	Shelled or unshelled; cracked, whole, or chopped	Alone, with seeds, or with fats; tray feeder at any height, or directly on ground
Mockingbird	Peanuts	Chopped	With fats; suet feeder or tray feeder
Nuthatches	All	Shelled; whole or chopped	Alone, with seeds, or with fats; any kind of feeder
Quail	Acorns, hickory nuts, pecans; may eat other nuts	Chopped	With seeds, chicken scratch, or cracked corn; low tray feeder or directly on ground
Thrashers	Peanuts	Chopped	Alone or with fats; suet feeder or tray feeder
Titmice	All	Acorns and pecans: shelled or unshelled; all others, shelled; whole or chopped	Alone, with seeds, or with fats; any kind of feeder
Woodpeckers	All nuts; particularly fond of acorns, almonds, beechnuts, pecans, walnuts	Acorns: in shell; all others, shelled; cracked, whole, or chopped	Alone or with fats; suet feeder or tray feeder

NATIONAL NUT FINDER

You can save significant dollars if you live in an area where nuts are grown commercially, or where they grow wild. Farm stands usually sell nuts at low prices, because there's no middleman involved. And wild nuts are free for the picking—but only if you ask first! Here's where you're most likely to find popular bird-feeding nuts!

NUT	WHERE IT'S GROWN COMMERCIALLY	WHERE IT GROWS IN THE WILD
Acorns	Not commercially grown	From oak trees; all across the country
Almonds	CA	Not in North America
Beechnuts	Not commercially grown	From beech trees; mainly in the East and Midwest
Black walnuts	IA, IL, IN, KS, KY, MD, MI, MN, NE, OH, OR, WI	East, Midwest, Southeast, Great Lakes
Chestnuts	CA, ID, MI, MN, OR, WA	Native chestnuts almost entirely wiped out by blight; commercial sources are for foreign varieties of this nut
English walnuts	CA	Not in America; but often grown on small farms or as a shade tree
Hazelnuts (filberts)	OR, WA	East, Midwest, Northwest
Hickory nuts	Not commercially grown	East, Southeast, Midwest
Macadamia nuts	HI	Not in continental North America
Peanuts	AK, AL, AZ, CA, FL, GA, MI, NC, NM, OK, SC, TN, TX, VA	Not in North America
Pecans	AL, AZ, GA, LA, NM, OK, TX	Southeast, South, Midwest
Pine nuts	Imported	Other species of nut-bearing pines grow in the Southwest
Pistachios	CA	Not in North America

CHAPTER 6

Sweets for the Tweets

Sweet stuff isn't just dessert to birds—it's the main dish! Adding sugar water, jelly, and fruit to your feeder menu will bring you some real beauts, including tanagers, orioles, bluebirds, and hummingbirds.

Sugar water is the bona fide bait for hummingbirds and orioles. In this chapter, you'll learn when and how to serve this nectar, and how to keep your feeder in fine fettle. As for those snazzy orioles, we'll talk about jelly as an extra enticement. You'll find out which fruits are most favored by bluebirds, robins, tanagers, and other songbirds, and how to offer them at the feeder. You'll also learn how to entice out-of-the-ordinary fruit eaters to your feeder. And, naturally, I've shared plenty of my secret recipes all along the way.

Surefire Sugar Water

Hummingbirds don't give a hoot about all the seeds, nuts, and fats at your feeder. It's nectar they need, which is why these birds are always buzzing around blossoms. Vivid orange or yellow orioles nosh on nectar, too, though not as exclusively as hummingbirds do. Natural nectar is very similar to sugar water—the same stuff you can mix up to pour in a feeder. In this section, you'll learn how to make it a staple at your feeding station.

Perfect Timing!

For most folks, midspring through early fall is the time to supply the sugar water. In the deep South and far West, hummingbirds stick around all year long, because the flowers never stop. But the rest of us (except for Floridians) will be bidding orioles goodbye for the fall and winter, and saying "Hello again!" in spring.

I use the emergence of big, yellow daffodils as my cue for putting out the hummingbird feeder. Daffodils are a sure sign of spring, so I know the birds won't be far behind. Orioles travel the comeback trail a little later, arriving when my apple trees are in bloom. It's always better to err on the early side, though, so you don't miss the rush of first arrivals. My general rule: As soon as you feel spring in the air, get out your feeders!

BULLOCK'S
ORIOLE

The Sweet-Tooth Tribe

Hummingbirds will be your first customers for nectar, and your most frequent sugar-water sippers. Orioles, too, are reliable regulars once they spot your supply. These gems would be reason enough to set up a nectar feeder, but sugar water attracts other incredible birds, too. More than 50 other kinds of birds, from tiny wood warblers to heavy woodpeckers, have occasionally been spotted bellying up to the bar!

Some experts tell us that birds generally have a poor sense of taste, but I'm not so sure about that. From the way they guzzle down the sweet stuff, I'm betting it's more than the high carbohydrate content that keeps 'em coming back for another hit. 🐦

Nectar Feeders

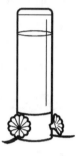

Folks used to fool around with test tubes, flower vials, and other contraptions to hold their sugar water, until some bright soul began making nectar feeders just for that purpose. A bottle of some sort holds the sweetened water, with a few feeding holes for the birds to sip from. Hummingbirds have become so accustomed to seeking sugar water in such feeders that they usually buzz over to check out a new one as soon as you hang it up. Select whatever style of feeder suits your fancy; basic models start at less than $10 and will give you years of reliable use. Orioles aren't up to speed on nectar feeders in all regions, so be patient; it may take them a while to investigate. 🐦

Color-Coded Cues

How can you tell if a strawberry is ripe? Why, you go by the color. Same thing with birds. They know just which colors are likely to spell "f-o-o-d." For hummingbirds, the magic

Succor for Stragglers

Birds don't usually change their time-honored habits because of our handouts, but hummingbirds may be a special case. In recent years, the migration patterns and home ranges of these tiny birds have begun to change, and so have their autumn departure dates. Some of the little buzzers have been showing up hundreds of miles from their usual homelands, happily sipping away at our sugar water. And in fall, when most hummers have left for warmer climes, a straggler may linger at the feeder, or stop in way past the usual season. I don't know whether I'm helping or harming things, but I don't like to risk starving a laggard hummingbird, or a stray. So I keep a nectar feeder hanging up until the daytime temperatures are regularly hovering below 32°F.

hues are red and red-orange. Nearly all flowers of this color range are tailored to the hummingbird's feeding habits, and they hold a hearty helping of nectar. Notice that flashy red plastic that decorates hummingbird feeders? The color is an advertisement for the wares within.

Orange is the eye-catcher for orioles. These birds eat a wide variety of fruits and other foods, but they absolutely adore oranges—to the extent that they can be pests in orange groves. A nectar feeder outfitted in orange trim will catch their eye sooner than one of a different color. ❧

Hover, or Have a Seat!

Hummingbirds are such amazing aerialists—up, down, forwards, back, hover, all at superfast speed!—that it's easy to believe they never need a break. They'll definitely use a feeder that has no perches at the feeding ports, because they can simply hover in place while they sip, just as they do at flowers. But if the model you select has a place to sit when sipping, they'll make use of the perch and linger a little longer. Besides, it's fun to see those teeny black feet grab on, while the bird rests its little wings a while. ❧

When a Perch Is Paramount

Orioles are agile, but they aren't the winged wonders that hummers are. Their bodies are much larger, too. You'll want to make sure that the nectar feeder you choose for your orioles includes sturdy, spacious perches so that the bird can easily take up a comfortable position and rest easy while feeding. All of us appreciate a comfy seat at the table! ❧

It's All Clear Now

Call me cranky, but I don't like straining my eyes to figure out whether or not my nectar feeders need a refill. That's why I pass up the pretty ceramic or painted feeders, or those made of plastic that's tinted so dark you can't see in. I want to be able to gauge the contents at a glance, and not have to hike across the yard to peer at the dang thing up close. And hummingbirds will keep coming to investigate the feeder, whether it has nectar or not. I don't want to play a cruel joke on my little friends, so I buy only those feeders that have clear nectar reservoirs. That way, I can tell at a glance when they need my attention.

Nectar Know-How

Making sugar water is a simple process, but it starts with a little bit of could-be-tricky math to get the proportions just so. In this section, I'll show you everything you need to know to be a good nectar-slinger, and how to adjust your formula for special seasons, or special effects. You'll also learn how to keep your feeder sparkling clean with some handy household helpers.

Fitting Formulas

One part granulated sugar to 4 parts water: That's the magic recipe that will satisfy the hummingbird habit. For orioles, the standard formula is a little less sweet. All species of orioles will eagerly guzzle down a mix of 1 part granulated sugar to 6 parts water.

Don't be surprised to see the birds trading feeders—both the hummingbird and oriole recipes result in a solution that's sweeter than nature's own. Natural nectar varies in sweetness according to the particular plant, the weather, and the time of year; but often, it's no sweeter than would be matched by a solution made of 1 part sugar to 10 parts water. No wonder a nectar feeder is such a hot spot for hummingbirds and orioles—it's significantly sweeter than the real thing!

COME 'N' GET IT!

Nectar of the Gods

Gods and goddesses of the kitchen, that is! Stir up these divine sugar-water solutions to seduce hummingbirds, orioles, and perhaps other nectar sippers to your backyard.

Heavenly for Hummingbirds

This is the gold standard for hummingbird nectar. Heating the water to the boiling point has no health benefit; it simply allows the sugar to dissolve quickly and completely.

4 parts water
1 part granulated sugar

Heat the water to or almost to the boiling point. Remove from heat, and stir in the sugar. Continue stirring until the sugar is completely dissolved. Cool, and fill your freshly cleaned feeder. If you've miscalculated the nectar capacity of your feeder (easy to do!), and you wind up with left-over nectar, just store the extra solution in the refrigerator in a tightly capped bottle or jar. It will keep for about three days.

Oriole Ambrosia

Oriole feeders usually have large reservoirs. Until you have a handle on how many orioles you'll be hosting and how much nectar they'll drink, start the season by filling the feeder only half-full.

6 parts water
1 part granulated sugar

Heat the water to or almost to the boiling point. Remove from heat, and stir in the sugar. Continue stirring until the sugar is completely dissolved. Cool, and fill your freshly cleaned feeder. If you've miscalculated the nectar capacity of the feeder, just store the extra solution in the refrigerator in a tightly capped bottle or jar. It will keep for about three days.

Protein Punch

Stuck with a straggler hummingbird that never departed on fall migration? If the weather turns nippy for this unseasonable visitor, add a protein boost to the nectar solution. This recipe yields a little over 1 cup of solution, which should be plenty to nourish a lone bird until he, too, gets packing!

1 cup of water
Pinch of low-sodium beef bouillon
granules
¹/₄ cup of granulated sugar

Heat the water to or almost to the boiling point. Sprinkle the bouillon granules into the hot water, and stir to dissolve. Add the sugar, continuing to stir until completely dissolved. Cool, then fill a clean feeder.

Don't Be a Drip!

I find it inconvenient to fill my nectar feeders outside, but carrying a freshly filled feeder from the kitchen to the yard can leave a sticky trail of drips along the way. The solution is simple: Hold a dishcloth below the feeder, and your journey will be drip-free. A quick rinse afterwards under the kitchen tap, and my dishcloth is ready to reassume its usual duties! 🐦

The Price of Convenience

You can buy packaged nectar mix right beside the feeders at your favorite store. It dissolves instantly in water, and it's just as nutritious as making your own. The only drawback? The price! Instant nectar costs about $3 for enough to make 6 cups of sugar solution. At my supermarket, 5 pounds of granulated sugar sets me back about the same amount of money—but there's enough in that bag to mix up half a bathtub full of bird nectar! 🐦

JERRY
TO THE RESCUE

Q. **How do I know how much sugar and how much water to put in my new feeder? The box says the feeder holds 18 ounces.**

A. A cup is equal to 8 fluid ounces, so your feeder holds $2^{1}/_{4}$ cups of sugar solution. But what if your next feeder holds 12 ounces? Or 24? Since all feeders seem to have different capacities, I figured out a cheat-sheet method so I don't get confused or have to refigure every time I refill! Here's how I do it:

Measure capacity in cups. I start by measuring the feeder's capacity by pouring in 1 cup of water at a time until the feeder is full or nearly full. If there's still enough space to squeeze in another half-cup, I do so to get the final capacity measurement. But I don't bother getting it down to quarter-cups!

Do the math. Take the total number of cups (plus the half-cup, if applicable), and divide by 4 for a hummingbird feeder; divide by 6 for an oriole feeder. This will give you the number of cups of sugar you'll need.

Write it down. Here's the most important time-saving part of this process! Use an indelible marker to write the recipe on the bottom of the feeder, where you can instantly check it when you refill. For instance, if my new "Humungo Hummingbird Feeder" (not yet made, as far as I know!) holds 12 cups of water, I write "12 c water, 3 c sugar" on its base. If it's a 12-cup "Oversized Oriole Feeder" instead, I write "12 c water, 2 c sugar."

Write it down again. What with rain, cleaning, and general use, the recipe you've written on the feeder bottom might get hard to read. Keep another record of it in a handy kitchen drawer, or tuck it in the front of your favorite cookbook. That way, you can double-check or re-ink the formula as needed.

Store the overflow. You'll notice that my rounding-off method may create a bit of overflow for the feeder's capacity; I just pour the extra into a glass jar with a tight lid and store it in the fridge to top off the tank whenever it's needed!

Bartender's Best Bet

Superfine white sugar is a staple behind the bar at many fine (and not-so-fine!) establishments, because it dissolves almost instantly when stirred into liquid of any temperature. If you want to eliminate the step of heating water to dissolve your regular sugar, take a tip from Bartender Jerry, and search your supermarket shelf for a box of sugar that's labeled "superfine"! 🐦

Mass Consumption

Don't say I didn't warn you! Hummingbirds can swamp your feeders, draining quarts of nectar dry in just a day or two. Spring and fall are the busiest seasons, because of the masses of migrants that stop in for a fill-up. But crowds can also be the rule all summer long if your yard, or your neighborhood, is a hot spot of hospitable flower gardens. To serve a horde of hummers in a hurry, make an extra-strong sugar syrup, and dilute it to fill feeders fast. It's the same principle used by soda jerks! Here's how to do it:

1. Heat 2 cups of water to the boiling point.

2. Meanwhile, measure 2 cups of granulated sugar into a deep, heat-proof container, such as a saucepan.

3. Pour the hot water into the sugar, and stir until completely dissolved. You now have a 1:1 sugar syrup.

4. Cool and store in the refrigerator until needed, or use immediately. When you're ready to fill the feeders, add 6 cups of water to the syrup. To prepare smaller quantities, combine 1 cup of water with each 1/3 cup of the syrup. Stir well before filling feeders. 🐦

WHITE-EARED HUMMINGBIRD

Boost It for a Bribe

Long ago, I used to be the only hummingbird feeder in my neighborhood, hosting a constant crowd of the busy little birds from sunup to sundown. Then came a year when I was plain baffled by my birds' behavior. They came in on spring migration just like clockwork, but instead of sticking around, the fickle little things fled the scene. A few days later, I found out why. Seems a neighbor had put up her own nectar feeder—and used a sweeter solution than my 1:4 mix. I was steamin', at least until I talked to her and we came to a truce. Now we both use the same strength of solution—and we share the customers!

Just in case you need to employ some sneaky tactics, you can safely increase the strength of your hummingbird solution to as much as 1 part sugar to 3 parts water without harming your friends or making the syrup too thick to sip. Likewise, if you have no competition other than flowers, you can save a little money on sugar, and mix it up at a 1:6 ratio. 🐦

"Gatorade®" for Guzzlers

Migrating hummingbirds follow the flowers, traveling north along with the first flowers of spring, and heading south again when blooms decline in fall. That little habit can get them into trouble. If a late-spring cold snap or an early frost catches them in inhospitable climes, your nectar feeder can be a serious lifesaver. At stressful times like these, boost the sugar-to-water ratio by adding an extra 2 to 4 table-spoons of sugar per cup of water, just to make sure the birds get enough calories to keep on buzzin'. That sugar rush will be as revitalizing to the birdies as a gulp of Gatorade® is to an exhausted athlete. 🐦

BIRD BITS

How Sweet It Is!

Hummingbirds have only about $1/1,000$ the number of tastebuds you and I have on our tongues, but theirs are finely tuned for detecting sweets. They're so perceptive, in fact, that hummers can tell the difference between different kinds of sugars (or so the experts tell us). But that sense of sweet isn't the main reason you'll want to stick to white granulated sugar, or superfine granulated, in your nectar solutions.

Honey is just as sweet as sugar, so why not use that? If you'd ever heard Grandma Putt cautioning against feeding honey to infants, you'd know that the anti-honey warnings aren't just an old wives' tale. Doctors now know that honey may contain spores that cause botulism in infants. Honey may also pass along a debilitating fungus to hummingbirds. Some researchers also suspect that hummingbirds cannot digest honey, and although they may drink it, they'll get no nutrition. Stick with white sugar, and you won't need to worry!

DO IT YOURSELF

Feeder Brush

Nifty little brushes made just for cleaning nectar feeders cost only a few dollars, but I have my pennypinching reputation to uphold. So, instead of investing in those tailor-made cleaning aids, I made do by adapting a bottle brush from my kitchen drawer. It does the trick just fine, and my rep is still intact! Here's how to make your own:

MATERIALS

Empty, dry nectar feeder, lid removed
Used bottle brush, with handle that extends at least 2 inches longer than your feeder
Scissors

DIRECTIONS

Step 1. Stick the brush into the empty nectar feeder reservoir (you'll have to push hard to get it through the opening), to make sure that it's long enough to swipe into all the corners.

Step 2. Pull the brush back out, and straighten out the now-flattened bristles with your fingers.

Step 3. Using the scissors and working over a trash can to catch the clippings, begin snipping about $1/4$ inch off the bristles, all the way around the brush.

Step 4. Poke the bush into the feeder again, and judge

whether it needs a "little more off the top." If the brush slides in with a reasonable amount of push behind it, you're all set. If it still bottlenecks at the entrance, trim off another $1/4$ inch or so.

I keep my doctored brush hanging on a hook, close to the kitchen sink. That way, when I need to scrub out a nectar feeder, I don't have to sort through the kitchen drawer! I'm proud of my homemade helper because it cost me exactly nothing, and it works just as well as the fancy ones.

Fresh Express

Sugar water doesn't stay fresh for long. Plan on emptying any leftover solution from your feeder and refilling at least once a week. In hot weather, it may need more frequent attention, especially if your setup is hanging in the sun. As the sugar water ferments or spoils, the water will turn cloudy; anything less than crystal clear means it's time for a change. Nectar sippers may continue to dine at fermented nectar, and we sure don't want to be the cause of any flying-under-the-influence incidents!

BLUE-THROATED HUMMINGBIRD

Squeaky Clean

A quick rinse may be all your feeder needs before refilling, if birds are emptying it every few days. I add a drop of dishwashing liquid and shake it up, then rinse several times to make sure every trace of the soap is gone. If your feeder needs further attention—maybe there's scum or black gook inside the reservoir or around the feeding ports, or dead insects trapped inside—you'll need to disassemble it to do a thorough job.

Rice Is Nice

To dislodge deposits within the feeder bottle, start by filling the bottle with warm water and a few drops of dishwashing liquid. Let it sit for about half an hour. Then, drop a few dozen grains of uncooked white rice into your feeder, add an inch or two of water, cover the opening with your hand, and shake, shake, shake, as fast as you can! The friction of the rice grains will help scrub off the scum. If stubborn spots remain, empty the rice and water, let the bottle soak again in warm, sudsy water, then repeat the rice-shaking operation. When the bottle is clean, rinse thoroughly before refilling.

Pipe Cleaner Pokey

Now that five-and-dime stores are no longer on every corner, you'll have to visit a craft store or discount chain to get your-self a pack of good old-fashioned pipe cleaners. They make ideal tools for getting the gunk out of feeder openings. Wash the pipe cleaner after use by rubbing it in a bit of dishwashing liquid with your fingers, and you can reuse it for several go-rounds. 🐦

Bleach It, Baby!

A weak solution of household bleach does a great job of neutralizing the nasties on glass or plastic feeders. Fill your kitchen sink with enough water to cover the feeder, then stir in 1 capful (or about 2 tablespoons) of bleach. Disassemble the feeder, and lay all of the parts in the bleach bath. Let the feeder parts soak for an hour or so, then rinse them under a strong stream of water. The dirt should wash right off. But if you have any stubborn hangers-on, give 'em the bottle-brush or pipe-cleaner treatment. Rinse thoroughly several times, until there's absolutely no trace of bleach scent left on any of the feeder parts. 🐦

JAMMING WITH JELLY

Orioles and other sweets-loving birds are learning to associate nectar feeders with food, and they're also learning to look for other goodies at feeders. Another sweet food that'll catch their eye is jelly, which is mostly sugar.

The Grapest Story Ever Told

G rape jelly is generally the sweetest of the sweet, with more sugar than most other preserves or jams. Spooned into a small container, super-sweet grape jelly is irresistible to orioles. Add a jar of grape jelly—NOT the low-sugar kind!—to your pantry in early spring so you're ready to go when you see that first flash of orange or hear that unmistakable loud, whistled song. 🐦

Weighing the Attraction

First, the bad news about offering jelly: You'll get ants. Bees and wasps will come, too. Now, the good news: Bugs? Who cares? When an eye-popping oriole arrives at your offering of grape jelly, you'll forget all about those little buggers. Tanagers may also take a taste of jelly, as may the yellow-bellied sapsucker and downy woodpecker. As more feeder hosts serve jelly, and as more birds learn to recognize its appeal, you can expect to see other sweet-toothed birds grabbing a bite, too.

COME 'N' GET IT!

Stroke of Brilliance

Some songbirds are so spectacular, they look like they should live in a jungle! They do—in winter. In the warmer seasons, these fancy-feathered friends move back north, and may even grace our feeders. Once a glowing red tanager—or an incandescent orange or yellow oriole—finds your feeder, the same bird is likely to return year after year, back from its winter vacation way down south. Try these treats to lure them in, from early to late spring, when songbird migration is at its peak. Trot them out again in early fall, when the singers fly southward.

Tanager Temptations

Consider yourself honored if a glorious red tanager shows up at your feeder. This recipe will help get their attention! Orioles and bluebirds may also nab a sample.

Half a ripe banana, mashed
1 cup of cornmeal, regular grind
$1/2$ cup of peanut butter
$1/2$ cup of suet or fat scraps, chopped

Mix together the mashed banana and cornmeal. Add the peanut butter and suet or fat scraps, and mix thoroughly. Mold into a shape to fit an accessible feeder, or put the mixture in a wire suet cage with a perch poked into it.

Good 'n' Fruity

Here's another sweet treat that's sure to draw the red tanager to your feeder:

¹/₄ cup of dried banana chips
1 cup of suet or fat scraps, chopped
¹/₂ cup of dried cherries, finely chopped
¹/₄ cup of raisins, chopped

Break the banana chips into bits with your hands or in a food chopper (don't chop with a knife; the brittle chips fly in all directions!). Combine all fruits with the suet, mixing thoroughly with your hands. Mold into a block to fit a wire suet cage, and add a perch by poking a stick directly into the fat.

All for Orioles

Mix up this recipe when orioles return in mid-spring. Continue refilling the feeder until they lose interest as natural foods become more abundant.

1 orange, peeled
1 cup of suet or fat scraps, chopped
¹/₄ cup of frozen blueberries

With a sharp paring knife, slice the orange along both sides of each section of membrane, cutting to the

center. Split the orange by pulling it apart with your fingers, and slice fruit pulp away from any remaining membrane. Finely chop the orange pulp, discarding the seeds. Combine the orange pulp and suet or fat scraps in a bowl, and mix well, using your hands. Stir the frozen blueberries (still frozen) into the mix. Form into a block to fit your suet feeder, and add a perch by poking a stick into the fat.

More Oriole Delights

Once you've got orioles coming to your feeder chowin' down on "All for Orioles," above, mix up this recipe for a change of pace:

1 cup of suet or fat scraps, chopped
¹/₂ cup of dried apricots, chopped
¹/₂ cup of dried currants

Combine all of the ingredients, mixing thoroughly with your hands. Mold into a block to fit your suet cage or other feeder.

A Little Dab'll Do Ya

Hang on to your hat, because it's easy to get carried away when you see an actual oriole eating your jelly offering. "Here, have some more!" we want to holler. "Bring your friends!" Before you know it, there's jelly everywhere: In each feeder, on the deck rail, on the ground, on your feeder birds' feet, on your dog's paws, and maybe even on you!

Instead of spreading it around, concentrate your jelly service in one small area, and start with just a paltry 2 tablespoons of the stuff. If the oriole—or better yet, orioles!—polishes it off lickety-split, then add another container and double the quantity to 4 good globs in each. No need to worry about scaring off the birds should you need to refill; they won't forget where they found that sweet stuff! 🐦

Stop the Jiggles

Hold that jelly still! You'll want to make sure that in whatever arrangement you rig up, or in whatever feeder you buy, the jelly container is held in place so that it doesn't tilt, slip, or slide when a heavy bird lands on it. A sudden shift will scare off your potential customer, and it can also make quite a mess! 🐦

BALTIMORE
ORIOLE

Finding a Feeder

My Jerry-rigged jelly-feeding method is to nail a few metal jar lids to a scrap of lumber (or my deck rail). It gets points for being cheap, fast, and utilitarian, but cleaning is another question. As for aesthetics? *Nada!*

Check your bird-supply store or go online to find jelly feeders that look like thoroughbreds compared to my old nag. Look for a simple design, with a roof to protect the food from rain. Expect to pay about $25 and up for a good-looking wooden feeder that can host four to six orioles or other birds at one time. 🐦

FRUITS FOR THE FEATHERED

 Robins, catbirds, thrashers, wrens, and a handful of other habitual fruit eaters are the bane of a fruit grower's life—but these birds' dining habits turn charming when they're transferred to the feeder. In this section, you'll learn how to serve some of the most favored fruits, and which wonderful birds you can expect to see nibbling at them. When you're ready to get fancy, you'll find a batch of fruit-boosted treats for your feeder regulars and your special guests.

An Apple a Day

A is for apple, and apples are a great beginning for your fruit feeder. Lots of your feeder regulars enjoy an occasional apple, so don't be surprised to see chickadees, titmice, woodpeckers, cardinals, or even juncos taking a nibble. Apples are also A-1 with the mockingbird and its relatives, the catbird and brown thrasher. Robins and bluebirds may sample apples, too. 🐦

Golden Delicious Decoy

I buy apples by the bushel, because they're one of my main anti-starling devices. No, I don't throw the fruit at them! I use apple halves to lure those ever-looting starlings away from my other feeders. When times are tough in winter,  and even starlings get my sympathy, I set out a half-dozen apple halves on the ground, far away from my feeders. The starlings will happily peck every last bit of flesh from the apple, until nothing is left but a thin, empty shell.

Farmers' markets and orchards are a great place to save money on apples. Look for the less than perfect ones, sold at a bargain price. Birds won't mind the blemishes one bit. 🐦

Oranges for Orioles

Oh my, orioles sure are spectacular birds! Their orange or yellow feathers practically glow. It's a good thing there are enough species to cover most of the country, so we all get a share of the beauty. The eastern half of the country gets the flashy orange-and-black Baltimore, while the western half hosts the similar Bullock's oriole. In the Southwest, Scott's oriole adds a dash of deep yellow, and along the California coasts and in the deserts, the flamboyant hooded oriole is the bird to watch.

All orioles adore nectar, and in the fruit department, it's oranges that are most appreciated. Service is simple: Just slice the fruit in half and set the halves, cut side up, in an open feeder.

Grabbing at Grapes

The smaller the grapes, the better for birds, because they like to gulp down these juicy fruits whole. If you're lucky enough to live near wineries, or have a farmers' market nearby, you may be able to scout out grapes in smaller sizes than some of those monsters at the supermarket. But if supermarket grapes are your only choice, you'll find birds can figure them out. Three related birds, the mockingbird, catbird, and brown thrasher, will probably be your prime customers for grapes. Watch for robins, too, especially in winter, and other fruit eaters including the Carolina wren, black-headed grosbeak, green-tailed towhee, fox sparrow, and white-throated sparrow.

JERRY
TO THE RESCUE

Q. **Every time I clean out the refrigerator, I find some fruit that's past its prime. Can I feed it to the birds, or should I add it to the compost pile?**

A. Unless the fruit is so far gone that it's nothing but mold-covered mush, it's still prime fodder as far as birds are concerned. In the wild, fruit isn't nearly as perfect as the pieces we buy at the grocery store. But there's still plenty of good eatin' in it! Soft, bruised, wormy, frozen—hey, it's all just part of the deal for fruit-eating birds. As long as they can find a few good bites, they'll take you up on that offering of slightly funky fruit.

But don't hesitate to toss that fruit on the compost pile, if you prefer. If your pile is exposed and the fruit isn't buried, birds will peck out the good bits at that "feeder," too!

COME 'N' GET IT!

Autumn Anticipation

Fall brings another wave of migrating songbirds, heading south this time. Catch the attention of long-haul travelers and win the loyalty of winter-resident songbirds with these fruity-sweet recipes. You may tempt an oriole, tanager, brown thrasher, bluebird, warbler, or catbird to your feeding station. Be sure to serve the food in a feeder that has a place to perch: These guys aren't as agile as chickadees!

Meow Mixture

Call in the catbirds with this fruit-rich specialty! They'll really appreciate it in late fall and winter, when natural fruits are hard to find.

1 cup of suet or fat scraps, chopped
1/2 cup of raisins
1/4 cup of currants
1/4 cup of blackberries, frozen
1/4 cup of strawberries, frozen
1/4 cup of fresh apple, chopped

Give the bags of frozen fruit a few whacks on the cutting board so that the solid lumps break apart. Combine all of the ingredients in a bowl. Use a large, sturdy spoon to mix lightly so that the fruit and suet are well distributed. Avoid crushing the fruit, and work quickly so that the frozen fruit doesn't thaw. Mold into a block, and serve in a wire suet cage with a perch added.

Thrasher's Thrill

And a thrill for you, too, when you spot an imposing, long-tailed thrasher at your bird table. This mockingbird relative is a solitary type, so you're only likely to see just one.

4 parts suet or chopped fat
2 parts cornmeal, coarse grind
2 parts raisins
1 part peanut butter
1 part fresh dark purple grapes, any variety, cut in half

Mix the suet or fat, cornmeal, raisins, and peanut butter, combining thoroughly. Mold the mix into large, flattened balls. Now for the tempting touch: Poke the grape halves partway into the suet balls so that they're highly visible to grape-eating thrashers!

Perchers' Paradise

Choose a low tray feeder to serve this special recipe in. It's suited to the tastes of robins, thrashers, thrushes, and other birds that prefer to dine at a lower table with a secure grip.

**6 parts cornmeal, regular grind
(not coarse or fine)**
2 parts suet or fat scraps, chopped
2 parts peanut butter
1 part peanuts, finely chopped
1 part raisins, chopped
**1 part fresh or dried cherries,
chopped**
1 part dried apples, chopped

Combine the cornmeal, suet or fat scraps, and peanut butter, mixing well with your hands. Add the peanuts, raisins, cherries, and apples, and mix well with your hands or a strong spoon until well distributed. Form into a block to serve in a low feeder for perching birds, or crumble 1 to 2 cups and serve directly on snow-covered ground.

Figgy Pudding

Unless you live in fig-growing country (mostly Texas, California, and other hot regions), figs are a pricey proposition. In my cold climate, fresh or dried figs are such a treat that it's hard to part with any for the birds. I turned to fig-filled cookies to add flavor to this mix—and to eliminate any guilt about keeping the fresh figs for myself!

**1 cup suet or fat scraps,
chopped**
$^1/_2$ cup peanut butter
**$^1/_2$ cup cornmeal, regular
grind (not coarse or fine)**
12 Fig Newtons®, crumbled

Combine the suet, peanut butter, and cornmeal in a deep bowl, and mix thoroughly to form a stiff dough. Add the crumbled cookies, using a spoon, an electric mixer, or your hands to lightly blend the cookies into the mix. Aim to distribute some figgy flavor throughout the mix, but avoid over-beating; stop while you can still see some recognizable brown, seedy streaks of fig. Mold into a block or balls to fit your suet feeder. Freeze any leftover balls, separately, in zip-top plastic freezer bags.

Cherries & Berries Jubilee

Small fruits are big temptations for fruit-eating birds. But unless you have your own blueberry/raspberry/strawberry/cherry farm, these special fruits are too high-priced to serve up every day. So I save them for special treats in the dead of winter or the first days of spring.

Of course, fresh berries and cherries cost even more in the off-season (if you can even find them). Not a problem! Just buy them dried or frozen, or process your own when the fresh supply is at its peak. I dry blueberries, blackberries, cherries and other small fruits, a pound at a time, on a cookie sheet in the oven. An hour or two at my lowest setting of 180°F usually does the trick. Why go to all this trouble and expen$e? The birds sure don't "need" a taste of summer in the cold season. But it's just plain fun to watch the surprise on a fox sparrow's face, when it stumbles across a blackberry in bitter winter!

Grandma Putt's BIRD BITS

Head 'Em Off at the Pass

Mockingbirds were mostly southern belles until recent decades, when their range gradually began to expand. This big, slim, gray bird is a possibility at feeders from coast to coast, as far north as Canada and way down into Mexico. Some stay put in winter, while others head for the warmer southern states. But wherever you live, mockingbirds can be a menace at the feeder!

When a mocker finds a well-stocked feeder, especially one that offers his beloved fruits, you can hear this greedy bird yell "Mine! Mine! All mine!" He'll vigorously chase off any intrepid bird that ventures near. And even when he's not eating, he'll perch nearby like a pit bull guarding a bone. No-nonsense Grandma Putt would have tried to scold the mocker into sharing, but when a mockingbird stakes its claim, there's no appealing to reason. She soon realized that the only recourse is to set up another feeder on the opposite side of the house—he can't guard both at once!

Cravin' Raisins

Raisins are cheap and easy to use, so stock up! But don't just empty that box into your feeder. I've found that raisins are often overlooked when I serve them plain, for reasons I haven't figured out yet. Save these good dried grapes for use in bird recipes, where they'll be eagerly eaten and not go to waste.

I like to add raisins to suet-based recipes to tickle the taste-buds of the bluebird, Carolina wren, catbird, brown thrasher, and mockingbird. When I crumble the treats at ground level, I can watch as towhees, sparrows, and robins wolf them down. 🐦

Exotic? Maybe Not!

I never considered trying tropical fruits at my feeder, until one balmy May day when I had a few extra bananas going brown. I peeled back a flap of skin, and nestled the 'nanners in the tray beside the apples and fruit treats. Was I surprised when a scarlet tanager fluttered down to take a taste! Tropical fruits, I learned, are just the ticket for our summer birds that winter in the Tropics. All tanagers are possible customers for your spare bananas. As for papayas, guavas, mangoes, and other exotic fruits—well, usually there just aren't enough of those in the Baker kitchen to share with the birds! 🐦

Bird-Tempting Trail Mix

Hey, can I have a date? Thanks! I'll add it to this trail mix I'm cooking up for my tanagers and thrushes. Birds eat dried fruits at the feeder with just as much relish as they do fresh ones, so I regularly patrol the bulk-foods aisle of my supermarket and natural-foods stores to see what's on sale. I've found great buys on chopped dates, apple slices, currants, apricots, peaches, and other goodies, including that classic, dried plums, a.k.a. prunes. It's all fair game for mixing with chopped suet and molding into bird-attracting treats! 🐦

Fall for Fruit

Fruit will be most eagerly gobbled when it's nearly nonexistent in nature. But in the height of summer, when birds can just as easily raid your garden or nearby orchards, everyone except those good ol' reliable starlings are likely to snub your stuff and get their own. So keep your fruit feeding minimal in summer, but ratchet it up as the natural harvest wanes. By September, most fresh fruit is a distant memory to birds. Your supply will be greeted with open beaks from fall through late spring, until natural fruit is once again in season.

CALLING ALL FRUIT EATERS!

Ever try to grow raspberries, strawberries, or—mmm!—blueberries? Day by day, you watch the green fruits swell and take on color, until you just know that tomorrow's the day. Hope you're an early riser! Birds have been keeping their eyes on your berries, too, and you're likely to discover that they've cleaned off a lot of the crop before you get out to the patch.

Just because birds eat fruit in the wild doesn't necessarily mean they'll come to your feeder as soon as you set out an apple. Fruit feeding is a little trickier, because many of the birds that love it best need coaxing to visit a feeder. Here are some of my tried-and-true tricks for tempting them into view.

Unknown Territory

Most fruit-eating birds are accustomed to foraging for themselves. They can zero in on a ripe strawberry or a bunch of grapes faster than you can beat 'em to it. But, when it comes to recognizing their favorite foods at the feeder, birds act like I do when I encounter my dentist in the grocery store: You look familiar, I'm sure I know you, but I can't think of who you are for the life of me!

The biggest hurdle in fruit feeding is to get your potential customers to notice the goodies. Unlike the chickadees, starlings, sparrows, and other feeder regulars who are willing to give anything you offer a try, many fruit-loving birds don't equate a feeding station with their food. 🐓

GRAY
THRASHER

Here, Kitty, Kitty

Want to call in catbirds? Then put out fresh, dried, or frozen fruit in fall and spring, when natural fruit is nearly nonexistent and fruit-eating migrants are plentiful. In no time at all, you'll be greeting that "kittybird," as well as an appreciative oriole, thrasher, tanager, wren, or other feeder newbie.

COME 'N' GET IT!

Winter Wonders

Natural fruit is a mighty scarce commodity in wintertime. Mix up these fruit-studded treats to add some sweet stuff, high in fruity carbohydrates, to the diet of your regular feeder birds.

Crush on Cardinals

Who wouldn't fall in love with those wonderful red birds? Cardinals are one of the cold-weather delights at feeders across the eastern two-thirds of the continent. Enliven the gray days of winter with a flash of red by offering this fruit-flavored treat.

4 parts black oil sunflower seeds
2 parts safflower seeds
2 parts cracked corn
2 parts dried cherries, chopped
2 parts grapes, cut in half

Combine the seeds and corn, stirring until well distributed. Gently stir in the dried cherries and grapes. Serve in an unroofed tray feeder so cardinals can spot the goodies.

Cardinal Come-On

Here's another fruity treat that's sure to entice cardinals to set a spell at your feeder.

4 parts black oil sunflower seeds
1 part cracked corn
1 part dates, chopped
1 part dried cherries, chopped

Combine all of the ingredients, and stir to mix thoroughly. Serve in a tray feeder.

Song Sparrow Specialty

Very few sparrows eat fruit at the feeder, but the reliable song sparrow, a small brown bird with a streaky breast, and its look-alike cousin, the bigger, darker fox sparrow, will appreciate the addition of fruits to their favored seeds.

2 parts millet
1 part dried cherries, finely chopped
1 part dried blueberries, finely chopped

Stir all of the ingredients together until well mixed. Serve in a low-level tray feeder to best suit the feeding habits of these ground-dwelling birds.

Bluebird Best

Bluebirds appreciate any soft foods, but in winter, they're swift to adopt an offering that's heavy on the fruits they love.

4 parts suet or fat scraps, chopped
1 part peanut butter
2 parts cornmeal, coarse grind
1 part oatmeal
1 part dried currants
1 part dried cherries, coarsely chopped

Mix the suet or fat scraps and peanut butter with the cornmeal and oatmeal. Add the currants and cherries, and mix to distribute the fruit throughout. Crumble the mix, sparingly at first, in a feeder with perching space.

Wrangle a Wren

The big, bright-eyed Carolina wren seems to be changing its habits in recent years, and sticking around for the winter season. Help this friendly bird stay in fine fettle with this fatty, fruity recipe.

1 cup of suet or fat scraps, chopped
1/2 cup of chopped apple, fresh or dried
1/4 cup of dried cherries, chopped
1/4 cup of prunes (dried plums), chopped

Combine all of the ingredients, using your hands to mix the fruits with the fat. Stuff a wire suet cage with the mix.

Mockingbird Mania

Long-tailed mockingbirds are related to catbirds and thrashers, but their personality is much different from their quiet cousins: These guys are just plain greedy! If a mocker lays claim to your feeding station, divert its attention by serving up this recipe on the far side of the house!

2 large apples, any kind
1 cup of raisins
1 cup of suet
   or fat scraps,
   chopped

Core the apples, then cut them in half and set them aside. Mix the raisins and suet or fat scraps with your hands until well combined. Using a spoon or your fingers, stuff the hollowed-out center of each apple half with the mixture, piling it on generously. Set the apple treats in an open tray feeder. Or hammer long nails through the back of a board, and push the apples onto the nails; hang the board against a post by fastening wire to the two outermost nailheads and making a hanging loop.

End-of-the-Trail Mix

Once fruit-eating birds find a feeder filled with this mix, they'll take off their boots and stay awhile! It's a winner for woodpeckers, house-finches, chickadees, catbirds, wrens, thrashers, robins, bluebirds—and for the tanagers that arrive in spring to announce that winter is behind us.

4 parts sunflower chips
4 parts hulled millet
4 parts peanuts, chopped
4 parts dried apples, chopped
4 parts raisins
2 parts dried apricots, chopped
2 parts prunes (dried plums), chopped
1 part dried cranberries

Measure all of the ingredients into a large bowl. Stir thoroughly to combine. Serve about 1 to 2 cups at a time, as a treat, in a tray feeder.

Fruit-Lovers' Leap

You'll have better luck gaining clientele at your fruit feeder if you set it among shrubs, near a bramble patch, or close to a hedge. That's because catbirds, thrashers, tanagers, thrushes, and other major fruit eaters are generally skulkers. They stick to the shrubbery, staying hidden within the leafy cover as they move about. Rarely do they spend much time out in the open. Once your intended guests learn to associate a tray or other feeder with their favored foods, they'll be more willing to make the leap across a scary stretch of open ground—your yard—to get to the goodies.

DO IT YOURSELF

String 'Em Up!

Got a bunch of loose grapes rolling around in your refrigerator? "Sew" them together with florist's wire to make a not-quite-natural bunch that is more appealing to birds than the loose fruit. You can find a spool of versatile florist's wire at any craft or discount store; it costs about $3 for what seems to be a lifetime supply!

Hang the bunch from a cup hook to attract the attention of any passing mockingbird, catbird, brown thrasher, or robin. Here's how:

MATERIALS

About 15–30 loose grapes, any kind or color (mixed colors are fine!)
Length of florist's wire, about 18" long
Screw-in cup hook

DIRECTIONS

Step 1. Attach the cup hook to any tree or post near your feeding station (if you prefer not to puncture a tree, you can instead loop the wire of your finished product around a branch).

Step 2. Don't worry about being all thumbs—there's no needle needed for this "sewing" job! Just poke one end of the wire through the center of each grape, as if you were stringing beads. Slide the fruit together with your fingers as you work.

Step 3. When you've threaded all of the grapes, snip off most of the extra wire and twist the two ends of the wire together. Loop the wire over the cup hook, and *presto!*—a funny-looking bunch of grapes that'll be devoured in no time!

Desperados

Desperate straits will inspire many a reluctant bird to venture to your feeder. That's why you'll want to make sure your own storehouse is well stocked with all the foods birds eat—you never know who'll show up in times of need!

Many fruit eaters leave town for the winter, but those that are left behind will be more apt to venture out and explore your offerings after a snow or ice storm, or in periods of extreme cold. Summer drought is another time that fruit-eating birds will be more willing to brave the feeder. When it's a choice between going hungry and seeing whether anything looks edible over there where all the other birds are hanging out, reticent fruit eaters are more likely to leave the hedgerow and visit the bird banquet.

FRUIT FLAVORS

Serving fruit at the feeder is different than "serving" fruit right on the tree. Fruit growers have to shoo birds from their bushes and trees, but feeder hosts know that birds can be fussy about digging into fruit at the feeder. If you want to lure birds to your feeder, use this guide to see which birds are most likely to be tempted, and which fruit may do the trick.

BIRD	FRUIT EATEN AT FEEDER	HOW TO PREPARE FRUIT
Black-headed grosbeak	Blackberries, blueberries, cherries, huckleberries, raspberries, strawberries	Fresh, frozen, or dried; mixed with sunflower seeds or in breads
Bluebirds	Apples, cherries, currants, grapes, raisins	Fresh, frozen, or dried; molded with fats or mixed into breads
Cardinal	All small berries, cherries, dates, grapes	Fresh or dried; alone or with seeds
Catbird	Apples, blackberries, blueberries cherries, currants, grapes, raisins; may also eat jelly	Fresh, frozen, or dried; alone, molded or mixed with fats, or in breads

(continued)

FRUIT FLAVORS, *continued*

BIRD	FRUIT EATEN AT FEEDER	HOW TO PREPARE FRUIT
Housefinch	Apricots, cherries, nectarines, peaches, plums; may also eat jelly	Fresh or dried; whole or chopped; alone or mixed with seeds
Mockingbird	Apples, blackberries, blueberries, cherries, figs, grapes, raisins; may also eat jelly	Fresh, frozen, or dried; alone or molded or mixed with fats or in breads
Orioles	All small berries, apricots, cherries, figs, grapes, oranges; fond of jelly	Oranges: fresh, alone or mixed with fats; all other fruits: fresh or dried; alone or mixed with fats
Robin	Apples, cherries, figs, grapes, raisins	Fresh, frozen, or dried; alone or mixed with fats or in breads
Sparrows, song and fox	Blueberries, cherries, grapes	Dried; chopped; mixed with seeds or mixed into breads
Tanagers	Bananas, blackberries, blueberries, cherries, grapes, oranges; fond of jelly	Oranges: fresh; alone or mixed with fats; all other fruits: fresh or dried; alone or mixed with fats
Thrashers	Blackberries, blueberries, cherries, figs, grapes, raisins; may also eat jelly	Frozen or dried; molded or mixed with fats or in breads
Titmice	Blueberries, cherries	Dried; chopped; molded with fats
Towhees	Blueberries, strawberries; may also eat jelly	Fresh, frozen, or dried; alone or mixed with seeds
Woodpeckers	Apples, bananas, blackberries, cherries, grapes, pears, raisins; fond of jelly	Apples and grapes: fresh or dried; other fruits: frozen or dried; molded with fats or mixed with sunflower seeds
Wrens	Apples, dried fruit, raisins	Apples: fresh or dried; alone or molded with fats; other dried fruits: chopped and molded with fats or mixed into breads

CHAPTER 7

Do-Si-Dough

Feeding birds sure was simple in the good old days. Toss a few crusts out the door in winter, and you'd see soon see red cardinals flashing against the snow. Shake out the crumbs from your tablecloth, and sparrows and snowbirds would happily peck away.

Now that our feeders are loaded with the most tempting seeds and other specialties, bread has dropped much lower on the list. Yet, despite all of the temptations at my bird-supply shop, I still depend on bread—and on cereal, crackers, pancakes, muffins, and other grain-based goodies—to make life more interesting for me and my birds. Why? Because it's a great way to use up leftovers and clean out the pantry shelf, and it's fun to get creative and cook up new bird treats! In this chapter, you'll discover how to choose and use leftovers from the breadbox and the pantry.

Golden Grains

Hard kernels of wheat, oat groats, and other unadorned grains often go begging at the feeder, because these seeds play a distant second fiddle to higher-oil selections, such as black oil sunflower seeds or millet. Yet bread, crackers, and other grain-based items are eagerly eaten. What makes the difference? Presentation! Bread products are ready-to-eat meals, so birds that can't crack seeds, or birds that appreciate an opportunity when they see one, are quick to take advantage of these goodies. Let's dig in by taking a look at the biggest fans of bread—and find out how you can lure them in, or fend them off!

Soft-Food Specialists

Birds that fancy soft foods can be tricky to tempt to a feeder. Many of them are accustomed to foraging for their own menu of fruit and insects. At the feeder, they'll eat suet and fruit treats—but it's bread-based goodies that work best as the bribe! Bread is easy to spot as the birds roam around the neighborhood, and these treats satisfy the birds' natural eating habit of grab-and-swallow.

Point of Pride

If bluebirds were as easy to entice as starlings, we'd lose all our bragging rights to these special birds. We treasure them not only because they're pretty and interesting, but because WE feel special when they grace our feeder! Bread-based treats will help make your feeder a hit parade of special birds.

When you serve goodies that suit their appetites, the dramatic long-tailed brown thrasher, the quiet gray catbird, or the cheery Carolina wren (all birds that

eat mainly soft foods) may check out your offerings every day. If you live in bluebird country, you may garner the attention of these treasured soft-food eaters, too. It's a great payoff for a handful of leftovers! 🐦

Dainty Habits

Good manners will get you an invitation to return to dinner at my house—or at my feeder. My favorite guests are those that don't hog the table; if they're colorful or charming besides, that's a bonus! Some bread eaters are well-mannered diners who visit feeders in small numbers to nibble daintily at their daily bread—or daily doughnut, cereal, or crackers. Add some bread-based foods to your menu, and you may also play host to these well-mannered guests:

✔ Black-headed grosbeak	✔ Chickadees
✔ Bluebirds	✔ Orioles
✔ Brown thrasher	✔ Robin
✔ Carolina wren	✔ Tanagers
✔ Catbird	✔ Titmice

Maniac Mockingbirds

Soft foods are favored by the elegant, long-tailed mockingbird, and that can cause a major problem. What harm can a single bird do at the feeder? Plenty, if he's a pit bull in disguise! The mockingbird is a ferocious defender of his food,

JERRY
TO THE RESCUE

Q. **Why do blackbirds always show up at my feeder in flocks? Every time I put out bread, I see lots of them, and often different kinds in the same group.**

A. Welcome to the land of the galloping gourmets, or should I say gourmands. Blackbirds aren't seeking extra-special food—they just want a lot of anything edible! I get masses of "black birds," too: the usual mix of starlings, grackles, cowbirds, and true blackbirds, depending on the season. All of them hang around in flocks except when they're raising babies—and sometimes even then, when they nest close together in colonies.

These ultra-common birds are constantly on the lookout for food, wherever they can find it. And because there's a lot of them and a lot of competition for every bite, they need to grab fast to get their share. Bread and bread-based treats are high on their list of favorite foods. Unless you serve such foods in feeders that are meant to keep them out, they'll be first in line and probably will stick around until every crumb is gone.

MOCKINGBIRD

and once this bird discovers a feeder stocked with his favorites, he'll vigorously chase away any other birds that dare to come near. When he's not eating, he'll perch nearby, guarding the feeder against all comers. The solution? Simple! Just add another tray feeder stocked with the mocker's favorite breads and other foods, far from your regular setup, to keep him away from the action. 🐦

Sneaky Treats for Nut Eaters

Nuts and fats are huge hits at the feeder, especially with chickadees, titmice, nuthatches, and woodpeckers. Bread? No thanks, say these birds, we'll just have some more of this great nutty suet mix!

Heh-heh—little do they know that I've used bread (or cereal or crackers) as the base of that penny-pinching suet mix (see page 184). My sneaky recipes, combining baked goods with chopped suet, peanut butter, and a handful of nuts, hold great appeal for birds that otherwise show little appetite for bread. The bread isn't the main draw for these birds—but it sure makes the treats go a lot further. And when I use up leftovers that have gone stale, it doesn't cost me a penny! 🐦

Full House at the Feeders

You'll go through a lot more bread-based treats in winter than in other seasons, because more birds will sample the stuff at that time of year. Natural foods are scarce, and birds are hungry, so your feeders will be bustling. During the cold season, you're likely to see cardinals, juncos, song sparrows, and other seed-eaters snatching a bite of bread or pecking at cracker crumbs. When harsh weather drives unusual birds to your welcoming spread, your treats might also attract meadowlarks, bobwhites, or red-winged or yellow-headed blackbirds.

Weeding Out Unwanteds

Abundant soft food will attract the attention of opportunistic birds, such as starlings and grackles, no matter where you serve it. If you prefer not to feed hordes of large, hungry birds, the only solution is to keep your soft foods in inaccessible feeders, where these birds will be unable to find a place to perch. If less desirable birds are particularly pushy at your feeding station, you may want to invest in a feeder with an outer cage of vertical bars: It will block starlings and other bigger birds from the food, while allowing small birds to get their share. Keep in mind, though, that this approach also prevents thrashers, catbirds, and maybe even bluebirds from sampling your soft-food treats. 🐦

Come One, Come All

I get a kick out of watching the free-for-alls of the starlings, grackles, and other frenzied flockers, so I keep a stock of stale bread on hand just for them. Plain bread, especially white or light-colored varieties, will catch their eye in a hurry. Rip it into pieces, toss it on the ground, and let the show begin! 🐦

THE STAFF OF LIFE

Cover your ears, Atkins® diet fans—it's carbohydrates that cause birds to crave bread! Although carbs aren't as high-calorie as fats, they're valuable nutrition and eagerly eaten by many birds, especially during winter. Doughnuts, muffins, and other bread-based treats also supply favored fats, and may include a bonus of nuts or fruits.

Nearly any kind of grain-based product, from cookies to pizza crusts, will have its takers. But my birds may not have the same standards as yours. If you're new to bread-feeding, try an assortment until you find the most popular product for your particular songsters. In this section, I'll share some of the favorites from my feeder, and pass along the tricks I've learned to make the offerings more tempting.

Here's a Corny One!

It's no joke: Cornbread, corn muffins, corn fritters, crumbled taco chips, and old reliable cornflakes are always a huge hit at my feeding station. Delightful wrens, catbirds, chickadees, red-

Mares Eat Oats

BIRD BITS

And so do birds! Oat kernels (a.k.a. groats) and raw oatmeal aren't favored by most birds, but cooked oatmeal is a surprise hit at my feeder. I've adopted Grandma Putt's habit of emptying the lump of leftovers from the oatmeal pot directly into the feeding tray, whenever I cook a batch from scratch. And if there's a spoonful or two left in the bottom of a bowl of the instant variety, I grab that for my feeder friends, too. Sparrows and juncos often nab a nibble, and so does my Carolina wren. Blackbirds and starlings love the stuff, too.

Uncooked oatmeal and oat-based cereals are devoured fast, too, but only if you mix them with suet or other fats. Add some chopped, dried fruit to the mix, mold it into blocks or balls, and bluebirds, robins, mockingbirds, and Carolina wrens will be delighted! And don't forget the oatmeal cookies—they follow the same principle of adding fats and fruit to boost appeal, and are also popular with these birds, as well as with chickadees, juncos, and sparrows.

bellied and red-headed woodpeckers, sparrows, juncos, and bluebirds eagerly peck away at anything with corn. Combine corn-based items with suet or fruit, and they're even more popular with special birds, such as thrashers or bluebirds. Blackbirds are big fans of corn products, too—so you'd better keep that scarecrow handy! 🐦

Wheat Workshop

Wheat kernels aren't a favorite at most feeders, because seed-eating birds seek out higher-fat selections. But wheat-based products are a bonanza for bread-eating birds. Here's how to use them at your feeder:

◆ Scatter pieces of highly noticeable white bread to catch the eye of robins, grackles, and other soft-food eaters.

◆ Crumble wheat crackers to serve juncos, sparrows, and other small seed-eating birds.

◆ Put a whole, unsliced loaf of stale wheat bread on the ground, away from feeders, to draw the trade of starlings, grackles, and other big-appetite birds.

◆ Thread chunks of bagels or other firm breads onto a wire for chickadees, the Carolina wren, or titmice to tug at.

◆ Tear whole-grain bread into pieces and drizzle with peanut oil to make an energy-boosting treat for thrashers, catbirds, and mockingbirds during the cold season.

◆ Spread a pizza crust or bagel with peanut butter or suet, and hang it up for a "feeder" that birds can eat! 🐦

From Breadbox to Bird Feeder

When I'm looking for possibilities to add to the feeder, the first place I investigate is my breadbox (or my counter, which often holds the overflow). I can usually dig up a few slices of sandwich bread, maybe a stale doughnut, and sometimes a real prize, such as a rock-hard bagel way back in the corner! All of those baked goods make prime fare for birds. In this section, you'll learn how to figure out which of your own "found objects" are fit for birds. Let's start by taking a closer look at the most likely option in that breadbox—bread!

Any Flavor Fits

Birds flock to bread for its food value, not its flavor. The biggest bread consumers, including blackbirds, grackles, starlings, and house sparrows, will devour any variety of bread you have on hand. But don't take my word for it—try your own taste test! Tear up a slice of two or more kinds of bread, and you'll see that white, wheat, rye, and even fancy, seven-grain artisan bread all have takers. 🐦

GRACKLE

Hold the Mold!

A patch of green or grayish mold on bread is no more enticing to birds than it is to you. Brushing off the mold won't fix the situation, unfortunately, because molds may extend much deeper into the bread, affecting the flavor and possibly the nutrition. As long as other foods are available, birds will let moldy bread sit untouched. So don't waste your time trying to salvage moldy bread—toss it in the trash or compost bin. 🐦

COME 'N' GET IT!

Dressed-Up Bread

Let the leftovers in your breadbox, or the bargains on the day-old rack, be the inspiration for your bird treats. Five minutes of prep time, and you're set for hours of frantic feeder antics. Try these treats, and then invent your own!

Bluebird Bounty Hunter

Bring in those blue-feathered rascals with this fruity bread treat, spiked with cherries to lure them into range.

4 to 6 slices of bread, any kind
1 cup of chopped suet or fat scraps
1/4 cup of peanut butter
1/2 cup of dried cherries

Use a food processor or knife to chop the bread into small morsels or large crumbs. Combine with the chopped suet or fat scraps and the peanut butter. Add the dried cherries. Mold into balls or blocks for serving, or break into chunks in a tray feeder.

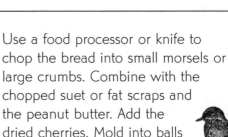

Chickadee Country

Fill a wire suet cage with this suet-stretching chickadee delight.

2 muffins, any kind
1 cup of suet or fat scraps, chopped
1/4 cup of extra-chunky peanut butter

Crumble the muffins or chop them with a knife. Stir in the chopped suet or fat scraps and the peanut butter. Mold into balls or blocks, and serve in a wire suet cage.

Woodpecker Welcome

Delight your downy woodpecker and his larger cousins with this nutty, corny mix. Chickadees, titmice, and nuthatches will approve, too!

1 loaf of bread, any kind
2 cups of chopped suet or fat scraps
1 cup of cracked corn
1/2 cup of walnuts, chopped

Tear the bread into pieces in a large bowl. Add the suet or fat scraps, the cracked corn, and the walnuts. Mix and mold firmly with your hands to fill two wire suet cages.

Hooked on Bagels

Sturdy bagels make perfect hanging feeders, accessible to chickadees, titmice, Carolina wrens, and other clinging birds. Give the bread some added nutrition with oil-rich extras.

2 bagel halves
1 commercial block of pure suet
1/2 cup of chopped walnuts
1/4 cup of sunflower chips
      (hulled seeds)
2 short lengths of string or wire

Spread the suet on the cut side of each bagel half. Sprinkle the walnuts and sunflower chips on top, and press them into the suet with the back of a tablespoon. Hang the bagels from loops of string or wire attached to a hook.

Songsters' Surprise

Here's a simple solution to use up leftover bacon fat from breakfast. Try it on a nippy spring day to attract songbirds such as robins, orioles, tanagers, catbirds, Carolina wrens, or mockingbirds.

4 to 6 slices of stale white bread
1/2 cup of bacon drippings,
      peanut oil, or melted suet
1/2 cup of grapes, coarsely chopped

Coarsely chop the bread. Put it in a large bowl and toss, as you would a salad, with the bacon drippings, peanut oil, or melted suet and the chopped grapes. Serve in small amounts in a tray feeder. Freeze the extras in a zip-top plastic freezer bag.

Mini Sandwich Squares

Ready for a quick lunch? Share this one with your chickadees, catbirds, and mockingbirds!

1 slice multigrain or
      sunflower-seed bread
2 tbsp. of creamy peanut butter
1/4 cup raisins, chopped

Spread the peanut butter on the bread, and sprinkle the raisins on top. Use the back of a spoon to push the raisins into place. Cut into bite-sized squares, and serve in an open tray feeder.

Hard As a Rock?

Unlike moldy crusts, stale bread is a story with a happy ending. No matter how hard the bread or muffin or other baked good is, birds will still make use of it. Their beaks are built for pecking, so stale bread isn't an obstacle. I use my food processor

DO IT YOURSELF

Vertical Breadboard

Try this quick project to make a serviceable feeder for your stale sandwich rolls. Getting the bread off the ground keeps your feeding station looking tidier, because it can take days of effort before birds manage to polish off every crumb from a roll that's hard as a rock. All you need is a scrap of board and a few great big nails.

MATERIALS

1 piece of 2x4 or 2x6
    wood board, about
    6" long
2 extra-large nails
1 nail for mounting

DIRECTIONS

Step 1. Hammer one of the extra-large nails entirely through the board, about 3 inches from the top, so that

the head of the nail is flush with the wood.

Step 2. Turn the board over so you are working on the side of the board with the nail point protruding. Being careful of the exposed nail point, hammer the other large nail into the board about 2 inches below and 2 inches to the left of the first nail. Drive it in only

far enough to anchor it solidly. Stop before the point protrudes through the other side. You've just made a nifty perch.

Step 3. Nail the board to a post with the mounting nail.

Step 4. Push a stale roll or other large chunk of firm-textured bread onto the exposed point of the top nail, until the roll is snug against the board. Don't worry if the nail tip extends a bit from the bread; birds will avoid it or use it as a mini-perch.

That's all there's to it. This simple breadboard will serve chickadees, wrens, titmice, and other bread eaters. You can also use it to secure half of an apple, a doughnut, or a suetty treat ball.

to break up chunks of stale bread into smaller pieces and crumbs, or I simply crumble stale muffins or other easy-to-squeeze bread products directly into the feeder. Stale breads also make an acceptable base for added-attraction recipes, such as those you'll find throughout this chapter. 🐦

Bargain Bread

I sometimes get carried away when I'm shopping at the day-old bakery store. After all, who can resist such bargains! Then, when I start to unload my bags of three-for-$1 loaves, I realize that, uh-oh, I now have several months' supply of bird bread on hand. That's because the visitors to my busy feeders eat only a few slices of plain bread a day, even in winter. No problem! Extra loaves just go in the freezer. 🐦

Day-Old du Jour

I could hang out the welcome sign to starlings by tossing my extra bread on the ground, but it's more fun to transform my loaves of plain bargain bread into my "Jerry Treat *du Jour*"! Here are the guidelines I use to inspire my concoctions:

Add fats. To increase the appeal to robins, tanagers, thrashers, wrens, and robins, combine bread with any of their favored fats. Chop, crumble, or tear the bread into pieces, then mix with any bird-favored fat, such as suet or fat scraps, peanut butter, or lard.

Add fruit and fats. Bluebirds, robins, thrashers, mockingbirds, and catbirds are big fans of fruit and fats, and bread works well as a binder to hold these ingredients together and supply additional nutrition.

LECONTE
THRASHER

Add nuts and fats. Earn the attention of chickadees, titmice, nuthatches, jays, and some woodpeckers with nutty treats. It's easy—just add any kind of shelled, unsalted nuts to a basic bread-and-fat foundation.

Add cracked corn and fats. Woodpeckers and flickers find this

JERRY
TO THE RESCUE

Q. Isn't feeding bread and cake to birds bad for their health? I thought they weren't supposed to eat sugar or salt.

A. There's no need to worry about dietary restrictions when feeding bread, because these foods aren't the staple of any bird's diet. They'll get plenty of more nutritious items to balance any of the things they grab a bite of at our feeders. The sugar in breads, cakes, or muffins isn't "bad" for birds: It just adds more carbohydrates to fuel their daily activities. And there's not enough salt in any of these foods to cause repercussions.

But there is one ingredient to beware of when feeding birds: chocolate. Substances in chocolate (methylxanthine alkaloids in the form of theobromine and caffeine, to be exact) can actually cause harm to animals by constricting blood vessels and overstimulating the heart, which is why candy's a no-no for dogs and cats. There's not much research into how it affects birds, but I play it safe and let them live without it. Besides, there's rarely a piece of chocolate anything in the Baker household that lasts long enough to make it out to the birdfeeder!

combo appealing; add nuts, too, and you may also draw chickadees, titmice, or nuthatches.

Add oils. This is a super-quick trick to add important fat calories for bread-eating birds in winter. Break the bread into bite-sized chunks, then drizzle with peanut oil or corn oil, and toss to coat well.

Dollars to Doughnuts

No need to bet the ranch on this one, pardners, because doughnuts are a winning hand every time! We're not the only ones flocking to Krispy Kreme®, it seems: Those greasy globs of fried dough are just as popular with the feathered tribe. Chickadees, especially, adore doughnuts. But titmice, nuthatches, downy woodpeckers, and, naturally, starlings will also gobble up your doughnut delicacies, unless you take measures to head them off, such as using a hanging feeder or a feeder with bars.

Don't Blame the Birds!

Keep in mind that avian doughnut-eaters eat like birds. No need to buy doughnuts by the dozen, unless you need an excuse to have extras for yourself! A single ring will serve 'em nicely, for several days or more. Plain cake doughnuts are my first choice, because they don't make a mess with sticky glaze or filling. But I also offer any variety of doughnut left in the box, as long as it's not chocolate. Peanut-coated doughnuts are a huge hit with nuthatches, and jelly doughnuts may attract a curious oriole.

Let Them Eat Cake!

Leftover birthday cake (no chocolate, please; it may be hazardous to birds' health—see "Jerry to the Rescue," opposite), coffeecake, sticky buns, and other sweet treats are beloved by the bread eaters with the heartiest appetites: starlings, grackles, and blackbirds. I pile them in the starling trough, er, I mean, feeder, which is located some distance away from my "regular" feeders.

When snow blankets the ground and feeder traffic is at its peak, I often toss sweet-bread leftovers directly on the ground, where any birds so inclined can peck away at will. I've noticed that juncos, song sparrows, white-throated sparrows, and other small birds will scour the area to pick up leftover crumbs.

Pantry Possibilities

Baked goods, as you've seen, are popular with soft-food eaters. But boxed and bagged goods, like those cereals or taco chips on your pantry shelf, have even more possibilities. In this section, you'll learn which boxed or bagged products work best as bird food, and how to make them more enticing to birds.

Singing the Praises of Cereal

Unsweetened cereal flakes are one of my favorite ingredients for bird treats. I mix them with suet, drizzle them with melted fat, and even serve

Stick to the Healthy Stuff

Battling the deluge of advertising for kids' cereals is frustrating for parents who want to avoid the artificial or the sugar-saturated. Birds seem to have more sense about this subject than most kids, because cereals that are more candylike than grainlike get few takers at the feeder. Marshmallow nuggets, sugary-sweet puffs of mostly air, and chocolate flavoring usually go to waste until starlings show up, and in the case of real chocolate, may even be harmful to their health (see "Jerry to the Rescue," on page 188). If these sugary "junk" cereals were around in Grandma Putt's day, I know she'd wag her finger and say, "Stay away!" So do what Grandma Putt would have done, and stick to "healthful" cereals based on grains, with or without nuts and fruits—your birds will be more likely to clean up every bite.

them as is when feeder traffic is heavy. Sparrows and juncos seem to be especially fond of them, but some of my cardinals enjoy their morning cornflakes just as much as I do! Lots of other cereals have bird potential, too, so I use just about anything that I can find sitting on my shelf. ✑

Premium Pays Off

Cereals are getting a lot more interesting these days, with dried cranberries, blueberries, pecans, or other extras spicing up the standard flakes and nuggets. You'll pay more for these premium cereals, but the added appeal to human palates translates to better bird food, too. You can sprinkle these high-class cereals straight from the box, which is a great solution when snow is on the way, the seed supply is looking slim, and birds are thick at the feeder. But I also like to make them stretch a little further by using fruit-and-nut cereals as the basis for some of my favorite recipes. Either way, they're a hit with birds! ✑

Cracker Crumbs

Oh, those irritating cracker crumbs! You'd think I'd learn not to snack in bed. Or maybe I should just shake out my sheets into the feeder, because birds adore these tiny bits of grainy goodness. Whenever I find a box of crackers with just a few left in the bottom, I crumble them into a corner of the seed tray. Cardinals, chickadees, juncos, and other seed-eaters crunch up both coarse and fine crumbs. Don't go overboard with crackers: Except in times of dire need, such as snowstorms, it's best to serve just a scant handful, to make sure they don't go to waste.

Experiment with any crackers you have on hand, except for saltines and oyster crackers. These bland crackers aren't big favorites with birds, and they'll usually go uneaten. ✒

Care for a Cookie?

Sure, especially if it's chock-full of raisins, dates, or nuts! Cookies make fast and easy bird treats, because they have the grains, the fat, and the little extras that add appeal. Avoid those with chocolate, but feel free to try any others that you can spare! Coarsely crumble the cookie if you want small birds to get a bite; otherwise, starlings or other large birds are apt to grab it and run. I also serve cookies in a hanging wire suet cage for chickadees, titmice, and other clinging birds to peck at. ✒

COME 'N' GET IT!

Crumbled Concoctions

A handful of crumbles is intriguing, not intimidating, to feeder birds. If you're just beginning to attract the attention of soft-food eaters, try a small serving of any of these treats to win their loyalty. If you already have a daily crowd of robins, wrens, bluebirds, or other customers, offer these recipes in whatever quantity your birds can quickly polish off. Keep in mind that starlings, blackbirds, and other big eaters love all of these concoctions, too.

Tanager Temptations

Here's a winning recipe that'll have tanagers coming back for more.

2 corn muffins
1 cup of suet or fat scraps, chopped

Crumble the corn muffins into the chopped suet or fat scraps. Mix gently but thoroughly with your hands, until the mixture holds together loosely. Crumble a small amount of the mix into a tray feeder. Bluebirds may also indulge!

Code Blue(bird) Emergency!

Getting caught short of bluebird food is a common problem, so don't waste time feeling guilty when a group of these lovely songbirds shows up in your yard, ready to eat. Just grab those stale corn chips from the shelf, and try my emergency recipe!

Crush the corn chips (an easy way to accomplish this is to pour them into a large zip-top bag and step on them!). Stir the crushed chips and the flour together until well mixed, then mix in the peanut butter, using your hands to make a soft dough. Serve in a tray feeder, or directly on the snow. That should hold them until you can restock the suet!

2 cups of stale corn chips
    (any brand; the less salt, the better)
¹/₂ cup of all-purpose flour
1 cup of peanut butter
    (substitute suet, lard, or,
    as a last resort, Crisco®)

Date-Bran Bird Muffins

Calling all you bran fans! If you can spare a cup of your favorite cereal, you can make some mouth-watering muffins for your special friends. Try this homemade treat to attract a catbird, brown thrasher, Carolina wren, or mockingbird. Any left-over crumbs will be quickly cleaned up by house sparrows and juncos!

1 cup of all-purpose flour
1 cup of bran flakes
³/₄ cup of milk
¹/₂ cup of chopped dates
¹/₄ cup of granulated sugar
¹/₄ cup of raisins
¹/₄ cup of peanut oil
2¹/₂ teaspoons of baking powder
1 large egg

Combine all of the ingredients, and mix by hand until thoroughly blended (the batter will be lumpy). Spoon the batter into a muffin tin, filling each cup two-thirds full. Bake in a 375°F oven about 30 minutes, or until browned. Remove from the oven, cool, and crumble into large chunks (and crumbs) in a tray feeder. *Makes 1 dozen muffins.*

Way Better'n Worms

I get a kick out of feeding cookies to robins, maybe because cookies seem like such a big improvement over earthworms! Whatever the reason, robins, thrashers, and other fruit eaters seem to be especially fond of this recipe. Notice that the fruit is first plumped up in water.

1 1/2 **cups of raisins**
1 **cup of water**
1/2 **cup of chopped apples**
1/2 **cup of butter**
1 **cup of all-purpose flour**
1 **cup of quick-cooking oats**
3/4 **cup of chopped walnuts**
1 **teaspoon of baking soda**
2 **eggs**

Combine the raisins, water, and apples in a saucepan and bring to a boil over high heat. Then reduce the heat to medium and cook, uncovered, for 3 minutes. Remove from the heat, and stir in the butter. Set aside to cool. Meanwhile, measure the other ingredients into a large bowl. Stir in the fruit mixture until well blended. Drop by rounded spoonfuls onto a greased cookie sheet, and bake at 350°F for 8 to 10 minutes, until golden brown. Cool the cookies on the baking sheet for 5 minutes, then carefully lift off the cookies to a wire rack to cool completely Serve whole or crumbled, in a low tray feeder. *Makes 24 cookies.*

PB-Raisin Cookies

I first made these cookies for the birds, but they looked so delicious, I had to try a bite myself. Funny, but ever since, it seems I make them more often for the chickadees, robins, wrens, and, um, other cookie lovers!

2 1/2 **cups of raisins**
2 **cups of quick-cooking oats**
1 **cup of brown sugar**
1 **cup of whole-wheat flour**
1 **cup of margarine or butter, melted**
3/4 **cup of bran cereal**
1/2 **cup of peanut butter**
1 **teaspoon of baking soda**
2 **eggs**

Use nonstick cookie sheets, or line your cookie sheets with aluminum foil: Raisins get very sticky when baked. Combine all of the ingredients, and mix thoroughly. Drop the dough by tablespoonfuls onto the cookie sheets. Dip a fork into water and press to flatten each ball of dough to 1/2-inch thickness. Bake for 15 minutes at 350°F, or until the cookies are lightly browned.
Remove from the oven, and cool on a wire rack. Serve whole or crumbled, in a tray feeder. *Makes 24 cookies.*

Tanager Two-Step

Tanagers love suet. Combine it with cereal or cornmeal, and you have nutritious crumbles that will get gobbled up fast on a spring or fall morning. Don't be surprised if black-headed grosbeaks or woodpeckers show up for a sample, too.

1 cup of unsweetened cereal flakes, any kind
1 cup of suet or fat scraps, chopped

Use your hands to mix the cereal flakes and suet together, until it forms a dough that holds together loosely. Crumble a small amount of the dough into an open tray feeder to serve perching songbirds. Save some to sprinkle in a ground-level feeder to tickle the taste-buds of robins, sparrows, and juncos.

Down the Dusty Trail

Flour of any kind is just too difficult for birds to eat. Unless no other food is available, they'll ignore the dusty stuff in favor of bigger crumbs or seeds. But flour and finely ground meal still have a place in bird feeding: You can mix either of them with suet, fat scraps, or peanut butter to make crumbly, greasy goodies. Toss some chopped nuts or fruit into the mix, and that dust turns to pure gold! 🐦

BLACK-HEADED GROSBEAK

Countertop Crumb Saver

My kitchen counter seems to be a magnet for crumbs, and until I smartened up, all that potential bird food went to waste. Now I keep a clean container on the counter so that I can swipe all those bits of bagels, toast, and muffins straight into my wide-mouthed crumb catcher. Wash and dry a plastic cottage cheese, ricotta, or deli container and its lid, and you can have your own. I tape a picture of a bird right on top, so I won't forget what's in it! Just make sure to either use up the contents within a week or freeze them, or you'll have yourself a container of moldy bread. 🐦

HOME COOKING

A dinner party sounds like one of my worst nightmares, but cooking for birds? Now, THAT I can handle! This appreciative audience makes such a fuss over the least of my efforts that I tie on my chef's apron proudly. Read on to learn about quick-and-easy treats that you can cook up in a flash to feed a hungry crowd. You'll also find tips on storing those extras, so you can pull them out whenever hungry beaks beckon.

Flapjack Fandango

Saturday morning pancakes are simple to jazz up for the birds. Save a bit of batter from your own breakfast makings, and stir in any—or all!—of the following. You'll have a feast that's fit for all of your favorite soft-food eaters. Look for robins, bluebirds, thrashers, Carolina wrens, and catbirds to do the fandango when you ring the dinner bell with this treat!

- ✔ Canned corn, drained
- ✔ Chopped apples
- ✔ Chopped dates
- ✔ Currants
- ✔ Raisins

Hoecake Hoedown

Even I can't recall anyone cooking cornbread on the back of a hoe. I'll take my cast-iron skillet any day, though: That long-handled hoe is just too awkward to maneuver around the kitchen!

Since cornmeal is the basis of hoecake, you can expect to spot corn-loving birds, including woodpeckers, cardinals, and blackbirds, pecking away at the cake, right alongside the usual soft-food eaters. Bluebirds and juncos may sample it, too. To make a bona fide hoecake, slowly mix water into cornmeal until it forms a stiff, thick batter. Pat into a flattened cake, and fry in

JUNCO

hot bear grease (use corn oil if you haven't "kilt a b'ar" lately); turn to cook the other side. The dense, heavy cake is a good bird food for a cold winter day.

Don't Let This Out of the Box!

Shhh...don't tell anyone, but boxed mixes are my secret arsenal for bird bread. I keep a stock of the small boxes of inexpensive mixes, such as JIFFY, to use as the foundation of lots of bird-flavored breads. Check your grocer's shelves for cornbread, date-nut bread, and muffin mixes, which you can dress up (if you like) with extra fruit or nuts. Serve a crowd of big eaters with the entire batch, or dole them out for special visitors. Watch for sales, and you can stock up for as little as 25¢ a box.

Serve-It-Up Secrets

The birds with the biggest appetites for bread—starlings and the like— need no special invitation to chow down at the feeder. They're always on the lookout for food, so they'll be super-quick to try the first bite of anything you put out. Bluebirds, thrashers, robins, and other more reserved birds are another story: These feathered treasures can be tricky to coax to the feeder, no matter how closely your offerings are tailored to their tastes. Even feeder regulars, including chickadees and woodpeckers, may require you to employ a trick or two to win their acceptance of this new food. In this section, you'll learn how to lure in wary customers, and how to prevent wasting your generous goodies.

Make It Look Familiar

Menu offerings that don't resemble the "real" foods that birds are used to are likely to get snubbed at the feeder, or at least ignored until one brave soul tries a sample. Reduce the learning curve by making your bread-based treats look as much like other familiar foods as you can. The simplest way to do this is to crumble your bread-based treats so that nuts, suet, fruit, and other additions are more visible. Crumbled foods are also easier for the true soft-food eaters to dine upon, since they require no heavy-duty pecking.

Suet-Feeder Switcheroo

Many birds are accustomed to finding yummy edibles in wire cage feeders, so take advantage of their conditioning by serving your goodies in that simple device. I use mine to hold muffins, cornbread, cereal mixed with fat, and other treats that are solid enough to stay put in the wire cage. Downy woodpeckers, chickadees, titmice, and other suet fans will quickly check out the new food, and that buzz of activity will draw other birds, too.

Spring for Fats

Winter is prime time for feeding bread because there's usually a hungry crowd at the feeder, and it helps stretch those seeds and other staples. But nesting season is also prime time for soft foods. Parent birds of any species may visit your feeder to grab a bite of bread for their youngsters, and when the babies are out of the nest, your soft-food feeder may be their first stop. To boost the nutrition during the nesting months of May and June, bolster your bread offerings with suet; parent birds will find it even more appealing when you add that extra fat.

Not by Bread Alone

No matter how yummy your bread treats are, they're only a side dish for most feeder birds. Chickadees will still eat sunflower seeds, no matter how delectable a doughnut you hang up. Woodpeckers will still head for the suet or the nuts, even though your date-nut bread is delicious. Even starlings, one of the biggest fans of bread, will leave the loaf after a while, to see what else is available.

So limit your servings according to the appetites of your customers, especially if you're feeding bread directly on the ground. Leftovers that linger overnight can attract rodents, raccoons, and other feeder pests.

Stingy Servings

Put out only what birds can easily eat in an hour or less. Start with a single handful of crumbs or crusts, or a single muffin or doughnut, or a single wire cage stuffed with goodies, and see how long it takes the birds to polish it off. You can always put out more bread, crackers, or cereal when the feeder is bare, but it's no fun to scoop out soggy leavings from the seed tray, or to pick up unwanted leftovers from around the yard. ✍

✖ DO IT YOURSELF ✖

Insta-Roof!

If you don't mind the DIY look, and I don't, you can make a wire suet-cage roof yourself from a waxed cardboard milk or juice carton. It takes just minutes to add this rain-shedding instant roof to a cage full of bread-based treats.

MATERIALS

1/2-gallon waxed cardboard drink carton, washed
Pocketknife or box cutter
1 nail

DIRECTIONS

Step 1. Using a sharp pocketknife or box cutter, cut out one of the sides of the carton, removing it entirely. Set aside the carton for another project, or toss it in the recycling bin.

Step 2. Fold the cardboard piece in half, with the printed side inside and the plain side on the outside, so it will make a little tent over your wire cage feeder.

Step 3. Using the nail, poke a hole in the middle of the fold. Push the chain of the feeder through the hole.

Step 4. Carefully push the roof down the chain, until its peak is about an inch above the feeder. Recrease the fold if the roof has flattened out in the process. (The hole may enlarge as you slide the roof down the chain, so that the roof rests directly on the feeder; it'll still serve the purpose, even without a peak.)

Step 5. Fill and hang the feeder.

High and Dry

Birds are about as fond of soggy sandwiches as I am, and that means... not at all! Once bread products get wet, only a desperate bird will eat them. Bread products easily absorb moisture, so save your bread-based goodies for a sunny day, or a freezing cold one. And always keep your servings on the stingy side to prevent waste.

I use a roofed feeder for my moisture-sensitive treats—AFTER the birds have discovered the goodies. I make the first offering of any unfamiliar food in an open tray feeder, where it's easily visible to curious birds that may fly over. But once the catbird is coming back, or the bluebirds are showing up every spring, I move the treats to a roofed feeder to help keep the bread dry.

Out of Harm's Way

Adept at acrobatics, chickadees, titmice, and Carolina wrens appreciate having their bread served in a hanging feeder. With no place to perch, such a feeder will bar the big eaters. The simplest "feeder" of this style? Just hang a doughnut or other bread product from a loop of string or wire. A long nail driven into a vertical post or a hanging-basket hook makes a quick, practical hanging "feeder," too! Or you can fill a hanging wire suet cage with your baked goodies.

Roofed against Rain

Those feeder-makers are getting pretty darn smart! Seems like all my old DIY tricks are now available ready-made—and for a price so reasonable, it hardly seems worth the trouble of pulling out the tape measure anymore. One of my favorite store-bought innovations is the roofed suet cage. Suet and fat-based treats aren't ruined by rain, because, as we all know, grease and water don't mix. But

I like to use my suet feeder to serve up bread-based goodies, too, and that can turn into a soggy mess when showers appear. Look for a neat, wooden or metal-roofed suet feeder at your bird-supply store, or from the sources you'll find in the back of this book (see page 324).

COME 'N' GET IT!

Tailored to Taste

Baking from scratch lets you fill your freezer with a winter's worth of treats, so you'll have plenty of bread-based goodies on hand when they're needed most. Or you can whip up a batch of these easy bird breads whenever you're in the mood: Most take only about half an hour from start to finish. These recipes are great for young cooks, too, because mixing is greatly simplified when you're cooking for birds. You can just measure all of the ingredients into a big bowl, and combine everything at once. Keep in mind that, although you *could* eat any of these treats, you probably won't want to: They're low on sugar, they have no spices or salt, and they may be flat or funny-looking, to boot!

Blueberry Cornbread

This treat combines that high-appeal peanut flavor with high-energy cornmeal, and adds the crowning touch of blueberries. Gather round, fruit lovers—it's just for you!

1¼ **cups of milk**
1 **cup of cornmeal**
¾ **cup of all-purpose flour**
⅓ **cup of peanut oil**
¼ **cup of sugar**
1 **tablespoon of baking powder**
1 **large egg**
½ **cup of fresh, dried, or frozen blueberries**

Combine all of the ingredients except the blueberries, and stir to blend thoroughly. Grease an 8-inch-square baking pan. Pour the batter into the pan, and sprinkle the blueberries on top; don't worry if they sink. Bake for 20 to 25 minutes at 400°F, until a knife inserted in the center comes out clean. Cut into 2-inch squares, and serve in a tray feeder. Freeze any leftovers in a zip-top plastic freezer bag.

Corny Banana Bread

Wrangle the attention of wood-peckers, tanagers, and orioles with this cereal-based quick bread. Sparrows, juncos, and other small birds may grab a bite, too.

2 cups of cornflakes
1 1/4 cups of all-purpose flour
1 cup of bananas, mashed
1/2 cup of firmly packed brown sugar
1/3 cup of milk
1/4 cup of peanut oil
1 tablespoon of baking powder
1 egg

Combine all of the ingredients, stirring until they are mixed thoroughly. The batter will be lumpy. Spoon into a greased 8-inch-square pan, and bake at 375°F for about 25 minutes. Remove from the oven, cool, and serve in chunks in a tray feeder.

Applesauce-Nut Bread

Dense and moist, this quick bread is favored by the Carolina wren, catbird, and brown thrasher. The nuts increase the allure for chickadees, titmice, and jays.

2 cups of all-purpose flour
1 cup of applesauce
3/4 cup of sugar
1/2 cup of chopped pecans or walnuts
1/4 cup of peanut oil
3 tablespoons of milk
1 teaspoon of baking soda
1 teaspoon of baking powder
3 egg whites

Stir all of the ingredients together, until well blended. Spread the batter in a greased 8-inch-square pan. Bake at 350°F for about 30 minutes, or until a knife inserted in the center comes out clean. Freeze any leftovers in a zip-top plastic freezer bag.

BREWER'S
BLACKBIRD

The Incredible Hulk

You may think you're being generous, but parking a giant hunk of bread in your feeder is more likely to scare the birds away than to draw them in. The bread may be delicious and nutritious, but it looks awfully strange, so most native sparrows and other bread appreciators will give it a wide berth. You can solve the standoff by serving bread products in small pieces or generous-sized crumbs, until birds get used to the idea. 🐦

Bigger Is Better!

On the other hand, if you want to distract starlings, blackbirds, or other voracious eaters from your feeder, an "incredible hulk" size of bread is a prize they can't resist. While your smaller birds dine in peace, these big eaters will tug and quarrel over the hulking bread. It's a neat trick! 🐦

BEST OF THE BAKERY

Who would have guessed that a slice of stale bread could draw in so many birds? Use this table to explore the possibilities of your pantry products, but remember that most of these birds also eat other foods, and they may take just a few bites of your bread-based treats if something they like better is available at the feeder or in the wild. Also keep in mind that starlings will gladly eat any and all of these offerings. And, finally, consider that particular birds have particular tastes, and what's good for the goose at my feeder may not be good for the gander at yours!

BAKED GOOD(S)	BIRDS ATTRACTED	HOW TO SERVE	COMBINATION PLATE?
Bread, any kind	Blackbirds, cardinal, catbird, crows, grackles, house sparrows, jays, magpies, mockingbird, robin, starling, thrashers	Break into medium to large pieces and serve in tray feeder or, in dry weather, directly on ground	Spread or mix with suet or other fat; add nuts or fruit if desired (will then also appeal to bluebirds and Carolina wren)

BAKED GOOD(S)	BIRDS ATTRACTED	HOW TO SERVE	COMBINATION PLATE?
Bread, quick, with fruit	Carolina wren, catbird, juncos, meadowlarks, mockingbird, robin, tanagers, thrashers	Break into pieces and serve in tray feeder or, in dry weather, directly on ground	Serve as is
Bread, quick, with fruit and nuts	Carolina wren, catbird, chickadees, grackles, jays, juncos, meadow-larks, mockingbird, robin, sparrows, tanagers, thrashers, titmice, woodpeckers	Break into pieces and serve in tray feeder or, in dry weather, directly on ground	Serve as is
Bread, quick, with nuts	Blackbirds, catbird, chickadees, jays, juncos, mockingbird, sparrows, thrashers, titmice, woodpeckers	Break into pieces and serve in tray feeder or, in dry weather, directly on ground	Serve as is
Cereal, flakes	Blackbirds, chickadees, house sparrows, juncos, mockingbird, sparrows	Serve in tray feeder	Combine with suet, peanut butter, or other fat; add nuts or fruit if desired (will then also appeal to bluebirds, Carolina wren, catbird, and thrashers)
Cookies, any kind but chocolate	Carolina wren, catbird, chickadees, grackles, house sparrows, juncos, mockingbird, robin, sparrows, thrashers	Break into pieces and serve in tray feeder or, in dry weather, directly on ground	Serve as is
Corn chips	Blackbirds, cardinals, grackles, house sparrows, magpies, meadowlarks, juncos, sparrows, tanagers	Crush or crumble and serve in tray feeder	Combine with suet, peanut butter, or other fat (will then also appeal to blue birds, Carolina wren, catbird, and thrashers)

(continued)

BEST OF THE BAKERY, *continued*

. . . .

BAKED GOOD(S)	BIRDS ATTRACTED	HOW TO SERVE	COMBINATION PLATE?
Cornbread	Blackbirds, Carolina wren, catbird, juncos, magpies, meadowlarks, mocking-bird, robin, sparrows, tanagers, thrashers	Serve whole or broken into pieces in tray feeder or, in dry weather, directly on ground	Combine with suet, peanut butter, or other fat; add nuts or fruit if desired (will then also appeal to bluebirds)
Doughnuts, glazed or plain	Carolina wren, chickadees, titmice	Serve whole, in a hanging feeder	Serve as is
English muffins	Blackbirds, cardinal, catbird, crows, grackles, house sparrows, jays, magpies, mockingbird, robin, starling, thrashers	Break into medium to large pieces and serve in tray feeder or, in dry weather, directly on ground	Spread or mix with suet or other fat; add nuts or fruit if desired
Muffins, any kind but chocolate	Carolina wren, catbird, juncos, mockingbird, robin, sparrows, thrashers	Break into medium pieces and serve, crumbs and all, in tray feeder	Serve as is
Piecrust, baked	Nearly all feeder birds, except for buntings, goldfinches, housefinches, and siskins	Crumble into large pieces and serve in tray feeder or, in dry weather, directly on ground	Serve as is
Tortillas, corn	Blackbirds, cardinals, grackles, house sparrows, juncos, magpies, meadowlarks, sparrows, tanagers	Crush or crumble and serve in tray feeder	Combine with suet, peanut butter, or other fat (will then also appeal to bluebirds, Carolina wren, catbird, and thrashers)

CHAPTER 8

Extra Enticements

Ready for a radical idea in bird feeding? Hold on to your hat, because the next big wave, I'm firmly convinced, is bound to be bugs! It's a natural choice: Not all birds eat seeds, but nearly all birds eat insects. So offering bugs at the bird feeder will draw in more kinds of birds, including some beauties that would otherwise never stop by.

In this chapter, you'll learn all about the benefits of bug feeding, and exactly how to do it. You'll also discover some other unusual items to add to your feeder feast, such as salt and eggshells, to fulfill various birds' needs for minerals and other supplements. Think of these extra enticements as the trimmings on your standard menu: They'll bring you bonus birds, and keep them lingering longer! So let's get busy by taking a closer look into the bizarre-sounding idea of feeding bugs.

IRRESISTIBLE INSECTS

Bugs in the bird feeder? I know, I know, my first response was "Yuck!", too. But feeding insects isn't as way-out as it sounds. In fact, it's more like common sense! Bugs are the number one food choice of almost every bird out there; in the wild, a single bird eats hundreds of these critters every single day. Adding insects to your feeder menu is guaranteed to bring you more birds.

In this section, you'll learn which fabulous birds can be lured in by bugs, and why this food is so popular. Once you're salivating for spectacular birds, I'll tell you exactly which insects and insect foods are a sensible choice at the feeder, and where to get them. You'll also learn when and how to serve your buggy bird foods, and how to safely store them. But let's begin by meeting some of the bug-brained birds you can attract.

Beauty and the Bugs

THRUSH

Think about it: Most of us live within the range of more than 100 species of birds. But only a dozen or so regularly show up at the feeder. The rest prefer to get their own food naturally, which mostly means out of our sight. Insects are the top temptation for those birds that usually say "no thanks" to our nicest feeder foods. By juicing up your menu with a small serving of their natural choice, you may lure birds you didn't even know existed in your neighborhood. And what birds they'll be! You might host delightful vireos, wood warblers, thrushes, and flycatchers, not to mention such classy customers as scarlet tanagers, bluebirds, and rose-breasted grosbeaks. Flamboyant colors, fabulous songs—insect-loving birds provide these plus a whole new world of beauty. 🐦

Imagine the Possibilities

Want a quick peek at the birds your bugs may attract? Check a field guide of birds for your region. Turn to the "perching birds" section, and look at all the dozens of species you haven't ever seen at your feeder. Nearly all of them may be potential customers for your new handouts. Why, it's enough to make me get my glasses checked, just so I can spot 'em better! Here's just a small sampling of the birds that go buggy for bugs:

WOOD PEEWEES

- ✔ Black-and-white warbler
- ✔ Common yellowthroat
- ✔ Great crested flycatcher
- ✔ House wren
- ✔ Kingbirds
- ✔ Myrtle warbler
- ✔ Purple martin
- ✔ Say's phoebe
- ✔ Scissor-tailed flycatcher
- ✔ Summer tanager
- ✔ Varied thrush
- ✔ Veery
- ✔ Vermilion flycatcher
- ✔ White-eyed vireo
- ✔ Wood peewee
- ✔ Wood thrush

Here Today, Gone Tomorrow

What's an insect eater supposed do in winter, when bugs are mighty hard to find? Why, take a vacation down South, of course! Most of the birds that rely mainly on insects are migratory songbirds, and they'll depart as soon as the nip of fall is in the air. (When you depend on bugs to fill your belly, you can't get caught in a cold snap that might make your banquet disappear.) They'll be back again in spring, as soon as the weather warms up and bugs are on the move.

Outlook: Warm and Buggy

Migration periods in spring, and again in fall, are when your insect feeder will attract the most traffic. Birds on the move are looking for easy eats in those seasons, so keep the feeder well stocked from March to early May, and from August through September. Keep in mind, though, that insect foods are welcome year-round by feeder regulars, even when the big migration rush is over for a while.

**RUBY-CROWNED
KINGLET**

Itty-Bitty Insect Eaters

A pair of tiny birds may very well show up at your feeder, once you begin serving mealworms. Watch for chubby, fast-moving kinglets, and, in the West, equally peripatetic bushtits. Both are mainly gray, and they never seem to sit still for long. Kinglets pal around in small groups in winter, joining forces with chickadees, titmice, and nuthatches, while bushtits roam the neighborhoods in bigger flocks of 20 or more birds.

Don't Forget the Old Reliables!

All of your usual feeder guests are insect eaters, too, even though they seek mostly seeds at your station. Once you set out the new fare, you can expect to see chickadees, titmice, nuthatches, woodpeckers, and other regulars grabbing a morsel of insect food, too. They'll keep your insect feeder hopping in winter, when nearly all of the mainly insect-eating birds have departed for warmer climes.

Natural Nutrition

Why all the fuss about bugs? Birds find insects irresistible for a couple of big reasons: They're superb food items, and there's an awful lot of them to go around! Eating bugs is a great way for birds to get the nutrition they need, all wrapped up in a tasty little package. The insects that birds feed on are high in protein and fat, exactly what those little feathered balls of energy need to keep them active and healthy.

Hey, Haven't We Met?

Insects are a natural food, so they're almost instantly accepted when served in their recognizable state, even by birds that don't usually frequent the feeder. Use mealworms, waxworms, and other larvae to grab the attention of insect-eating birds; then, follow up with insect-enriched suet and spreads, such as those in "Come 'n' Get It," on the opposite page.

COME 'N' GET IT!

Bonzo Bug Spreads

Want more woodpeckers, bluebirds, tanagers, or chickadees? Sure you do! Try these insect-boosted blandishments to attract those birds, and many more, to your backyard feeders.

Housefly Hash

One of the simplest ways to supply insects to your birds is to mix dried bugs in with suet. This combo is high in protein and beneficial fat, and will have the birds coming back for more.

4 parts suet or fat scraps, melted
3 parts dehydrated *Musca domestica* (houseflies)
2 parts cracked corn
2 parts sunflower chips

Stir all of the ingredients together until well mixed, using a mixing bowl and spoon reserved specially for bird recipes. Set aside until the mix solidifies. Then scoop out chunks, and stuff them in a suet cage, drilled log, or other feeder.

"Fruity" Suet

Fruit fly infestations are awful—it seems like even after I chuck the fruit, they just keep coming! Maybe next time, I should just open the window and invite the birds in to give me a hand. Fruit flies make great bird food, but I buy mine from insect suppliers for this recipe. It's a boon to thrashers, orioles, tanagers, woodpeckers, and lots of other birds.

2 parts suet or fat scraps, melted
1 part cornmeal
1 part dried fruit flies

Stir all of the ingredients together until well mixed, using a mixing bowl and spoon reserved specially for bird recipes. Set aside until the mix partially solidifies but is still spreadable. Spread on a pinecone, corncob, or feeder post, or the corner of a feeder.

Fly This Way!

A hearty dose of flies is just what Dr. Jerry ordered to keep birds happy during early spring! Watch for orioles and other migrant songbirds to seek out this high-protein treat.

2 parts suet or fat scraps, melted
1 part dehydrated *Musca domestica*
   (houseflies)
1 part dried fruit flies

Stir all of the ingredients together until well mixed, using a mixing bowl and spoon reserved specially for bird recipes. Set aside until the mix solidifies. Cut into chunks, and serve in a tray feeder for perching birds, or in a hanging feeder for chickadees, bushtits, wrens, and other clinging birds.

Eeek! A Bug!

Now I know that some folks have a hard time handling insects, dead or alive, and that goes for bird food with insects, too. I find that a pair of disposable plastic gloves is a big psychological help. And when I think about all the good reasons there are for feeding bugs to my bird visitors, it's a lot easier to get over the "ick" factor. Insects are the coming thing in bird feeding—not because bugs are highly nutritious for birds, which they are, but because WE get major benefits! Here's why the notion makes so much sense:

More diversity. Wouldn't you like to see a speckled-belly hermit thrush or a great crested flycatcher grabbing a bite right beside your faithful sparrows? When you think about it that way, grubs don't look so bad!

Year-round delights. Feeder traffic drops off dramatically in summer, because even the tastiest seeds pale in comparison to the insects that are everywhere for the taking. Serve up a helping of juicy bugs at your feeder, and birds will regularly scout it out, even in the usually slow summer season.

Neighborhood competition. When there's more than one feeding station on the block, the birds you see are just as likely to grab their usual seeds and suet next door, and never cross the fence for your similar selection. But birds naturally forage over a wider area to find the most desirable foods, and a ready-to-eat banquet of insects is hard to beat.

Bluebirds, bluebirds, bluebirds! If you live near bluebird terri-tory, I give you my word, cowboy's honor, that insect foods will bring bluebirds to your door. They simply can't resist! And they're so fond of the food and such tame birds, to boot, that you can get up close and personal while they chow down. Just wait till they bring the babies!

Rustle Up Some Grubs

Feeding bugs to birds is a recent innovation in bird feeding, but it has gained a dedicated following in a short time. Bluebirds, purple martins, thrashers, woodpeckers, and other shy birds will quickly learn that yours is the place to go for good eats. And the insect that's most favored? Why, the mealworm, of course! High in protein and fat and readily available, mealworms are your secret weapon for having the most popular feeder on the block.

Meet the Mealworm

You fishermen and -women need no introduction to this grub, because mealworms have been an ultrapopular fishing bait for years. Mealworms are also the food of choice for reeling in birds—without the rod, of course!  Mealworms are the larvae form of the darkling beetle (*Tenebrio molitor*). The thin grubs are about half an inch to 1 inch long, and their color ranges from white to brown. The eastern bluebird is a huge fan of mealworms, and so are dozens of other kinds of birds. 🐦

Trading One Worm for Another

No one would have ever dreamed of feeding bugs to birds in years gone by. Fewer people had feeders, for one thing, and, more important, more yards had bugs. I remember noticing a Jenny wren looking very interested in our broccoli plants one day, when I was helping Grandma Putt with the weeding. Just as I was about to chase the bird away, she put her finger across her lips and pointed to the wren. That's when I saw that the tiny brown bird actually had a beakful of bright green caterpillars, the same "cabbageworms" I often spent an afternoon seeking and destroying!

Nowadays, I cover my own broccoli plants with a lightweight cover to keep the egg-laying cabbage butterflies away, but I make up for it by offering my wrens a daily helping of equally yummy mealworms at the feeder. I figure it's the least I can do to make up for all the missing bugs that have been sprayed into oblivion with pesticides. Even the organic kind, like highly popular *Bacillus thuringiensis (Bt)*, wipes out zillions of plump caterpillars across the country. Mealworms are one small way to fill the gap.

Start Small

The easiest way to give mealworms a try is to visit a bait shop. Buy a small amount, 50 or 100 mealworms, for starters. They're sold in small, tidy containers, just like those you get at the deli. Feed stores, pet shops, aquarium shops, and some bird-supply stores also sell mealworms in whatever quantity you prefer. They're also  widely available on the Internet, but usually in large quantities. Expect to pay about a penny or two per mealworm for quantities under 500, and about a penny apiece for larger quantities. If you're buying humongous amounts of mealworms (say, more than 5,000), shop around; prices vary considerably for large quantities.

Penny-Pinching Counts

Here's a funny thing I've noticed: Mealworms are a lot cheaper when they're sold as bait than as bird food! Also, on the Internet, I've noticed that companies that deal only in bird food, as opposed to those that exclusively sell insects, generally slap a significantly higher price tag on their wares. One online insect supplier, for example, offers

1,000 mealworms for $6.25, while a bird-supply website carries a sticker price of $14.95 for the same amount! Although the difference is minor when you're buying small quantities, those pennies add up fast when you're shopping for masses of mealworms. So be a bargain hunter and save. 🐦

WHITE-EYED VIREO

Temptation Island

U nless you have your own mealworm farm—and I'll tell you intrepid souls just how to do that, a little later on—you'll want to serve mealworms as a treat, not as a main dish. Offering them at an all-you-can-eat buffet can eat up your budget fast! Instead, designate a single feeder as the mealworm feeder so that birds learn to look there for their goodies. Keep the feeder somewhat apart from your regular seed and treat trays so that the grubs stay isolated and visible. That way, your discerning guests can eat without competition from the masses at the seed feeders. 🐦

Cold-Weather Munchies

Mealworms will be a hit with your birds any time of the year, but especially during one of those cold-weather spells in spring. It's not unusual to have unseasonably cold weather at least one time in March or April, and this can spell doom for some birds. Birds that feed only on insects, or get the majority of their nutrition from bugs, will have a hard time finding enough food. Here's where you can help! Keep a supply of mealworms ready, and the purple martins and bluebirds, back from migration, will thank you.

It's Just Food

S erving up a dish of grubs is a popular tactic on TV reality shows, because nearly all of us in modern society find them disgusting and repulsive. But in other countries, grubs are a desirable delicacy. It's all a matter of conditioning. And, really, it's not so hard to get over that initial hurdle once you set your mind to it. Get over the grossness factor if you possibly can, at least long enough to give grubs to your birds. Mealworms are the easiest way to attract unusual songbirds to your feeder setup. As soon as you see how much your feathered friends like mealworms, that dish of grubs will start to look like a dish of gold! 🐦

**CRESTED
FLYCATCHER**

Mealworm Stampede?

No need to get out the branding iron for your mealworms—these wiggly critters are going nowhere. Commercially available mealworm feeders are all designed to keep the mealworms where you, and the birds, want them. Homemade mealworm feeders can also be built with containment in mind. My favorite homemade mealworm feeder is the sawed-off bottom of a plastic 2-liter soda bottle. (See "Mmm—I See Grubs," below.) The smooth sides prevent the mealworms from escaping. Even if mealworms do somehow manage to get out of their confines, the birds will happily take care of the problem.

Tip for the squeamish: Roasted mealworms are super-simple to feed to birds, because they're dead. So you can serve them in any kind of feeder or container. 🐦

Mmm–I See Grubs!

Most insect eaters are not accustomed to finding bugs at a feeder, so they don't come looking. You'll have to draw the birds in, and the key is to allow the birds to see the insects. Make your first mealworm feeder a clear one, with sides at least 1½ inches high—such as my homemade soda-bottle device! Here's how to make one:

1. Using a sharp kitchen knife, slice the bottom off a plastic 2-liter soda bottle to form a wide cup about 2 inches deep.

2. Nail the feeder right through its bottom to a post about 3 feet high, in a highly visible area, without overhanging trees. Your feeder will be easy to spot by birds in your yard, as well as those just passing overhead. 🐦

Wanted, Dead or Alive!

If the thought of storing a container of live mealworms next to your salad dressing makes you squirm, you may want to give roasted mealworms a try. Birds also find these delectable, and you can serve them in any

kind of feeder because they won't be able to get away! Prices may be a bit higher than for the live variety, but the difference is generally negligible.

Same Time Tomorrow

Make it a routine to put out your mealworms at the same time every day. Birds will learn when this time is, and they will start waiting for you. When I began feeding mealworms, it only took two days before a male bluebird was perching on my fence, waiting for me to emerge with his new favorite food. Warning: Once you see how eagerly birds await their serving of mealworms, your budget for grubs is apt to expand!

How Many Mealworms?

That all depends! Start with a small amount (I'd say "a handful," but I can already hear the "Eww"s!), about a quarter cup (there, is that better?). Add more mealworms, or more mealworm feedings, as the traffic increases. If you have a lot of customers, you may want to offer a lot of mealworms, in more than one feeder. If you only have a few birds checking out the grubs, keep your servings small until traffic picks up. At my busy feeder, I put out about 100 to 200 mealworms, twice a day.

JERRY
TO THE RESCUE

Q. Does it matter what time of day I put out my mealworms? I've noticed that when I offer them in the afternoon, they often get no takers.

A. Ever hear about those early birds getting the worms? That's your cue! Backyard birds are up and at 'em bright and early. Birds are hungriest in the early morning, and you'll see the most activity until about two to three hours after sunrise. It's the best time to catch the eye of those mealworm-appreciating migrating birds, too, because that's when they'll be ranging through neighborhood shade trees and other greenery to find their daily breakfast, before they get on the road again. So, be an early bird yourself and get those (meal)worms out as early in the day as you can! Then, once the resident birds are used to finding them at your feeder, you can serve them at other times, too.

DO IT YOURSELF

Mealworm Ranch

Raising mealworms is a simple process. I use a plastic storage container, about shoebox-sized, for my "plantation." Make sure that whatever home you choose for your wormlets has a tight-fitting lid so that you don't find the residents of the ranch roaming over your own abode! You can buy a starter kit for about $20, with everything you need for a supply of these bird treats, or you can make your own setup. Here's how I did it:

MATERIALS

2 plastic shoebox- or sweater-sized storage containers with tight-fitting lids
Potatoes
Whole-wheat flour, cornmeal, or wheat bran (available at feed stores)
Small container of mealworms (about 50)

DIRECTIONS

Step 1. Pour about an inch of flour, cornmeal, or bran into one of the containers. This is your mealworms' "bedding," which they will live in and eat.

Step 2. Cut two or three slices from a potato, the long way, about $1/4$ inch thick. Set the slices on the bedding. These will supply moisture to the mealworms.

Step 3. Dump in the mealworms, and snap on the lid.

Step 4. Choose an accessible location for your ranch, with a temperature that doesn't fall below 45°F or rise above 85°F. You can set it outdoors, but make sure it's not exposed to direct sun. Your garage may be the perfect location.

Step 5. Open the lid and check on your ranch hands

(continued)

START WITH BEDDING AND POTATO SLICES

TRANSFER HALF OF THE BEETLES TO A NEW BOX

❌ Mealworm Ranch, continued

every few days; you'll need to replace the potato slices as they dry out. Add another $\frac{1}{4}$ to $\frac{1}{2}$ inch of bedding about every 10 days, or whenever you notice that the level has decreased.

Step 6. In a couple of weeks, the grubs will pupate, going into a resting stage as they begin the transformation to beetles.

Step 7. When beetles emerge, you're ready for the ranch "addition." Fill the second container with an inch of bedding, add three more potato slices, and transfer about half of the beetles to their new home.

Step 8. You now have two mealworm setups, each with adult beetles. Keep replacing the potato slices when they start to dry out, and add bedding as needed. The beetles will mate and lay eggs, and in a few weeks, they will die. Don't worry about removing the carcasses. Soon, tiny mealworms will be visible, having hatched from the eggs.

Step 9. Each female beetle can lay up to 500 eggs, so you're about to become a rancher rich in mealworms! Whenever you need some to stock your birdfeeders, simply remove mealworms from either container with a small net, such as the kind sold at aquarium-supply shops.

Step 10. Continue adding fresh bedding and potato slices as needed.

Mealworms go from egg to worm to beetle in only 12 weeks, so you may soon have more mealworms than you know what to do with (if 25 of the original 50 lay eggs, you may have more than 10,000 mealworms after just one cycle!). If you're feeling overwhelmed, open a bait shop, or give gift containers to your bird-feeding friends!

Just for Bluebirds

If your intention is to attract bluebirds with mealworms, you'll need to keep other birds from scarfing down the grubs. The best way I know of to keep out unwanted feathered guests is to invest in a bluebird feeder. This hopper-style roofed feeder has openings cut into the sides so that the bluebirds can enter to eat in peace. Chances are, your bluebirds will be the first ones to figure this out, although chickadees, nuthatches, and other birds that can fit through the holes may also give it a try. Place a small dish of mealworms on top of the feeder to get the bluebirds' attention at first, then move the mealworms inside the

feeder once the bluebirds know the location of their favorite treat. A woodpecker feeder, made from a long wooden box with access holes in the sides, is also an option. 🐦

Good Grubs

Other kinds of grubs, or beetle larvae, are also available online, at pet-supply stores, and at some bird-supply stores. Most common are wireworms and waxworms, roasted or live. All kinds of grubs are relished by birds, so you may want to give these a try if the price is right and you want to add a little variety to the menu. Serve them just as you would mealworms. 🐦

Store 'Em Away

You probably won't use all your mealworms in a week, or even in a month, depending on how many you bought or raised. To slow them down so they don't transform into adult beetles, keep the container in the fridge or in an unheated garage. In nature, these insects often overwinter as larvae, so they'll do just fine in cold storage for a while! 🐦

INSECT-ENRICHED TREATS

Treat your feeder regulars and gain new customers with foods that contain plenty of high-protein insects. You can buy several types commercially, or you can make your own. In this section, we'll take a look at these bird-favored foods, and find out when and how to serve them.

Open Wide for Flies

Now here's an occupation I never considered in my formative years: fly farmer! Luckily, some folks have taken up the trade, and they raise tons of houseflies and other insects for use in pet foods—or by savvy bird feeders! Check the shelves of pet- or bird-supply stores to find a selection of the most popular feeder insects, or look for the finished product. As bugs become big business at the bird feeder, they're becoming more widely available. One of my favorites is called "Wild Bird Magnet Food"; ask for it by name if you can't find it at your local shop, or look for it on the Internet. This spreadable concoction of flies, pecans, soybeans, and calcium is a big hit with lots of birds at my feeder, including woodpeckers, chickadees, titmice, and nuthatches. Sounds almost good enough to eat!

Bug-Boosted Suet

One of the easiest ways to feed bugs to your birds is to use an "insect-augmented" block of suet—suet that contains dried insects. When birds discover that the suet feeder holds an added treat, they'll be ecstatic! Suet with birdseed in it has been offered for a while now, but a few companies have started to sell suet that contains bugs. You can also make your own special blends. Check the pet store or online sources to find dried flies (often sold for reptile food), and use them in any suet recipe.

GREEN-TAILED TOWHEE

Mulch Madness

Let's face it, birds can be pretty messy sometimes, and it's not always a joy to see a mound of seed shells around your feeder area. But that messy conglomeration can be a boon, so don't be so quick to rake it away! Leave a few inches of the birds' discards on the ground, and sowbugs, beetles, centipedes, earwigs, and other savory insects will soon be burrowing among the mulch. Messy mulch gets a lot of attention in early spring, when feeder traffic is still high. Towhees, robins, sparrows, cardinals, and other birds spend quite a bit of their feeding time hopping about on the ground then, digging through the munchie-filled mulch to find juicy treasures. By early summer, when bugs are everywhere in abundance and the feeder has fewer customers, the mulch loses its appeal; that's when I tidy up.

Mineral Musts

Many feeder-keepers worry about their birds eating a balanced diet, because the birds seem to spend most of their time pecking at whatever we put out. Maybe we should add vitamin and mineral supplements to the feeding tray, like what we serve to our kids? I figure birds are smarter than us, though, because I often see them pushing away from the table to search out natural foods in my yard and garden. I do serve a few minerals "straight up," though, because some birds have a big appetite for them. In this section, I'll show you how you can coax in crossbills, purple finches, purple martins, and some other songsters with a smattering of mineral musts.

Old Salts

I'm forever preaching "Hold the salt," whether it's at the bird feeder or at the dining room table, so this suggestion definitely goes against my better nature. But a giant block of pure salt will certainly get the attention of certain birds, who apparently have never heard of high blood pressure. Natural salt licks were great gathering places for now-extinct passenger pigeons; their modern kin, the mourning dove and common city pigeon, are just as fond of the salty stuff, which they often glean along the sides of roads that have been salted in winter weather. Goldfinches, house finches, house sparrows, pine siskins, evening grosbeaks, and crossbills are also drawn to salt. 🐦

Separate Servings

Because many feeder birds don't need extra salt, it's not a good idea to pour the Morton's® directly into your feeder. Instead, set up a separate "salt lick," where you can set a block of salt for any birds that are inclined to take a taste. Keep in mind that a salt block will also attract deer and possibly other animals, so think twice if you live in an area that's plagued by deer. 🐦

Think Big

If you can carry it—it will weigh about 80 pounds!—pick up a block of salt at any feed store or horse-supply shop. Salt will kill any surrounding vegetation as it seeps into the soil after a rain, so don't set your block near any plants you want to keep. I kill two birds with one stone, so to speak, by keeping my salt block in an unused area of a gravel driveway: The birds can easily spot it, and the runoff destroys those pesky weeds that are always popping up in among the gravel!

RED CROSSBILL

Just Call It "Art"

Just to see who might come calling, I picked up a chunk of bricks-and-mortar at a local demolition site and set the piece at the base of a feeder, like a work of art. (See "Mortar Mania," at right, for the details on birds and bricks.) Sure enough, the house finches went to town on the stuff! Later that winter, I had the thrill of seeing my first crossbills, which were chowing down on that mineral-rich mortar. Seems the crumblier it is, the better they like it. If you're feeling a bit adventurous, try some edible art at your feeding station!

Clambake at the Old Corral

Save the clam or oyster shells from your next shellfish bake, or donate those souvenirs from the beach, and you can make calcium-hungry birds extra happy! You'll need to crush them first,

Grandma Putt's BIRD BITS

Mortar Mania

It's hard to believe that bird beaks could destroy a brick wall, but some folks can attest that it's true! Grandma Putt used to tell stories about flocks of "red" birds descending on a brick house in her town, and pecking it apart until the wall needed serious repair work. Here's how it happens: The mortar between the bricks is ambrosia to some birds, including crossbills (Grandma Putt's red birds), evening grosbeaks, pine siskins, and house finches, and they'll work away at every bit they can reach, until the wall needs help in a hurry. It's the calcium and other minerals in the mortar that the birds are after. And, when they discover a good pecking place, these flocking foragers will work away diligently for weeks. If their demolition derby goes unnoticed and the birds aren't shooed away, they may eat so much that the mortar needs repair.

**BARN
SWALLOW**

which isn't an easy task. I use my car to do the job. Just sweep a section of paving clean, place a shell or two in the tidy spot, and drive over it until it's pulverized.

You can also buy crushed oyster shells at many garden centers or farm-supply stores. Offer a handful at a time in a tray feeder set in an open area. You may see purple martins, barn swallows, or other birds stopping by for their calcium. This enticement is most effective in spring and summer. ✐

Eggshell Excitement

Purple martins have some of the staunchest fans around. Maybe it's because a colony of martins is a lot like an apartment house of people! They sun themselves on the porch, they chatter back and forth constantly, and they're great parents. If you're lucky enough to have a martin colony in your neighborhood, you can enjoy nurturing these birds at your feeding station. They may come for mealworms, which you can read all about earlier in this chapter, and you can also beckon them with crushed eggshells, which may also attract barn swallows and other birds.

Now I've heard some scary stories about the deadly salmonella disease being contracted from uncooked eggshells, so I take extra measures to help make my eggshells safe for my feathered friends. Here's how I do it:

1. Rinse the cracked, but not yet crushed, shells in cold water, then spread the wet shells on a paper plate (for microwaving) or cookie sheet (for the oven).

2. Zap on high for 2 minutes in the microwave. Or heat in a 200°F oven for about 10 minutes.

3. When the shells have cooled, crush them with your hands, and scatter them in an open tray feeder that has easy access to swooping swallows. ✐

INSECT EATERS' MENU

For every insect, there's a bird just waiting to nab it! Which bird eats which bug has more to do with where that bird lives than with the sophistication of its palate. Birds that live low to the ground, such as thrushes, eat insects that live near the ground, such as centipedes. In this table you'll see a sampling of insect eaters and their natural menu items, and find out what you can offer at the feeder to suit their tastes—and their eating styles.

BIRD	SAMPLING OF INSECTS EATEN	FEEDER SUBSTITUTES	SERVING SUGGESTION
Bluebirds	Caterpillars, crickets, grass-hoppers, katydids, millipedes, sowbugs	Mealworms or similar larvae; suet or peanut butter with insects	Bluebird mealworm feeder, open dish, or tray feeder
Flycatchers	Bees, butterflies, caterpillars, cicadas, crickets, flies, katydids, moths, wasps	Mealworms or similar larvae	Open dish or tray feeder
Kingbirds	Bees, butterflies, crickets, dragonflies, flies, grass-hoppers, moths, wasps	Mealworms or similar larvae	Open dish or tray feeder
Kinglets	Ants, aphids, beetles, caterpillars, flies, scale insects, small moths	Mealworms or similar larvae; suet with insects	Open dish, tray feeder, or hanging feeder for suet mixes
Meadowlarks	Ants, beetles, caterpillars, crickets, grasshoppers, spiders	Mealworms or similar larvae; suet with insects	Open dish or low tray feeder
Orioles	Ants, beetles, caterpillars, leafhoppers, scale insects, weevils	Mealworms or similar larvae; suet or peanut butter with insects	Open dish, tray feeder, or hanging feeder for suet or peanut butter mixes
Purple martin	Butterflies, dragonflies, flies, grasshoppers, moths, wasps	Mealworms or similar larvae	Open dish or tray feeder

(continued)

INSECT EATERS' MENU, *continued*

BIRD	SAMPLING OF INSECTS EATEN	FEEDER SUBSTITUTES	SERVING SUGGESTION
Tanagers	Aphids, bees, cicadas, caterpillars, dragonflies, wasps	Mealworms or similar larvae; suet or peanut butter with insects	Open dish or tray feeder
Thrushes	Ants, beetles, caterpillars, crickets, flies, sowbugs, wasps	Mealworms or similar larvae; suet with insects	Open dish or low tray feeder
Vireos	Beetles, butterflies, caterpillars, flies, moths, stink bugs, wasps	Mealworms or similar larvae	Open dish or tray feeder
Wood warblers	Butterflies, caterpillars, flies, small moths, small wasps, spiders	Mealworms or similar larvae; suet with insects	Open dish, tray feeder, or hanging feeder for suet mixes
Wrens	Aphids, beetles, caterpillars, small moths, weevils	Mealworms or similar larvae; suet or peanut butter with insects	Open dish, tray feeder, or hanging feeder for suet or peanut butter mixes

CHAPTER 9

The Old Watering Hole

I doubt I'd feel half as refreshed as I do in the morning if I didn't step into the shower first thing. Splashing water is a great pick-me-up. And, as for guzzling a glass—why, it's the first thing I reach for when I come inside on a hot summer day, or after shoveling a lot of snow.

Birds are as fond of water as we are, which is why I make sure water is at my feeding station. In this chapter, you'll find out why water can be an even bigger draw than feeder foods in some seasons and for some special birds, and you'll learn how to make those shy types feel at home. You'll discover ingenious ways to offer birds water, even on a balcony or deck, all year long. We'll also consider how to cater to the water needs of hummingbirds, who are pure delight at the bath.

Sip and Splash

Better-designed birdbaths bring better birds: It's that simple. In the pages to come, you'll discover why investing in a pricier model is well worth the extra bucks. Still, you can enjoy plenty of daily activity with a budget-priced bath, and I'll show you how to choose a good one, too. I'll also share some bright ideas for making your own for free. But let's begin by taking a look at the best.

Au Naturel

That's fancy French for "in a natural state." And what it means in bird terms is that the more your birdbath looks like the real thing, the more the birds will love it. Now, you could just keep a big puddle going, but that's harder than it sounds, since puddles have a way of drying up. Or you could build a stream with boulders and complicated piping. That's too much work for me, and, besides, I like results that are just about instant.

So I bit the bullet, and, for about $60, I bought one of the fancified new birdbaths. It's made of plastic, but it looks just like natural rocks, with several shallow pools. It even has a trickle of water running down one side. The results were amazing! Read on, and I'll tell you why I think this style is worth its weight in gold. 🐦

High-Class Clientele

Half an hour after setting up my premier natural-style bath one fine May day, I took a peek and was stunned to find a bright scarlet tanager splashing with abandon, a handful of evening grosbeaks crowding another shallow pool in the bath, and a white-throated sparrow taking dainty sips from the side. Whoopee! The next day, things got even more interesting. Now there were bluebirds taking their turn, with a wood thrush waiting nearby.

Why all the fuss by birds that had never graced my old pedestal-style birdbath? This style of birdbath hits all of the high points of their natural drinking habits. To learn what exactly those are, see "Sophisticated Simplicity," below. 🐦

WOOD THRUSH

Sophisticated Simplicity

Birds will drink from just about anything when they're thirsty, which may be why most birdbaths are made to look pretty, rather than suit the needs of the birds that use them. In recent years, the trend is shifting. When you shop for a birdbath, look for a candidate that covers these bird needs:

Ground level. Birds naturally seek water right at ground level. A molded bath that sits directly on the ground, or on a very low pedestal, will garner more customers than a higher style.

Places to perch. Molded faux rocks provide places to perch both beside the water and protruding from it, just like the natural stones in a stream.

Shallow water. Birds are vulnerable when they're in water. They'll stay away from anything that's uncomfortably deep. Make sure the bath is shallow, so they feel safe when using it. Two inches of water is good for larger species.

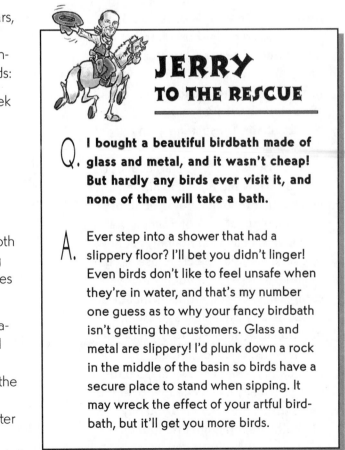

JERRY
TO THE RESCUE

Q. I bought a beautiful birdbath made of glass and metal, and it wasn't cheap! But hardly any birds ever visit it, and none of them will take a bath.

A. Ever step into a shower that had a slippery floor? I'll bet you didn't linger! Even birds don't like to feel unsafe when they're in water, and that's my number one guess as to why your fancy birdbath isn't getting the customers. Glass and metal are slippery! I'd plunk down a rock in the middle of the basin so birds have a secure place to stand when sipping. It may wreck the effect of your artful birdbath, but it'll get you more birds.

More than one pool. Smaller birds need shallower water than larger robins, jays, and the like. A bath that includes more than one water area allows you to have baths of different depths so that more kinds of birds will use it.

Rough surface. I feel insecure in a slippery shower stall, and so do birds. Look for a surface that's rough, so their feet can find solid ground when they're using the bath, or when they're perching.

Call of the Wild

You'll get more birds faster if they can hear your watering hole as well as see it. The trickling water in my new rig, which dribbles from an arched copper tube hooked up to my hose, is the clincher: It advertises the new bath to any bird within hearing distance. I'm convinced the sound of water is why my setup attracts so many unusual migrating birds. When they're traveling over a long haul, anything that helps them home in faster and not waste energy getting their needs met will catch their attention in a big way.

Please, Be a Drip!

Want to boost the drawing power of your current birdbath? Look for a "drip tube," or dripper, which you can find at bird-supply stores or online, to add

Grandma Putt's BIRD BITS

A Bath Worth Its Price

"You get what you pay for," Grandma Putt always told me, usually right after scolding me for spending my hard-earned pocket cash on some gadget or other that fell apart after a few uses. Eventually, frugality became my middle name, which is probably why I get a bad case of sticker shock just about every time I shop for a new birdbath. These items aren't exactly cheap!

The simplest models start at about $30, and they rapidly climb higher, until you reach the point where you're paying for a work of art, not a simple water saucer. I still have fun figuring out how to put household objects to use as supplemental sippers, but for my everyday setup, I now go for birdbaths that offer me bona fide value, just as Grandma Putt drummed into me. To overcome my natural reluctance to part with my cold, hard cash, I remind myself that a birdbath is actually much cheaper over the years than a feeder: Once you buy the birdbath, the refills are just about free!

that all-important sound of water to your setup. Drippers, which consist of an arched tube, a sturdy base to set in the bath, and a valve that reduces hose water pressure to a mere trickle, start at about $35, but I consider that a reasonable admission price for the entertainment of the extra birds it will draw. You'll need to attach a hose to supply the dripper. More expensive models (around $50) include a spray unit, which produces a fine mist that birds also adore. 🐦

Back to Basics

Pedestal birdbaths have been a fixture for longer than I've been around, and that's a long time indeed! Come to think of it, my old birdbath, a typical pedestal style, is a family heirloom—it's been used by at least two generations, and it's still going strong! Thanks to that long history of use, this style of birdbath is quickly accepted by many birds, because they recognize it as a source of water. Mine is used every day by robins, cardinals, house finches, and some sparrows. I've even seen a squirrel trying to climb the pedestal during a drought. 🐦

Down the Slippery Slope

Old-time pedestal birdbaths were commonly made of concrete, the perfect material from a bird's-eye view. It's a rough surface, ideal for making birds feel secure when they perch to take a sip, or when they step into the bath. Many newer models are made of other materials, and some have slick or shiny finishes. That makes them less appealing to birds, which strongly prefer a better grip. No need to toss that art glass birdbath into the trash, however: Just add a rock to the basin, to give birds a secure place to stand. Make sure the rock protrudes above the water line. 🐦

Simple Saucers

Ready to test your imagination? Cast a look around the house, garage, and yard, and you're likely to find several objects suitable for use as a birdbath or drinking station. Any kind of shallow, saucer-shaped object that holds water and won't tip when birds land on it is worth a try. Here are some of the ones I've tried with satisfying results:

- ✔ Clay or plastic saucers from flowerpots
- ✔ Frying pan that had lost its handle
- ✔ Soup or cereal bowls

- ✔ Glass or metal pie pans
- ✔ Salad plates
- ✔ Old hubcap

High Waters

One of the most important things I've learned in my years of feeding birds is that the location of the feeders or birdbaths depends on my convenience as well as theirs! That's why I like the many styles of deck birdbaths that are flooding the market in recent years. They're lightweight and easy to clamp onto the rail or the corner post. I use them mainly from fall through early spring, when they require less cleaning than in summer. My favorite model is a heated plastic one with an ingenious bracket that allows me to tilt the bath to empty it—look out below!—for easier cleaning and refills. You'll find deck-mount birdbaths at bird-supply shops, at home stores, and online. 🐦

Winter-Wise Storage

Plastic or resin birdbaths are so rugged and so simple to care for that it's all too easy to forget that they may need protection when cold weather comes. Some of these materials are made to withstand below-freezing temperatures; but others may chip, crack, or split if you leave them outside for the winter. Pottery or terra cotta birdbaths are likely to be susceptible to damage in severe cold, too. You may find information about winter care of your birdbath on the label (or in the fine print in the catalog that you ordered it from), but if you peeled that label off long ago, your best bet is to move the birdbath indoors for the cold season. Give it a thorough cleanup before you put it into storage, so it's all ready to go next spring.

WATER HABITS

Birds will become accustomed to finding water at your feeding station, so don't disappoint them. Keep your birdbath filled with fresh water, especially when times are tough. In this section, you'll learn when water is needed most, and how birds will make use of your supply.

Double Dipping

HOUSE WREN

Drinking from the bathtub? The sensibilities of birds must not be quite as delicate as mine! Maybe it's because they don't lather up when rinsing off the grime, or maybe they simply know that water is a prize commodity, and it makes sense not to waste it. Whatever the reason, you can expect to see plenty of birds quenching their thirst at the same water supply they use for taking a dip.

That double-dipping habit makes it easy for us bath-masters. You'll only need to provide one water source for both sipping and splashing. But I'll wager you won't stop with one, because double the birdbaths means double the fun! 🐦

Letting Loose

Watching backyard birds in the water is just as much fun as seeing them eat seeds, maybe even more so! Birds are all business when they're eating, but in the bath, they really kick loose. There's as much splashing and flapping as there is in a kiddie pool. And those wet heads look just plain comical, especially on the most regal of our friends. Once you've seen a cardinal in the bath, you'll have a whole new take on its personality. 🐦

Bath or Shower?

Birds revel in a bath, but, oh boy, wait'll you see them in the shower! I like to set up my lawn sprinkler, pull up a comfy outdoor chair, and watch the robins discover the spray. They puff and ruffle their feathers, and sometimes hold their heads up just like I do in a gentle rain. I've

DO IT YOURSELF

Pump It Up

Here's a beautiful way for birds to get a drink on your patio, and advertise your welcoming yard at the same time. All you need is a pretty pot, a small recirculating pump, and an electrical outlet. I like the simple and inexpensive dull-glazed Vietnamese pots you can find at any discount store or garden center; a large one costs $15 to $20.

MATERIALS

Glazed ceramic pot, at least 8" in diameter at the mouth

Tube of waterproof caulk or a wine cork, if your pot has a drainage hole

Small recirculating pump (check the water garden aisle at a home-supply store)

Water

DIRECTIONS

Step 1. If your pot has a drainage hole, fill it with the caulk, following the directions on the tube. You can also plug the hole with a cork pared to size; it may leak a bit until it swells to seal the hole.

Step 2. Set the pot in your selected location on the patio. Place the pump in the bottom of the pot. Attach the tubing supplied with it, so that the open end of the tube is about $3/4$ inch below the rim of the pot.

Step 3. Fill the pot with water to about $1/2$ inch below the rim, making sure the open tube end is under the water.

Step 4. Plug in the pump. It will create a gentle, but audible, burble. Back away, and watch for birds to perch on the rim and take a sip. Be sure to top off the pot every few days, as the water evaporates. Birds won't use this drinking hole if they have to bend too far to reach the water.

seen grosbeaks gather around a sprinkler, too, shuffling their wings and dipping their shoulders as though they're making sure every inch gets a good splashing.

Sprinkler showers are a boon for birds, but they waste water unless I'm tending plants at the same time. So I added misters to my repertoire, to even better effect. Read on to learn how to use these novel devices. 🐦

Call Me "Mister"!

Mister heads break water into superfine droplets, creating a cascade of refreshing, but not intimidating, spray. Attach one to your garden hose, and secure it in a tree or over your birdbath, and you'll soon see a circus of birds jostling for their turn. Hummingbirds are huge fans of misters, which was why I investigated using this $20 attachment to begin with. But once I saw how my client list expanded, I added misters in other spots, too, to supply a cooling spray to wood warblers, grosbeaks, finches of every description, buntings, and tons of other beautiful birds. 🐦

Simple Setup

A mister is easy to put into action. The small spray head is attached to a section of tubing with a connection at the end for your garden hose. I add an on/off valve to the end of the hose so that I can simply throw the

Grandma Putt's BIRD BITS

Good Timing Pays Off

I've been guilty of wasting water many a time in my years of gardening, mostly due to getting distracted and forgetting that I left the hose running. Grandma Putt was none too happy whenever she discovered that, yet again, I'd forgotten to turn off the hose after watering the garden. But she never scolded me for it, because she sometimes did the same thing herself!

All that water could have been saved with the use of an inexpensive device that I now attach to the end of every hose: a timer. You can get plenty of fancy "programmable" gadgets that take as much time to set up as a VCR, but I stick to the simpler models, which I can set to turn on for as long as I want and then shut off automatically. Timers are especially useful for a misting device, because the birds soon learn when the spray will be available. Look for a timer at any garden center or discount store, where you'll find them for about $15 and up.

switch at bath time, and turn it off just as easily a half-hour later.

You can leave your mister spraying all day, if you're so inclined, but I reserve mine for late-morning showers; on summer days, I add late-afternoon refreshers. When frost threatens, disconnect your mister for the season, and store it away until the milder weather returns. 🐦

WATER FOR ALL SEASONS

Water is a year-round necessity—and delight!—for birds. In this section, you'll learn why every season is a good time to offer H_2O, and you'll discover special equipment to keep your water flowing, even in the coldest winter.

Spring Fling

It may be "April showers" season, but you'll still want to keep your birdbath brimming during this time of year. Migrating songbirds are the big thrill in spring, and water is one of the best ways to tempt them into view. Look for colorful songsters at the bath, including orioles, tanagers, goldfinches, and indigo buntings, and watch a little more closely for quiet-colored thrushes and native sparrows. Nearly every bird that moves through your neighborhood—and it's a list of a hundred or more—may stop in to check out your bathing area, especially if you signal its presence with a dripper, or include a burbling fountain. 🐦

LUCY'S
WARBLER

Summer Sustenance

During the long, hot days of summer, water is definitely not everywhere. Like cattle on the dusty trail, birds are superthirsty this time of year and quick to dive into your welcoming birdbath. Housekeeping is important now, because algae (that's "scum" to you and me!) grows fast in hot weather, and mosqui-toes are looking for water to lay their eggs in. Empty and scrub the basin every two days with warm soapy water, then rinse thoroughly several times, and you won't have a buildup of either pesky problem.

Misters and sprinklers get a lot of use in summer. I like to let my grandkids have the job of switching on the misters. They're as tickled as I am to see those hummingbirds zipping through the spray! 🐦

Fall Flurry

Bird traffic increases in fall, as migrant birds head south. Food is foremost on their minds now, but they'll also take advantage of your convenient birdbath. Just as in spring, an audible dripper will boost your chances of seeing some special birds. And keep using your mister or sprinkler, too, until the cold weather moves in. But switch the shower schedule to late morning or early afternoon; night falls fast as the season advances, and birds like to be nice and dry when bedtime nears. 🐦

JERRY
TO THE RESCUE

Q. **I'd like to heat my birdbaths this winter. Any advice?**

A. Well, bless your heart! Birds are extra appreciative of a bath in winter, when it's bitter cold and just about everywhere they land is covered in ice and snow. Birdbath heaters are simple to use, and amazingly powerful, with some models effective even when it's −40°F! You can buy a heating unit to set in a birdbath, or a heated birdbath, which has the heater hidden inside its walls and the cord concealed in the base. Heaters cost from $20 to about $50. Heated birdbaths start at about $50 and go up. Both are equally efficient, so the choice is yours!

I use a separate heater with an automatic on/off mechanism in my pedestal birdbath; it kicks on whenever the temperature of the water falls to 40°, and shuts off when the water reaches 50°F. But as soon as I can clear some space, I plan to try a new-fangled heated birdbath that clamps to my deck rail. It'll be just the ticket for the chickadees and finches that visit the tube feeders I have hanging there.

Winter Water

I can't help saying "Brrr" when I see birds splashing in a puddle rimmed by ice or snow, but my little pals don't seem to mind the temperature. Their downy inner coats probably keep them from feeling chilled to the bone. Still, they forsake those freezing puddles mighty fast when I serve up some steamin' water. Not too hot, now! Lukewarm to medium warm (like a half-cooled cup of coffee) is just right.

Creatures of Habit

My chickadees are so clever, they learned my schedule within days when I began a new routine of setting out a shallow clay saucer of warm water on winter mornings. Now they holler at me if I'm slow to deliver, just as they scold me when the sunflower seeds are running low! Meanwhile, most other birds have figured out the schedule, too. If the chickadees are running late, the titmice or goldfinches quickly jump ahead of them in line.

WHERE TO PUT THE WATER

Bath or shower? Our refreshing routine is a matter of personal preference, and that's the case with birds, too. Some like an elevated basin to splash around in, while others are attracted to a ground-level bathing spot. Many birds also like to ruffle their feathers under a shower. Try these suggestions and see who comes to splash. Of course, when water is scarce during dry times, just about any source of wet stuff will do the trick!

TYPE OF BATH OR SPRAY	HEIGHT	BIRDS MOST EASILY ATTRACTED
Pedestal birdbath	About 3 feet up	Cardinal, catbird, chickadee, goldfinch, grackle, house finch, house sparrow, jays, mockingbird, orioles, robin, starling, titmice, wrens
Basin birdbath	Ground level	Cardinal, catbird, chickadees, goldfinch, native sparrows, purple finch, quail, starling, thrashers, titmice, towhees

TYPE OF BATH OR SPRAY	HEIGHT	BIRDS MOST EASILY ATTRACTED
Basin birdbath	On a deck	Cardinal, chickadees, goldfinch, house finch, jays, purple finch, siskin, titmice
Naturalistic faux-rock birdbath	Ground level	Bluebirds, cardinal, catbird, finches, jays, native sparrows, quail, siskins, thrashers, thrushes, towhees
Naturalistic faux-rock birdbath with dripper	Ground level	Bluebirds, buntings, cardinal, catbird, finches, grosbeaks, jays, native sparrows, orioles, quail, siskins, tanagers, thrashers, thrushes, towhees, vireos, warblers, waxwings
Lawn sprinkler	Ground level	Blackbirds, bluebirds, flickers, grackles, robins, thrushes
Mister	Ground level	Buntings, catbird, grosbeaks, native sparrows, thrashers
Mister	In a tree, 3–6 feet up	Cardinal, catbird, chickadees, grosbeaks, hummingbirds, jays, mockingbird, orioles, tanagers, thrashers
Mister	At a birdbath, about 3 feet high	Cardinal, catbird, goldfinches, house finches, purple finches, hummingbirds, mockingbird, orioles, robins, thrashers, wrens
Mister	On a deck	Hummingbirds

CHAPTER 10

Vamoose, You Varmints!

Stock the feeders with seed, hang out the suet, and get ready for the siege! Pesky visitors are just as much a part of the feeding station as those chickadees that cheer you up every morning. Some of these hombres will come for the seed or other supplies—but others will be drawn to dine on the dinner guests!

In this chapter, we'll talk about the pests, both feathered and furred, that most feeder-keepers face. I'll share my tricks for making your setup less inviting to mauraders, and safer for your songbirds.

WEARING OUT THEIR WELCOME

Too much of a good thing? Hard to buy into that notion, when the good thing is bluebirds or chickadees, or any of the smaller birds that make life interesting. But when a mob of raucous jays descends on your feeder, or a single feisty hummingbird blusters every competitor away from the nectar feeder, you may find yourself ready to pin on your sheriff's badge and call out the posse.

In this section, you'll discover which "good birds" can turn into bad boys, and which less-desirable birds can become the bane of the bird feeder. Of course, you'll also learn custom-tailored tips for discouraging the unwanteds, or at least encouraging them to adopt better manners. We'll start with the good birds gone bad, and then we'll tackle the hungry hordes that can clean you out of house and home in a hurry.

Aggressive Antics

It takes just a few minutes of watching your feeder to discover that the arrival of jays spells "See you later" for other birds. Jays are one of the biggest birds at the feeder, and they sure know how to throw their weight around. Unlike doves or pigeons, which peck away industriously, jays let everyone know that they're arriving. They screech and squawk in a flurry of excitement, and they don't settle down during their visit, either. It's a grab for the biggest and best of the likely offerings, and never mind who gets shoved out of the way!

If you're one of those who prefer that jays not partake of your treats, consider the ideas on the following couple of pages for keeping them away. 🐓

SCRUB JAY

INDIGO
BUNTING

Jam Up the Jays

Jays are smart, but not smart enough to outwit a feeder that blocks their entry. If you don't want to share your offerings with jays, skip the open feeders entirely, and make all of your food inaccessible. These anti-jay feeders will do the trick:

Feeders with bars. Feeders with an outer cage of vertical metal bars cost more than the unbarricaded type, but they're worth every penny. They may look like a jail, but native sparrows, juncos, chickadees, and other small birds quickly learn to slip between the bars to reach the treats within. And jays just as quickly learn to give up and search for a more accessible spread.

Covered hanging feeders. Jays don't like to bump their heads any more than you do. Try a hanging feeder with an adjustable roof to keep them from getting grabby. These dome-shaped feeders are inexpensive, and some models allow you to adjust the height of the overhanging half-dome so that you can accommodate only the smallest birds, or leave space for slightly larger ones.

Tube feeders. Jays just can't get a grip on the stubby perch of a tube feeder. Their big bodies aren't a comfortable fit, so they'll leave the seed inside to the chickadees, siskins, and finches. Just be sure to use a tube feeder made of slick plastic, not one made of grabbable metal mesh! ✍

Small-Seed Solution

Another effective way to discourage jays, but still enjoy the company of many other birds, is to limit the menu instead of changing the feeder style. Jays are only interested in certain foods, including nuts, corn, and sunflower seeds. Offer them the seemingly tempting spread of millet, niger, or other small seeds, and they'll fly right on by to see what your neighbor is offering!

Sticking to small seeds will still hold out a welcome to goldfinches, native sparrows, doves, and fabulous indigo buntings and tanagers. But your cardinals, grosbeaks, chickadees, and other sunflower seed lovers will be gone with the wind. 🐦

Distraction Device

I wouldn't want to keep jays away from my feeders, because I like their high-energy antics. Besides, they're great watchdogs for the whole bird community, raising the alarm whenever a dangerous cat or hawk comes prowling. But I hate to see the other birds waste their energy in panicked getaways when jays arrive. So I follow a three-pronged plan: I make some feeders off-limits, I limit the menu at others, and I distract jays with their very own tray feeder stocked with the most tempting tidbits, such as peanuts in the shell, other nuts, corncobs, and sunflower seeds. 🐦

Mine, Mine, All Mine!

Two types of birds, with very different tastes, qualify for the crown of "King Greedy" at the feeder: the mockingbird and the humming-bird. Both birds are notorious bullies. Few birds will stand up to the onslaught of a mockingbird, who's not afraid to use his sharp beak to

JERRY
TO THE RESCUE

Q. **I've read that jays eat baby birds. Is this true?**

A. It's true, I'm sorry to say. Jays—and crows, grackles, some blackbirds, and even meadowlarks—do occasionally dine on a baby bird or an egg fresh from the nest. They're just doing what comes naturally, though, so I don't hold it against them. Such losses are built into the bird population; if every egg grew into an adult bird, we'd soon have way more birds than the world could handle! A robin, for instance, may nest three or more times every year, laying three to six eggs in every batch. That's math even I can do: as many as 18 additional robins per adult pair; then next year, if they all survive, my neighborhood could be hosting 162 more Robin Red-breasts from just that one family!

And jays are probably responsible for saving just as many birds as they destroy. They're the superheroes of the neigh-borhood birds, warning everyone with loud cries as soon as they spot trouble. That early warning system gives birds time to hide from hawks, or fly from cats, or defend their nest from a snake. All in all, I'd say it's an even exchange— though definitely not a pleasant one to think about!

COWBIRD

make his point. A tiny hummingbird is an unpleasant adversary, too, what with that supersonic speed, not to mention that built-for-business bill! When either of these territorial birds claims a feeder, the other customers will quickly go elsewhere for a less frightening dining experience. Teaching a territorial bird to share is a lost cause, so I solve the standoff another way. Read on to learn my simple secret. 🐦

Out of Sight, Out of Mind

Here's the secret to dealing with a, shall we say, over-enthusiastic hummingbird or mockingbird: Set up another feeder—out of sight! Not out of your line of vision, that is, but out of the bully bird's view from the feeder it's claimed as its own. Keep in mind that both birds may guard "their" feeder from a high perch, so hide the new feeder under the overhanging branches of a tree or shrub. 🐦

Where's the Nest? Ask a Cowbird

Cowbirds are parasitic nesters: The female lays her eggs in another species' nest, and lets them do all the work of raising her babies! Watch for these blackbirds to show up at your feeder in late spring, about the same time as goldfinches come flocking. The drab gray female cowbird can be an excellent aid in finding out where other birds are nesting in your yard. Keep an eye on her when she leaves the feeder, and you're likely to see her skulking about; a particular area of interest in a bush or other greenery may very well hold the nest of her soon-to-be victim. Sorry to say, there's no good way to discourage cowbirds at the feeder; they eagerly eat any of the seeds, corn, or other foods you supply.

SEASONAL SUGGESTIONS

Can't Say No to This!

I use an open tray of favorite foodstuffs to lure a troublemaking mockingbird away from my main feeding area. These birds are fools for fruit, bread-based treats, and other soft foods, so I take advantage of those tastes to lead the mockingbird on—right around the corner of the house! For hummers, I simply stick in another iron hook elsewhere, and hang a second (or third, or fourth!) inexpensive nectar feeder. These birds may be bullies, but they have their limits; they won't patrol a large area when there's a feeder that's all theirs. 🐦

Flocking Frenzy

Now that we've dealt with the bullies, that leaves us with the hungry hordes. Some birds are just too gregarious for our sensibilities! Feed a single starling, and next day, you'll be hosting 10 or more. Ditto with grackles, blackbirds, and house sparrows, all big eaters with a large number of friends and family. My plan of attack is similar for all of these birds, even though their eating habits are different: I simply control 'em with kindness! 🐦

Non Gratis Number One!

Starlings are the number one not-wanteds at most feeding stations. Whether you love 'em or hate 'em, they're the birds that everyone loves to complain about most. They're not raving beauties, they're noisy, they have bad manners, they show up in crowds, and as for their droppings, well, let's not even go there!

You can eliminate starlings from your feeding station by using the same kinds of feeders that bar boisterous jays (see "Jam Up the Jays" on page 240). But since that tactic will also trim your trade of cardinals, grosbeaks, and other large desirable birds, you may want to try a sneakier solution: the distraction feeder. Read on to find out how I put this plan into action. 🐦

Minimize the Opportunity

To make sure that the starlings follow my plan, I take a few extra steps to boost my chances of success. Start with these preliminaries to accomplish your goal of keeping starlings in their place:

Add anti-starling feeders. Increase the accommodations for non-starling visitors by adding tube feeders for both small and large seeds, wire mesh nut feeders, barred feeders, and domed-roof feeders. That'll keep your small birds and your nut-loving woodpeckers happy.

Stock tray feeders with only sunflower seeds. Starlings will seek out edible bits among the seeds, but only if they have to. Meanwhile, your cardinals, grosbeaks, jays, and other larger sunflower seed lovers will revel in the repast.

Turn suet topsy-turvy. Starlings will work hard to get a bite of suet, so wire suet cages aren't the answer. But you can outfox them by using a suet feeder that gives them no place to reach the goodies. Try an upside-down model, where the suet is on the bottom of the feeder, with no access to the top or sides of the block. 🐦

Cheap Feast for a Flock

The fate of the "four-and-twenty blackbirds" in the old Mother Goose rhyme, "Sing a Song of Sixpence," was vivid enough to stick with me all these many years, ever since Grandma Putt read out the lines with relish: The birds were baked into a pie! Seems a little extreme, until blackbird flocks show up outside your own castle. But instead of pulling out your cookbook when the hordes arrive, pour out the cracked corn for grackles, red-winged blackbirds, cowbirds, and other birds with black feathers. I scatter their feast directly on the ground when the masses are at their peak in winter and early spring, or in a low tray feeder in other seasons. That's usually all it takes to keep them from infiltrating other feeders, but for extra insurance, you can also use tube feeders and other inaccessible serving devices for your other feathered friends.

Bring Out the Bribe

Now for the *pièce de résistance* of the starling plan! But first, a word in favor of these oft-scorned birds: Starlings may not be the best feeder guests, but they're a great aid in the yard and garden; Japanese beetle larvae are one of their favorite foods. At the feeder, soft foods are first in line: bread and bread-based treats, suet and fat-based treats, and fruit (half an apple will keep them busy for an hour). Bolster the menu with millet, cracked corn, and chicken scratch, and they'll have a feast. Be sure to set up the starling feeder some distance from your other feeders so that less-aggressive birds aren't disturbed by all the activity. And keep it away from decks and sidewalks so you won't have to haul out that scrub brush! 🐦

Grin and Bear It

House sparrows are impossible to disinvite from the feeding station, unless you stop feeding birds altogether. They eat sunflower seeds, they eat small seeds, they eat suet—why, they eat any kind of treat you can name. On occasion, they've even been spotted sneaking a sip of nectar!

Luckily, these birds, although plentiful, aren't a problem as far as other feeder guests are concerned. Juncos, native sparrows, cardinals, chickadees, and every other feeder bird will not be deterred from visiting your feeding station, no matter how big the house sparrow brigade gets.

BIRDSEED BANDITS

Wild animals are just as happy to make use of a handout as our favorite birds are. Raccoons, squirrels, deer, and other birdseed bandits can be charming, but they can also be destructive, and they'll eat through your supplies faster than wildfire. Here are my best suggestions for discouraging furry diners.

Raiders in the Night

Except for squirrels, which grab their goodies in the daytime, furry feeder raiders mainly do their dastardly deeds under cover of darkness. Focus on that habit for the starting point of your campaign. If you're sparing with the seed and treats, and limit the offerings in open feeders to the amount that birds can clean up during daylight hours, there won't be many edibles left to tempt nighttime raiders. You won't eliminate their visits, but you will save your wallet from being emptied!

DO IT YOURSELF

El Diablo Sauce

When pests get a little too fond of my feeders, I turn to my own recipe of hot sauce to make them vamoose in a hurry. If you grow your own peppers, you'll have a ready supply. But you can also find dried hot peppers, sold by the pound for very low prices, in Latino or Mexican grocery stores, and in some supermarkets. Ultra-hot habaneros are my top pepper choice.

MATERIALS

1 pound of dried hot peppers—the hotter, the better!
5-gallon bucket
Thick rubber gloves
Protective goggles
Garden hose
Yardstick or similar long, sturdy stick
Large soup ladle or cup with handle
3 clean 1-gallon plastic milk jugs, with caps
Permanent marker
Large funnel
Masking tape
Plastic trash bag
Empty spray bottle

DIRECTIONS

Step 1. Hot peppers are extremely irritating to the skin and eyes, as well as the mouth. Wear long sleeves and sturdy rubber gloves to handle them, and don a pair of protective goggles to remind you not to touch your eyes! When you're finished with each step of this project, wash any part of your skin or your clothes that have been exposed to the fiery peppers or the juice.

Step 2. Empty the bag of peppers into the 5-gallon bucket. Immediately dispose of the bag.

Step 3. Fill the bucket about halfway with water, using a hose. Avoid splashing. Then carefully carry the bucket to an unused corner of the yard, and let it sit to stew out the juices from the peppers.

(continued)

⊗ El Diablo Sauce, continued

Step 4. Wearing gloves and long sleeves and using the yardstick, stir the mix at least once a day. Let the stick rest in the bucket between stirrings.

Step 5. After three full days, prepare to ladle off the brew. Work in an area where you have access to a hose. First, label each gallon jug with the permanent marker. I make a skull-and-crossbones above the words "Hot Peppers!" just so there's no mistake.

Step 6. Insert a large funnel into the mouth of the first gallon jug. Tape it in place for extra stability.

Step 7. Put on your protective gear, including the goggles. Carefully pour the liquid from the 5-gallon bucket into the funnel, until the gallon jug is about two-thirds full. Cap the jug tightly, and set it aside. Discard, in a plastic trash bag, any peppers that have poured out and stayed in the funnel.

Step 8. Repeat until all that is left in the bucket is mostly a mass of peppers. Pour the remains into the plastic trash bag. Close the trash bag, and put it in your outdoor trash can.

Step 9. Using the hose, wash off each of the plastic jugs with a generous stream of water. Thoroughly rinse out the 5-gallon bucket and the funnel. Let the containers sit outside to dry. Meanwhile, remove your gear and clothes, and wash thoroughly.

Step 10. When you're ready to treat your seeds, pour some of your home-made hot sauce into the spray bottle. Use the funnel and, as always when working with hot peppers, put on your protective gear.

Step 11. Pour a shallow layer of untreated sunflower seeds or millet into an open tray feeder. Spray lightly, but thoroughly, across the surface with the hot-pepper solution. The seeds will soon dry and you can set them out for feed.

Outfox Their Appetite

Feeder makers do a brisk business in styles that guard against animal use. Check your bird-supply store or a discount store or garden center, or shop online, and you'll find a variety of anti-this, anti-that feeders. Look for these features:

Weight-sensitive. When a heavy customer steps onto the feeding platform, the door drops down, cutting off access to the seed supply.

MEADOWLARK

Chew-proof metal. Gnawing teeth make short work of wood or plastic feeders, especially when hunger is the driving force. The best anti-pest styles are made with metal that resists munching molars.

Anti-theft attachments. Dexterous paws often resort to carrying off feeders, hook, line, and suet! Look for feeders that attach with nails, screws, or other permanent moorings to prevent wholesale highway robbery.

Make 'Em Sweat

"Mouthwatering" takes on new meaning when you use spicy hot sprays to keep pests away. Hot peppers provide the pest-deterring heat that will make feeder thieves think twice before trying again. Look for sprays and powders that you apply directly to seed supplies (see "El Diablo Sauce," on page 246). Birds avidly eat treated seeds, but animals are highly sensitive to the burning capsaicin of hot peppers.

Think You Have Problems?

So coons are crunching on your sunflower seeds, and possums are poaching the suet? Ho-hum. Even dastardly deer depredations are small potatoes for the customers who buy one of the most rugged pest-proof feeders around: the anti-bear model!

Fondly referred to as the Humvee® of home feeders, this surprisingly good-looking feeder is made of sturdy metal that's apparently impervious to claws and jaws. I haven't had the need to give it a test drive; but if you live in bear country, it's nice to know that feeder manufacturers have made it possible to entertain 2-ounce birds—and keep 300-pound bruins away! Expect to pay $50 and up for such a heavy-duty feeder.

PREDATOR PROTECTION

Boy, it sure gets my goat when pesky critters start considering my feeding station as a supplier OF birds, instead of FOR birds! When goldfinches go into the clutches of hawks, or roaming cats start stalking my sparrows, I see red. And I'm not talking rose-colored glasses, either!

Discouraging bird-eaters is way more difficult than dealing with other feeder pests. You can't just change your feeder styles to make birds less appetizing. And, since the shotgun isn't an option, your other choices will have limited effectiveness. Let's consider the habits of feeder-stalkers, and take a look at the methods I use to keep my birds off their menu.

Hello, Kitty!

Dear kitty is such a wonderful pet—when she's inside the house. Outdoors, she turns into the number one threat to songbird populations across the board. It's hard for scientists to get a handle on exactly how many birds fall prey to cats, but they estimate that the slaughter is in the billions per year. Judging from my own experience, I know that a single cat left to its own devices outdoors can easily snag three or four birds at a feeding station, each and every day! Even well-fed pets turn into killers as soon as they see a bird.

Keeping your own cats indoors is the place to start. Eventually, they'll get used to their limited confines, even if they do occasionally complain about it.

Range Wars

Ask your neighbors to keep their cats indoors, and you'll instantly be branded the grump of the block. For some reason, most folks simply don't consider their free-roaming felines to

Hold Your Fire

What do cats hate most? Why, getting wet, of course! That's why a squirt gun or motion-activated spritz of water is so effective at getting the "No Trespassing" message across to neighborhood cats that stray into your yard. But getting soaked in cold weather is no fun, and it can cause those kitties to come down with a case of the sniffles, or worse. Limit your anti-feline water maneuvers to times when the weather is well above freezing, just to make sure you have no sniffling cats weighing on your conscience. After all, we're not trying to be cruel to the cats; we just want to keep our birds safe.

be a problem, though they'd turn 15 shades of purple if your Fido romped in their yard every morning. Unless you don't mind icy relationships with those nearby, I wouldn't even advise trying this approach. Keep mum, smile at your neighbors, and try other anti-cat measures within the confines of your own territory. 🐦

Riding Herd

Cats despise getting wet, especially when the spray is unexpected. I keep a squirt gun in my anti-kitty arsenal, and it's highly effective. Except that it works only when I'm keeping an eye on my feeder friends. As soon as I go indoors, the cats are back. They've learned to associate me with the super soaker, which is a good thing, but they've also figured out that when I'm not around, neither is the wet stuff. I've thought about making a dummy dressed like me (no comments, please!), to sit in a lawn chair when I can't be there keeping watch. It might work. But then again, the cats would probably figure that one out, too. 🐦

BROWN CREEPER

Hot-Footin' It

Pepper spray helps keep away animals that eat birdseed, and those spicy peppers can also help discourage barefooted trespassers. Sprinkle a wide band of ground hot peppers around your feeder area. When cats cross it to stalk the birds, they may feel its effects on their paw pads. It's not a lethal dose, just a temporary hot foot, but it may be unpleasant enough to discourage them from a return engagement. 🐦

Do Fence Me In

If you have the bucks, you can barricade your entire yard with a cat-discouraging fence—and maybe add a yappy dog inside, too! But for most of us, living inside a stockade isn't an appealing answer. I depend on a halfway method that puts the fence where it's most needed: right around the feeding station.

Anti-Stalker Corral

A corral of stiff wire fencing about 4 feet high, which you can find at any garden center, will do the trick for keeping stray cats away from your feeder. You'll need only a few stakes to keep it upright, since it will naturally coil in a circle when you remove it from the roll. To close the mini-corral, simply overlap the ends of the wire fencing. That way, you can easily get in or out (watch for sharp ends of wire when you handle the fence, or snip them off to prevent scratches). Expect to pay about $1 a foot for such fencing, and keep an eye out for sales to help trim the cost.

JERRY
TO THE RESCUE

Q. **I've tried everything to chase cats away from my feeder, but as soon as I go inside, they come back. They even learned to climb my fence. What can I do?**

A. I have one more trick up my sleeve, and it's a dandy! This newfangled device uses a motion detector to aim water their way. At $50 to $90, it's not a cheap solution, but it is effective. Installation is simple: You push a plastic stake into the ground, hook up a hose to the outlet, and attach the battery-powered sensor. A range of sensitivity settings allows you to adjust the sensor for a slew of other yard pests besides cats, including deer, raccoons, and dogs. When an animal wanders into its sights, the device lets loose with a short burst of water. Then it turns itself off, and resets to wait for the next invasion.

Anti-Hawk Hideout

Compared to the number of birds killed by roaming cats, hawk predation is a minor blip. But give your birds a fighting chance by adding more protective cover around the feeder and in your yard. Hemlocks, spruces, and other evergreens are perfect hiding places, where feeder birds can make a fast dive for shelter. Try placing your discarded Christmas tree near the feeder for birds to retreat into when a hawk approaches, or spread seed on the ground below bushes and low trees. 🐦

Remove the Temptation

If a hawk does grab dinner on the wing, it can be exciting to get an up-close-and-personal look at nature in action. But if a hawk begins a daily patrol, or perches frequently near your feeders, do your birds a favor and remove the temptation—for both parties! Take down your feeders so that the birds disperse, and the hawk will go a-hunting elsewhere. Once the predator has moved on to better bird pastures, you can replace the feeders. 🐦

CHAPTER 11

Oh, Give Me a Home

Once you have birds accustomed to visiting your yard to find food and water, putting up a birdhouse is a natural next step. Nesting birds add a new dimension to those friends at the feeder: Now we *really* get to see how they engage in family life! And having birds move into the birdhouse you put up will definitely make you feel special.

In this chapter, you'll learn which birds use a birdhouse, so that you can tailor your offerings to the birds in your own backyard. And you'll find out exactly what kind of nest box (another name for birdhouse) they prefer. There's also an entire section dedicated to starlings and house sparrows, a pair of potential tenants that can be mighty pesky—or just plain fun! We'll take a look at the kinds of birdhouses you can buy, and you'll discover why keeping predators out is as vital as picking the right box.

TOP TEN TENANTS

 Cheerful Jenny wrens, perky chickadees, and those beauteous bluebirds are among the backyard birds that might call your birdhouse home. In this section, you'll meet our birdhouse friends, and learn which of them are easy-to-please possibilities, which are a bit persnickety, and which are long shots that have special needs. You'll find plenty of tips along the way for tempting these birds to set up housekeeping in the homes you provide.

PYGMY
NUTHATCH

The Few, the Proud— The Birdhouse Birds!

Let's get the bad news out of the way first: Only a handful of birds will make their home in a birdhouse. Most birds happily make their nests in trees, shrubs, or weedy patches, no matter how deluxe the accommodations you offer are. Now, for the good news: Nearly all of the birds that nest in birdhouses are our favorite friends, the kind we coax to our feeders. Some can't even be tempted to feeders (because they eat mostly insects), but if you nail up a nest box, they'll soon be knocking on the door! Here's the list of possible takers for a backyard birdhouse:

- Bluebirds, all species
- Chickadees, all species
- Nuthatches, white- or red-breasted
- Purple martin
- Robin (nesting shelf, not box)
- Screech owl

- Swallows, tree or violet-green
- Titmice, all species
- Woodpeckers, nearly all species
- Wrens: Bewick's, Carolina, or house wren

Bluebird Dreams

Dream on, city dwellers and the rest of us who don't live near bluebird country! No matter how pretty or how perfect your bluebird house is, you won't get any bluebirds unless you live close to their natural territory. But if you have bluebirds visiting your feeder, or if you've spotted one on a nearby golf course or other open area, you have a chance of attracting this premier birdhouse bird.

Even if you haven't seen a bluebird within miles of your place, you can still put up a bluebird house. If those beautiful blues don't move in, a chickadee, a downy woodpecker, or someone else is apt to claim it. 🐦

Bewildering Boxes

So many folks are fans of bluebirds that a whole cottage industry (not to mention scientific research) has sprung up to figure out exactly what kind of nest box is best. You'll find a bewildering array of bluebird nest box styles, from the standard rectangular model to a slanted-front style, a box with a slot instead of an entrance hole, and even a birdhouse with a screen roof (seems a little soggy to me!). Each type has its ardent defenders, it appears, with no general consensus on the "best" style. So choose whichever kind you like. 🐦

A Long Winter's Night

Bluebirds may use birdhouses in fall and winter, as well as in spring and summer. They won't be singing lullabies in winter, though—they'll be snoozing! Like other cavity-nesting birds, bluebirds often seek out a snug shelter on chilly or snowy nights. Several birds may pile into the box, where their body heat will keep the whole batch as snug as bugs in a rug!

Bluebirds Galore

The eastern bluebird, a beauty with a reddish breast, gets most of the press. But in other parts of the country, where the eastern species doesn't roam, the western and mountain bluebirds pick up the slack. All three species are among the easiest birds to attract to a nest box—if

JERRY TO THE RESCUE

Q. Why don't robins or cardinals ever use my birdhouse? The picture on the label showed a robin on the perch by the hole, and a cardinal on the roof. What's up?

A. False advertising! Robins and cardinals, along with most other songbirds, just don't feel comfortable climbing through that entrance hole into a dark, enclosed box. They're used to building their nests in the great outdoors, hidden in a shrub or saddled to a tree limb. You may get a taker if you put up a simple shelf to support a robin's nest, but as for birdhouses—forget it!

"Cavity nesters" is the official term for birds that readily use birdhouses. The cavity that makes some birds feel comfy is a hole in a tree, such as in a dead branch or where a limb has broken off. Birdhouses, or nest boxes, as they're often called, are simply a reasonable facsimile of the natural holes that these birds seek out for nesting. No one knows why some birds nest in cavities. But one guess is that it may give them an extra bit of protection against predators, by making it more difficult for marauders to nab helpless nestlings or eggs.

they live within a short distance of your house. All of them will freely visit suburban backyards as well as country homes when they're looking for a handout of food or a new roof over their heads, so keep your hopes up, and hang up those birdhouses!

Bluebird High-Rise?

Bluebird fanciers recommend placing your birdhouse 4 to 5 feet above the ground, but that's more for your ease of use than theirs! A lower box is easier to peek into, and to clean and repair when needed. In the wild, bluebird nesting cavities may be only a few feet from the ground, or they may be high up in old oaks, apple trees, or pines.

House sparrows don't seem interested in high-rise houses. A friend tells me the sparrows fight over her lower bluebird boxes. But they never raise their sights to a box that's mounted about 20 feet up on a tree. There, her bluebirds can raise their family unmolested.

Into the Great Wide Open

Give your bluebirds a view of wide open spaces, and they'll feel right at home. You can mount their birdhouse on a post, along a fence, or on a tree; but make sure it faces into open territory, such as your lawn or a neighboring field. Bluebirds seem to prefer unimpeded access to and from their domicile, even when the box is nestled in a hedgerow or along the edge of a woods. I like to position the box several yards away from a shrub or small tree so that baby bluebirds have a sheltered landing site for their first flight. 🐦

Easy Chickadeesy

Perky little chickadees are among the easiest birds to tempt with a nest box. And, you won't have to deal with house sparrows or starlings, because the 1¹⁄₈-inch entrance hole is small enough to get the "No Vacancy" message out, loud and clear, to the bigger, pesky birds.

Chickadees are almost everywhere in winter, but their nesting ranges in summer are more limited, though still large. Check a field guide to see whether your backyard falls into their breeding territory. If it does, your chance of attracting a pair of these agreeable birds is very good! 🐦

Trees Are Tops!

Think trees when it comes to placing the box, because that's where chickadees will check first for homesites. Grand old shade trees or a woods are ideal locations, but they're not neces-

---

Grandma Putt's

BIRD BITS

Privacy, Please

Talk about Jekyll and Hyde personalities—the same chickadee that fearlessly eats nuts from your hand will put up the "No Trespassing" sign around its nest. Privacy is important to nesting birds, even when they're extra friendly at the feeder. So mount your birdhouse in an undisturbed area of your yard, away from the comings and goings of kids, dogs, and lawnmowers.

"Shhh! The baby's sleeping," was a caution I heard often from Grandma Putt, whether we were visiting friends or having our own gatherings. If you put your birdhouse where there's plenty of peace and quiet, the parent birds won't need to remind you to tiptoe around the nursery.

sary to make chickadees happy; a dogwood, young maple, or other small tree will serve the purpose just as well. Mount the box right on the tree, or on a post. A good height for chickadee homes is 2 to 10 feet high, but they'll also adopt homes at higher levels. They might even venture into setting up housekeeping in a box mounted discreetly beneath the railing of your second-story deck! 🐦

Stumped by Chickadees

Got a stump in your yard that you've prettified with flowers or a forest-creature lawn ornament? How about adding a lively chickadee family to the arrangement?

Chickadees often make their home just a foot or two off the ground, and they'll quickly investigate a nest box mounted on the side of a stump. The mountain chickadee, a species found in the Sierras and other western mountains, is especially keen on stumps, sometimes excavating its home only a few inches above the ground. The black-capped, Carolina, boreal, and other chickadee species often check out stumps, too, perhaps because it's easy to peck out a home in the dead wood. And if your stump has trees nearby, you're almost guaranteed to host a chickadee family. 🐦

Feed 'Em First

A hearty supply of nuthatch favorites at the feeder in winter can sway the vote when it's time for a pair of birds to select a homesite. Check a field guide to find out whether nuthatches nest in your area of the country. If they do, then mount a campaign to sweeten the deal. Offer abundant chopped nuts and suet, and other fat-based treats favored by the birds. Once they become familiar with your yard, they may check out the nest boxes after they chow down on the eats.

SEASONAL SUGGESTIONS

Nasal, Natty Nuthatches

No one would ever mistake a nuthatch's voice for a sweet chanteuse (a nasal "ank" is about the best they can manage, plus some quiet little conversational murmurs), but when it comes to fancy dress, nuthatches would be right at home in a swanky night-club—they look like they're wearing little tuxedos! And they have such a comical way of moving: They're upside-down birds, crawling headfirst down tree trunks. Besides, these birds are among the most faithful visitors to my feeders, so on that basis alone, I reward their loyalty with a custom-made nuthatch house. 🐦

BROWN-HEADED NUTHATCH

One Size Fits All

Four kinds of nuthatches roam the trees, and the same size nest box will accommodate all of them. An entrance hole of 1¼ inches is all a nuthatch needs to squeeze inside the box.

Now, that same size hole will also allow titmice and chickadees to use the box; but if you plan to coax nuthatches to your place, too, you'll have better luck putting up two boxes this size at different heights. Chickadees and titmice readily use a birdhouse that's placed relatively low to the ground, but you'll need to haul out that ladder to put up the nuthatch box. Mount it 12 to 20 feet above the ground, and cross your fingers! 🐦

Near a Woods?

Even if nuthatches are daily customers at your feeder setup, they may not be so eager to take advantage of your backyard as a nesting site. In fall and winter, nuthatches range far from their usual haunts to find food, but at nesting time, they usually retreat to woodsy areas to bring up their babies.

A nuthatch nest box is worth a try if you live within easy flying distance of woods or tree-studded hedgerows, or a city park or riverside with lots of old trees. But if your backyard is surrounded by suburban backyards with only very young trees, your chances of netting a nesting nuthatch are pretty slim. 🐦

Few and Far Between

I'll bet you've never hosted a flock of nuthatches, of any kind, at your feeder. Me neither! Nuthatches usually visit by ones or twos, although in winter, my feeder offerings can draw in half a dozen. Because nuthatches are in relatively short supply, your chance of attracting a pair of the birds to a nest box is slimmer than it would be for chickadees or other more populous birds. Don't let that discourage you, though. Nuthatches may be few and far between, but so are ideal nesting holes. Your tailor-made birdhouse could be just the ticket for a house-hunting pair! ✍

JERRY TO THE RESCUE

Q. **I live in the city, and I often see a titmouse at my feeder in winter. Do I have any chance of attracting one to a birdhouse?**

A. Sure, but make that two titmice, not just one. Titmice are feeder regulars year-round because they don't migrate. If titmice are cracking sunflower seeds and nibbling the nutty treats at your feeder in winter, you can bet they'll be nesting somewhere in your neighborhood in spring. Why not in *your* yard?

City or country? It makes no diff to these mousy-gray birds, who will happily raise a family in a backyard, no matter where it is. Just put your birdhouse near the shelter of a large or small tree, as you would for chickadees, and wait for the moving van to appear!

Sticky Subject

If your birdhouse is adopted by a red-breasted nuthatch, you'll soon see the evidence, even if you haven't yet spotted the tiny bird. This species has the oddball habit of smearing sticky pitch from pines or other conifers all around the entrance hole. It's weird, all right, but pretty darn smart, too! Should an egg-eating coon or snake try to cross the stuff, their sticky feet (or slithery skin) will soon beat a retreat. ✍

Twice the Titmice

Instant gratification is almost guaranteed when you put up a birdhouse for titmice. These little gray birds, with a feathered crest on their heads that makes them look like miniature cardinals of a different color, are so quick to appreciate new digs that they're likely to start moving in as soon as you move out of the area. ✍

Same Size, Same Site

I like to put up at least three bird-houses suitable for titmice around my place, because the 1¼-inch entrance hole that fits their bodies also does the trick for chickadees and nuthatches.

Titmice, like their close relatives, the chickadees, will quickly adopt a box mounted so low that you don't even have to haul out the ladder to put it up. About 3 to 6 feet above the ground will do the trick, or you can mount the box as high as 15 feet if you like, where you may also catch the attention of a house-hunting nuthatch. 🐦

Early Birds

Your titmice will tell you when it's time to get out there with the hammer and nails! They're among the earliest birds to begin courtship, tuning up with love songs by late winter. When you hear a loud, clear, whistled "Peter! Peter!" (easy and fun to imitate!), you'll know it's tit-mouse time. By Valentine's Day, the titmouse pair is acting like a just-married couple, and beginning the search for a hospitable home, where they may start raising a brood as early as March. 🐦

Grandma Putt's BIRD BITS

Picky Woodpeckers

Grandma Putt liked to put up nest boxes for woodpeckers, even though in most years a squirrel claimed possession, instead of the hammerheads she had in mind. I, too, put up the boxes in hopes of attracting a mating pair. I figure the reason there's usually not much immediate interest in my woodpecker houses is because these strong-beaked birds are so adept at whacking out their own living quarters in a dead tree or utility pole.

With more than 20 species of wood-peckers chipping away across North America, and most of them year-round residents, there's little doubt you live in woodpecker territory! So it's still worthwhile to try to coax a pair of these interesting birds into calling your yard home. But if your birdhouse isn't selected by a pair of woodpeckers, don't take it personally.

A Deeper Look at Custom Fit

Shopping for a woodpecker house is like buying clothes for a big family. You may have to visit the children's department, the juniors', and maybe even the big-and-tall. Not only do wood-

TUFTED TITMOUSE

**HAIRY
WOODPECKER**

pecker requirements differ for the size of the entrance, but the depth of the box is significant, too. Here's how to decide just what you need to accommodate different sizes of woodpeckers:

Small. An entrance hole of 1¼ inches and a depth of 8 to 10 inches, the same size box as you use for titmice and nuthatches, will allow a downy woodpecker to claim the birdhouse as its own, without competition from starlings or larger woodpecker relatives.

Medium. The hairy woodpecker, a larger look-alike of the familiar downy, can't squeeze in through a 1¼-inch entrance; this bird needs a hole at least 1½ inches across, and it prefers a much deeper box, about 12 to 15 inches deep. Other medium-sized species, such as the Nuttall's woodpecker of the West, may also use the box.

Large. Choose a box with an entrance hole of 2½ inches, and a depth of about 12 to 15 inches, and you've found a flicker home. The box will also suit redheaded and red-bellied woodpeckers, as well as a slew of other large woodpeckers. 🐦

An Iffy Proposition

Put up a wren house in your yard, and a house wren will come. But whether it stays or not is another story! The male house wren builds several trial nests before the female arrives to select her favorite. So, watching a bird carefully poke twigs through the hole isn't a guarantee that babies

will soon be on the way. But even if your birdhouse isn't selected as the real thing the first time around, it may be just perfect for a later batch of babies, or for next year. 🐦

The Joys of Jenny Wrens

Just watch a little brown house wren when it sings, and you'll see that the bird throws everything it's got into the perform-ance. Head back, throat bulging, wings fluttering, and beak wide

DO IT YOURSELF

One-Season Wren House

Here's a fast, fun birdhouse that requires no handyman capabilities to put together. It's simple enough for kids, but a satisfying project for grown-ups, too.

MATERIALS

$\frac{1}{2}$-gal. waxed cardboard drink carton with plastic cap, rinsed and dried thoroughly
Stapler
1"-wide masking tape
Small can of paste-type brown shoe polish
Penknife or box cutter
Ruler
Nail
Sturdy twig, about 5" long
Twine

DIRECTIONS

Step 1. Screw the cap back on the carton tightly, or, if your carton had no cap, use the stapler to fasten the top back together securely.

Step 2. Cover the entire carton with masking tape, but not in big strips: Use small pieces so that the final texture resembles natural bark. Just tear off pieces about an inch or two long, and stick them all over the carton, until every bit is covered. Don't worry about overlaps!

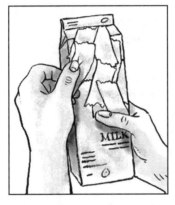

Step 3. Using a soft cloth, rub the brown shoe polish all over the carton so that it covers all the tape. See? Looks like bark, doesn't it? (At least from a distance!)

Step 4. Cut a 1-inch-diameter entrance hole about 6 inches above the bottom of the carton.

Step 5. Use the nail to poke a few drainage holes in the bottom of the carton. Also poke two holes in the top of the carton, on each side, to allow ventilation.

Step 6. Again, using the nail, poke a hole into the box about 1 inch below the entrance hole. Insert the twig, leaving most of it outside the box as a perch.

Step 7. Staple each end of a piece of twine securely to the top of the container to form a handle for hanging. Hang your wren house in a sheltered location, such as under a porch roof.

JERRY
TO THE RESCUE

Q. I watched a wren move lots of sticks into my birdhouse, but after a while, it stopped coming, and I never saw any babies. What happened?

A. You were watching the wrong wren! That one was a male, and he was working hard to impress a girl. Winning the favors of his intended isn't simply a matter of singing a good song or showing off his feathers. Nope, this poor guy has to build a bunch of nests and then take the maybe-Missus on a tour, hoping that one of his trial nests will catch her fancy.

Not until the lady shows up and gives my birdhouse her stamp of approval do I know for sure that I'll be playing doting uncle to baby wrens. Male and female house wrens look alike, so how do you know which one you're watching? Simple! Just take a close look at what's in that beak. If it's sticks, sticks, and more sticks, chances are you're watching a male. But if the building materials include feathers, hair, fuzzy cocoons, or other soft bits and pieces—even pussywillow catkins!—you're watching a female add the finishing touches to her mate's pile of sticks.

open, it's as full-throttle as any soprano in the church choir!

But house wrens aren't just pretty voices. They're hard workers, too, cleaning our yards and gardens of thousands of insects. And with their appetite for the caterpillars of the white cabbage butterfly, they're one of the best friends a vegetable gardener could ever ask for!

Pinch an Inch

I know that house wrens are little birds, but when I watch them fluttering around the yard, it seems that there's no way they could ever squeeze into that tiny front door of their birdhouse. Must be mostly feathers, I figure, because an entrance hole just 1 inch in diameter is all they need.

And then there's the matter of moving in the nesting material. House wrens build big, bulky nests, with a foundation of hundreds of sticks. Not just small twigs, either: Some of these sticks are 6 inches long! All I can say is that house wrens are much better at finagling large objects into tight quarters than I am. Just take a look at my doorway, and you'll see the nicks from the last time I tried to wrangle a new bookcase inside!

The Dark Side

Bluebird fans shudder when house wrens are mentioned, because the dark side of the cheery wren comes into full play in territorial fights over nesting areas. When there are a lot of house wrens in the neighborhood, the birds may take it in mind to start their own seek-and-destroy mission, puncturing the eggs or stabbing the nestlings of other wrens, bluebirds, or other song-birds nesting in what they consider "their" home grounds. Scientists consider this a natural process of population control, but bluebird keepers get understandably upset at such dire tactics. 🐦

Wrens of a Different Stripe

If the wren in your yard sports a dashing white stripe by its eye, you may be lucky enough to be playing host to a Carolina wren (or a Bewick's wren, if you live in the West). Originally a bird of the Southeast, the Carolina wren could now be called the Florida-to–New England–to-Nebraska-to-Texas wren! 🐦

Thanks, but I'll Make It Myself

Ah, that doggone independent streak! Carolina and Bewick's wrens would be a lot easier to entice to a birdhouse if they weren't so darn fond of making their own cozy hangouts. Like house wrens, both of these birds have a penchant for building nests in odd places: baskets, mail-boxes, cow skulls, pockets of clothes left hanging on a peg, or anyplace else that seems like a good spot to stuff to the brim.

To make a birdhouse more appealing to these master builders, make it a big one! The hole should be small—1½ inches will fit either bird—but select a box that's at least 8 inches

Put Out the Welcome Mat

SEASONAL SUGGESTIONS

The similar Carolina and Bewick's wrens live year-round in their large range, but in severe winters, the birds may retreat south-ward. Even if your Carolina or Bewick's wrens disappear for the winter, they'll come back again next spring at nesting time. So be ready with a bird-house—which they may adopt instantly, or com-pletely ignore!

TREE SWALLOW

deep. Don't worry: Although they'll soon cram it full of grass, moss, dead leaves, and other goodies, their young'uns will have no problem scrambling out when it's time to make their exit. 🐦

Easy to Swallow

Tree swallows are simple to attract to a birdhouse—IF you live in the right place! That means practically anywhere in America, but only near water: a stream, pond, or lake, where they can be found skimming insects above the surface nearly all day long.

In the West, the similar violet-green swallow often adopts birdhouses, and it's not nearly so particular. These pretty birds, with their pristine white undersides, are common in towns and countrysides, whether there's water nearby or not. 🐦

⊗ DO IT YOURSELF ⊗

Robin Nesting Shelf

Ask for a nesting shelf at any birdhouse supplier, and you're likely to be surprised at what you see: Instead of a simple shelf, the item looks more like a typical birdhouse, with the front removed. I have good luck using an unroofed version that I make myself from a shelf and bracket available for a few dollars at any craft store. Don't give me credit for this idea: The

plan is all the birds'! They started it by adopting a knickknack shelf I had fastened to the outside wall of my porch.

Robins nest from March though July, and raise at least two batches of youngsters a year, generally building a new nest for each family. Early March is a good time to get this shelf in place, but don't worry if you miss the early-nesting birds—you may catch the next round!

MATERIALS

1 unpainted wooden shelf, at least 4" long and 3" wide (bigger is fine), with a decorative wooden bracket, available at any craft store
Pencil
Screws for mounting
Screwdriver, or power drill with screwdriver bit

DIRECTIONS

Step 1. Select a site for the nest shelf. Because it has

(continued)

⊗ Robin Nesting Shelf, continued

no roof to protect the birds from rain, you'll need to attach it to a wall under a porch roof, or beneath an overhanging eave of the garage or shed. Robins don't mind people walking or sitting nearby, as long as you don't show too much interest in their home. Choose a location that doesn't get direct sun in the afternoon, so the baby birds will stay cool.

Step 2. You can mount the shelf about 6 feet above the floor or ground, so that you can get a glimpse of the family at home, or place it as high as 15 feet, if you prefer. Hold the shelf against the wall, using the siding boards (or a level) to make sure it's straight. Mark a line on the wall at the top of the shelf.

Step 3. When you've finalized the position, use a screwdriver or power drill to attach the bracket to the wall.

Step 4. Some shelves of this type are already attached to the bracket when you buy them; for others, you'll need to

secure the shelf to the bracket after you screw it to the wall.

Step 5. Ignore the shelf. With any luck, it will soon be adopted by a pair of robins, phoebes, or perhaps even barn swallows.

Open Access

Part of the pleasure of having swallows as tenants is watching their graceful, swooping flight as they approach or exit from the house you've provided. That's why you'll need to make sure there's a wide open stretch in front of the box, such as a lawn or driveway area. A swallow birdhouse is just what the doctor ordered for a barren new subdivision yard!

You can also perch the birdhouse on top of a hill or fence in your yard so the swallows can soar in and out without braking for bushes. And don't forget to look up to see your friends at work: They spend most of their daylight hours patrolling the skies for flying insects. ✐

First Come, First Served

Planning to attract bluebirds to your welcoming, open-access area? Then you may soon have a different opinion of swallows, which are likely to claim the boxes you intended for your blue-feathered friends, thanks to the 1¹⁄₂-inch entrance hole that accommodates both kinds of birds. Some bluebird aficionados detest the competing swallows, but I follow the open-door policy: Whoever comes first gets the house. Because there are many more swallows than bluebirds, and because bluebirds quickly give up when challenged for possession, you can guess who usually wins the war. ✐

Welcome to the Colony

Swallows like to nest in a neighborhood of other swallow families, called a colony. In the wild, they may adopt the edge of a woods or a fence line, making their homes in separate holes that may be only several feet apart. So, you'll increase your chances of attracting the birds if you supply more than one birdhouse. When you run out of room, or if you prefer a less hodgepodge look, you can even mount them back to back on a post or tree. ✐

BANK SWALLOW

Rooms to Let

Purple martin landlords are a different breed altogether. It's not a matter of simply investing in a martin apartment house and erecting it on a tall pole. Nope, martin-hosting often moves quickly from the casual to the obsessed. Some folks put up a martin house and let the birds look after themselves. But many other landlords invest hours of care, worry, and even medical treatment in their colonies. Whether you want to go casual or are looking for an involving new hobby, you'll find tons of additional info about purple martins from the places you'll find listed in the Sources section of this book, starting on page 324.

Add the Pole

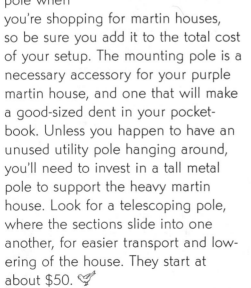

It's all too easy to overlook the price of the pole when you're shopping for martin houses, so be sure you add it to the total cost of your setup. The mounting pole is a necessary accessory for your purple martin house, and one that will make a good-sized dent in your pocketbook. Unless you happen to have an unused utility pole hanging around, you'll need to invest in a tall metal pole to support the heavy martin house. Look for a telescoping pole, where the sections slide into one another, for easier transport and lowering of the house. They start at about $50.

Grandma Putt's

BIRD BITS

House Hunting

Martin houses are elaborate buildings, with individual compartments for six or more pairs of birds, often complete with "front porches" and perching rails. In the old days, folks made their own houses out of wood, and maybe you have your own Grandma Putt, who'll be willing to let you move her martin house to your yard if maintenance has become too much of a chore.

Wooden martin houses are charming, and they make an appealing yard ornament even if you never get any martins. You can still find wooden houses for sale, at about $135 and up—and UP. How about a lovely, Victorian-style house for 24 martin families, made of painted rot-resistant cypress wood, with a patined copper roof, for $1,200? It's out there, if you decide your martins deserve a luxury suite!

Modern metal houses may not have as high a quaintness quotient as the wooden ones, but they're less expensive and easier to clean. Expect to pay $70 and up for a metal martin apartment house.

THE DASTARDLY DUO

In the old days, when more land was forested and dead trees were free for the finding, bluebirds and other cavity-nesting birds had it easy. Now that our subdivisions, shopping centers, and farm fields cover a lot of the land, suitable homesites are harder to find. Another factor is at work, too: the presence of house sparrows and starlings, two cavity-nesting species that were imported into America. In this section, you'll discover some tricks you can try to outsmart these birds, or to learn to live with them.

STARLING

Near and Not-So-Dear

House sparrows and starlings live only where people do. You won't find them far out in the wilds; they stick to our back-yards, parking lots, or other sites that are within a short jaunt of human habitation. That's one of the reasons for their success: They adapted quickly to making the best of such cozy quarters, and learned to live on our leftovers. These birds find their daily bread outside fast-food restaurants, along roadsides, and in other prime litter locations. Farmyards, fields, and feed mills are favored, too, thanks to all that inviting grain scattered on the ground. They're feisty birds, accustomed to fighting for every crumb, as well as for nest sites. So, unless a disease of some sort runs through their ranks, these birds are here to stay.

Trying It On for Size

It seems to me that house sparrows are none too bright in the bird-brain department. One of these birds may hop about on the roof of a too-small birdhouse for days, complaining loudly to all its friends, repeatedly trying out the hole, in case it has magically increased in size. Even-tually, though, even a house sparrow will give up on a birdhouse that just won't fit.

Starlings, on the other hand, look like Einstein compared to sparrows. A starling may stick its head into the entrance hole of a birdhouse, but if the bird can't wiggle the rest of itself inside, it'll quickly give it up as a lost cause.

Stick to Extra-Small

Want to eliminate any chance of hosting house sparrows or starlings? Then stick to birdhouses with extra-small entrance holes. Chickadees, titmice, nuthatches, house and Bewick's wrens, and the downy woodpecker can all comfortably slip into a box with an entrance that's 1^1/$_4$ inches or smaller. Sorry, house sparrows—guess you'll have to find a home elsewhere!

Go Low

Get that liniment ready, because one of my favorite tricks for outwitting house sparrows and starlings calls for some back bending! Most of our favored birdhouse birds will happily accept a nest box at a very low level; house sparrows, on the other hand, are less interested when the box is less than 3 feet from the ground, and starlings will usually say "No thanks" when your box is less than 5 feet off the ground. So keep your birdhouses less than 3 feet off the ground, and say goodbye to sparrows and starlings.

JERRY
TO THE RESCUE

Q. Why can't I just use a birdhouse with a big hole, so that any bird that wants to use it can fit inside the entrance?

A. I, too, used to wonder why I couldn't use the same birdhouse for all the birds I wanted to attract. Since nearly all of them could fit through a 2-inch hole, it seemed silly to invest in other houses with smaller holes. Then I realized that although a chickadee, say, may use a box with a front door that's 2 inches in diameter (much larger than the minimum 1^1/$_8$ inches it requires), it probably wouldn't be my tenant. The petite chickadee would face more competition from larger, desirable birds, as well as from the ubiquitous house sparrows and starlings.

So keep the entrance at the minimum size for the species you want to attract. If that hole is smaller than 2 inches, starlings won't be able to enter. If it's less than 1^1/$_2$ inches, you'll bar both of the nuisance birds from getting in—even if it does take the house sparrow a long time to say, "Duh! I don't fit!"

DO IT YOURSELF

Bluebird Box Protection

Bluebird lovers keep finding new tricks up their sleeves, and this one is looking like a winner for deterring house sparrows. All you need is some fishing line plus a fence for mounting your bluebird box. You attach three pieces of thin fishing line, two vertically and one horizontally, making a crisscross effect across the front of the house, but not blocking the entrance.

MATERIALS

Bluebird house
Wooden fence with
    wooden posts
Spool of monofilament
    fishing line
Scissors
2 wood screws, about
    2" long
Screwdriver

DIRECTIONS

Step 1. Attach the screws to the front corners of the roof of the birdhouse, near the front edge. Screw them in only enough to anchor them solidly; leave at least an inch of the shank exposed.

Step 2. Attach the bluebird house to a fencepost, facing away from the fence. Position it so that the entrance hole of the box is 6 inches or more below the top of the post.

Step 3. Tie the fishing line to the next post, and stretch it across the front of the bluebird house, about 2 to 3 inches below the entrance hole. Tie the other end to the next fencepost on the other side of the box.

(continued)

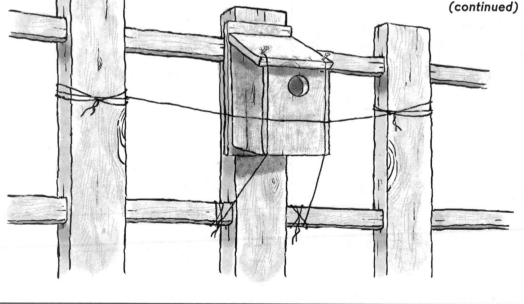

⊗ Bluebird Box Protection, continued

Step 4. Tie another piece of fishing line to the screw sticking up from the left corner of the roof, and stretch it downward. Tie the other end of this piece of line to a fence rail below the house, so that the line is about 2 to 3 inches from the left side of the entrance hole.

Step 5. Repeat with another piece of fishing line, tying it to the screw on the right corner of the roof and stretching the line to the right of the entrance hole.

I haven't tried this myself yet, but I've heard that the house sparrows apparently blunder into the line when they approach the entrance, become frightened, and depart. The bluebirds, meanwhile, seem to be able to see the line, and they aren't deterred by it. See you later—I'm goin' fishin' for bluebirds!

Please, Make Yourself at Home!

B ack in the 1920s, when it still seemed possible that every last house sparrow could be done away with, folks tried their darndest to wipe out the species. As you can see, it didn't work! I figure that my kind has done way more to upset the natural order of things than these "nuisance" birds have. Besides, I appreciate their willingness to make themselves at home in my world. So, I include housing for house sparrows and starlings in my backyard plan.

Naturally, I also have a couple of ulterior motives: By supplying the kind of nest boxes these birds like best, I steer them away from my other birdhouses. And I also help deter them from wriggling into loose flaps of siding, chimney crevices, or other nesting places where they could really cause me problems. 🐦

Two for the Road

S tarlings may hang out in big, companionable flocks, but when it comes to raising a family, they do it two-by-two. Paired birds select a nesting site well away from other starling couples. Any large woodpecker birdhouse will suit them just fine, and once they're settled, they just may leave your other birdhouses alone. 🐦

Room for the Relatives

House sparrows often live in large colonies, like you'll sometimes see on the ivy-covered wall of an old building. Although a single pair will often take over an isolated birdhouse, a nesting site that's cheek-by-jowl with other house sparrows is way more appealing. So why not make a folk art display guaranteed to attract the eye of passersby—including house sparrows? Mount several flat-backed birdhouses of various kinds and colors, all with entrances of at least 1½ inches, on a wall, in whatever arrangement suits your eye. Place their apartment complex out of sight of your other birdhouses, and you may distract them from their usual takeover tactics.

BEST BIRDHOUSES ON THE BLOCK

Birdhouses are everywhere these days, including *inside* our homes! You can find sturdy, suitable models at bird-supply, discount, and hardware stores, or from mail-order suppliers, and fun, inexpensive styles at craft shops and farmers' markets. Or, for direct access to the mother lode, turn to the Internet and search for "birdhouses".

In this section, you'll learn why it's better to pay more for a well-made model, and where to comparison-shop to sniff out the best deal. You'll also discover tips that will make your shopping expedition a pleasure, and your purchase a success!

Built to Last

I used to buy cheap birdhouses whenever I saw one I liked—only $5.99? Who could resist? And it even has a sunflower painted on the front! But after a few too many experiences with replacing boxes that had split after just one winter outdoors, I decided to pay the price for quality, instead of getting peeved.

You'll pay more for better-made birdhouses, but they'll last longer and stay in good shape for years, needing no maintenance. Here's what to look for when you're shopping for a durable nest box:

Skip the plastic. Plastic birdhouses usually don't last as long as wooden ones, and they can look junky in your yard, especially if their colors fade. Plastic also lacks the insulation power of wood, which protects the birds inside from getting too hot on sunny days, or too cold on chilly nights.

Shop for Bargains

Watch the newspaper or community notice boards for advertisements of upcoming craft shows and sales, where you can often find sturdy birdhouses at paltry prices. For about $5 apiece, I was able to outfit my yard with strongly built, solid-wood birdhouses that show every promise of lasting for years. In stores, a birdhouse of the same quality might cost as much as $25. Scout groups, garden clubs, retirees, and other folks who make good birdhouses often sell their wares at such sales in fall, or near the Christmas season.

Choose real wood. Take a pass on plywood or oriented-strand board (OSB). Solid wood holds up better than other woodlike materials, which may split, splinter, or disintegrate. Look for boxes made of boards at least $1/2$ inch thick.

Look for rot resistantance. Birdhouses get wet. A lot. And that means rot can set in. Select one made of cedar, cypress, or redwood, and it will probably last years longer than a pine model. But if pine is all you can find, don't fret: It should still hold up well for a few years.

Nix staples. Staples have a tendency to pop out, causing gaps that allow rain or snow to enter, hastening the decline of the box. Nails may also lose their grip as the wood absorbs water or dries out. Screws are a sign of good workmanship, and they make it easy to replace any parts that may need repair.

Seek a sensible mount. If you intend to attach the house to the side of a post, wall, or tree, you'll need a back that extends above and perhaps below the house itself, into which you can drive mounting screws. If your birdhouse is going to sit proudly atop a post, you'll need a base that allows you to hammer it home. Make sure the model you pick allows you to mount it where you intend to.

Opt for pre-drilled mounting holes. To avoid the risk of splitting the wood of my brand-new birdhouses, I buy nest boxes that come with mounting holes already drilled in place. Then all I need to do is attach the screw through the hole to the post. ✑

Cheaper by the Years

Soften the blow of whatever price you pay by dividing it by 5: In my experience, that's the number of years the typical birdhouse will last, without needing repairs. Of course, you'll buy birdhouses that fit your budget, but even a $25 house can feel like a bargain when you figure out its annual cost. Hey, $5 a year for the privilege of hosting my favorite chickadee family is a price even *I'm* happy to pay! ✑

Call On a Carpenter

Find a carpenter or a handyman who works with wood in the "Home Services" ads in your newspaper's classified section. Then, gather your courage and make the call. Many of these fellows are happy to put together a birdhouse or two in their spare time from scrap lumber that's already lying around their place.

By the way, if you have a Skil® saw, an electric drill, and a screwdriver at your disposal, you can easily make your own avian housing. You'll find a bevy of birdhouse plans at your library or on the Internet. Once you have the wood cut to size, assembly is easy. ✑

Simplify the Schlock

I know, I know, a lot of us have a Nehru jacket or a pair of go-go boots lost in the dim reaches of the closet (and probably worth big money now on eBay!), but when it comes to bird-houses, it's better to use restraint than to give in to fads. Today's sunflower decorations are all too likely to become yesterday's black-and-white cows.

A single decorated birdhouse can add a homey, country touch to your yard, but five of them staggered around the place are likely to look as gaudy as a flock of pink flamingos. I buy basic, unadorned, unpainted models for my staple housing needs. Birds can easily spot them, but they blend right into the scenery for human passersby. Then, of course, I glitz up the scenery a bit with a fancy painted birdhouse that just jumped into my hands at the last craft show I attended. 🐦

The Cradle Could Fall

All birds that use birdhouses will use a box that's solidly mounted to a post or tree. A few of those birds will also make their home in a birdhouse that's able to sway in the breeze. Want to play it safe? Batten down the hatches, and secure all your houses to stable supports. Since you can never be sure just which bird will choose which birdhouse, you're broadening the audience by making it appealing to all. And, mounting the house in a nonmoving position also eliminates any chance of a windstorm or a prowling cat or coon knocking the whole shebang to the ground. 🐦

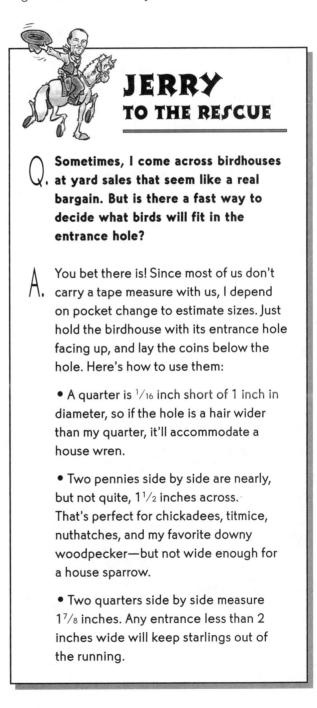

JERRY
TO THE RESCUE

Q. Sometimes, I come across birdhouses at yard sales that seem like a real bargain. But is there a fast way to decide what birds will fit in the entrance hole?

A. You bet there is! Since most of us don't carry a tape measure with us, I depend on pocket change to estimate sizes. Just hold the birdhouse with its entrance hole facing up, and lay the coins below the hole. Here's how to use them:

• A quarter is $^1/_{16}$ inch short of 1 inch in diameter, so if the hole is a hair wider than my quarter, it'll accommodate a house wren.

• Two pennies side by side are nearly, but not quite, $1^1/_2$ inches across. That's perfect for chickadees, titmice, nuthatches, and my favorite downy woodpecker—but not wide enough for a house sparrow.

• Two quarters side by side measure $1^7/_8$ inches. Any entrance less than 2 inches wide will keep starlings out of the running.

NESTS IN NUMBERS

Lots of backyard birds raise more than one batch of babies every year, and many of them build a new nest for each family, or start from scratch if their nest is destroyed. That means your birdhouses (or nesting materials, which you'll learn about in the next chapter) may have takers at any time during the spring-to-summer nesting season. Here's the scoop on the typical family life of some of our familiar fine-feathered friends.

BIRD	BROODS PER YEAR	NESTING SEASON
Barn swallow	2	April–July
Bluebirds	2 to 3	March–July
Cardinal	2 to 4	March–August
Carolina wren	2	April–July
Chickadees	1	April–June
Goldfinch	1	June–September
House finch	2 to 4 or more	February–August
House sparrow	2 to 3	Usually April–September
House wren	2 to 3	April–July
Jays	1	Most species, March–July
Mourning dove	2 to 5; even more in areas with warm winters, where they may breed year-round	April–August
Nuthatches	1	Most species, April–June
Orioles, Baltimore and Bullock's	1	May–June
Robin	2 to 3	April–July
Song sparrow	2 to 3	February–August
Starling	2 to 3	April–July
Titmice	1, sometimes 2	March–May (plain titmouse, March–July)
Tree swallow	1, sometimes 2	April–June

CHAPTER 12

Feathering the Nest

Feeder traffic drops off as birds move into nesting season, and that means it's time to make the transition from shopping for seeds to setting up a building-supplies outlet! From early spring through midsummer, a supply of nifty nesting materials is popular with birds of all kinds.

Instead of beginning with the basic foundation materials, such as twigs and leaves, I've started with the finishing touches. That's because these materials, such as feathers, string, and fur, are harder for birds to find. After you've learned all about the most tempting materials, including why they appeal to birds and where you can find them, you'll also find plenty of info about setting out a supply of the basics. Finally, you'll discover some clever ways to offer your supplies, so that you can have the thrill of seeing nest builders shopping at your own "store."

Sweetening the Deal

Looking forward to sinking into that featherbed tonight, are you? Then be glad you weren't raised by mourning doves or blue jays! These birds don't bother to soften their sleeping quarters in any way, so their youngsters have to use a bedroll made of nothing but sticks. Ouch!

But many birds do add a lining to the basic structure of their nest, weaving a soft inner cup of fine fibers, feathers, thistledown, or other soft-as-a-cloud materials, so their youngsters snooze as gently as you do. In the following pages, you'll find lots of suggestions for nesting materials that go beyond the basics. You'll discover what materials are most prized and where to look for them around the house or in the stores. Sweet dreams, y'all!

Fabulous Fibers

Birds are weavers deluxe, so add any kind of fibers you can find to your cache of nesting materials. Orioles are renowned for fashioning string, twine, and yarn into their complicated nest pouches, and many other birds will work a few pieces of fiber into their construction, too. In the wild, birds strip fibers from plant stems, but anyone who spots your supply will quickly take advantage of it.

Shoestring Budget?

Being a packrat at heart, I save everything I come across throughout the year that even remotely looks like it might have possibilities for fiber-loving birds. Snippets of string from the bakery box, pull strings from pet food bags, cords from discarded window blinds—anything that's thin and stringy goes into the grab bag. My broken shoelace, for instance, was such a hit that a wren and an oriole actually fought over it, with each bird hanging on to one end of the prize! ✑

Avoiding Accidents

Keep your pieces of string, twine, or yarn short so that you don't unwittingly cause a disaster. Orioles, robins, and other birds may be good weavers, but they can be klutzes when it comes to handling the stuff. Sometimes, they become so enmeshed in a long length of fiber that they can't get free. Discarded monofilament fishing line, when it gets tangled in the bushes or trees, is a deadly trap for orioles and other birds.

Never, ever offer extra-long lengths of string (over about 10 inches). And if you happen to spot any while you're out walking, do the birds a favor and slice them up with your pocket knife, or take them home with you to cut up. ✑

Eight Is Enough

I use the short edge of a sheet of 8 × 11-inch paper as a quick guide when I'm snipping string or other fibers. That's long enough for master weavers to work into their creations, and short enough to prevent accidents. I also make sure to put out a selection of shorter pieces for smaller birds that like to use the materials. Any piece of fiber from 2 inches to 8 inches long will have its takers. ✑

Spotlight on White

White is definitely the quickest color to get a nesting bird's attention, because it stands out

Under Construction

Expect to see birds fishing for finds at your nesting supplies pile throughout the spring and summer, not only during the peak of the first go-round in mid-spring. Many birds make more than one nest each season, and every time they build, they usually start from scratch.

Nests are also prone to construction disasters. Sudden storms can blow a nest right out of the tree, or a predator may claw it to shreds. What's a bird to do? Why, rebuild, of course! If you keep your stash of supplies refreshed throughout spring and summer, any birds shopping for nesting materials may very well stop on by.

Friendly Fabrics

BIRD BITS

Monday, wash day; Tuesday, ironing: You didn't need a calendar to check the days of the week when Grandma Putt was at work! Now, with all the easy-care man-made fabrics on the market, laundry is no longer a full-time occupation, thank goodness. But for the most appealing fabrics for birds, you'll want to use all-natural fibers, not the man-made miracles.

Plant fibers are rated tops by nesting birds, and your home is full of them. Just look for anything made of 100 percent cotton, linen, or ramie. Stick to non-knitted fabrics, so they don't stretch and sag once they're part of a nest. Snip lightweight natural fabrics into strips of about 1/2 inch wide and 6 to 8 inches long, and you'll find plenty of takers, from cardinals to house sparrows. Coarsely woven fabrics, such as "home-spun"-type tablecloths, make great raw materials for birds that do fine weaving. And they'll unravel the threads them-selves: Just fasten one end of the fabric to a post or tree branch so the birds can tug away at it.

like a spotlight from a distance. So I try to include as many white and light-colored fibers in my collection as I can. I've noticed that as long as birds can find white or whitish fibers, they don't even bother with those strips of snazzy red in my pile! ✎

Rags to Riches

Cotton fabric is a terrific source of nesting material. How about those 300-thread-count sheets? That's 300 threads in every inch, just beg-ging to go into a bird nest! Relax, I'm just kidding: There's no need to shred your sheets, when your rag bag holds such opportunities. Lightweight fab-rics, like shirts and blouses, are most appealing. Don't worry if the edges of your strips unravel; birds may pull out loose threads to use singly, too.

Rag bag looking slim? You can find cheap shirts at garage sales and thrift shops; in this instance, stains won't matter! ✎

Crinkly Cellophane

Save the cellophane wrapping from that fancy fruit basket, and you'll find house spar-rows, cardinals, and other birds eagerly

recycling it. Cellophane is also sold in packages or on rolls at a cost of a couple of dollars. Cut it into fluttery strips about 1/2 to 1 inch wide and 8 to 10 inches long, and snag it among the branches of a shrub. Clear cellophane is highly appealing, but birds will also make use of yellow or other light-colored stuff. ✍

Drugstore Cowboy

One of my favorite places for rustling up nesting materials is the discount drugstore. I scout the sewing aisle, the household department, and the makeup area to collect a season's worth of specialty materials. Here are some of the treasures I round up along the drugstore trail:

CHIPPING
SPARROW

✔ Cotton balls

✔ Mylar balloons or other mylar decorations (see "Jerry to the Rescue," on page 284)

✔ Spool of white butcher-type string

✔ White or tan carpet thread or other coarse thread.

Crafty Shopping

Craft and hobby stores can be overwhelming, thanks to the huge selection of products they stock to keep hobbyists happy. Make a list before you go so that you won't forget what you came for. Then if anything else grabs your eye while you're wandering the aisles, you won't lose track. Here's what I snap up on my forays:

✔ Bagged spaghnum moss

✔ Bagged Spanish moss

✔ Clear cellophane

✔ Faux fur

✔ Feathers, especially white ones

✔ Natural-color linen yarn

✔ Unwoven wool (not yarn)

✔ White or natural-color cotton yarn

✔ White pompom trim

Wanted: Rapunzel's Hairbrush

Chipping sparrows, song sparrows, and many other birds use long hairs, such as those from your hairbrush or a horse's tail, to weave a soft circlet for the inside of their nests. Each hair is usually handled individually by the deft little weaver, who joins them together in a tidy cup by tucking in loose ends with her beak. It's as seamless as one of those well-advertised hair weaves for balding fellers, and just as strong.

JERRY
TO THE RESCUE

Q. I've heard that some birds use snake skins in their nest. Why on Earth do they do that?

A. One theory is that it may scare away predators, but that's a wild guess. And nobody can get a straight answer from the birds themselves! But we do know that modern materials are making headway as substitutes. Great crested flycatchers, indigo buntings, titmice, and other snakeskin aficionados are equally fond of skinny strips of cellophane or shiny mylar, the material used for balloons and other decorations. A single mylar balloon or sheet of cellophane is plenty to supply a neighborhood of such nesting birds. Just slice it into strips about 1/2 to 1 inch wide and 6 to 8 inches long, and nestle it among some rocks in your yard, where it will look like Mr. Snake just wriggled out of it.

The Long and Short of It

Fur is really hair, too; it's just shorter. Fur, or short hair, like that from your dog, is usually tucked into nests in tufts of several to many hairs, especially by birds that use birdhouses, such as titmice and chickadees. They use fur for the innermost lining of the nest to form an ultrasoft resting place for eggs and babies. I've never seen birds show any interest in cat hair, but dog hair is eagerly plucked up.

The Pony Express

Long, flexible horsehair is a prized commodity for backyard birds, but now that station wagons and SUVs have replaced stallions, it's not so easy to come by. But it's worth making a special trip, if you have a stable within easy reach of your home. Check the Yellow Pages of your local phone book, or simply keep your eyes open for horses in pastures. Ask nicely, and you're likely to find a horse owner who will be happy to share whatever's in the currycomb! 🐦

GREAT CRESTED FLYCATCHER

Don't Bother with Dryer Lint

Even though that nice, fluffy handful of dryer lint sure looks like prime nesting material, it's not. Birds rarely make use of lint, maybe because the individual pieces are so small that they can't be woven or secured into place. And dryer lint gets soggy when the rains come, and dries into a stiff film that looks like slime mold. So save your yard from the mess created when unwanted dryer lint gets wet, and toss the lint in the trash, instead of saving it for the birds. 🐦

Rein 'Em In

Collecting nesting materials is so much fun—it's a scavenger hunt!—that it's easy to get carried away and gather way more than the birds on your block will be able to use in one season. Keep in mind that you don't need to stock up on a lifetime supply. Just a few handfuls, enough to loosely fill an empty wire cage suet feeder, will be plenty to satisfy the birds in your backyard. I follow these guidelines to keep my generosity within reasonable bounds:

Cotton string. 1 spool (put out 10 to 20 2"–8" pieces at a time)

Cotton yarn. 1 small skein (put out 10 to 20 2"–8" pieces at a time)

Fabric strips. 1/4 yard (put out 5 to 10 1/2" strips at a time)

Feathers. About 2 cups (several dozen, assorted sizes)

Fur. About 2 cups (2 handfuls)

Hair. About 1 cup (1 handful)

Linen yarn. 1 small skein (put out 10 to 20 2"–8" pieces at a time)

Unspun wool. About 1 handful

PHOEBE

Must-Have Moss

Moss is a must for phoebes, jays, summer tanagers, and other nesting birds. They'll seek it themselves in the wild, or they'll grab what you've got if you add it to your offerings. Two kinds will serve the purpose: spaghnum moss and Spanish moss. Both are often used around the base of potted floral arrangements, so moss may already be lurking in your house, ready for recycling. If not, then you can buy bagged moss at craft shops for a buck or two. Oh, and if your backyard happens to be festooned with long streamers of Spanish moss, or if you live among the moss-bedecked trees of the Pacific Northwest, there's no need to offer a supply; it would probably go untouched because birds can easily gather their own.

Early Supplies Catch the Birds

Catch the early birds by setting up your nesting-supplies station *before* spring has officially sprung. Titmice, chickadees, and other birds may begin making a home as early as late February. By the time the calendar says that it's officially spring, they may no longer be in need of your carefully collected nesting materials. Beat these eager beavers by making your stash over the winter months, and set out the first temptations as soon as you notice that birds are singing again. Or remember that Valentine's Day is a good time to show the birds how much you care about them by putting out materials for their happy homes-to-be.

The Touch, the Feel of Cotton

Cotton balls are another popular item, but be sure to read the fine print on the bag before you add them to your shopping basket: Many of them are now made from synthetic fibers. Birds prefer the all-cotton variety, which is still available at many drug and discount stores.

I always add cotton balls to my nest supplies, just because it's so much fun to watch the chickadees, titmice, and other birds tear them apart! They'll spend many minutes pulling out tufts of fibers from the balls to carry away to their nesting holes or birdhouses. You can expect to pay about $3 for a bag of 200 cotton balls—and that's enough to last for several seasons.

Mary Had a Little Lamb

And everywhere that Mary went, the birds were sure to go! That's because tufts of sheep fleece are hugely popular with wrens, orioles, and other birds that fashion soft, cuddly nests. I like to take a small bit of woolen fleece and snag it on a splintery post or fence rail, where birds have to work a bit to tug it free. Look for unspun wool at shops that supply home weavers and spinners, or at craft shops. White, pale tan, and gray fleece are the most popular with birds, but they'll use other colors, too—even if it comes from a real black sheep! 🐦

Fussin' over Feathers

Feathers are so popular with swallows and other nesting birds that you can expect these items to be among the first to go. The best kind to offer are small to medium-sized "body feathers," the kind that have a wide, slightly curled-under end and a short, flexible quill. Wing and tail feathers aren't nearly as appealing to birds, probably because they're so stiff. I use natural, undyed feathers just to make sure I'm not exposing my friends to any possibly harmful chemicals. 🐦

Grandma Putt's BIRD BITS

Safety First

"Don't be a bird-brain," as Grandma Putt would say, whenever she reminded me to wash my hands before dinner. Protecting ourselves against germs is only common sense. And with all the warnings about West Nile virus and other avian diseases, it makes good sense to take a few precautions when you collect feathers or set out your supply of previously used plumage. Wear disposable plastic gloves whenever you're handling feathers, and avoid touching your face or eyes until after you've thoroughly washed your hands. Store feathers in a zip-top plastic bag in a dry place away from most family activity, such as in a shed or garage.

Feather Collecting

Federal laws protect most of our birds from human interference, and that includes collecting their feathers, even if they shed them in your front yard. So stay on the right side of the law by sticking to waterfowl or poultry feathers.

Try the following places to find feathers:

In pillows. Look for bargain throw pillows or bed pillows at thrift shops and garage sales.

At duck ponds. Visit the local park to collect soft feathers from ducks and geese.

At poultry farms. Scour nearby roadsides, and you're likely to find windblown feathers. Or ask permission to collect a few near the barns.

At craft shops. Cleaned feathers are sold in bags for a few dollars. Just be sure they're natural and not dyed.

Back to Basics

Bird nests are so distinctive that with some experience, you can look at an empty nest and tell just who it belonged to. Yet all nests are made of just a few basic materials. Come to think of it, so are the houses in my neighborhood. Yet my house is as different from the house next door as a robin's nest is from a jay's!

Even though our friends are skilled at seeking out the building materials on their own, many of them will gladly take advantage of a generous supply of nesting basics that YOU provide! You'll find plenty of ideas for "raw" materials in the following pages.

The Big Four

Nearly all birds make their nests from just four materials: sticks, leaves, grass, and plant stems. Some birds use only one of the materials, but many combine two or more of them to form the housing for their family-to-be. Just as you'd expect, the basic building materials are in abundant supply wherever birds live, including your own backyard. If you create a place where birds can find a bountiful supply of their favorite foundation materials, they're likely to stop on by and check out the offerings. 🐦

Hey, That's My Stick!

I offer a stash of sticks in clear view of my window, so my ego gets a thrill when a jay or other stick-seeker comes to sort through the offerings. I love thinking about MY twigs forming the foundation for a homey haven! Not to mention that it's a lot of fun to see just who shows up; sometimes, I get a glimpse of a towhee or a thrush that I didn't even know was in the neighborhood!

Dozens of birds use twigs, or small sticks, in their nests, including these common backyard dwellers:

- ✔ Cardinal
- ✔ Catbird
- ✔ Doves
- ✔ Jays
- ● Mockingbird
- ✔ Robin
- ✔ Thrashers
- ✔ Wrens

Slight Case of Sloppiness

One fine, spring day, I spent a couple of hours watching a wren, a jay, and a cardinal scour the yard for sticks. Those birds worked so doggone hard to find just a few twigs in my tidied-up yard that I changed my ways, then and there. Oh, I still sweep and rake the paving and lawn, just to keep things looking good. But now I no longer clean up beneath my shrubs or hedges, which are the prime locations for stick-collecting songbirds. 🐦

Right This Way

I also stoop to a slightly sneakier trick to bring stick-seeking birds into better view. I collect handfuls of those twigs myself, and pile them loosely in an area where I can watch the birds sorting through to find their favorites. You can do the same by gathering dropped twigs from privet, willows, oaks, dogwoods, lilacs, or just about any other tree or shrub that you happen to have in the

JERRY
TO THE RESCUE

Q. Where should I put my nesting supplies? Is it okay to put them near the feeder?

A. It's not just "okay" to offer nesting materials near the feeding station, it's perfect! For one thing, your feeder regulars will be quick to check out the offerings. And for another, the temptations of those supplies may attract tanagers or other birds that wouldn't normally frequent the feeder—and they may stick around to sample the food. Either way, it's a win-win situation.

Once you see how popular nesting materials can be, you'll probably want to put up more than one holder for them. I use a couple of hanging wire suet cages (clean, of course!), plus an empty tray feeder on a post to serve up my strings-'n'-things near the feeding station. My stash of sticks goes on the ground near some shrubs, where stick-using birds are apt to scout for materials.

yard. Those bits and pieces are naturally shed by plants as they die. If you're not in the habit of raking under your shrubs, you'll be amazed by how many there are to collect, year after year!

Anything Goes

A study of Florida scrub jay nests revealed that nearly all of the sticks they used were from oaks. That makes sense to me because birds use what grows nearby. In the scrublands where these jays nest, shrubby oaks are about the only deciduous tree there is. No wonder they snatch up the twigs, rather than do battle with a wide fan of saw palmetto!

But don't let that study fool you into thinking that all birds are such specialists. In my own yard, I've noticed that the birds collect twigs from azaleas, privet, and many other plants that aren't native to my region. So I don't worry about separating the twigs I put out for birds: In my yard, anything goes!

Size Matters

Some birds use slender, short twigs, while others seek out sturdier, longer sticks that can be more than a foot in length. Many birds combine all sizes and lengths in their construction. As long as you gather sticks that are about

¹/₄ inch or less in diameter, in an assortment of lengths from 3 to 10 inches, you'll have lots of takers.

Big sticks of ¹/₂-inch diameter or better are also collected by birds—but that's the size used by large hawks, ospreys, and eagles. So watch out! 🐦

The Thornbirds

If you live in catbird country, you might get a meow of appreciation for supplying the birds with thorny twigs. Prickly sticks are all the rage with catbirds and their kin, the mockingbird and brown thrasher, perhaps because the spines discourage trespassers. Birds of all three species will quickly take advantage of a supply of prickly twigs, if they're planning to raise their families in your neighborhood. 🐦

Handle with Kid Gloves

On second thought, make those rawhide gloves! An encounter with a thorny stick can quickly leave your own hide pretty raw, so be sure to protect your hands and wrists with stout gloves before you handle these prickly subjects. By the way, this inhospitable building material is used in the outer part of the nest, not near those unfeathered babies. 🐦

Leave the Leaves

Here's another reason that a less-than-perfect yard is tops with birds: dead leaves! Now, I'm not suggesting that you quit raking altogether, but there's no need to collect every last leaf. Those strays that wind up in the corners of our yards, or under the hedge, are in high demand come nesting season. I don't bother

Recycle Those Cuttings

SEASONAL SUGGESTIONS

When you cut back your perennials after blooming season is over, you're left with quite a heap of potential nesting material. Many garden plants, including butterflyweed (*Asclepias tuberosa*) and asters (Aster *spp.* and *cvs.*), have fibrous stems that can be used in nest building. Pile those plants where you can see them, and you may spot orioles or other fiber seekers tugging at the dead stems to strip off the usable fibers.

ROBIN

trying to corral the windblown leaves; birds are perfectly adept at tracking them down without my help. Besides, there are plenty of other more-prized materials that I can use to coax them into view. But I do like knowing that my stray leaves are going to a good home. Dead leaves worked into a twiggy foundation help keep the nest insulated on chilly nights, and won't hinder air circulation on stuffy days. 🐦

Grapevines and Great Vines

A grapevine is a popular source material for nest builders because the flexible stems and bark are ideal for creating a nest foundation. If you can sacrifice some snippings from your own grape arbor, try clippings of stems, a few of the brown corkscrew tendrils, and some strips of bark (look on the ground at the base of the vine to find pieces that shed naturally). They're all prized property!

If you don't have a grapevine growing in your yard, try another great vine, such as clematis, honeysuckle, trumpet vine, or anything else that's twining around a support in your yard (but no poison ivy, please!). Just remember that dead or woody stems are preferred to green ones.

Golden Grasses

Whether golden, russet, beige, tan, or any other shade that grass takes on after it's dead and dried—all of these colors are equally appreciated by nesting birds, including titmice, nuthatches, and native sparrows. But green is a no-no, because birds need

Grandma Putt's
BIRD BITS

Thorny Lures

Thorns are a great deterrent to cats and other predators of nesting birds, and parent birds put that advantage to good use. Some, like the cardinal that came every year to nest in one of Grandma Putt's climbing roses, build their homes in a thorny plant, while others use thorny sticks for the nest itself. When I cut back my roses or trim the barberries in late winter, I save some of those prickly clippings. Thorny sticks are as good as gold for tempting an elegant brown thrasher right up to the window. I snip the leafless clippings into lengths of about 6 inches, and lay them directly on the ground or in an empty tray feeder, so that I can see the birds better when they come to gather their prickly sticks.

dry materials for nesting.

Birds prefer longer blades of grass, which lend themselves to weaving, rather than short clippings. Look for grass blades that are 6 inches and longer. You won't need to worry about birds possibly getting tangled in extra-long grasses; although these materials are strong, they can be pecked apart should a bird get tangled up.

Fine Focus

Offer a selection of various-sized grass blades, and you'll win approval from a wider variety of birds. Robins and larger nest builders appreciate wide blades of miscanthus and stout grasses. Titmice and other small birds go for the fine grasses, such as blades of ornamental fescue.

The bottom line: Include more fine grasses than wide-bladed ones in your offerings, because fine grasses get more takers. Big and small birds alike make use of fine or wiry grasses to weave an inner cup within the bulkier nest foundation.

Adobe Abodes

Barn swallows and a few other species forgo the usual sticks and stems, and build their homes mostly from mud. Their architecture

JERRY
TO THE RESCUE

Q. Can I offer any kind of grass for use as nesting material?

A. Sure! Well, as long as its leaves are long and strong, that is. The leaf blades of ornamental maiden grass (*Miscanthus* spp.), fountain grass (*Pennisetum* spp.), blue fescue (*Festuca* spp.), or whatever special grasses you have in your yard are prime material for nesting birds. So are the dead leaf blades of big clumps of "weedy" grasses, such as orchard grass or timothy, which may be growing along your fence or in an overlooked corner. But skip the crabgrass and lawn clippings; few birds bother to collect them. Now, if your lawn is so overgrown that the clippings are 6 inches long or more, you may want to collect some! By the way, the dead foliage of "grassy" plants, such as liriope or crocuses, may also be used by nesting birds.

Set aside a few handfuls of clippings whenever you cut back any of your ornamental grasses, and you'll be the best friend of birds seeking nesting materials in the months to come. Coil the dry, but flexible, blades into a loose circle, and store your treasure in a dry place. Then offer small amounts of it throughout the spring-to-early-summer nesting season.

is so unusual that their oddball nests are easy to identify. But most birds that use mud in their nests add it toward the end, on top of a foundation of the basic building materials. All-adobe abodes may not be a popular style with backyard birds, but even mud will have its takers at your nesting-materials station. (See "Making Mud Pies" on page 298 for details on making a mud puddle these birds will love.) 🐦

HOLDERS FOR THE HEIST

Figuring out how to proffer your offerings is part of the fun of setting out nesting supplies. Because birds have different styles of perching and foraging, you'll need more than one type of setup to satisfy everyone. Here are the considerations I keep in mind to make sure all of my clients are accommodated, and the devices I use to keep the customers satisfied.

Shopping Habits Revealed

Offering nesting materials is another step in your education about bird habits; but don't worry, it's a pleasurable and painless one! All you need to remember is that just like at the feeder, some birds are fearless and will instantly investigate your material offerings, no matter how unnatural the holder or the setting. Other birds, however, are shyer and more comfortable shopping when the materials are placed in a way that's close to natural.

What does that mean for you? Well, unfortunately, the birds that prefer to select their goodies from beneath shrubs or among branches will be harder to observe—and you're likely to forget just where you put the items! But your "unnatural" stash will also get plenty of takers. 🐦

Suet Cage Cache

A clean wire suet cage is my favorite holder for most of my special nesting materials, including feathers, fur, moss, wool, and other soft supplies. The wire grid prevents the items from spilling out willy-nilly, and it gives the birds a secure place to cling to while they extract their favorites.

Chickadees, titmice, nuthatches, and other clinging birds that typically use the same style of wire cage when it's filled with food will be the first to explore this kind of a setup. If you fasten the cage to a solid support, so that it doesn't swing freely, you may also spot orioles, tanagers, and other larger birds making use of it. 🐦

Blowin' in the Wind

If you live in the Plains, or in any other region where daily winds are a fact of life, lick your finger and do a little test to see which way the wind blows. Often, winds blow one way in winter and in another direction in summer. Knowing which way the winds blow will help keep feathers and other lightweight nesting materials from being scattered all over the neighborhood. Just put your offerings on the leeward side of a bush or fence, where they're protected from the direct force of the wind.

On the Level

The simplest way to offer supplies is to put them right on the ground. That's just fine with robins, thrushes, towhees, native sparrows, and other birds that prefer to forage at low levels. The drawback to this method is that lightweight materials, such as feathers and wool, will easily blow away on a windy day. Counter that problem by putting out only a scanty amount of materials; you can always refresh the supply as needed. 🐦

A-Tisket, A-Tasket

A nesting-materials basket! A shallow wicker basket makes a handsome holder for your stash of twigs, grass, or soft specialty items. Set it directly on the ground, either in the open or tucked under a shrub, for robins, thrushes, sparrows, and other low-level birds to discover. If your basket

Coming Unraveled

You don't have to get any fancier than a nail when it comes to supplying a piece of coarse fabric for birds to unravel by themselves. Just hang a loosely woven scrap of coarse cotton or linen fabric on a nail, and watch for orioles or house sparrows to begin the unraveling process. Determined string-collecting birds have even been known to peck apart items that were left hanging on a clothesline—as well as the frayed end of the clothesline itself! I'll never forget the beautiful oriole that incurred Grandma Putt's wrath by shredding a corner of one of her favorite crocheted curtains that was hanging on the line!

Clotheslines are becoming pretty much a thing of the past, but you can still put them to work by hanging a piece of coarsely woven cloth on the line. Just be sure to use plenty of clothespins to keep the fabric secure for tugging birds. And, if you can find an old crocheted curtain or doily at the thrift shop, those delicate strings are as good as gold to orioles. Just don't tell Grandma Putt I told you so!

has a handle, you can hang this supply of nesting materials from the branch of a tree or from an iron hook for chickadees, jays, and other birds.

Baskets are available at any discount store; check a "dollar store" for super-duper bargains, or keep your eyes open for sales. There's no sense in spending more than a couple of bucks on such a holder, since it won't last more than a season or two out in the weather.

Open Space

Feathers, especially white ones, are so effective at catching the eye of nesting swallows and purple martins that I make sure to set out a few in an area that's accessible to their swooping, free-flying style. An open area of lawn or a gravel driveway will do the trick for these birds, which require unimpeded access for landings and takeoffs. Just scatter several feathers across the area, and be sure to include at least a few white ones so the birds will spot them quickly.

A Bird in the Bushes

I use the shrubs in my yard as holders for fibrous nesting materials, such as twine and yarn. It's simple to drape the strings onto the shrub, poking them into the branches a bit for a more secure hold. Orioles, tanagers, jays, and many other birds are happy to pluck them loose and carry them home. I also drape a few offerings on the very lowest branches for ground-dwelling birds. ✑

Up in the Trees

Cedar waxwings are notoriously difficult to tempt to a feeding station, but during nesting season, you may get their attention with lengths of white string. Dangle the string over the branch of a tree, where there's plenty of room for the bird to land. A small tree, such as a dogwood, hawthorn, or holly, is perfect because it's within easy reach for you, and it's a natural perching place for the waxwings. The string will be more visible there than on the branch of a large shade tree, where the canopy of foliage would block the string from the view of any waxwings that fly over.

Attracting cedar waxwings is a great argument for supplying nesting materials throughout the season. These birds are very late nesters, and often don't get started until midsummer. ✑

Be a Kid Again

Making a mud puddle for robins and other nesting birds to use for nest building is just as much fun as squishing mud pies was way back when. But this time, you'll have a great excuse for getting sloppy! Be sure to maintain your mud puddle throughout the nesting season because swallows, robins, and other takers are likely to build a nest more than once. ✑

Pre-Stuffed Holders

Bird-supply companies are jumping into the nesting-materials market in a big way because some folks prefer to buy a holder that's already filled, rather than collect supplies themselves. If the notion of convenience appeals to you, look for prefilled holders at bird-supply stores, in catalogs, or on the Internet. You'll find some suppliers listed in the Sources section of this book, too (see page 324). The contraptions are reasonably priced at about $10, but if you're pinching pennies, you'll have equal success doing it yourself with recycled finds. ✑

⊗ DO IT YOURSELF ⊗

Making Mud Pies

Birds usually have no problem finding mud for their early nests because the spring rains leave puddles everywhere. But by early summer, when they're working on the start of yet another home, drought may have dried up all the likely spots. If that's the case, then this modest mud pie will suddenly look like a grand prize.

MATERIALS

Plastic dishpan or similar
    shallow container
Soil
Garden trowel
Water
A few rocks, the same
    height to about an inch
    taller than the dishpan

DIRECTIONS

Step 1. Set the dishpan in an open area, where birds that use mud are more likely to check it out.

Step 2. Fill the dishpan to about 3 inches from the rim with regular soil. Unim-proved soil from your yard is perfect for this project, unless it's sandy. Clay soil will work just fine. But don't use peat moss or packaged topsoil, which is too "good" for this mix; its high content of lightweight humus will prevent the mud from reaching the thick, sloppy consistency we're after.

Step 3. While stirring with the garden trowel, pour in water. Aim for a thick, wet mix that slides slowly off your trowel with a viscous "thwop." If the mud pours easily from the trowel, you need more soil to thicken it up; if the mix stays put on the trowel blade and needs a nudge to dislodge it, add a bit more water.

Step 4. Mud pie mixed to perfection? Way to go! Now it's time to add perching places so that robins and other birds can easily grab a beakful. Settle two or three good-sized rocks into the mud so that their tops protrude an inch or two above the "swamp." Place them so that there's plenty of open mud near their edges.

Step 5. Why, it's a master-piece! Move away, and wait for your first curious customers to arrive. In the days to come, as the mud dries out, water it with a sprinkling can or hose to keep it usable. And if drenching rains arrive and cause your dishpan to over-flow, don't worry: The spill will quickly sink into the surrounding soil, and the soupy mix in the container will thicken up when the sun comes out.

BIRD BUILDING SUPPLIES

Put out an enticing supply of nesting materials, and you never know who might come shopping for home improvements! Here are the birds you might get a peek at, and the materials that will interest them the most. (Because twigs are commonly used by so many birds, only thorny twigs are listed in this table.) Keep in mind that these are only guidelines; your birds may select other materials to finish off their masterpieces.

BIRD	NESTING MATERIAL OFFERINGS	"SERVING" SUGGESTION
Blue grosbeak	Cellophane, mylar	Draped on shrubs or tree branches, among rocks, or directly on ground
Brown thrasher	Fur, grass, hair, short fine string, thorny twigs, wool	In low basket, draped on shrubs, or directly on ground; near protective cover
Buntings, indigo or lazuli	Cotton balls, horsehair, Spanish moss	In wire cage or other elevated container
Cardinal	Bark strips, hair	In tray or low basket
Catbird	Grass, vines	In low basket, draped on shrubs, or directly on ground
Cedar waxwing	String	Draped on small tree
Chickadees, all species	Cotton balls, feathers, fur, hair, milkweed fluff, moss, wool	In wire cage or other elevated container
Finches, Cassin's, purple, and rosy	Hair	In wire cage or other elevated container
Goldfinch, American	Cattail down	In wire cage or other elevated container
Goldfinches, lesser or Lawrence's	Feathers, hair, wool	In wire cage or other elevated container
Great crested flycatcher	Cellophane, mylar	Draped on shrubs or tree branches, among rocks, or directly on ground

(continued)

BIRD BUILDING SUPPLIES, *continued*

BIRD	NESTING MATERIAL OFFERINGS	"SERVING" SUGGESTION
House sparrow	Cellophane, feathers, hair, string	In tray or directly on the ground
Jay, blue	Moss, string, twigs	In tray or directly on the ground
Jay, gray	Bark strips, feathers, fur, hair	In tray or directly on the ground
Jay, scrub	Hair, moss, twigs	In tray or directly on the ground
Jay, Steller's	Moss, mud, twigs	In tray or directly on the ground; near protective cover
Juncos	Hair, moss, possibly feathers	In low basket, draped on shrubs, or directly on the ground; near protective cover
Magpies	Mud	On the ground
Mockingbird	Hair, moss, thorny twigs	In tray, draped on shrubs, or directly on the ground
Native sparrows, including chipping, field, song, white-throated, white-crowned, and others	Hair, long fine grass	In low basket, draped on shrubs, or directly on the ground; near protective cover
Nuthatches, most species	Feathers, fur, grass, hair, moss, wool	In wire cage or other elevated container
Orioles, Baltimore and Bullock's	Cotton balls, grapevine bark, hair, Spanish moss, string, wool	In wire cage or other elevated container, draped on shrubs or trees, or directly on the ground
Orioles, hooded or Scott's	Spanish moss	In wire cage or other elevated container, or draped on shrubs
Pine siskin	Feathers, fur, hair, moss, twigs	In wire cage or other elevated container
Purple martin	String	Directly on the ground or in tray; in open area

BIRD	NESTING MATERIAL OFFERINGS	"SERVING" SUGGESTION
Pyrrhuloxia (the "cardinal" of the Southwest)	Thorny twigs	Directly on the ground
Red-eyed vireo	Vine tendrils	In elevated open tray; near protective cover
Robin	Cloth strips, long fine grass, mud, string	In low basket, draped on shrubs, or directly on the ground
Swallows, most species	Feathers, mud	Directly on the ground, in open area
Tanager, summer	Spanish moss	In wire cage or other elevated container, or draped on shrubs
Titmice, most species	Bark strips, cellophane, fur, grass, hair, moss, mylar, short fine string, thread, wool	In wire cage or other elevated container
Towhees	Grasses	In low basket, draped on shrubs, or directly on the ground; near protective cover
Vermilion flycatcher	Cotton balls, feathers, fur, hair	In wire cage or other elevated container
Warblers, chestnut-sided and other species	String	In wire cage or other elevated container
Wood thrush	Grasses, moss, mud	In low basket or directly on the ground; near protective cover
Wren, canyon	Feathers, fur, pussywillow catkins, wool	In low basket or tray, or directly on the ground; in wire cage or other elevated container
Wrens, Bewick's, Carolina, or house	Cellophane, feathers, hair, leaves, moss, mylar	In wire cage or other elevated container

CHAPTER 13

Mighty Fine Station Design

Setting up a feeding station seems so simple when you start. You buy a feeder, and you hang it up. Why, it's a snap! I can see you experienced feeder-keepers nodding, because you know what happens next. Another feeder, then another one, and before you know it, you have a hodgepodge that looks more like a junkyard than an attractive feeding station.

Well, my friends, help is on the way! In this chapter, I'll show you how to set up a feeding station that's not only practical, but has some class. You'll learn how to select a feeder for its function as well as its form, and how to install your collection of feeders so that they're easy to maintain and look good together. I'll share my suggestions for setting up feeders on your upper deck or balcony, too.

FUNCTIONAL FEEDING STATIONS

Choosing the right feeders and the right combination of feeders is the key, whether you have one place to feed the birds, or one on every side of the house. I like to think of a feeding station as a meal: There's the main course, the side dishes, and the dessert. Here's how to put the parts together to make a full-course meal that'll have you AND the birds saying "Ahhh."

The Main Dish

That main course is supposed to be hearty and filling, right? So start your station with the biggest feeder that will fit into your space and your budget. One big feeder is better than a bunch of dinky ones in three BIG ways:

1. It needs refilling less often.

2. Its hefty size gives it a feeling of permanence in the landscape.

3. Its visual weight will balance an assortment of smaller auxiliary feeders, if you decide to add them later on.

Keep It Simple

The main seating area of your bird restaurant, where a whole bunch of birds can dine at once, is the natural focus of your feeding station. As you learned in Chapter 2, this seed feeder will most likely be a spacious tray or hopper-style model. Look for a feeder that's simply and sturdily made, but also easy to fill. You won't want to be fumbling with fancy contraptions on a frosty morning or when you're running late for work, so get one that lets you pour and run!

JERRY TO THE RESCUE

Q. I only have a small yard. How do I set up a feeding station?

A. A small yard is plenty big enough for a feeding station! Just keep these vital points in mind:

Empty space. You won't need much room for a feeding station, but you will need enough empty space to make refills fast and easy. An open area about 5 by 10 feet will give you plenty of room to install feeders—and to move around to refill them without bushwhacking through shrubs or squeezing up against the house. Remember, the feeding station needs to be inviting for both you and the birds to use!

Room with a view. I guarantee you'll take better care of feeders that you can see up close than those that are hidden, even partially, from view. So set up your station outside a window where you can spend time watching.

Easy access. The sun may come out tomorrow, but right now, a north wind is howling in, and the snow is flying! Or maybe it's raining cats and dogs, or your knees just aren't what they used to be. For convenience considerations, pick a spot that's not too far from your door.

No Wasted Motion

The way you mount your main dish feeder—and all your accessory models—has a lot to do with how easy it will be to use. A hanging feeder is harder to fill, and often harder to reach, than a stationary feeder. With a mounted feeder, you can do a fast, one-handed refill job.

All of the birds that visit a hanging feeder will readily come to a stationary one, but more kinds of birds will visit a mounted feeder than will come to one that swings under their weight. So put in some extra work and support your "main dish" feeder on a solidly anchored post or railing.

Side-Dish Standards

Feeder-keepers are feeder collectors: Once we see how much the birds like our setup, we can't resist adding more. And besides, there's always something new on the market to tempt us. But before you go hog wild, make sure you have the basic side-dish bases covered. A roster of five side-dish feeders is all your well-outfitted feeding station needs to serve every bird in the neighborhood, as well as protect your birdseed budget and make maintenance easy. But you can get away with as little as one side dish added to your main-course feeder. 🐦

Cagey Suet Feeders

Suet and other fats are such a big hit with birds that I consider a suet cage an absolute must. All other bird foods, from niger to nuts, can be offered in your main-dish feeder. But suet needs a place to itself, both because it's messy and because unprotected suet will quickly be gobbled up by starlings.

We're not talking big bucks here, which is why most feeding stations include two or more suet feeders. The basic wire-cage style costs basically pocket change, although substantial wood-mounted models are pricier. And remember, the feeder is also suited to serving peanut butter treats, bread-based goodies, and fruity fat mixes. You'll have customers daily from early fall through spring at a suet feeder, and usually throughout the summer, too. 🐦

One Terrific Tube

You'll need a tube feeder to serve niger and other small specialty seeds, and you can expect goldfinches and other birds to visit it daily throughout the year. Although you could feed niger and other specialty seeds in your main-dish feeder, a tube will save you money because it targets the audience and safeguards the seed.

I know you won't stop at just

LAZULI
BUNTING

Go for the Gold

A handful of goldfinches are likely to stick around all year at your feeding station, but the boom times happen during goldfinch migration in early spring and fall. If your tube feeder is brimming with their favorite niger and other specialty seeds, you can bet you'll have a bounty of loyal customers. Loyal for a while, that is: As soon as their inner clock tells them it's time to move on, they'll be saying "So long!"

I keep a stock of cheap, plastic tube feeders (which you can pick up for as little as $5), ready to press into service when those sunny yellow finches swamp my investment-quality tube feeder. It's a motley assortment that I hang wherever I can find a handy tree limb, but who cares how slap-dash the setup looks, when there's a gang of 100 goldfinches gobbling away?

one terrific tube, because tube feeders are simply so easy to use. But, invest in the best for your primary model so that you get years of nonfrustrating use from it. Buy a tube with sturdy metal trim around the feeding holes, a securely attached handle, an easy-to-remove lid—and a capacity of at least 1 quart. Downsized versions may be mighty cute, but their need for frequent refills will make them quickly lose their charm. 🐦

Nut Miser

Slowing down runaway consumption is the main reason for adding a nut feeder to your feeding station. Nuts aren't cheap, so these wire mesh cylinders (often with wood trim) will help stretch your feed budget by making birds work for it. To cut down on nut consumption more drastically, look for a model that bars blue jays and other large birds (not to mention squirrels) from gobbling up the nuts.

Nut feeders are hot spots at the feeding station year-round. Chickadees, woodpeckers, nuthatches, and other nut lovers will visit early and often. 🐦

Select Company

Figuring out how to un-invite undesirable birds is a common dilemma. You can make sure the birds you like best have a protected place to dine by adding a selective feeder, with restricted entry, to your feeding station. Older models depend on weight-activated doors or perches, but you'll find a wide variety of "caged" feeders now on the market. They're just as effective as weight-sensitive feeders, but they're better for bird watchers because smaller birds can continue dining without interruption. A restrictive feeder isn't a must for your station, but it will give some of your favorite birds a better shot at the feast. 🐦

Nectar Knowledge

You'll definitely want a nectar feeder in your yard, but you may not need to make it part of your feeding station. Here are the things to consider:

Hummingbirds. Hummingbirds will happily use a nectar feeder no matter where you put it. If it's part of the feeding station, they usually won't interfere with birds at other feeders. Just make sure to keep it at least 3 feet from other feeders so you don't antagonize their territorial instincts!

Orioles. The larger nectar feeder that attracts orioles will also get used, whether it's part of the feeding station, or it's located elsewhere in your yard. But I keep mine near other feeders so that the orioles (and possibly tanagers) can easily investigate the suetty goodies and other offerings I custom-make for them.

Seasonality. Hummers and orioles are warm-weather friends in many regions. When they head south, you can simply take down a nectar feeder that's in your feeding station area, and hang a suet cage or tube feeder from the same support.

CALLIOPE
HUMMINGBIRD

The Icing on the Cake

Once you have the standard feeders in place, you can start adding any of the gotta-have-it gadgets that catch your eye. Here's a sampling of what's out there:

- ✔ Dome feeders
- ✔ Expandable wire-mesh feeders
- ✔ Fruit feeders
- ✔ Inside-the-window feeders
- ✔ Jelly feeders
- ✔ Mealworm feeders
- ✔ Mini feeders
- ✔ Niger "socks"
- ✔ Squirrel-proof feeders
- ✔ Suction-cup window feeders
- ✔ Sunflower seed tube feeders

Grandma Putt's

BIRD BITS

Keep It Neat

Grandma Putt was a big fan of a tidy garden, so I would spend an afternoon each spring spreading straw over her strawberry patch. She'd stand back when I had finished, look over the little patch, and announce that now she could tell where the patch began and ended. That's the principle I put into action at my feeding station, too. Instead of straw, I use wood chip mulch to define the feeding area and tie everything together. The tidy layer instantly makes my assortment of poles, posts, and feeders look like they're all part of a whole. And, just like in the strawberry garden, the mulch keeps down weeds and gives the area a well-tended look. It announces to all that someone has put a little TLC into this!

DO IT YOURSELF

Lifesaving Window Treatment

Windows are deadly traps for birds because they never see the glass, only the reflection of the outside world. And one bang is all it takes to permanently remove a bird from your feeder clientele. Naturally, none of of us sets out to lure birds into danger, which is why I use this coverup to make my windows death-defying. Inexpensive black plastic garden netting, is the miracle worker. You'll still have a clear view through it from the inside, but the netting will deter birds from head-on collisions.

MATERIALS

Black plastic garden netting with a grid of about 1" x 1", big enough to cover the window and its frame*

4 suction-cup, stick-on metal or plastic hooks

DIRECTIONS

Step 1. The most time-consuming part of this project is the first step: Wash and dry your window. A squeegee is fun to use and does quick work. I like to follow up with a wadded-up sheet of newspaper to dry the window streak-free.
(continued)

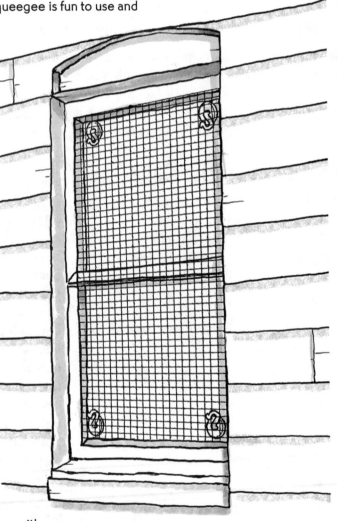

*If your window is too big to cover with one piece of netting, just add more pieces and suction-cup hooks as needed.

⊗ Lifesaving Window Treatment, continued

Step 2. Mount the suction-cup hooks, following the package directions. Put one in each of the corners of the window, as close to the frame as you can. Mount the upper hooks so that they are facing upward; but reverse the bottom hooks so that the hooks are facing downward. This will help keep the netting in place on windy days.

Step 3. The netting will curl at the edges because it was wrapped on the roll. Holding the netting at the top, so the edges curl toward the house, and keeping it moderately taut but not stretched super-tight, hold it in position to fully cover the window. Then, hook the netting over the upper two hooks mounted to the window. Be sure the hooks are inserted in the same horizontal row of the grid so that the netting hangs straight.

Step 4. Gently pull the netting downward, and hook it onto the two lower hooks. Be sure that the hooks are inserted in the same horizontal row of the grid, as well as in the same vertical rows as the upper hooks.

Kissin' Cousins

You'll cut down on refill time by grouping your feeders closely together. Birds will cheerfully visit feeders that are only a couple of feet apart, which means that you can mount your main dish, plus a couple of specialty feeders, practically within arm's length of each other.

But before you poke in those poles or set up those platforms, make sure there's enough room for you to easily maneuver between the feeders. Keep those kissin' cousins separated by about 4 feet of space, so you can move around without getting conked in the head by a hanging tube or tripping over a ground feeder. 🐦

Feeders of a Feather

Another way to reduce refill time and trouble is to make "flocks" of the feeders that you fill with the same food. Keep your soft-food servers in one area, your sunflower tubes and trays in another, and your suet holders all within shouting distance of each other. Then when it's time to refill, you only need to carry that kind of food to one small area, instead of zigzagging from one far corner to the other. This approach makes sense to birds, too, because birds of a feather that flock together appreciate feeders that do the same thing! 🐦

Feeder Siberia

When you're setting up a decoy feeder to lure away starlings, jays, or other troublesome customers from the main feeding area, you'll want to relegate it to the outer reaches of your feeding station—or to another side of the house altogether. That way, the less-wanted birds won't be tempted to check out all the other offerings, and will be more content to stick to their own serving tray. Just don't tell them they've been sent to Siberia! 🐦

INSTALLATION INSIGHTS

Take some time to arrange your feeding station, instead of just adding feeders wherever, whenever you buy them. Start with the main-dish feeder as the center of attention, then fill in around it with your side-dish setups and those little extras that we all like to have. Here's the scoop on setting up a good-looking station with the right supports, the ideal hardware, and the least amount of work!

Plant a Post

If you can dig a hole for a rosebush, you can plant a post! For some reason, lots of folks are scared off by the idea of installing a wooden support for their feeders, and they end up hanging a heavyweight feeder from a flimsy-looking pole. Metal poles that you quickly push into the ground make installing feeders a snap, but save them for lightweight tubes and smaller feeders. Use a wooden 4-by-4 for a substantial feeder, and your setup will instantly look better and be easier to use. Here's how I cut the job down to size:

Have your supplier cut the post. Home-supply stores and lumber-yards are generally happy to cut a 4-by-4 to the length you need. A good length is 5 feet: It'll fit in the backseat of most vehicles, it won't be too heavy for one person to carry, and when it's in the ground, it'll put feeders at an easy-to-reach height, making them easy to fill.

Skip the concrete. Buy a treated post or one made from rot-resistant cedar or cypress, and it should last for several years when it's set directly in the soil. That way, you won't need to mix up any quick-setting concrete to anchor it in.

Bury the bottom at least 18 inches deep. Dig a hole, set in the post, and have a helper hold it straight while you refill the hole. Tamp the soil thoroughly after every couple of shovelfuls that you put in the hole so that the post will be anchored solidly in place.

Mound the soil away from the wood. When you're finished refilling the hole, mound the soil at the top so that the post sticks up from the center of a sloping hill of soil. That'll help keep water from settling around the wood. 🐦

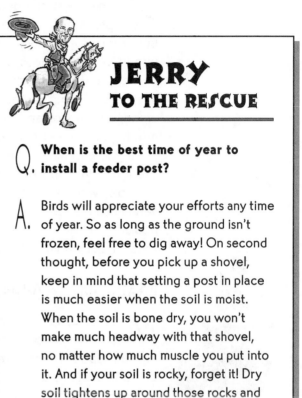

JERRY
TO THE RESCUE

Q. **When is the best time of year to install a feeder post?**

A. Birds will appreciate your efforts any time of year. So as long as the ground isn't frozen, feel free to dig away! On second thought, before you pick up a shovel, keep in mind that setting a post in place is much easier when the soil is moist. When the soil is bone dry, you won't make much headway with that shovel, no matter how much muscle you put into it. And if your soil is rocky, forget it! Dry soil tightens up around those rocks and makes them almost impossible to budge.

Not only is it harder to penetrate dry soil with a shovel or a pole, but dry soil will offer poor support for the post. You can't stomp dry soil into a hard-packed mass. (Just try to mold a ball from dry soil sometime, and you'll see what I mean!) So the post or pole for your feeder will probably begin to lean as soon as you add some weight to it. Wait until the soil is wet deep down after a soaking rain to install your post, or, if rain is scarce, soak the area overnight with a hose set to a trickle.

Added Attractions

A wooden post can double as an impromptu feeder for peanut butter mixes and other smearable bird foods. Chickadees, wood-peckers, and other birds will find it easy to get a grip on the rough wood, and juncos and other low-level birds will be able to peck at a high-fat smear placed near the base of the post.

If you can manage to transport a taller 4-by-4 post, you can use it to attach more than one feeder. An 8-foot-tall post, for example, when set 2 feet into the ground, has 6 inviting feet of vertical space for nailing or hanging feeders from. You can attach hooks on all sides for hanging feeders, or mount flat-backed styles directly against the wood. *Voila*, it's a feeder tree! 🐦

Make Mine Metal

Metal poles for hanging or holding bird feeders come in two basic types: solid iron about 1 inch in diameter, with a hooked top for instant use; and hollow metal 1-inch poles that come in sections to be fitted together, usually with a threaded top or clamp for attaching a feeder.

Both are easy to install: You just push the end of the pole into the ground until the pole is standing straight and secure. Hooked poles are less expensive, but heavier, and may be difficult to fit into your car. Both types will give you years of reliable use. 🐦

Clamp Adapters

You can double the usefulness of a metal pole by adding an inexpensive clamp-on device that lets you attach another feeder. These clamps, which fit poles 1 inch in diameter and larger, start at about $5 and are available at bird-supply stores as well as from the suppliers listed in the Sources section (see page 324). Look for snap-on and screw-on styles; both will support a feeder securely. 🐦

Stiffen That Backbone!

Without a little extra support, metal poles can have problems keeping their posture perfectly straight. Add a feeder to the hook, drop in some bread or other bird treats, and before you know it, you have the leaning pole of pizza crusts. The birds won't mind, but the slumping pole will make your feeding station look shabby.

Many of these popular poles now include an extra "leg" at the base for better support. Look for these styles so that your poles always stand up nice and straight. You can also stack bricks or rocks around the base of a pole to help improve its posture. 🐦

Hooks and Hangers

Playing the hanging judge can be fun, thanks to the array of hooks and other hanging devices that will support a feeder. But before you go shopping, think about where you're going to put the feeder. If you're going to mount it on a wooden post, you'll want a screw-on hook. Want to suspend it from a tree limb? Look for extra-long, solid wire hangers that will hug the limb, or swing it from a chain. Just make sure the wire hanger or chain doesn't interfere with refilling the feeder.

Choose hooks and hangers that are weatherproof and won't need painting or other treatments to prevent rust. And whatever kind of hanging device you choose, make sure it will put the feeder at a convenient height so that you won't have to stand on your tiptoes to refill it! 🐦

SEASONAL SUGGESTIONS

Get 'Em While You Can

Black iron poles with a hook on top for hanging feeders or plants are sold at just about every garden center, discount store, and home-supply center—in spring and summer. But by the time fall and winter roll around, they're often packed up in some dim corner of the storage room, their precious former shelf space replaced with Christmas decorations or other more-in-demand products.

The off-season for garden poles, however, isn't the off-season for feeder-keepers. So think ahead, and outwit the merchants by buying your poles in spring and summer, when you'll often find them featured as sale items. Then keep them in your own storage area until you're ready to set up your feeding station.

DO IT YOURSELF

Double Tubes

Inexpensive iron poles with double (or even triple) hooks on top make the most of your space, and cut down on the time it takes to refill feeders. Double-hook poles seem to disappear much faster than the single-hook style at my garden center, so I discovered a simple trick to make one out of two. The poles sell for as little as $6.99, so this is an inexpensive (and good-looking!) solution, as well as a super-swift installation. Here's how I did it.

MATERIALS

2 iron poles, single-hook style
3 pieces of flexible, but heavy-gauge, aluminum wire, each about 8" long (available at hardware and home-supply stores)
Needlenose pliers
2 tube feeders

DIRECTIONS

Step 1. Choose a location for your double-tube feeder. Push one of the poles into the ground until it is securely anchored.

Step 2. Holding the second pole so that the hook faces in the opposite direction as the hook of the first pole, push it into the ground right beside the first one.

Take care to hold the second pole as straight up vertically as possible while you insert it, to avoid dislodging the first pole. Insert the pole so that its top is aligned with that of the first pole; or, let it extend above

(continued)

⊗ **Double Tubes, continued**

or be lower than the first one, if you prefer that effect. Firm the soil around the poles with your feet.

Step 3. Wrap a piece of wire around the bottoms of both poles, about 6 inches above ground level. Twist the ends as you would a bread twist-tie, until the poles are tightly bound together. Needlenose pliers make quick work of twisting the wire; use it to bend the ends of the wire into a loop, and bend it down against the poles so that no sharp ends stick out.

Step 4. Repeat, wrapping wire near the center of the two poles.

Step 5. Finally, twist one more wire in place at the uppermost point of the parallel poles.

Step 6. Fill and hang one tube feeder from each of the poles. Finches will soon spot your new feeders. They'll appreciate the extra feeding perches, as well as the generous amount of waiting room on the tops of your conjoined poles.

Block Booster

B irdseed sitting directly on the ground overnight is an open invitation to every hungry rodent in the neighborhood. Keep your seeds out of their little paws by setting your low tray or saucer on a concrete block or a few bricks. Try a couple of paving stones as a booster seat for a clay saucer that's a seed tray in winter and a birdbath in summer. Concrete blocks may not be handsome head-on, but they look just fine as a simple foundation for a low-level feeder. 🐦

Porch Posts

I f you set up your feeder near your porch, you can use the posts and rails to hold additional feeders. Stick to seed feeders there, rather than ones that hold fats or fruit, so your posts and porch don't get stained. Waste-free seeds, such as sunflower chips or hulled millet, are perfect for serving near the porch because you won't have any messy collection of shells. This is a good place to install one of those artsy feeders you've been eyeing, because it will make a good ornament hanging from the post.

You can also attach a nectar feeder to your porch for the summer season, when you're most likely to be sitting in that wicker rocker, sipping a mint julep and taking in the sights.

PRETTIFY THE PRACTICAL

Now it's time to put everything together so that your backyard feeding station looks good, as well as serves its purpose. In these pages, we'll look at the finer points of feeding station design. Now don't get all hot and bothered: Good feeding station design is so simple that even *I* can do it! And I'll pass along what I've learned, one step at a time.

Simple Style Wins by a Mile

Stick to classic feeder models: the less decoration, the better. That's because an assortment of ornamented styles can quickly create a higgledy-piggledy effect, even if those fancified feeders cost you a bundle. Clean, uncluttered design is the way to go when you're setting up multiple feeders. Think utilitarian, not froufrou, and let the birds be the real stars at your feeding station.

YELLOW
WARBLER

Mr. Natural

The reason that many feeders are so attention-grabbing is that they're so obviously man-made. Any shiny or bright-colored materials are where our eyes turn to first. (White plastic is the worst offender!) And when there's a batch of unnatural feeders competing for our gaze, the total effect is like an outfit of bold plaids and stripes: It's just too loud and busy to appreciate any of its parts. Choose from feeders with the following quiet qualities when you're buying specialty feeders, and you'll be well on your way to creating a classy feeding station:

✔ Dark-colored metal, either painted or coated

✔ Dull-finish metal trim

✔ Dull-finish plastic in natural colors

✔ Mixed metal-and-wood feeders

✔ Painted feeders in natural colors, such as brown or deep green

✔ Plain wooden feeders

✔ Simple metal designs

Put It on a Pole

I wouldn't be without my tube feeders, but those plastic cylinders can sure make a feeding station look junky in a hurry. Not only are tube feeders made from unnatural-looking materials, they also hang in midair and move about in the breeze or under the weight of birds, which only adds to their impact. Solve this part of the problem by putting your tube on a pole, instead of letting it dangle in the air.

Many tube feeders have a bottom plate that allows you to screw the feeder to a discreet black metal pole, about waist-high. Filling is just as easy as ever: Simply lift the lid, and pour in the seed. And cleaning is only a little more complicated, because you'll need to unscrew the feeder from its base. This solid support looks best with single tube feeders of short to medium height; those with an extra-tall tube or with multiple tubes look ungainly perched atop the relatively skinny pole. ✒

Plain, Please

Often, I have more trouble finding an unadorned style of bird feeder (or practically anything, for that matter) than buying one with all the decorations you could ever dream of. Yet, plain and simple is always in good taste—so much so, that uncluttered objects, if you can find them, often sell for more than their fancy counterparts. I bet Grandma Putt never dreamed that simple wooden kitchen chairs, like the ones she got as hand-me-downs from previous generations, would be fetching sky-high prices at antiques auctions! To her, they simply served their purpose well. And that's the reason for buying a classic style of bird feeder, too: It's made to do the job without calling attention to itself.

Use It or Lose It

An empty or nearly empty tube feeder is way more eye-catching (in a negative way) than a feeder that's kept filled, mostly because those dark seeds help disguise the plastic cylinder. And an empty feeder isn't only unattractive: It's also an advertisement of your lack of attention to refilling chores.

It's easy to accumulate more tube feeders than you can handle regularly, and it's all too tempting to let the empty ones hang until you get around to refilling all of them. If you find yourself looking at nearly empty tube feeders frequently, take it as a hint that you should take down those extras and stick to just one or two that you can keep chock-full of niger, sunflower seeds, or other goodies. 🐦

JERRY
TO THE RESCUE

Q. I can't quite put my finger on it, but my hanging tube feeder looks all wrong. What's the matter?

A. How's it hanging? A tube feeder may look "wrong" because either it's not hanging straight or it's too close to (or too far away from) its supporting post. Or it could simply be at the wrong height. Hang it near eye level, so that your gaze hits the feeder near the middle, or slightly below. You'll want to be able to get a good look at your customers, not have to crane your neck to see their underbellies. And don't let a tube feeder dangle from a long length of chain or wire; for a more attractive effect, snug it up closer to the hook or hanger, with only a few inches of suspension. That way, your feeder should be lookin' good!

Line Up the Lineup

A simple trick for avoiding a slapdash look at your feeding station is to hang all of your tube feeders at about the same height. But what if one feeder is taller or shorter than another? Just hang them so that the shorter feeders are roughly centered, vertically, on the longer ones. Sounds kind of fussbudgety, doesn't it? Yep, it sure is. But being a fussbudget about the details is what good design is all about. And sometimes, moving a feeder a few inches can make a big difference. So if your feeders look funny, but you can't put your finger on exactly why, try adjusting their hanging heights, and see for yourself! 🐦

See Ya Later, Slim!

Multi-tube feeders are a hit with feeder-keepers because they can accommodate more birds at one time, and because you put different kinds of treats in each tube. But if you hang one of these XXL feeders on a slim metal pole shoved into the ground, it will look as awkward as a watermelon hanging on an apple tree. To give a big feeder a bulky backup that's much more pleasing to the eye, fasten a stout metal hook near the top of a wooden 4-by-4 post set into the ground. 🐦

One Is Art; Two Is Too Many

Have you fallen in love with a Victorian-style domed bird feeder with beautiful curlicues? Great! But if you want a good-looking feeding station, stop right there, and keep your other feeders as simple as possible. That way, your ornate masterpiece will get the attention it deserves, instead of competing with a jumble of other pretty things.

Of course, you can carry the theme of your fancy feeder to another feeding area: There's still room—on the other side of the house—for that Victorian gazebo feeder you just have to have! 🐦

Color My World

Even my rules are made to be broken! That's why I call them "guidelines," because I know we all have our own ways of doing things. As much as I prefer my feeders to look as natural as possible, that preference flies right out the window in winter, when **I love to see** a touch of color in the yard. If you live in a gray or snowy climate, **try a few inexpensive plastic feeders with red or green trim for the season. They look great full of snowbirds, chickadees, and cardinals!**

Painted Ponies

Ever notice how a spotted horse stands out in a stampede? They aren't called "paints" for nothing, you know. There's no need to call attention to posts or feeders by painting them bright colors, because most of them are better left to fade into the background. But if you want to make a pretty feeder a real standout in the feeding station stampede, just paint its post or pole to match. 🐦

Second-Story Solutions

Good eats, and plenty of 'em, will encourage many birds to go to great lengths, er, I mean, heights—such as your upper deck. Goldfinches, purple finches, chickadees, cardinals, jays, and a whole laundry list of your favorite birds will have no qualms about becoming regular customers at a second-story sitdown.

Setting up a feeding station on a deck or balcony is different from installing feeders at ground level. Read on for the details on how to select attractive, low-maintenance feeders, and the right kind of hardware for long-lasting attachments.

BLUE
GROSBEAK

Room for Everyone

Keep in mind that you'll be using the area for your own activities, too! You'll want to make sure that your feeders and feeder traffic don't interfere with dining, entertaining, barbecuing, or whatever else you may use the space for. That means, for example, saving birds from hot tootsies by installing feeders well away from the gas grill.

Your upper-level feeding station will probably be much smaller in scope than one that's in the yard, because the space is limited. To keep the bird traffic to a manageable level, you may want to use only limited-access feeders, such as tubes or feeders with an outer cage of bars. A flock of starlings is definitely *not* on the wanted list for a balcony!

Riding the Rails

The railing around your upper-level space is the logical place to attach feeders, and hardware suppliers have taken notice. You'll find a selection of clamps and supports that attach to the rails. But before you buy one, take a close look at

DO IT YOURSELF

High-Rise Hummingbirds

Zippy little hummingbirds are so tuned in to the color red that you can use it as a signal to draw their attention to your balcony or deck, no matter where you live. If there's a hummer in the neighborhood, he'll find it! Have a nectar feeder ready and waiting as the reward, and the bird is likely to become an everyday regular. Real flowers need daily watering in summer, so I use silk blossoms to get their attention. But my nectar solution is no fake!

MATERIALS

Flowerpot or windowbox
Hook for hanging
Nectar feeder
Florist's foam (available at craft stores)
6 or more stems of bright red or orange-red silk flowers, any style, on wire stems
Spanish moss

DIRECTIONS

Step 1. Set the flowerpot or windowbox near the edge of the deck or balcony, where it will be visible from the ground or from the air.

Step 2. Install the hook and hang the freshly filled nectar feeder from the railing near the pot.

Step 3. Set a block (or blocks) of florist's foam into the flowerpot or windowbox and poke the wire stems of the faux flowers into the foam, making sure that the blossoms are above the rim.

Step 4. Nestle the Spanish moss around the top of the pot to disguise the bare stems and the foam.

It may take a week or two for hummingbirds to discover your setup. For fastest results, plan this project for daffodil time in spring, when hordes of hungry migrating hummingbirds are on the move.

how your railing is made; not all supports fit all rails.

If you can't find a clamp-on feeder support to fit your railing, you can still attach feeders to hooks on posts, or on the wall of the house. Or, you can poke a metal feeder pole into an extra-large patio pot that's full of soil and artificial or real flowers.

Lookin' Good

Design details aren't nearly as important at an upper deck feeding station because at this close range, you'll be viewing the feeders individually, not as a whole. And they won't be settled in the landscape, they'll be silhouetted against the sky. This is the place to indulge your desire for any fanciful feeders you take a hankerin' to. Beautiful art-glass tubes, metal curlicues, rustic log cabins, or folksy paint jobs: Go ahead, go wild—it's *your* outdoor art gallery!

SOLID GROUND OR SWINGING FREE?

Most birds prefer to dine at a feeder that doesn't leave them twisting in the wind. Although many species will use hanging feeders when there are no nearby alternatives, you'll get a bigger crowd at stationary feeders, where birds feel more secure. Use these guidelines to make the call when you decide whether to fasten it tight, or hang it up.

FEEDER TYPE	HOW TO MOUNT	BIRDS MOST EASILY ATTRACTED
Nectar	Hanging	All nectar eaters, including house finch, hummingbirds, orioles, small woodpeckers, warblers
Nut	Hanging	All woodpeckers; chickadees, nuthatches, titmice
Nut	Stationary; on post, tree, or railing	All woodpeckers; chickadees, jays, nuthatches, titmice

FEEDER TYPE	HOW TO MOUNT	BIRDS MOST EASILY ATTRACTED
Suet	Hanging	Bushtit, chickadees, nuthatches, small woodpeckers, titmice
Suet	Stationary, on post or railing	All woodpeckers; all soft-food eaters, including bluebirds, bushtit, juncos, orioles, tanagers, wrens
Tray or hopper	Hanging	Bluebirds, cardinal, chickadees, finches, nuthatches, pine siskin, titmice
Tray or hopper	Stationary, on post or railing	All feeder birds (dozens of species)
Tube, large seeds	Hanging	Cardinal, chickadees, goldfinches, grosbeaks, house finch, nuthatches, pine siskin, purple finches, titmice
Tube, large seeds	Stationary, on post	Cardinal, chickadees, goldfinches, grosbeaks, house or pole finch, nuthatches, pine siskin, purple finches, some small and large wood-peckers, titmice
Tube, small seeds	Hanging	Chickadees, goldfinches, house finch, nuthatches, pine siskin, purple finch, redpolls, titmice
Tube, small seeds	Stationary, on post or pole	Buntings, chickadees, goldfinches, house finch, juncos, nuthatches, pine siskin, purple finch, redpolls, titmice

Sources

I usually shop in person so that I can judge the quality of the products with my own eyes. You can find all of the products mentioned in this book at bird-supply stores, discount stores, pet superstores, garden centers, or other outlets that sell supplies for feeding backyard birds. And if your store doesn't happen to have the item you're looking for, they may be willing to order it—if you just ask!

Many mail-order and online companies also sell the supplies you'll need for feeding birds. Their catalogs or websites are a convenient way to comparison-shop, so you can see what options are out there. (I'm kind of partial to jerrybaker.com myself.) That way, you don't have to leave home to lay in your bird feeding supplies!

In this section, you'll find mail-order and online sources for the bird feeding supplies I've mentioned throughout this book. Of course, these sources barely scratch the surface of all the suppliers you might find online. I've selected suppliers that have been in business for at least a few years, with a good reputation for satisfied customers. Happy shopping!

A Bird's World

10645 N. Tatum Blvd.
Ste. 200-273
Phoenix, AZ 85028
abirdsworld.com
877-725-1965

Birdbaths (ground, hanging, heated; drippers, misters, and sprinklers) **bird feeders** *(all-weather, anti-squirrel, domed, fruit, globe, ground, hopper, nectar, platform, suet, tube,* **woodpecker)** *birdhouses (bluebird, chickadee, nuthatch, purple martin, swallow, titmouse, warbler, woodpecker, wren)* **seeds; suet**

A. S. WebSales Corp.

27449 U.S. Highway 59
Shady Point, OK 74956
BirdAndYard.com
800-451-4660

Birdbaths (heated, natural style; bath drippers, heaters, and misters); **bird feeders** *(anti-bear, anti-pest, anti-racoon, anti-starling suet, bluebird, bread, deck-rail, fruit, jelly, mealworm, nectar, roofed, suet, suet-peanut butter log, tray, upside-down suet, upside-down tube, wire cage, woodpecker);* **birdhouses** *(bluebird, chickadee, nuthatch, purple martin, swallow, titmouse, woodpecker, wren; hummingbird nest support,*

robin nesting shelf); **clamp adapters for mounting poles; cleaning brushes; hot pepper spray/powder; instant nectar**

Berkshire Biological

264 Main Road
Westhampton, MA 01027
berkshirebio.com
413-527-3932

Mealworm kits

Berry Hill Irrigation, Inc.

3744 Highway 58
Buffalo Junction, VA 24529
berryhilldrip.com
800-345-3747

Garden hose timer

BestNest.com

4750 Lake Forest Dr.
Ste. 132
Cincinnati, OH 45242
bestnest.com
877-369-5446

Bird feeders (anti-starling suet, bluebird, bread, deck-rail, fruit, hanging, jelly, nectar, roofed, specialty seed, suction-cup, suet, tray, upside-down tube, wire cage, woodpecker); **clamp adapters for mounting poles; cleaning brushes; instant nectar; mealworms; mounting posts and poles; suet blocks**

Jerry Baker

P.O. Box 805
New Hudson, MI 48165
jerrybaker.com
800-888-0010

Labels that say thistle seed, niger seed, or Nyjer™ seed refer to the seeds of Guizotia abyssinica. Good ol' Guizotia is a tall, bushy, yellow-flowered daisy, most definitely not a thistle. I'd wager that "thistle seed" was somebody's idea of how to grab the birdseed market, because true thistle seeds were widely known to be a favorite of goldfinches. Seed sellers later switched to "niger," an English variation of the name used for the plant in its homelands. Nowadays, "niger" is beginning to give way to "Nyjer," a name trademarked by the Wild Bird Feeding Industry of North America. The new phonetic spelling eliminates any chance of an offensive mispronunciation of niger.

Birdola Products

1650 Broadway NW
Grand Rapids, MI 49504
birdola.com
800-BIRDOLA

Bird feeders (finch, hummingbird, suet, thistle, woodpecker) birdhouses; feeder cleaners; seeds

The Bird Shed

6 High Street, Unit 5
Plainville, MA 02762
thebirdshed.com
866-BIRDSHED

Birdbaths (corner, hanging, heated, mister); bird feeders (anti-squirrel, bluebird, hopper, hummingbird, nut, oriole, suet, thistle, tray, window); birdhouses (bluebird, purple martin, woodpecker, wren-chickadee- nuthatch)

ChefShop.com

305 9th Ave. North
Seattle, WA 98109
chefshop.com
877-337-2491

Superfine sugar

Diaz Rock and Pet Supply, Inc.

23907 West Industrial
   Drive N.
Plainfield, IL 60544
diazrock.com
815-609-0888

Seeds; Suet

Do It Best

P.O. Box 868
Fort Wayne, IN 46801
doitbest.com
260-748-7175

Bagged Spanish moss

Droll Yankees

27 Mill Road
Foster, RI 02825
drollyankees.com
800-352-9164

Bird feeders (anti-starling suet, tube seed catcher tray, wire cage); clamp adapters for mounting poles; cleaning brushes; mounting posts and poles

Drs. Foster & Smith, Inc.

2253 Air Park Road
P.O. Box 100
Rhinelander, WI 54501
drsfostersmiths.com
800-381-7179

Birdbaths; birdfeeders, birdhouses; seed; suet

drugstore.com

411 108th Ave. NE, Ste. 1400
Bellevue, WA 98004
drugstore.com
800-378-4786

100% cotton balls

Duncraft, Inc.

102 Fisherville Road
Concord, NH 03303
duncraft.com
800-593-5656

Birdbaths (deck-rail, heated, natural style; bath drippers, heaters, and misters); bird feeders (anti-bear, anti-pest, anti-racoon, deck-rail, fruit, hanging, jelly, mealworm, nectar, nut, specialty seed, suction-cup, suet, upside-down suet, wire cage); birdhouses (bluebird, chickadee, nuthatch, purple martin, swallow, titmouse, woodpecker; hummingbird nest support, robin nesting shelf); mealworms; metal feeder-mounting poles; niger socks; pre-filled nesting materials holders; seeds; suet

eBirdseed.com

27823 86th Avenue S.
Hawley, MN 56549-8982
ebirdseed.com
218-486-5607

Birdseed (canary, flax, hulled millet, hulled sunflower, niger, and other specialty seeds)

Home Harvest Garden Supply, Inc.

4870 Dawn Ave.
East Lansing, MI 48823
homeharvest.com
517-332-5016

Bagged sphagnum moss; black plastic garden netting

Bird-Related Books and Websites

Field guides are available at any bookstore, at bird-supply stores, or from Internet sources, such as amazon.com. Bird feeding websites abound. Here are a few of the most popular guides and websites to get you started.

Field Guides

Birds of North America: A Guide to Field Identification, by Chandler S. Robbins, Bertel Bruun, Herbert S. Zim, and Arthur B. Singer (Golden Guides from St. Martin's Press, 2001)

A Field Guide to the Birds of Eastern and Central North America, edited by Roger Tory Peterson (Houghton Mifflin Co., 2002)

A Field Guide to Western Birds, by Roger Tory Peterson (Houghton Mifflin Co., 1998)

The Sibley Guide to Birds, by David Allen Sibley (Knopf, 2000)

Bird Feeding Internet Sites

birdforum.net

birds-n-garden.com

petco.com

gardenweb.com

purplemartin.org

purplemartins.com

Insect Lore
Box 1535
Shafter, CA 93263
insectlore.com
800-548-3284

Mealworm kits

J.S.C.
971 E. Village Way
Alpine, UT 84004
flaxseedpro.com
801-319-9445

Birdseed (canary, flax, and other specialty seeds)

Mag Enterprises
P.O. Box 210334
Montgomery, AL 36121-0334
magent.com
877-824-5037

Motion-sensitive spray device

Maine Bird & Critter Food
11 Bangor Mall Boulevard
Box 342
Bangor, ME 04401
www.mainebirdfood.com
207-848-2577

Seeds; suet

Nashville Wraps
242 Molly Walton Drive
Hendersonville, TN 37075
nashvillewraps.com
800-547-9727

Cellophane

Nature Hills Nursery, Inc.
3334 North 88th Plaza
Omaha, Nebraska 68134
naturehills.com
888-864-7663

Bagged sphagnum moss

Nu-World Amaranth, Inc.
Nuworldamaranth.com
630-369-6819

Birdseed (canary, flax, and other specialty seeds)

Oregon Feeder Insects, Inc.
oregonfeederinsects.com
208-642-8190

Fruit flies; house flies; insect-enriched suet

Petco
9125 Rehco Road
San Diego, CA 92121
petco.com
877-738-6742

Birdbaths (clamp, hanging; drippers) bird feeders (finch, hummingbird, platform, seed, suet); nectar; seeds; suet

PETdiscounters.com
346 Twin Bridge Road
Ferndale, NY 12734
petdiscounters.com

Crushed oyster shells

PETsMART, Inc.
1989 Transit Way
P.O. Box 910
Brockport, NY 14420-0910
petsmart.com
888-839-9638

Bird feeders (finch, platform, suet); seeds

ShopNatural
350 S. Toole Avenue
Tucson, AZ 85701
shopnatural.com
520-884-0745

Hulled millet

Smarthome
16542 Millikan Avenue
Irvine, CA 92606-5027
smarthome.com
800-762-7846

Motion-sensitive spray device

Songbird Station
Forum Shopping Center, Suite 15
Columbia, MO 65203
songbirdstation.com
888-985-2473

Anti-bee guards

Sunrise Seeds
P.O. Box 501
Union City, IN 47390
sunriseseeds.com
765-964-3956

Suet-peanut butter log

Wild Birds Forever
27214 Highway 189
P.O. Box 4904
Blue Jay, CA 92317-4904
wildbirdsforever.com
800-459-2473

Birdbaths (deck-rail, hanging pedestal, heated; drippers, heaters, and misters) bird feeders (anti-squirrel, fruit, globe, hopper, nectar, platform, specialty seed, suction-cup, suet, tube) birdhouses (bluebird, chickadee, purple martin, wren; robin nesting shelf) nest materials; seeds; suet

Favorite Backyard Birds

B irds at your feeders will feel more like friends when you can call them by name. Here, in living color, you'll find out who's who among more than 60 of the birds that may drop by for a handout.

Each entry in this section includes a map so you can see whether you live in the bird's home zone. But remember, during spring and fall migration, birds often show up beyond their normal range, so you'll never know which birds'll grace your feeders. In addition, each entry tells you what your chances are of hosting the species, and what foods it loves best. Also, to add extra spice to the menu, you'll learn the best homemade recipes (found throughout this book) to tempt the taste buds of each species. Follow my suggestions, and you'll be well on your way to hosting well-fed beauties right in your own backyard!

MAP KEY: ■ Summer ■ Winter ■ Year-round

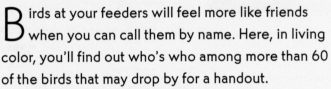

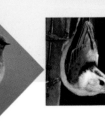

AMERICAN GOLDFINCH

RELIABLE REGULAR: Count on goldfinches showing up daily, year-round.

PEAK SEASON: Crowds (possibly 100 or more) during spring and fall migration.

BEST EATS: Niger, black oil or hulled sunflower seeds, canary and other small seeds.

HOMEMADE TREATS: Finch Favorite (page 29), Grainy Goodness (page 66), Every Finch's Fave (page 75), Cheep Crowd-Pleaser (page 75), Suburban Savories (page 78)

TIDBITS: Accommodate the crowds during migration with an open tray feeder. The male's bright yellow changes to olive green for winter, like the female's year-round color.

ANNA'S HUMMINGBIRD

RELIABLE REGULAR: Many sips of nectar every day keep these birds buzzin'.

PEAK SEASON: Year-round in much of its range; otherwise, spring through fall.

BEST EATS: Nectar.

HOMEMADE TREATS: Heavenly for Hummingbirds (page 153), Protein Punch (page 154)

TIDBITS: Watch the bright pink feathers of a male Anna's hummingbird as it moves its head in sun, and you'll see the feathers flash with hints of gold to pink to magenta to deep purple. In shade, all hummingbirds look black; sunlight makes their iridescent colors come alive.

BALTIMORE ORIOLE

SPECIAL GUEST: May take a while to discover your feeder; then, will visit daily.

PEAK SEASON: Spring. But one to a few orioles may visit at any season if they are present in your area.

BEST EATS: Grape jelly, oranges, nectar, mealworms, fruit, other soft foods.

HOMEMADE TREATS: Oriole Ovals (page 117), Oriole Ambrosia (page 153), All for Orioles (page 162), Perchers' Paradise (page 167), Figgy Pudding (page 167), Corny Banana Bread (page 201)

TIDBITS: Birdbaths are popular with orioles from spring through fall. Females are yellowish green with tinges of orange.

BLACK-CAPPED CHICKADEE

RELIABLE REGULAR: Everyday visitors to the feeder, in pairs or groups.

PEAK SEASON: Year-round.

BEST EATS: Nuts, suet, fat-based treats, black oil and hulled sunflower seeds, bread-based treats.

HOMEMADE TREATS: Suet 'n' Sunflowers (page 90), Suet Snowman (page 100), Good 'n' Pretty (page 136), Extra Incentive (page 137), Super Stuffing (page 143), Chickadee Country (page 184), Hooked on Bagels (page 185)

TIDBITS: Traffic slows in summer, but picks up again when the young leave the nest—and are brought to the feeder!

BLACK-HEADED GROSBEAK

RELIABLE REGULAR: Visits daily, in pairs or small groups.

PEAK SEASON: Spring through fall.

BEST EATS: Sunflower seeds of any kind.

HOMEMADE TREATS: Souped-Up Sunflowers (page 67)

TIDBITS: Unlike many other feeder birds, grosbeaks don't switch to other seeds when the sunflowers run out. Instead, they leave in search of a better-stocked feeder or available natural foods. This species often strays far outside its usual range, so keep an eye open for it, no matter where you live. Female grosbeaks are streaky brown.

BLUE JAY

RELIABLE REGULAR: Visits feeders often, usually every day.

PEAK SEASON: Year-round; more birds from fall through early spring.

BEST EATS: Nuts, acorns; striped, hulled, or black oil sunflower seeds.

HOMEMADE TREATS: Gorgeous Gluttons (page 127), Good 'n' Pretty (page 136), Blue Jay Bounty Hunting (page 138), Acorn Bash (page 138)

TIDBITS: Other birds at a feeder are likely to briefly flee when brash jays arrive, a good reason to have more than one feeder. Male and female jays look alike.

BOBWHITE

SPECIAL GUEST: If you live near grass-lands, these chubby cuties may come to visit daily.

PEAK SEASON: Visits most frequently from fall through early spring.

BEST EATS: Cracked corn, chicken scratch, millet, grain of any kind.

HOMEMADE TREATS: Quail Ho! (page 30), Farms & Fields (page 78)

TIDBITS: Bobwhites are secretive birds that prefer to stay sheltered in tall grass or among shrubs. They may use flower beds as a way to travel between the feeder and wild places.

BROWN CREEPER

SPECIAL GUEST: Reclusive and independent, the brown creeper only occasionally visits feeders. If any come to your feeder, it will be singly.

PEAK SEASON: Winter, in most areas.

BEST EATS: Suet, insect-enriched suet.

HOMEMADE TREATS: Acrobats Only (page 143), Housefly Hash (page 209), Fly This Way! (page 210)

TIDBITS: The creeper has the unusual habit of crawling up tree trunks, in an upward spiral, to spot insects hidden in the bark crevices. When one tree is checked over, the creeper flies to the bottom of the next one and does it again.

BROWN THRASHER

SPECIAL GUEST: This bird is becoming more common at feeders, so be on the lookout for a visit. Usually visits singly.

PEAK SEASON: Fall through spring; may visit year-round.

BEST EATS: Fruit, fruit-based treats, mealworms, suet, other soft foods.

HOMEMADE TREATS: Come One, Come All (page 90), Thrasher's Thrill (page 166), Figgy Pudding (page 167), Date-Bran Bird Muffins (page 192), Way Better'n Worms (page 193), Blueberry Cornbread (page 200), Housefly Hash (page 209), "Fruity" Suet (page 209)

TIDBITS: The thrasher is a great singer, but he often hides in a bush to perform. Male and female look alike.

BUSHTIT

RELIABLE REGULAR: Small to large groups visit sporadically, but reliably.

PEAK SEASON: Year-round.

BEST EATS: Suet, suet-based treats.

HOMEMADE TREATS: Suet Snowman (page 100), Acrobats Only (page 143), "Fruity" Suet (page 209), Fly This Way! (page 210)

TIDBITS: Don't blink or you'll miss 'em! Bushtits don't linger at the feeding station; they grab a few bites and leave within minutes. They do announce themselves, though, with a constant chatter of high, short calls uttered by members of the flock. They're one of the smallest birds in America.

CARDINAL

RELIABLE REGULAR: Visits feeders often, usually every day.

PEAK SEASON: Year-round. Higher numbers (a dozen or more!) in winter, when cardinals flock together.

BEST EATS: Black oil, striped, or hulled sunflower seeds; cracked or whole corn kernels.

HOMEMADE TREATS: Craving Cardinals (page 38), Souped-Up Sunflowers (page 67), Tube-Feeder Treat (page 128), Crush on Cardinals (page 171)

TIDBITS: Once cardinals get used to it, safflower seed is a popular treat. In late winter, the males become brighter red for breeding season.

CAROLINA WREN

RELIABLE REGULAR: A daily visitor, if one lives in your neighborhood. Visits singly or in pairs.

PEAK SEASON: Year-round.

BEST EATS: Mealworms, suet, fruit-based treats, bread-based treats, millet.

HOMEMADE TREATS: Suet Snowman (page 100), Wrangle a Wren (page 172), Hooked on Bagels (page 185), Songsters' Surprise (page 185), PB-Raisin Cookies (page 193), Applesauce-Nut Bread (page 201), Housefly Hash (page 209), Fly This Way! (page 210)

TIDBITS: Much more willing than the house wren to visit feeders. Male and female look alike.

CATBIRD

SPECIAL GUEST: The gray catbird appears to be getting more accustomed to eating at feeders, so keep your eyes open. Usually visits singly.

PEAK SEASON: Fall through spring.

BEST EATS: Mealworms, suet-, fruit-, and bread-based treats, and other soft foods.

HOMEMADE TREATS: Meow Mixture (page 166), Perchers' Paradise (page 167), Songsters' Surprise (page 185), Mini Sandwich Squares (page 185), Date-Bran Bird Muffins (page 192), Blueberry Cornbread (page 200), Housefly Hash (page 209), "Fruity" Suet (page 209)

TIDBITS: The gray catbird can sound just like a meowing cat, but it also has a pretty song. Male and female look alike.

CHIPPING SPARROW

RELIABLE REGULAR: One to a few of these birds will visit daily.

PEAK SEASON: Fall, spring; winter in its southern winter range.

BEST EATS: Millet, canola and other small seeds, chicken scratch.

HOMEMADE TREATS: Sparrows Supreme (page 38), Budget Breakfast (page 66), Sparrow Style (page 76)

TIDBITS: One of the smallest feeder visitors. Look for its jazzy reddish brown cap. Unlike many sparrows, the little "chippy" usually eats at raised feeders, rather than near the ground.

COMMON GRACKLE

RELIABLE REGULAR: Expect to see a few to several grackles strutting around at the feeder every day.

PEAK SEASON: Year-round in many areas; otherwise, spring through fall.

BEST EATS: Cracked corn, chicken scratch, millet, and just about any other seed they can crack. Also eats soft foods, including bread-based treats.

HOMEMADE TREATS: Cheepest Trio (page 38), Farms & Fields (page 78), Blackbird Buffet (page 101)

TIDBITS: The sleek black feathers of the common grackle flash with bronze or purple in the sun.

DARK-EYED JUNCO

RELIABLE REGULAR: Juncos are a part of winter feeder life just about everywhere. You'll host several to many.

PEAK SEASON: Daily visitor from fall through spring.

BEST EATS: Millet, chicken scratch, cracked corn. Eats suet if it's accessible, such as crumbled in the feeder tray.

HOMEMADE TREATS: Cheepest Trio (page 38), Budget Breakfast (page 66), Sparrow Suet (page 91), Acorn Bash (page 138)

TIDBITS: Juncos, also called "snowbirds," often scratch on the ground below feeders to ferret out dropped seeds. Male and female are very similar.

DOWNY WOODPECKER

RELIABLE REGULAR: One of the daily stalwarts at feeders across the country. One to a few birds will visit.

PEAK SEASON: Year-round.

BEST EATS: Suet, fat-based treats, sunflower seeds of any kind, nuts.

HOMEMADE TREATS: Downy's Dream (page 118), Extra Incentive (page 137), Woodpecker Windup (page 137), Woodpecker Welcome (page 184)

TIDBITS: Keep that suet going in summer, when downy woodpeckers often take pieces to feed their babies. Later, they may bring the young'uns to show them where to find the good stuff for themselves. Downy woodpeckers may also drink nectar.

EASTERN BLUEBIRD

SPECIAL GUEST: Likely to make their first visit to your feeder when snow or ice causes them to seek other food sources. May become reliable regulars. Usually visits in pairs or small groups.

PEAK SEASON: Fall through early spring.

BEST EATS: Mealworms, suet-based treats, peanut-butter-based treats, other soft foods.

HOMEMADE TREATS: Got the Blues (page 107), Ultramarine Dream (page 107), Sapphire Supply (page 108), Bluebird Best (page 172), Bluebird Bounty Hunter (page 184), Code Blue(bird) Emergency! (page 192), "Fruity" Suet (page 209)

TIDBITS: Bluebirds are tame at the feeder, allowing you to approach up close.

EASTERN TOWHEE

SPECIAL GUEST: One to a few may visit, especially after a snowstorm.

PEAK SEASON: Fall through spring.

BEST EATS: Millet, chicken scratch, cracked corn, canola and other small seeds.

HOMEMADE TREATS: Cheepest Trio (page 38), Every Finch's Fave (page 75), Sparrow Style (page 76)

TIDBITS: In the West, this species is replaced by the similar spotted towhee. Towhees often feed on or near the ground, and are strong "scratchers"; they can dig through snow with their feet to get to seeds underneath. Female towhees are brown.

EVENING GROSBEAK

SPECIAL GUEST: It's feast or famine with these guys: If they come, they'll arrive by the dozen.

PEAK SEASON: Fall through spring. Notorious for inconsistent migration patterns.

BEST EATS: Sunflower seeds of any kind, and plenty of them!

HOMEMADE TREATS: Souped-Up Sunflowers (page 67)

TIDBITS: I keep an extra bag of sunflower seeds on hand, just in case grosbeaks decide to drop in, because once the seeds run out, the birds are gone. Females are gray-green.

FOX SPARROW

SPECIAL GUEST: Once a fox sparrow finds your feeder, it may drop in for a visit daily for weeks.

PEAK SEASON: One to a few may visit from fall to spring, especially when a snow or ice storm hits.

BEST EATS: Millet, canola and other small seeds, chicken scratch, cracked corn. Also eats suet if it's accessible.

HOMEMADE TREATS: Sparrows Supreme (page 38), Budget Breakfast (page 66), Sparrow Style (page 76), Sparrow Suet (page 91)

TIDBITS: It's always a thrill when this big, plump sparrow shows up. Fox sparrows are great at digging through snow with their feet to get to seed below.

GAMBEL'S QUAIL

RELIABLE REGULAR: A daily visitor at feeders and birdbaths. Small groups visit the feeder area together.

PEAK SEASON: Year-round.

BEST EATS: Cracked corn, chicken scratch, millet, grain of any kind.

HOMEMADE TREATS: Quail Ho! (page 30), Farms & Fields (page 78)

TIDBITS: Water is a huge draw for these birds of the Southwest. Don't be surprised to see one or more perched on the rim of a pedestal birdbath! To make these ground-dwelling birds more at ease, add a low-level bath.

HAIRY WOODPECKER

SPECIAL GUEST: Even more widespread than the downy woodpecker, but much less numerous. If one finds your feeder, it'll generally visit daily. You'll most likely host just a single bird.

PEAK SEASON: Year-round.

BEST EATS: Suet, fat-based treats, sunflower seeds of any kind, nuts.

HOMEMADE TREATS: Woodpecker Windup (page 137), Acorn Bash (page 138), Woodpecker Welcome (page 184), Housefly Hash (page 209)

TIDBITS: Take a close look at the beak to tell hairy from downy. The hairy is a larger bird, with a bill to match.

HERMIT THRUSH

SPECIAL GUEST: Seen in yards more often than seen at feeders, but may check out the eats in winter.

PEAK SEASON: Fall through early spring, especially during migration or in harsh winter weather.

BEST EATS: Mealworms, possibly soft foods made with fruit.

HOMEMADE TREATS: Perchers' Paradise (page 167)

TIDBITS: Water is often a bigger attraction than food. Thrushes are big fans of ground-level birdbaths, particularly those with dripping or running water.

HOUSE FINCH

RELIABLE REGULAR: Too reliable and too regular, in many folks' opinion. Expect a few to dozens daily.

PEAK SEASON: Year-round.

BEST EATS: Black oil or hulled sunflower seeds, niger, millet, other small seeds, chicken scratch.

HOMEMADE TREATS: Finch Favorite (page 29), Cheapest Trio (page 38), Budget Breakfast (page 66), Grainy Goodness (page 66), Suburban Savories (page 78)

TIDBITS: House finches are plentiful. To separate them from similarly colored purple finches, look at the females—they're streaky brown.

HOUSE SPARROW

RELIABLE REGULAR: Ubiquitous daily visitor, several to many at a time.

PEAK SEASON: Year-round.

BEST EATS: Chicken scratch, cracked corn, millet and other small seeds, bread-based treats.

HOMEMADE TREATS: You won't need "treats" to attract this bird, but you can use Cheapest Trio (page 38) to serve a multitude.

TIDBITS: If house sparrows were a beautiful color, feeder hosts would be a lot fonder of them. Still, they're a cheerful presence in inner cities and other places where few types of birds visit the feeder.

INDIGO BUNTING

SPECIAL GUEST: This bright blue bird makes it a red-letter day. One to a dozen or more may stop in for days to weeks during migration.

PEAK SEASON: Spring migration.

BEST EATS: Millet, canola and other small seeds, chicken scratch.

HOMEMADE TREATS: Finch Favorite (page 29), Budget Breakfast (page 66), Every Finch's Fave (page 75), Cheep Crowd-Pleaser (page 75), Suburban Savories (page 78)

TIDBITS: Once a rarity at feeders, this incredible bird is becoming a regular spring harbinger at many feeding stations. Females are plain brown.

LAZULI BUNTING

SPECIAL GUEST: Groups of a few to several may visit daily. In some areas, the birds are reliable regulars.

PEAK SEASON: Spring migration; possibly fall migration, and also possibly in summer if you live near their nesting territory.

BEST EATS: Millet, canola, and other small seeds.

HOMEMADE TREATS: Budget Breakfast (page 66), Grainy Goodness (page 66), Cheep Crowd-Pleaser (page 75)

TIDBITS: At first glance, it's easy to mistake this bunting for a bluebird. Females are gray-brown, with a buff breast.

MEADOWLARK

SPECIAL GUEST: One to a few birds may visit, especially after heavy snow or ice storms.

PEAK SEASON: Winter to early spring.

BEST EATS: Millet, cracked corn, chicken scratch. In bitter winter weather, chop some suet to help them boost their body heat.

HOMEMADE TREATS: Cheepest Trio (page 38), Farms & Fields (page 78)

TIDBITS: Meadowlarks are divided into eastern and western species, but they look almost exactly the same. The big difference is in their songs. In fall, the birds lose their bright yellow breast and black chest V; in spring, they brighten up again.

MOCKINGBIRD

SPECIAL GUEST: If a mockingbird claims your feeder, it'll visit every day; usually one bird per feeding station.

PEAK SEASON: Fall through spring.

BEST EATS: Millet and other seeds, fruit, baked goods, suet-based treats.

HOMEMADE TREATS: Come One, Come All (page 90), Mockingbird Mania (page 173), Songsters' Surprise (page 185), Date-Bran Bird Muffins (page 192), Applesauce-Nut Bread (page 201)

TIDBITS: The mockingbird's talent for singing (even at night) may make up for its greed—unless the mocker is singing right outside your bedroom window!

MOUNTAIN BLUEBIRD

SPECIAL GUEST: At most feeders, only an occasional delight. But even if a few of these bluebirds visit daily, they're special.

PEAK SEASON: Fall through early spring, especially during harsh winter weather.

BEST EATS: Mealworms, suet, fat-based treats, fruit and fruit-based treats.

HOMEMADE TREATS: Got the Blues (page 107), Ultramarine Dream (page 107), Sapphire Supply (page 108), Bluebird Best (page 172), Bluebird Bounty Hunter (page 184)

TIDBITS: Just as fond of birdhouses as other bluebirds, this species may bring its youngsters to your feeder.

MOURNING DOVE

RELIABLE REGULAR: Day in, day out, mourning doves are regular clients at the feeding station. They visit in pairs or small groups.

PEAK SEASON: Year-round, except in the North, where doves reside from spring through fall.

BEST EATS: Cracked corn, chicken scratch, millet, any other small seeds.

HOMEMADE TREATS: Pigeon-Toed Treat (page 37), Cheepest Trio (page 38), In-Town Treats (page 79)

TIDBITS: During breeding season, a male mourning dove's thoughts turn to love. Watch him strut and stretch his pretty neck to impress his lady love.

NORTHERN FLICKER

RELIABLE REGULAR: One to a few birds will visit daily.

PEAK SEASON: Year-round in most areas.

BEST EATS: Suet, fat-based treats, nuts, corn, sunflower seeds of any kind.

HOMEMADE TREATS: Corny Suet (page 92), Flicker Flapdoodle (page 101), Good 'n' Pretty (page 136), Woodpecker Windup (page 137)

TIDBITS: Western birds, like this one, sport a red moustache; the eastern bird has a black one. Western or red-shafted flickers are reddish under the wings; the yellow-shafted flickers of the East are golden underneath. Flickers often feed on grubs in lawns.

PIGEON (ROCK DOVE)

RELIABLE REGULAR: While an infrequent delight at suburban feeders, the pigeon is an everyday visitor to city spreads. You'll host one to several daily.

PEAK SEASON: Year-round.

BEST EATS: Cracked corn, chicken scratch, millet and other small seeds.

Homemade treats: Pigeon-Toed Treat (page 37), Cheepest Trio (page 38), In-Town Treats (page 79)

TIDBITS: Unlike starlings and house sparrows, pigeons are all-American, descended from wild birds that nested on cliffs before there were city ledges. They're easy to recognize as individuals because of variations in their coloring.

PINE SISKIN

RELIABLE REGULAR: Expect several to many of these birds to visit daily.

PEAK SEASON: Many areas, fall to spring; in areas where they live year-round, they visit feeders year-round.

BEST EATS: Niger seed, black oil sunflower seeds, millet and other small seeds.

HOMEMADE TREATS: Grainy Goodness (page 66), Every Finch's Fave (page 75), Cheep Crowd-Pleaser (page 75), Pumped-Up All-Purpose Mix (page 76), Suburban Savories (page 78)

TIDBITS: Streaky brown siskins are easy to confuse with female house finches. Males have yellow wing bars.

PURPLE FINCH

SPECIAL GUEST: The visits of these pretty birds are usually fleeting, just a few days or weeks before they go on their way. You'll host one to several birds; sometimes, a dozen or more.

PEAK SEASON: Spring and fall migration in most areas; winter or year-round.

BEST EATS: Sunflower seeds of any kind, niger, millet and other small seeds.

HOMEMADE TREATS: Finch Favorite (page 29), Every Finch's Fave (page 75), Suburban Savories (page 78), Forest Fauna (page 79)

TIDBITS: Males look much like house finches at first glance, but females are easier to I.D., due to a bold eyestripe.

PURPLE MARTIN

SPECIAL GUEST: You'll be visited by purple martins only if a colony lives nearby, with a few to many birds arriving, depending on the colony size.

PEAK SEASON: Spring through early fall.

BEST EATS: Mealworms, crushed eggshells.

HOMEMADE TREATS: None

TIDBITS: Make sure these large swallows have room to swoop in for their food, and to take off unimpeded. An open tray feeder—or your lawn!—fills all the requirements for beautiful martins, and also gives you a good view of their shining plumage.

RED-BELLIED WOODPECKER

RELIABLE REGULAR: One to a few birds will visit daily.

PEAK SEASON: Year-round. More birds visit in winter.

BEST EATS: Suet, fat-based treats, corn, nuts, sunflower seeds of any kind.

HOMEMADE TREATS: Corny Suet (page 92), Woodpecker Windup (page 137), Recipe for Redheads (page 139), Woodpecker Welcome (page 184), Corny Banana Bread (page 201)

TIDBITS: Red belly?! It's the red on head and neck that you'll notice; the small patch of reddish feathers on the belly is usually hidden when the bird perches.

RED-BREASTED NUTHATCH

RELIABLE REGULAR/SPECIAL GUEST: Can be a daily visitor or an infrequent, short-term guest.

PEAK SEASON: In some areas, a frequent visitor year-round; in others, a treat during spring and fall migration time.

BEST EATS: Black oil sunflower seeds, hulled sunflower seeds, suet, fat-based treats.

HOMEMADE TREATS: Suet 'n' Sunflowers (page 90), Suet Snowman (page 100), Nuthatch Hustle (page 118), Big Treat for Little Guys (page 137), Extra Incentive (page 137)

TIDBITS: Known for being plentiful at feeders one year, scarce in other years.

RED-HEADED WOODPECKER

SPECIAL GUEST: If you're lucky enough to live in red-headed woodpecker territory, one to several birds will visit daily.

PEAK SEASON: Year-round in some areas; spring through fall in others.

BEST EATS: Corn, suet, fat-based treats, nuts.

HOMEMADE TREATS: Corny Suet (page 92), Woodpecker Windup (page 137), Recipe for Redheads (page 139), Pileated Possibility? (page 144)

TIDBITS: These birds live in colonies throughout their large range. But the colonies are widely scattered, so the birds aren't common everywhere.

REDPOLL

SPECIAL GUEST: In the North, redpolls may be reliable regulars, but in most of the country, they're erratic surprise visitors. They will visit in groups of several to many.

PEAK SEASON: Winter.

BEST EATS: Niger, black oil sunflower seeds, millet, canola and other small seeds.

HOMEMADE TREATS: Grainy Goodness (page 66), Forest Fauna (page 79)

TIDBITS: Keep an eye on those tube feeders: Redpolls may be occupying some of the perches! These little birds are noted for straying outside their usual range, and may turn up in just about any state across the country.

RED-WINGED BLACKBIRD

SPECIAL GUEST: If you live near where redwings nest, they may be daily visitors. Otherwise, they usually visit only during migration. Expect several to hordes!

PEAK SEASON: Year-round; in the North, spring through fall.

BEST EATS: Millet, cracked corn, chicken scratch, other small seeds.

HOMEMADE TREATS: Cheepest Trio (page 38), Farms & Fields (page 78), Blackbird Buffet (page 101)

TIDBITS: Although redwings are one of the most numerous birds in the country, they usually stay near fields or water. Females are streaky brown.

ROBIN

SPECIAL GUEST: Robins find plenty of natural food to eat in your yard.

PEAK SEASON: Winter to early spring, when the ground is frozen and natural food is harder to find.

BEST EATS: Soft foods, including mealworms, bread, suet-based treats, fruit, fruit-based treats.

HOMEMADE TREATS: Robin Roundabout (page 102), Perchers' Paradise (page 167), Songsters' Surprise (page 185), Way Better'n Worms (page 193), PB-Raisin Cookies (page 193), Blueberry Cornbread (page 200)

TIDBITS: A helping hand can save a robin's life in wild winter weather.

ROSE-BREASTED GROSBEAK

SPECIAL GUEST: Look for one to several of these beauties to visit for a few days or weeks.

PEAK SEASON: Spring migration; may also visit during fall migration.

BEST EATS: Black oil sunflower seeds, hulled sunflower seeds, striped sunflower seeds.

HOMEMADE TREATS: Souped-Up Sunflowers (page 67)

TIDBITS: Not many years ago, the rose-breasted grosbeak was a rarity at feeders. Now becoming more common, the birds often arrive about the same time as indigo buntings. Females are streaky brown.

RUBY-CROWNED KINGLET

SPECIAL GUEST: Infrequently visits feeders, but may adopt a nectar feeder or come for suet in winter.

PEAK SEASON: Winter, unless the bird discovers the joys of nectar, in which case one or a few may visit as long as the feeder is hanging.

BEST EATS: Insect-enriched suet, possibly nectar.

HOMEMADE TREATS: Heavenly for Hummingbirds (page 153), Fly This Way! (page 210)

TIDBITS: Grab binoculars to spot the small bright patch of red head feathers that gives this bird its name.

RUBY-THROATED HUMMINGBIRD

RELIABLE REGULAR: Put out a nectar feeder anywhere within their range, and you're bound to attract hummingbirds.

PEAK SEASON: You'll host several to many during spring and fall migration; resident birds will visit all summer long.

BEST EATS: Nectar.

HOMEMADE TREATS: Heavenly for Hummingbirds (page 153), Protein Punch (page 154)

TIDBITS: Keep the feeder filled until the sugar water threatens to freeze, in case any migrating slowpokes happen by. Females lack the flashy throat feathers.

RUFOUS HUMMINGBIRD

RELIABLE REGULAR: Count on these hummingbirds to visit daily.

PEAK SEASON: You'll host many during spring and fall migration; fewer, but still reliable, regulars will appear all summer.

BEST EATS: Nectar.

HOMEMADE TREATS: Heavenly for Hummingbirds (page 153), Protein Punch (page 154)

TIDBITS: Early evening is prime time for hummingbirds to drink up at the nectar feeder, to fuel up for the night before the sun goes down. Females are green and lack the fancy throat color.

SCARLET TANAGER

SPECIAL GUEST: Wow, what a thrill to see this brilliant bird at the feeder! One to a few may visit for a few days or weeks.

PEAK SEASON: Spring migration.

BEST EATS: Millet, mealworms; other soft foods, especially fruit-based treats.

HOMEMADE TREATS: Tanager Treat (page 29), Tanager Tantalizer (page 117), Tanager Temptations (page 161), Perchers' Paradise (page 167), Figgy Pudding (page 167), End-of-the-Trail Mix (page 173), Tanager Two-Step (page 194), Corny Banana Bread (page 201), Applesauce-Nut Bread (page 201)

TIDBITS: Females are olive green. Birdbaths are a hit with tanagers.

SCOTT'S ORIOLE

SPECIAL GUEST: May take a while to discover your feeder; then, it may be a daily guest. One to a few may visit at any season if they are present in your area.

PEAK SEASON: Spring.

BEST EATS: Nectar, grape jelly, oranges, mealworms, fruit, suet, soft foods.

HOMEMADE TREATS: Oriole Ovals (page 117), Oriole Ambrosia (page 153), All for Orioles (page 162), Corny Banana Bread (page 201)

TIDBITS: As with all orioles, the male is the show-off with his coloring; females are much duller. Birdbaths are popular with orioles, especially in dry summers.

SCRUB JAY

RELIABLE REGULAR: A few to several will visit the feeder daily.

PEAK SEASON: Year-round.

BEST EATS: Nuts, sunflower seeds of any kind.

HOMEMADE TREATS: Gorgeous Gluttons (page 127), Goober Boost (page 128), Good 'n' Pretty (page 136), Blue Jay Bounty Hunting (page 138), Acorn Bash (page 138), A&W Float (page 142)

TIDBITS: Scrub jays are generally gray-blue, but those along the Pacific show off brighter color. Florida scrub jays have lighter markings, including a pale back and whitish forehead.

SONG SPARROW

RELIABLE REGULAR: One to a few of these small brown birds visit feeders daily.

PEAK SEASON: Year-round, or winter only, depending on where you live.

BEST EATS: Millet, canola and other small seeds, chicken scratch, cracked corn.

HOMEMADE TREATS: Sparrows Supreme (page 38), Budget Breakfast (page 66), Sparrow Style (page 76), Song Sparrow Specialty (page 172)

TIDBITS: A quiet guest, the song sparrow often gets overlooked among the more colorful or pushier birds at the feeder. Look for this one pecking at seeds below the feeder.

STARLING

RELIABLE REGULAR: Daily visitor, with a few to many visiting the feeder.

PEAK SEASON: Year-round.

BEST EATS: Just about anything! The starling became so successful in America because of its non-fussy food habits. Chicken scratch, stale bread, fat scraps, and other inexpensive foods will easily satisfy them.

HOMEMADE TREATS: Cheepest Trio (page 38), Feedbag Full o' Oats (page 91), Strictly for Starlings (page 101)

TIDBITS: Use starling-proof feeders if these birds are too numerous at your place, or give them a generous feeder full of the foods they like.

TUFTED TITMOUSE

RELIABLE REGULAR: Everyday visitors, singly or in pairs.

PEAK SEASON: Year-round. Highest numbers occur in winter.

BEST EATS: Nuts, suet, fat-based treats, black oil and hulled sunflower seeds, bread-based treats.

HOMEMADE TREATS: Suet 'n' Sunflowers (page 90), Bottom Line (page 96), Titmouse Time (page 100), Good 'n' Pretty (page 136), Big Treat for Little Guys (page 137), Peanutty Porcupines (page 142), Super Stuffing (page 143), Hooked on Bagels (page 185)

TIDBITS: Adults bring adorable youngsters to the feeder when the young'uns leave the nest.

VARIED THRUSH

SPECIAL GUEST: If your yard is near woods, one of these beautiful birds may become a regular.

PEAK SEASON: Usually winter, but may visit year-round in some areas.

BEST EATS: Millet, other small seeds, chicken scratch, fruit-based treats.

HOMEMADE TREATS: Cheepest Trio (page 38), Budget Breakfast (page 66), Perchers' Paradise (page 167)

TIDBITS: This songbird of the West looks like a robin in fancy dress. It is often spotted far afield from its usual range, so take another look if that "robin" looks a little duded up.

WHITE-BREASTED NUTHATCH

RELIABLE REGULAR: One to several will visit daily.

PEAK SEASON: Year-round. Numbers usually increase in winter, though it's hard to tell unless multiple birds visit at the same time.

BEST EATS: Nuts, sunflower seeds of any kind, suet, fat-based treats.

HOMEMADE TREATS: Suet 'n' Sunflowers (page 90), Suet Snowman (page 100), Nuthatch Hustle (page 118), Good 'n' Pretty (page 136), Big Treat for Little Guys (page 137), Extra Incentive (page 137)

TIDBITS: Sexes look alike. Nuthatches often bring their young ones to the feeder after the youngsters leave the nest.

WHITE-CROWNED SPARROW

RELIABLE REGULAR: A daily feeder appreciator. You may have a single bird, or several.

PEAK SEASON: Fall through spring.

BEST EATS: Millet, canola and other small seeds, chicken scratch.

HOMEMADE TREATS: Sparrows Supreme (page 38), Budget Breakfast (page 66), Sparrow Style (page 76), Sparrow Suet (page 91)

TIDBITS: This small brown bird gets an A+ for posture. It's easy to sort out from other sparrows, thanks to its alert-looking upright stance and brightly striped head.

WHITE-THROATED SPARROW

RELIABLE REGULAR: A few to dozens of these birds visit feeders daily in winter.

PEAK SEASON: Fall through spring.

BEST EATS: Millet, canola and other small seeds; eats suet in winter if accessible.

HOMEMADE TREATS: Sparrows Supreme (page 38), Budget Breakfast (page 66), Sparrow Style (page 76), Sparrow Suet (page 91), Song Sparrow Specialty (page 172)

TIDBITS: Sparrows can be mighty tricky to tell apart. This one has a white bib and striped head, to make I.D. matters a bit easier. It often scratches on the ground alongside juncos.

WILD TURKEY

SPECIAL GUEST: If you live near fields and forests, you may be surprised to spot this big feeder guest—or his entire flock!

PEAK SEASON: Winter, but may visit at any time of year.

BEST EATS: Corn, corn, and corn! It's cheap and goes a long way. Turkeys also peck at millet, nuts, and many other grains and seeds, and will eat chicken scratch.

HOMEMADE TREATS: Cheepest Trio (page 38), Turkey Trot (page 39), Acorn Bash (page 138)

TIDBITS: Gangly baby turkeys are a sight to behold. Keep pouring out the feed, and you may be treated to a visit.

YELLOW-BELLIED SAPSUCKER

SPECIAL GUEST: A single bird may stop by occasionally, or visit daily once it discovers your nectar feeder.

PEAK SEASON: Winter to early spring.

BEST EATS: Nectar; may sample jelly or other sweets.

HOMEMADE TREATS: Heavenly for Hummingbirds (page 153), Oriole Ambrosia (page 153)

TIDBITS: One of the first species to learn that sipping from hummingbird feeders is easier than drilling holes in trees for sap. Appreciates a big, heavier-duty nectar feeder, such as those made for orioles.

YELLOW-HEADED BLACKBIRD

RELIABLE REGULAR: It may take a while for your setup to be discovered, but once found, a few to several birds will visit daily.

PEAK SEASON: Spring and fall migration; also winter, in areas where the birds spend that season.

BEST EATS: Cracked corn, millet and other small seeds, chicken scratch.

HOMEMADE TREATS: Cheepest Trio (page 38), Farms & Fields (page 78)

TIDBITS: During nesting season, these bold-colored birds stick close to the marshes where they raise their families. Females lack the vivid yellow hood.

YELLOW-RUMPED WARBLER

SPECIAL GUEST: This pretty little bird is showing up at more and more feeders, but its visits are always a surprise.

PEAK SEASON: Winter, unless the bird has adapted to drinking nectar from a feeder.

BEST EATS: Suet and suet-based treats, especially in winter; nectar in warmer seasons.

HOMEMADE TREATS: Yo-De-Lay-Hee-Hoo! (page 97), Heavenly for Hummingbirds (page 153), "Fruity" Suet (page 209)

TIDBITS: The photo shows Audubon's warbler, the western variation of this species, which has a yellow throat.

YELLOW WARBLER

SPECIAL GUEST: Another bird that's learning to sip from nectar feeders. If one that knows the trick shows up at yours, it may linger for several days or weeks.

PEAK SEASON: Spring and fall migration.

BEST EATS: Nectar.

HOMEMADE TREATS: Heavenly for Hummingbirds (page 153)

TIDBITS: Yellow warblers are insect eaters, so if you keep mealworms on hand at your feeder, you may find a warbler expanding its diet beyond the sugar water! Meanwhile, hang another nectar feeder so hummingbirds don't have to wait in line.

Index

Note: Page references in *italic* indicate illustrations or photographs; those in **boldface** indicate tables.

A

Acorn Bash, 138
Acorns, 128, 138–139, **147**
Acrobats Only, 143
All for Orioles, 162
Almonds
    recipes using, 100,
        136–138, 142
    shell-on, 130
    where grown, **147**
Aluminum pie pans, as feeders,
  26
Amaranth seed, 59, 63, 66–67
Animal pests, 98, 245–248
Anti-bear feeders, 248
Anti-house-finch feeders, 77
Anti-jay feeders, 240
Anti-pest feeders, 247–248
Anti-starling feeders, 243
Aphids, 5–6
Apples
    birds attracted to, 164
    dried, 169
    recipes using, 166–167,
        172–173, 193
Applesauce-Nut Bread, 201
Apricots, 162, 169, 173

Aster cuttings, 291
Avian diseases, 287
Awesome Twosome, 96
A&W Float, 142

B

Bacon fat, 102, 113, 185
Bagels, 61, 182, 185
Baked goods. See Breads
Bakeries, 64
Balconies, 10–11, 320–322
Banana Bread, Corny, 201
Bananas, 161–162, 169
Barred feeders
    to discourage jays, 240
    to discourage starlings, 48,
        180–181
    in feeder station, 306
Baskets, as nesting-materials
  holder, 295–296
Beaks, 27–28, 36
Beechnuts, **147**
Beef bouillon, in sugar water,
  154
Beetle larvae. See Mealworms;
  Waxworms; Wireworms
Beetles, 5–6, 244
Beneficial insects, 6
Berries
    dried or frozen, 168
    recipes using, 162, 166,
        172–173

Big Treat for Little Guys, 137
Birdbaths
    bird behavior in, 231–232
    bird preferences for,
        236–237
    buying, 226–228
    heated, 235
    homemade, 232, *232*
    from household items,
      229–230
    location of, 230
    pedestal-style, 229
    seasonal considerations for,
      234–236
    sound of, 228–229
    sprinklers and misters as,
      232–234
    surface of, 229
    winter care of, 230
Bird-eaters, 241, 249–252
Birdhouses
    birds attracted to, 254
    for bluebirds, 255–257,
      272–273, *272*
    buying, 274–277
    for chickadees, 257–258
    discouraging bird pests
      from, 270–274
    entrance hole size for, 271,
      277
    for house wrens, 262–265,
      263
    making, 276

Birdhouses *(continued)*
    mounting, 269, 275–277
    for nuthatches, 258–260
    for purple martins,
        268–269
    on stumps, 258
    for swallows, 266–268
    for titmice, 260–261
    for woodpeckers, 261–262
Bird netting, on feeder, 132
Blackberries, 166
Blackbird Buffet, 101
Blackbirds
    birdbath preferences of,
        237
    bread preferences of,
        195–196, **202–204**
    Brewer's, *202*
    cake for, 189
    feeder placement for, **49**
    habits and characteristics of,
        179
    milo for, 37
    nut preferences of, **145**
    oats for, 60
    recipes for, 101
    Red-winged, 350, *350*
    seasonal food preferences
        of, **17**
    Yellow-headed, 359, *359*
Bleach, for cleaning feeders,
    160
Blenders, 134
Blizzards. *See* Snowstorms
Block mounts, 315
Blood pressure, effect of
    bird-watching on, 2–3
Blueberries, 162, 172
Blueberry Cornbread, 200
Bluebird Best, 172
Bluebird Bounty Hunter,
    184
Bluebird feeders, 217–218

Bluebirds, *86*
    birdbath preferences of, **237**
    birdhouse protection for,
        272–273, *272*
    birdhouses for, 255–257
    bread for, 178, 181–182
    Eastern, 255, 338, *338*
    fat preferences of, **121**
    feeder placement for, **49,**
        109
    fruit preferences of, 164, **175**
    habits and characteristics of,
        34, 196
    insect preferences of, 211,
        223
    Mountain, 255, 345, *345*
    natural habitat of, 109, 255,
        257
    nest competitors of, 256,
        265, 268
    nesting habits of, **278**
    nut preferences of, **145**
    oats for, 182
    peanut butter for, 106
    recipes for
        bread-based, 184, 192
        fat-based, 90, 96,
            107–108
        fruit-based, 173
        insect-based, 209–210
    seasonal food preferences
        of, 15, 16, **17**
    Western, 255
Blue Jay Bounty Hunting, 138
Bobwhites, 37
    milo for, 37
    profile of, 333, *333*
Body temperature of birds, 23
Bottom Line, 96
Bran muffins, 192
Bread eaters, 17, 178–179,
    202–204
Bread feeders, 186, *186*

Breads
    additions to, 187–188
    corn-based, 181–182,
        195–196
    health concerns about, 188
    mixes for, 196
    moldy, 183
    for nut-eaters, 180
    recipes for, 192, 200–201
    recipes using, 102,
        184–185, 191
    seasons for, 180, 197
    serving, 196–198, 202,
        202–204
    stale, 186–187
    storing, 187
    wheat-based, 182
Bribes, for birds, 134
Budget Breakfast, 66
Bulk foods, 63–64, 140, 144
Bungee cords, for suet feeders,
    99
Buntings
    birdbath preferences of,
        237
    corn for, 43
    Indigo, *240*
        feeder style and place-
            ment for, **83**
        nesting materials for,
            284, **299**
        profile of, 343, *343*
        seed preferences of, **83**
    Lark, *61*
    Lazuli, *305*
        feeder style and place-
            ment for, **83**
        nesting materials for,
            299
        profile of, 343, *343*
        seed preferences of, **83**
    migration of, 57
    Painted, *47,* **83**

recipes for, 75–76
seasonal food preferences
of, **18**
small seeds for, 59, 60
Bushtits
fat preferences of, **121**
habits and characteristics of,
97, 208
profile of, 334, *334*
recipes for, 143
seasonal food preferences
of, **18**
Butcher shops, 93
Butterflyweed cuttings, 291

C

Cage feeders. *See* Suet feeders
Cake, leftover, 189
Canary seed
birds attracted to, 56
described, **70**
recipes using, 67, 78–79
sources for, 63
Canola seed (rapeseed)
described, 56–57, **70**
recipes using, 67, 78–79
sources for, 63
Cardinal Come-On, 171
Cardinals, *4, 65*
birdbath preferences of,
236–237
bread preferences of,
195–196, **202–204**
cereal for, 190
corn for, 43
feeder placement for, **49**
fruit preferences of, 164,
175
habits and characteristics of,
219
nesting habits of, 256, **278**
nesting materials for, **299**

profile of, 335, *335*
recipes for
fruit-based, 171
nut-based, 128
seed-based, 38, 67
seasonal food preferences
of, **18**
unfamiliar seeds and, 65
Carpet thread, as nesting
material, 283
Catbirds
birdbath preferences of,
236–237
bread preferences of, 178,
181–182, **202–204**
fat preferences of, **121**
feeder style for, 107
fruit preferences of, 164,
165, **175**
Gray, *130*
habits and characteristics of,
174
meat for, 115
nesting materials for, 291,
299
nut preferences of, **145**
peanut butter for, 106–107
profile of, 336, *336*
recipes for
bread-based, 185, 192
fat-based, 90, 96
fruit-based, 166, 173
seasonal food preferences
of, 15, 16, **18**
Cat hair, as nesting material,
284
Cats, 98, 249–251
Cavity nesters, defined, 256
Cellophane, as nesting material,
282–283, 284
Cereals
as bird food, 189–190, **203**
recipes using, 194, 201

Charity sales, 141
Cheep Crowd-Pleaser, 75
Cheepest Trio, 38
Cherries
dried or frozen, 168
recipes using, 162, 167,
171–172, 184
Chestnuts, 139, 143, **147**
Chickadee Country, 184
Chickadees
benefits of, 6
birdbath preferences of,
236–237
birdhouses for, 257–258
Black-capped, 258, 331,
331
Boreal, *108*, 258
bread preferences of,
181–182, 188, **203–204**
Carolina, *141*, 258
fat preferences of, 108, 112,
122
feeder style and placement
for, **49**, 312
fruit for, 164
habits and characteristics of,
129, 199
insects for, 208
Mountain, *2*, 258
nesting habits of, **278**
nesting materials for, 286,
295, 296, **299**
nut preferences of, **146**
oats for, 182
peanut butter for, 108
recipes for
bread-based, 184–185,
193
fat-based, 90, 96, 100
fruit-based, 173
insect-based, 209–210
nut-based, 128,
136–139, 142–144

Chickadees *(continued)*
 seasonal food preferences
 of, **18**
Chicken scratch, 38–39, 44, 101
Children, bird-watching and, 11,
 134
Chinet® plates, as feeders, 23
Chocolate, warning about, 188
Clamp-on feeders, 320–322
Clotheslines, as nesting-materials
 holder, 296
Code Blue(bird) Emergency,
 192
Coffee can feeders, 47, *47*, 132
Coins, as measuring device,
 277
Cold, extreme, 14
Colors
 for nectar feeders, 150–151
 for nesting materials,
 281–282
 for winter feeders, 319
Come One, Come All, 90
Comparison shopping, 62
Cookies
 as bird food, 182, 190–191
 birds attracted to, **203**
 recipes for, 193
Cookie sheets, as feeders, 34
Cooking oils, 61, 115, 188
Corn
 added to bread, 187–188
 as menu mainstay, 42–45
 as pest distraction, 244
 recipes using
 bread-based, 184
 fat-based, 92, 100–101
 fruit-based, 171
 insect-based, 209
 nut-based, 137, 139
 seed-based, 30, 37–39,
 76, 78–79
 with suet, 103

Cornbread
 birds attracted to, 181–182,
 204
 hoecake, 195–196
 recipes for, 200–201
 serving, **204**
Corn chips, 192, **203**
Cornmeal
 in feeders, 45
 with peanut butter, 109–110
 recipes using
 bread-based, 200–201
 fat-based, 90–91, 96,
 100–101, 107–108,
 117–118
 fruit-based, 161,
 166–167, 172
 insect-based, 209
 nut-based, 143
Corn oil, 101, 188
Corny Banana Bread, 201
Corny Suet, 92
Cotton balls, as nesting material,
 283, 286
Cotton fabric, as nesting
 material, 282, 296
Cowbirds, 242, *242*
Crackers and cracker crumbs,
 182, 190–191
Craft shows, 275
Craft stores, 283, 288
Cranberries, dried, 173
Craving Cardinals, 38
Creepers, Brown, *250*
 profile of, 333, *333*
 seasonal food preferences
 of, **17**
Crossbills, 220, 221, *221*
Crows, **202–204**
Crumbs, saving, 194
Crush on Cardinals, 171
Currants
 buying, 169

recipes using, 162, 166–167,
 172
Cuttings, as nesting material,
 291

D
Daffodils, as migration cue, 149
Dandelions, as migration cue, 57
Date-Bran Bird Muffins, 192
Dates, 169, 171
Decks
 attracting birds to, 10–11
 birdbaths mounted to, 230
 feeder stations for, 320–322
Decoy feeders
 in feeding station, 310
 for house sparrows, 44
 for hummingbirds, 242–243
 for mockingbirds, 168,
 179–180, 242–243
 for starlings, 44, 97, 164,
 202
Deer, salt licks and, 220
Diablo Sauce, 246–247
Dickcissels, 25, *25*
Dog hair, as nesting material,
 284
Doughnuts, 188–189, **204**
Doves
 corn for, 43
 milo for, 37
 Mourning, 220, **278,** 345,
 345
 nut preferences of, **146**
 oats for, 60
 seasonal food preferences
 of, **18**
Downy's Dream, 118
Dried fruit, 168, 169. *See also*
 Raisins
Drippers, for birdbaths, 228–229
Drugstores, 283

Dryer lint, as nesting material, 285

Duck ponds, nesting material from, 288

E

Eagles, nesting material for, 291

Eggshells, as food, 222

Electric mixers, 118–119

End-of-the-Trail Mix, 173

English muffins, **204**

Ethnic grocery stores, 64

Every Finch's Fave, 75

Experimentation, with seed mixes, 69

Extra Incentive, 137

F

Fabrics, as nesting material, 282, 285, 296

Fall season
  birdbaths in, 235
  considerations for, 12
  feeder traffic during, 207
  first-time feeders in, 10
  foods for, **17–20**, 85–86, 169
  goldfinches during, 80
  migrations, 24
  recipes for, 166–167

Farm outlets, 140

Farms & Fields, 78

Farm-supply stores, 63

Fats. *See also specific fats*
  added to bread, 187–188
  bacon, 102, 113
  bird preferences for, **121–123**
  in insect foods, 208
  from kitchen scraps, 113–114, 115

lard, 97, 112–113

meat, 114–115

in nuts, 125

peanut butter, 96–97, 100–112, 118, 312

seasons for, 13, 14

serving, **121–123**

suet, 85–105, 117–118, 120–121, **145,** 219

in sunflower seeds, 22, 24

working with, 116–121

Faux fur, as nesting material, 283

Faux wild setting, 8

Feathers, as nesting material
  amount needed, 285
  serving, 296
  sources for, 283, 287–288

Feedbag Full o' Oats, 91

Feeder brush, homemade, 158, *158*

Feeders. *See also* Feeding stations; *specific birds; specific types*
  anti-house-finch, 77
  anti-jay, 240
  anti-pest, 247–248
  anti-starling, 243
  birds' dependence on, 11
  checklist for, 45–46
  competition at, 156–157, 210–211
  cost of, 7
  design of, 316–319
  for first-time or new locations, 7–12, 134
  homemade, 23, 26, 47, 47
  monitoring and filling, 6, 31, 55
  mounts for, 304, 310–316, *314,* 317, **322–323**
  placement of, **49–50,** **82–83**

size of, 46–47, 48

Feeding stations. *See also* Feeders; *specific feeder types*
  auxiliary feeders for, 305–307
  decoy feeders in, 310
  filling feeders in, 303, 304, 309–310
  grouping feeders in, 309–310
  main feeder for, 303
  number of feeders in, 304–305
  for small yards, 304

Feed stores, 63

Fencing, as pest control, 251

Field guides, using, 3

Figgy Pudding, 167

Fig Newtons®, 167

Filberts. *See* Hazelnuts

Finches
  birdbath preferences of, **236–237**
  Cassin's, **82, 299**
  feeder styles and placement for, 71–82, **82–83**
  habits and characteristics of, 29, 52–53
  House
    discouraging from feeders, 77
    feeder styles and placement for, **50, 83**
    fruit preferences of, **176**
    minerals for, 220, 221
    nesting habits of, **278**
    nut preferences of, **146**
    profile of, 342, *342*
    recipes for, 173
    seed preferences of, **83**
  migration of, 57
  Purple, **83, 299,** 347, *347*

Finches (continued)
recipes for, 29, 66–67, 75–76
Rosy, **299**
seasonal food preferences of, **18**
seed preferences of, **82–83**
small seeds for, 54–61
taste test for, 58
Finch Favorite, 29
Finger millet, 41. See also Millet
Fishing line, 281
Flaxseed
described, 57, **70**
recipes using, 67, 75–76, 78–79
sources for, 63–64
Flicker Flapdoodle, 101
Flickers
birdbath preferences of, **237**
birdhouses for, 262
feeder placement for, **49**
Northern, 346, 346
recipes for, 101, 136–139
Flour, 194
Flour & Pantry Moth Traps, 41
Flowers, attracting humming-birds with, 321, 321
Flycatchers
Crested, 214
Great crested, 284, 285, **299**
insect preferences of, **223**
Least, 68
nesting materials for, **299**
Vermilion, **301**
Fly This Way!, 210
Food choppers, 133, 134
Food processors, 118–119, 134
Forest Fauna, 79
Freezing suet, 120–121

Fruit. See also specific fruits
added to bread, 187
attracting birds to, 170–175
recipes using, 166–167, 171–173
seasons for, 17, 169
serving, **175–176**
types to feed, 164–169
Fruit flys, 209–210
"Fruity" Suet, 209
Full Flavor for Finches, 67
Funnel, homemade, 43, 43
Fur, as nesting material, 284, 285

G
Gardens, benefits of bird in, 5–6, 212, 244
German millet, 57, 67, **70**. See also Millet
Germs, avoiding, 287
Gloves, 95, 210, 287
Goldfinches, 71
American, 52, **299,** 330, 330
birdbath preferences of, **236–237**
feeder style and placement for, **49, 82,** 305
habits and characteristics of, 53, 80
Lawrence's, 54, **299**
Lesser, 56, **299**
minerals for, 220
nesting habits of, **278**
nicknames for, 56
recipes for, 75–76
seed preferences of, **82**
small seeds for, 57, 59, 60
winter feathers of, 16
Goober Boost, 128
Good 'n' Fruity, 162

Good 'n' Pretty, 136
Gorgeous Gluttons, 127
Got the Blues, 107
Grackles, 183
benefits of, 5
birdbath preferences of, **236–237**
bread preferences of, **202–204**
cake for, 189
discouraging from feeders, 180–181
feeder placement for, **50**
profile of, 337, 337
Grains, 60–61, 178. See also Bread eaters; Breads
Grainy Goodness, 66
Grape jelly, 160
Grapes
birds attracted to, 165
recipes using, 166, 171, 185
stringing, 174, 174
Grapevines, as nesting material, 292
Grasses, as nesting material, 292–293
Grass seed, 63, **70,** 75
Grocery stores, 63–64
Grosbeaks
birdbath preferences of, **237**
Black-headed, 165, **175,** 194, 332, 332
Blue, **299,** 320
Evening, 28, 220, 221, 339, 339
feeder placement for, **50**
nut preferences of, **146**
recipes for, 67
Rose-breasted, 351, 351
seasonal food preferences of, **19**
Ground feeding, 69, 81–82

Ground serving, of nesting materials, 295
Grouse, **146**
Grubs. See Mealworms; Waxworms; Wireworms

H

Hair, as nesting material, 284, 285
Hamburger, 114–115
Ham fat, 113–114
Hand-feeding, 134–135, 140
Hand mixing methods, for fats, 116
Hand washing, 287
Hanging feeders, 199, 240, 313
Hardware stores, 63
Hat feeding, 140
Hawks, 77, 252, 291
Hazelnuts (filberts)
    recipes using, 100, 128, 136, 138
    shell-on, 130
    where grown, **147**
Health benefits
    of bird-watching, 2–4
    of flaxseed, 57
    of nuts, 125
Health-food stores, 63
Heart rate, effect of bird-watching on, 2–3
Heavenly for Hummingbirds, 153
Hickory nuts, **147**
Holidays, nut prices during, 141
Home-supply stores, 63
Honey, warning about, 157
Hooked on Bagels, 185
Hooks and hangers, 313
Hopper feeders, 47–48, **323**
Horsehair, as nesting material, 284–285

Hot peppers, as pest control, 246–247, 248, 250
Hot sauce recipe, 246–247
Houseflies, 209–210
Housefly Hash, 209
Houseguests, bribing birds for, 134
Household items, as birdbaths, 229–230
Hummingbirds. See also Nectar feeders; Sugar water
    Anna's, 330, 330
    anti-honey warning for, 157
    attracting with flowers, 321, 321
    birdbath preferences of, **237**
    Blue-throated, 159
    Calliope, 307
    decoy feeder for, 242–243
    feeders for, 150–152, 307
    habits and characteristics of, 241–242
    migration patterns of, 150
    nectar preference of, 149
    perches for, 151
    recipes for, 153–154
    Ruby-Throated, 352, 352
    Rufous, 353, 353
    seasonal food preferences of, 15, 17, **19**
    White-eared, 156

I

Ice storms, 12, 13, 14
Insect eaters, 206–208
Insect foods. See also Mealworms
    benefits of, 210
    bird preferences for, **223–224**
    commercial, 218–219
    grossness factor of, 210, 213

nutritional content of, 208
    recipes using, 209–210
    seasons for, 13, 14, 15, 16, 207, 210
    serving, **223–224**
    in suet, 219
Insects
    beneficial, 6
    in birdseed, 41
    as garden pests, 5–6, 244
Internet resources, 4, 65
In-Town Treats, 79

J

Japanese beetles, 5–6, 244
Jays
    birdbath preferences of, **236–237**
    Blue, 31, **300,** 332, 332
    bread preferences of, **202–204**
    discouraging from feeders, 132, 239–241
    fat preferences of, **122**
    feeder style and placement for, 31, **50,** 133
    Gray, 12, **300**
    habits and characteristics of, 33, 126–127, 241
    nesting habits of, **278**
    nesting materials for, 286, 296–297
    nut preferences of, **146**
    Oregon, 133
    recipes for, 127, 136–139
    Scrub, 239, **300,** 354, 354
    seasonal food preferences of, **19**
    Steller's, 32, **300**
Jelly, 160–163
Jelly feeders, 163
JIFFY mixes, 196

Juncos, *196*
    bread preferences of,
      181–182, **203–204**
    cereal for, 190
    corn for, 43
    Dark-eyed, *40, 337, 337*
    fat preferences of, **122**
    feeder style and placement
      for, **50,** 312
    fruit for, 164
    nesting materials for, **300**
    niger for, 55
    oats for, 182
    recipes for, 91, 139
    seasonal food preferences
      of, **19**

K

Kids, bird-watching and, 11, 134
Kingbirds, **223**
Kinglets
    habits and characteristics of,
      208
    insect preferences of, **223**
    Ruby-Crowned, *208,* 352,
      352
    seasonal food preferences
      of, **19**

L

Labels, on seed mixes, 68–69
Lard, 97, 112–113
Lawn furniture, as shelter, 13
Learning, as benefit of bird-
    watching, 3, 4
Leaves, as nesting material,
    291–292
Lifting and moving techniques,
    for bags of seed, 27, 32–33
Linen fabric, as nesting material,
    282, 296

M

Macadamia nuts, **147**
Magnifying lens, 68–69
Magpies, **201–204, 300**
Martins, Purple, *14*
    birdhouses for, 268–269
    insect preferences of, **223**
    minerals for, 222
    nesting materials for, 296,
      300
    profile of, 348, *348*
    seasonal food preferences
      of, 15, **20**
Meadowlarks, *247*
    bread preferences of,
      203–204
    insect preferences of, **223**
    profile of, 344, *344*
Meal moths, 41
Mealworm feeders, 214
Mealworms. *See also* Insect
    foods
    birds attracted to, 206–208
    buying, 212–213
    described, 211
    raising, 216–217, *216*
    roasted, 214–215
    seasons for, 13, 14, 15, 16
    serving, 213, 215
    storing, 218
Meat and meat scraps, 113–114,
    115
Mental acuity, effect of bird-
    watching on, 3
Meow Mixture, 166
Metabolism, of birds, 23
Microwaves, for melting fat, 119
Migration patterns, changing, 150
Migration seasons
    goldfinches during, 305
    insect feeders during, 207
    nectar feeders during, 149
    seed feeders during, 24, 57

Millet
    birds attracted to, 39
    described, **70**
    German, 57
    as menu mainstay, 35–42
    recipes using
      fat-based, 91
      fruit-based, 172–173
      nut-based, 128
      seed-based, 29–30,
        37–38, 66–67,
        75–76, 78–79
Milo, 30, 37
Minerals, 220–222
Mini Sandwich Squares, 185
Misters, as birdbaths, 233–234
Mixing methods, for fats, 116,
    118–119
Mockingbird Mania, 173
Mockingbirds, *180*
    birdbath preferences of,
      237
    bread preferences of,
      202–204
    corn for, 43
    decoy feeders for, 168,
      179–180, 242–243
    fat preferences of, **122**
    feeder style and placement
      for, **50,** 107
    fruit preferences of, 164,
      165, **176**
    habits and characteristics of,
      241–242
    nesting materials for, 291,
      300
    Northern, 43
    nut preferences of, **146**
    oats for, 182
    profile of, 344, *344*
    recipes for
      bread-based, 192
      fat-based, 90, 185

fruit-based, 173
seasonal food preferences
of, 17, **18**
More Oriole Delights, 162
Mortar, as food, 221
Moss, as nesting material, 283,
286
Motion detectors, as pest
control, 251
Mounts
for birdhouses, 269, 275–277
for feeders
bird preferences for,
322–323
ease of use and, 304
versus hanging, 317
types of, 310–316, *314*
Mud, as nesting material,
293–294, 297, 298
Muesli, 97
Muffins
birds attracted to, **204**
mixes for, 196
recipe for, 192
recipes using, 184, 191
serving, **204**
Mulch, 219, 307
Mustard seed, 56–57, 64, **70**
Mylar, as nesting material, 283,
284

N

Nails, as nesting-materials
holder, 296
Nectar. *See* Sugar water
Nectar eaters, 149–150
Nectar feeders
brush for, 158, *158*
cleaning, 159–160
in feeder station, 306–307
filling, 154, 155
mount for, 316, **322**

seasons for, 15, 17, 149
types of, 150–152
Nest boxes. *See* Birdhouses
Nesting habits, 256, 264, **278**
Nesting materials
bird preferences for,
299–301
finishing materials
amount needed, 285
cellophane, 282–283
feathers, 283, 285,
287–288, 296
fibers, 280–283
hair or fur, 284–285
moss, 283, 286
sources for, 283, 288
foundation materials
grasses, 292–293
leaves, 291–292
mud, 293–294, 297,
298
sticks, 289–292
thorny twigs, 291
vines, 292
location for, 290
prefilled holders of, 297
serving, 294–298, *298*,
299–301
Nesting shelf, 266–267, *267*
Net bags, as feeders, 93
Net-wrapped feeder, 132, *132*
Niger
buying, 54, 62
described, **70**
ease of use, 54–55
names for, 53
recipes using, 66–67,
75–76, 78–79
Niger socks, 80
Nutcracker, Clark's, *125, 126*
Nut-eaters, 125–126,
145–146, 180. *See also*
specific birds

Nut feeders, 131, 306, **322**
Nuthatches
benefits of, 5
birdhouses for, 259–260
bread for, 188
Brown-headed, *259*
fat preferences of, 112, **122**
feeder placement for, **50**
habits and characteristics of,
129, 258–260
insects for, 208
natural habitat of, 259
nesting habits of, **278**
nesting materials for, 292,
295, **300**
nut preferences of, **146**
Pygmy, *254*
recipes for
fat-based, 90, 96, 118
nut-based, 136–139,
142, 144
Red-breasted, 260, 349, *349*
seasonal food preferences
of, **19**
White-breasted, 357, *357*
Nuthatch Hustle, 118
Nuts. *See also specific nuts*
added to bread, 187
bird preferences for,
145–146
as bribes, 134
buying, 135–145
chopped, 127–128, 129,
133–134
conserving, 130–135, 306
fat content of, 125
human health benefits of,
125
most popular, 129
recipes using, 100–101
salted, 131
serving, **145–146**
shell-on, 130, 135

Nuts *(continued)*
  where grown, **147**
Nyjer seed. *See* Niger

O

Oats
  birds attracted by, 60
  recipes using, 91, 142, 172,
    193
  serving, 182
Opossums, 98
Orange juice, 117
Oranges, 162, 165
Oriole Ambrosia, 153
Oriole Ovals, 117
Orioles. *See also* Nectar feeders;
  Sugar water
  Baltimore, *163*
    fruit for, 165
    nesting habits of, **278**
    nesting materials for,
      300
    profile of, 331, *331*
    birdbath preferences of,
      237
  Bullock's, *149*
    fruit for, 165
    nesting habits of, **278**
    nesting materials for,
      300
  fat preferences of, **122**
  feeders for, 307
  Hooded, 165
  insect preferences of, **223**
  nesting materials for, 280,
    281, 287, 291, 295,
    296–297
  perches for, 151
  recipes for
    bread-based, 185
    fat-based, 90, 96, 117
    fruit-based, 162

insect-based, 209–210
  nectar, 153
Scott's, *120*
  fruit for, 165
  nesting materials for,
    300
  profile of, 354, *354*
  seasonal food preferences
    of, 15, 16, 17, **19**
  sweet preferences of, 149,
    161, 165, **176**
Ospreys, nesting material for,
  291
Oyster shells, 221–222

P

Pancakes, 195
Pan drippings, 114
Paper plates, as feeders, 23
Parent birds, 16, 17
PB-Raisin Cookies, 193
Peaches, dried, 169
Peanut butter
  birds attracted to, 106–108,
    110
  buying, 110–112
  with cornmeal, 109–110
  creamy versus chunky,
    108–109
  feeders for, 111, *111*, 312
  recipes using
    bread-based, 184–185,
      192–193
    fat-based, 96–97,
      100–101, 107–108,
      118
    fruit-based, 161,
      166–167
    nut-based, 142–143
  safe feeding of, 110
  seasons for, 17
  serving, **121–123**

Peanut oil, 107, 117, 188
Peanuts
  economy of, 130
  popularity of, 129
  recipes using
    fat-based, 118
    fruit-based, 167,
      172–173
    nut-based, 127–128,
      136–138, 142–143
  with suet, 102–103
  where grown, **147**
  for woodpeckers, 128
Peanutty Porcupines, 142
Pecans
  recipes using, 128, 138,
    144, 201
  where grown, **147**
Peewees, Wood, *207*
Pepperoni, 115
Perchers' Paradise, 167
Perches
  on birdbaths, 227
  on nectar feeders, 151
  on suet feeders, 99
Perching pole, 111, *111*
Perennial cuttings, as nesting
  material, 291
Pest-control, birds as, 5–6
Pesticides, 15, 212
Pests
  bird food eaters, 98,
    245–248
  birds as, 5–6, 239–245,
    270–274 (*See also specific
    birds*)
  predators, 249–252
Pet-supply stores, 63
Pheasants
  corn for, 43
  feeder placement for, **50**
  nut preferences of, **146**
  Ring-necked, *45*

seasonal food preferences of, **20**
Phoebes, 286, *286*
Photography, 8, 9
Piecrust, baked, **204**
Pie pans, as feeders, 26
Pigeons
    corn for, 43
    minerals for, 220
    nut preferences of, **146**
    oats for, 60
    profile of, 346, *346*
    recipe for, 37
    seasonal food preferences of, **18**
Pigeon-Toed Treat, 37
Pileated Possibility, 144
Pillows, nesting material from, 288
Pine nuts, **147**
Pipe cleaners, as feeder cleaner, 159–160
Pistachios, **147**
Pizza crust, 182
Plastic, for birdhouses, 278
Plastic bags, as gloves, 95
Plastic netting
    to discourage jays, 132, *132*
    as feeders, 93, 117
Plastic soda bottles
    as feeders, 26, 72–73, *72*, 214
    as funnel, 43, *43*
Pocket change, as measuring device, 277
Pole mounts
    for feeders, 312–315, *314*, 317
    for martin houses, 269
Pompom trim, as nesting material, 283
Poppy seed
    buying, 60, 64

described, **70**
    recipes using, 67
Porch posts, as feeder mount, 315–316
Possums, 98
Post mounts, 310–312
Poultry farms, nesting material from, 288
Pre-blizzard conditions, 13
Proso millet, 35, 41. *See also* Millet
Protein, in insect foods, 208
Protein Punch, 154
Prunes, 169, 172, 173
Pumped-Up All-Purpose Mix, 76
Pyrrhuloxia, **301**

Q

Quail
    birdbath preferences of, **236–237**
    feeder placement for, **50**
    Gambel's, 340, *340*
    milo for, 37
    nut preferences of, **146**
    oats for, 60
    seasonal food preferences of, **20**
Quail Ho!, 30

R

Raccoons, 98
Rain, 28
Raisins
    recipes using
        bread-based, 185, 192–193
        fat-based, 100–101, 107
        fruit-based, 162, 166–167, 173

serving, 168–169
    with suet, 104
Ramie fabric, as nesting material, 282
Rapeseed. *See* Canola seed
Recipe for Redheads, 139
Recipes
    bread-based, 184–185, 191–194, 200–201
    fat-based, 90–92, 96–97, 100–102, 107–108, 117–118
    fruit-based, 161–162, 166–167, 171–173
    insect-based, 209–210
    nectar, 153–154
    nut-based, 127–128, 136–139, 142–144
    seed-based, 29–30, 37–39, 66–67, 75–76, 78–79
Redpolls, 62
    canola seed for, 57
    feeder styles and placement for, **83**
    habits and characteristics of, 64
    profile of, 350, *350*
    seed preferences of, **83**
Rice, as feeder cleaner, 159
Robin Roundabout, 102
Robins, *292*
    birdbath preferences of, **237**
    bread preferences of, **202–204**
    fat preferences of, **122**
    fruit preferences of, 164, 165, **176**
    habits and characteristics of, 196, 219
    nesting habits of, 256, **278**
    nesting materials for, 281, 293, 295, **301**

Robins (continued)
  nesting shelf for, 266–267, 267
  oats for, 182
  profile of, 351, 351
  recipes for
    bread-based, 185, 193
    fat-based, 90, 102
    fruit-based, 167, 173
  seasonal food preferences of, **20**
Roofed feeders, 47, 198, 198, 199–200

S

Safflower seed, 59, **70,** 171
Salt, on nuts, 131
Salt licks, 220–221
Sapphire Supply, 108
Sapsuckers, Yellow-bellied, 161, 359, 359
Saucer, seed-catching, 81
Sausage, 115
Seasons. See also specific seasons
  for first-time feeders, 10
  food guide for, **17–20**
  for nectar feeders, 307
  nesting, **278**
  for setting posts, 311
Second-story feeders, 10–11, 134, 320–322
Seed-eaters, 25, 39, **49–50**
  See also specific birds
Seed mixes, 68–71, 133
Seeds. See also specific seeds
  amaranth, 59, 66, 67
  canary, 56, 63, 67, **70**
  to discourage jays, 240–241
  flaxseed, 57, 63–64, **70**
  millet, 35–42, 57, **70**
  niger, 53, 54–55, 62, **70**

poppy, 60, 64, **70**
safflower, 59, **70**
sesame, 60, 62, 64
storing, 69–70
sunflower, 22–34, 67, 244
Seed sources, 62–64
Seed spillage, from tube feeders, 76–77, 81–82
Serve-'Em-All Seed Mix, 30
Sesame seed
  feeding, 60
  recipes using, 67
  sources for, 62, 64
Sheep fleece, as nesting material, 287
Shelf feeders, 34, 46
Shelter
  lawn furniture as, 13
  roofed feeders for, 47, 198, 198, 199–200
Shoelaces, as nesting material, 280–281
Shrubs, as nesting-materials holder, 296–297
Shut-ins, bird-watching and, 10
Siskins, Pine, 74
  birdbath preferences of, **237**
  feeder styles and placement for, **83**
  migration of, 57
  minerals for, 220, 221
  nesting materials for, **300**
  profile of, 347, 347
  recipes for, 67, 75–76
  seasonal food preferences of, **19**
  seed preferences of, 57, 59, **83**
Sledding saucers, as birdseed mover, 27
Snakeskins, as nesting material, 284

Snowbirds (human), 55
Snowstorms
  feeders during, 14
  preparing for, 12, 40
  warning of, 13
Sock feeders, 80
Song Bird Specialty, 172
Songsters' Surprise, 185
Soup bones, 114
Souped-Up Sunflowers, 67
Sparrows
  bread preferences of, 181–182, **203–204**
  cereal for, 190
  Chipping, 283, 336, 336
  fat preferences of, **122**
  Fox, 165, **176,** 340, 340
  habits and characteristics of, 219
  House, 6
    benefits of, 5–6
    birdbath preferences of, **236–237**
    in bluebird houses, 256
    bread preferences of, **202–204**
    colonies of, 274
    decoy feeder for, 44
    discouraging from birdhouses, 270–274
    minerals for, 220
    nesting habits of, **278**
    nesting materials for, 296
    oats for, 60
    as pests, 245
    profile of, 342, 342
  native
    birdbath preferences of, **236–237**
    corn for, 43
    feeder placement for, **50**

identifying, 36
nesting materials for,
292, 295, **300**
niger for, 55
recipes for, 76
oats for, 182
recipes for, 38, 91
seasonal food preferences
of, **20**
Song, *89*
fruit preferences of,
176
nesting habits of,
278
profile of, 355, *355*
recipes for, 172
White-crowned, 357, *357*
White-throated, *35,* 165,
358, *358*
Sparrows Supreme, 38
Sparrow Style, 76
Sparrow Suet, 91
Specialty seeds. *See also specific*
seeds
bird preferences for,
64–65
buying, 62–64
types of, 54–61
Spring season
birdbaths in, 234
birdhouses in, 265
considerations for, 14–15
feeder traffic during,
207
foods for, **17–20,** 86,
113, 197, 213
migrations, 24, 57
mulch in, 219
nesting materials during,
281
Sprinklers, as birdbaths,
232–233
Squirrels, 98, 131

Starlings, *114, 270*
benefits of, 5–6, 244
birdbath preferences of,
236–237
bread preferences of, 181,
188, **202–204**
cake for, 189
decoy feeders for, 44, 97,
164, 202
discouraging from
birdhouses, 270–274
discouraging from feeders,
25, 48, 98, 180–181,
243–244
habits and characteristics of,
273
nesting habits of, **278**
profile of, 355, *355*
recipes for, 101
Stick-on feeders, 81
Sticks, as nesting material,
289–292
Storage
of mealworms, 218
of seeds, 69–70
of suet, 120–121
Strawberries, 166
Strictly for Starlings, 101
String, as nesting material,
280–281, 283, 285
Stumps, for birdhouse location,
258
Suburban Savories, 78
Suction-cup feeders, 81, 132
Suet
additions to, 87–88,
102–105, 145
avoiding mess from, 95
buying, 86–89, 92
chopped, 87
defined, 85
handling, 95
insect-augmented, 219

for parent birds, 17
recipes using
bread-based, 184–185,
191, 194
fat-based, 90–92,
96–97, 100–102, 107,
117–118
fruit-based, 161–162,
166–167, 172–173
insect-based, 209–210
nut-based, 142–144
seasons for, 13, 14, 15,
85–86, 95, 197
serving suggestions,
121–123
storing, 120–121
thieves of, 98
Suet feeders
for breads, 197
commercial, 92–93
for controlling jays, 132,
132, 133
in feeding station, 305
homemade, 93, 94, *94,*
104–105, *105,* 117
mounts for, **323**
as nesting-materials holder,
295
perches for, 99
placement of, 88
roofed, 198, *198,*
199–200
stabilizing, 99
stringing together, 99
upside-down, 98, 244
Suet logs, 93
Suet 'n' Sunflowers, 90
Suet Snowman, 100
Sugar, superfine, 156
Sugar water
birds attracted to, 149–150
making, 152–157
packaged mix for, 154

Sugar water *(continued)*
seasons for, 15, 17, 149
spoilage of, 159
Summer season
birdbaths in, 234–235
considerations for, 15–17
feeder traffic during, 59,
210
foods for, **17–20,** 86, 149,
210
nesting materials during, 281
Sunflower chips
described, 33–34
recipes using
bread-based, 185
fat-based, 90, 100, 118
fruit-based, 173
insect-based, 209
nut-based, 136–137
seed-based, 29
Sunflowers, 33
Sunflower seed
birds attracted to, 25
black versus striped, 26
buying, 31–32
to discourage starlings, 25,
244
hulled (See Sunflower chips)
lifting heavy bags of,
32–33
as menu mainstay, 22–28
recipes using
fruit-based, 171
nut-based, 127–128,
137–139
seed-based, 29–30,
37–38, 67, 75–76,
78–79
Super Stuffing, 143
Suppliers, 324–328
Swallows
Bank, *268*
Barn, *222,* **278,** 293–294

birdhouses for, 266–268
colonies of, 268
nesting materials for, 287,
296, **301**
Tree, 266, *266,* **278**
Sweets
fruit, 164–175, **175–176**
jelly, 160–163
sugar water, 149–160

T

Tanagers
birdbath preferences of,
237
bread preferences of,
203–204
fat preferences of, **123**
fruit preferences of, **176**
habits and characteristics of,
29, 174
insect preferences of, **224**
nesting materials for, 286,
295, 296–297, **301**
recipes for
bread-based, 185, 191,
194
fat-based, 90, 96, 117
fruit-based, 161–162,
173
insect-based, 209–210
seed-based, 29
Scarlet, 353, *353*
seasonal food preferences
of, **20**
Summer, **301**
Western, 99
Tanager Tantalizer, 117
Tanager Temptations, 161, 191
Tanager Treat, 29
Tanager Two-Step, 194
Taste test, for finches, 58
Thistle birds. *See* Goldfinches

Thistle seed. *See* Niger
Thorny twigs, as nesting
material, 291
Thrashers
birdbath preferences of,
236
bread preferences of,
202–204
Brown
bread for, 178
feeders for, 107
fruit preferences of,
164, 165
nesting material for,
291, 292, **299**
profile of, 334, *334*
seasonal food
preferences of, 15
corn for, 43
fat preferences of, **123**
feeder style and placement
for, **50,** 107
fruit preferences of, **176**
Gray, *170*
habits and characteristics of,
174, 196
Hermit, 341, *341*
Leconte, *187*
nut preferences of, **146**
recipes for
bread-based, 192–193
fat-based, 90, 96
fruit-based, 166–167,
173
insect-based, 209
Sage, *289*
seasonal food preferences
of, 15, 16, **18**
Thrasher's Thrill, 166
Thread, as nesting material, 283
Thrushes, *206*
birdbath preferences of,
237

fat preferences of, **123**
habits and characteristics of, 174
insect preferences of, **224**
nesting materials for, 295
recipe for, 167
Varied, 9, 356, *356*
Wood, *227,* **301**
Time of day, for feeding, 9, 24, 215, 245
Timers, for water hoses and misters, 233
Titmice
    birdbath preferences of, **236–237**
    birdhouses for, 260–261
    bread preferences of, 188, **203–204**
    Bridled, *48*
    fat preferences of, 112, **123**
    feeder placement for, **50**
    fruit preferences of, 164, **176**
    habits and characteristics of, 129, 199, 260
    insects for, 208
    nesting habits of, **278**
    nesting materials for, 284, 286, 292–293, 295, **301**
    nut preferences of, **146**
    recipes for
        bread-based, 185
        fat-based, 90, 96, 100
        nut-based, 128, 136–139, 142–144
    Tufted, *261, 356, 356*
Titmouse Time, 100
Tortillas, corn, **204**
Towhees
    birdbath preferences of, **236–237**
    Eastern, *339, 339*
    fruit preferences of, 165, **176**

Green-tailed, *219*
habits and characteristics of, 219
nesting materials for, 295, **301**
niger for, 55
seasonal food preferences of, **20**
Spotted, *82*
Tray-type feeders
    mounts for, **323**
    for overflow crowds, 73
    recipes for, 75–76, 78–79
Tropical fruit, 169
Tube feeders
    buying, 71, 74
    to discourage jays, 240
    double, 314–315, *315*
    in feeding station, 305–306
    filling, 318
    hanging, 318
    homemade, 72–73, *72,* 80
    mounts for, 317, **323**
    multi-tube, 319
    placement of, 74
    recipes for, 78–79, 128
    seeds for, 73, 74
    seed spillage from, 76–77, 81–82
Tube-Feeder Treat, 128
Turkeys, wild
    corn for, 43
    feeder placement for, **50**
    nut preferences of, **146**
    profile of, 358, *358*
    recipes for, 39, 139
    seasonal food preferences of, **20**
Turkey Trot, 39
Twine, as nesting material, 280–281, 296–297

U
Ultramarine Dream, 107
Unusual or unfamiliar foods, 58, 64–65

V
Valentine's Day, 286
Victorian-style feeders, 319
Vines, as nesting material, 292
Vireos
    birdbath preferences of, **237**
    insect preferences of, **224**
    nesting materials for, **301**
    seasonal food preferences of, **20**
    White-eyed, *213*

W
Walnuts
    recipes using
        bread-based, 184–185, 201
        fat-based, 100
        nut-based, 128, 137–139, 142–143
    where grown, **147**
    for woodpeckers, 128
Warblers
    birdbath preferences of, **237**
    Lucy's, *234*
    nesting materials for, **301**
    Wood, **224**
    Yellow, *316, 360, 360*
    Yellow-rumped, 15, **20, 123,** *360, 360*
Waxwings
    birdbath preferences of, **237**
    Cedar, *297, 297,* **299**

Waxworms, 218

Way Better'n Worms, 193

Weather considerations, 28. *See also specific seasons or conditions*

Wheat-based products, 182

Wild Bird Magnet Food, 219

Wild canaries. *See Goldfinches*

Wild nuts, 141, **147**

Wild turkeys. *See Turkeys, wild*

Wind
    protecting nesting materials from, 295
    seed spillage from, 76–77

Window treatment, lifesaving, 308–309, *308*

Winter blahs, 3–4

Winter season
    birdbaths in, 230, 236
    bluebird houses in, 255
    colored feeders for, 319
    considerations for, 12–14
    feeder traffic during, 180
    foods for, **17–20**, 85–86, 95
    nesting materials during, 286
    nuthatch houses in, 258
    preparing for, 40, 120
    recipes for, 171–173

Wireworms, 218

Wood, for birdhouses, 278

Woodpeckers
    Acorn, *22*
    benefits of, 5
    birdhouses for, 261–262
    bread preferences of, 181–182, 188, 195–196, **203**
    corn for, 43
    Downy, *95*
        birdhouses for, 262
        jelly for, 161

profile of, 338, *338*
        recipes for, 118, 137
    fat preferences of, 112, **123**
    feeder style and placement for, **50**, 94, *94*, 312
    fruit preferences of, 164, **176**
    habits and characteristics of, 129
    Hairy, 262, *262*, 341, *341*
        insects for, 208
        meat for, 115
        nut preferences of, 128, **146**
    Pileated, 144
    recipes for
        fat-based, 90, 92, 96, 100, 184
        fruit-based, 173
        insect-based, 209–210
        nut-based, 136–139, 144
    Red-bellied, 139, 262, 348, *348*
    Red-headed, 139, 262, 349, *349*
    seasonal food preferences of, **20**

Woodpecker Welcome, 184

Woodpecker Windup, 137

Wool, as nesting material, 283, 285

Worms, in birdseed, 41. *See also Insect foods; Insects*

Wrangle a Wren, 172

Wrens
    Bewick's, 265, **301**
    birdbath preferences of, **236–237**
    bread for, 181–182
    Canyon, **301**
    Carolina
        bread preferences of, 178, **203–204**

described, 265
        feeder placement for, **49**
        fruit preferences of, 165
        habits and characteristics of, 199
        insect foods for, 15
        meat for, 115
        nesting habits of, **278**
        nesting materials for, **301**
        nut preferences of, **145**
        oats for, 182
        profile of, 335, *335*
        recipes for, 90, 96, 172, 185, 192
        seasonal food preferences of, 16, **18**
    fat preferences of, **123**
    fruit preferences of, **176**
    House, *231*
        birdhouses for, 262–265, *263*
        habits and characteristics of, 265
        nesting habits of, **278**
        nesting materials for, **301**
    insect preferences of, **224**
    nesting habits of, 264
    nesting material for, 287
    recipes for, 173, 193

Y

Yard maintenance, 289, 291

Yards
    benefits of birds in, 5–6, 244
    small, 304

Yarn, as nesting material, 280–281, 283, 285, 296–297

Yo-De-Lay-Hee-Hoo!, 97